PEARSON CUSTOM BUSINESS RESOURCES

Compiled by

Strategic Analysis: The Capstone Course
MGMT 162
Santa Clara University

Pearson Custom Publishing

New York   Boston   San Francisco
London   Toronto   Sydney   Tokyo   Singapore   Madrid
Mexico City   Munich   Paris   Cape Town   Hong Kong   Montreal

Senior Vice President, Editorial and Marketing: Patrick F. Boles
Senior Sponsoring Editor: Robin J. Lazrus
Development Editor: Abbey Lee Briggs
Marketing Manager: Jack Cooney
Associate Editor: Ana Díaz-Caneja
Operations Manager: Eric M. Kenney
Database Product Manager: Jennifer Berry
Art Director: Renée Sartell
Cover Designer: Renée Sartell

Cover Art: Courtesy of EyeWire/Getty Images and PhotoDisc/Getty Images. Photodisc, "Globe surrounded by business people on computer monitors," courtesy of Photodisc/Getty Images. Dave Cutler (Artist), "Man Dropping Coins Into Glass Jar," courtesy of David Cutler/Images.com. Dave Cutler (Artist), "Three Coins in Glass Jar," courtesy of David Cutler/Images.com.

This special edition published in cooperation with Pearson Custom Publishing.

Printed in the United States of America.

Please visit our web site at *www.pearsoncustom.com.*

Attention bookstores: For permission to return any unsold stock, contact us at *pe-uscustomreturns@pearson.com.*

**Pearson
Custom Publishing**
is a division of

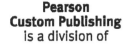

www.pearsonhighered.com   ISBN 10: 0558461190
ISBN 13: 9780558461195

Editorial Advisory Board

Contents

What Is Strategy and the Strategic Management Process?

What Is Strategy and the Strategic Management Process?

The Music Download Industry

It all began with Napster—uploading digital music files and then sharing them with others on the Web. Nothing could be easier. Hard drives around the world began to fill with vast music libraries, all for free. There was only one little problem: It turned out that such downloading was illegal.

Not that this stopped illegal downloads. Indeed, even today there are 40 illegal music downloads for every legal one. Not surprisingly, the music industry continues to sue those engaging in this practice; over 12,000 such lawsuits have been filed around the world so far.

But declaring some music downloads illegal only created a new market, with new competitive opportunities: the legal download market. After just a few years, iTunes has emerged as a clear winner in this legal download market. In 2006, iTunes had over 88 percent of the legal download market. In 2008, iTunes surpassed Best Buy and Wal-Mart to become the largest music seller in the United States. The second most successful firm in the online music market—eMusic—has less than 10 percent of the market. Other contenders, including Amazon's digital music store and MusicPass (owned by Sony BMG), have less than 5 percent of the market.

So, why has iTunes been so successful? iTunes is a division of Apple and understanding iTunes' success begins by recognizing the link between the iTunes Web site and iPod, Apple's incredibly successful MP3 portable music player. The iPod is generally recognized as one of the simplest, most elegant music listening devices ever created. Efforts to imitate iPod's simple interface and software have, according to most reviewers, simply failed. So Apple began with a great music-playing product, the iPod.

Apple made it easy to link the iPod to its iTunes Web site. Even technological neophytes can download songs from iTunes to their iPods in just a few minutes. Of course, to make this transfer as seamless as possible, Apple developed proprietary software—called FairPlay. This software restricts the use of music downloaded from iTunes to iPod MP3 players. That means once you start downloading music from iTunes to your iPod, you are unlikely to change to another music Web site because you would have to download and pay for the music a second time.

Pretty clever. Build a great player—the iPod—develop proprietary download software—iTunes—and you have built-in customer loyalty. It is also pretty profitable. As the number of iPod or iTunes users continued to grow, more and more music producers were willing to sign agreements to let Apple distribute their music through

2

iTunes. The result was Apple's dominance of the legal music download industry.

So, can anyone catch iTunes? Several firms are trying.

Some people think that the future of the music download industry is going to depend on the extent to which restrictions on the use of downloaded music are eliminated. These restrictions are created by the digital rights management (DRM) software that is "wrapped" around each song downloaded from iTunes. Initially, music companies insisted on DRM protection, to ensure that they were compensated for the use of their music. But now Apple's proprietary DRM system seems to be one reason that iTunes has been able to create and sustain a huge advantage in the music download industry.

Enter Amazon. In 2007, Amazon.com announced that it would start selling music without DRM restrictions on its online music store. As important, most of the big music companies signed up to sell music on Amazon. Shortly thereafter, SonyBMG, eMusic, and Rhapsody all announced the creation of non-DRM music download sites. Would legal downloads without use restrictions begin to erode iTunes' huge advantage?

It's early days, but so far iTunes' competitive advantage seems to be secure. Of course, Apple did not ignore this potential competitive threat. Almost immediately, it began to sell non-DRM music downloads on iTunes, albeit at a price higher than its DRM-restricted downloads. As important, Apple continued to invest in its MP3 player and related technologies. First there was the iPhone, then more advanced iPods that played videos and games. Now some iPod models have the same "soft touch" interface system as Apple's iPhone. All this has made iPods and related products more

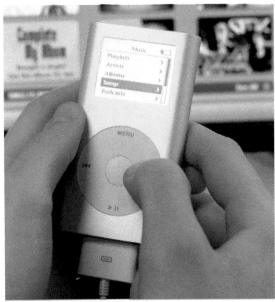

Virginia Mayo/AP Wide World Photos

attractive than competing MP3 players, and people who buy Apple MP3 players are more likely to download music from iTunes than any other Web site. So Apple matched the non-DRM offer and simultaneously reinforced its perceived hardware advantages—essentially implementing many of the same strategies that enabled it to gain its advantages in the music download industry in the first place.

But competition in this industry continues to evolve. What's next? Watch for Nokia and other cellphone manufacturers!

Sources: E. Smith (2006). "Can anybody catch iTunes?" *The Wall Street Journal*, November 27, pp. R1 +; J. Chaffin and A. van Duyn (2006). "Universal backs free music rival to iTunes." August 29, www.ft.com/cms/s; P. Thurrott and K. Furman (2004). "Illegal music downloads jump despite RIAA legal action." January 22, www.connectedhomemag.com. David Kravets (2007). "Like Amazon's DRM-free music downloads? Thank Apple," wired.com/entertainment/music/news/2007/09; Peter Kafka (2008). "iTunes competitors: We're number 2, we're number 2," *Silicon Alley Insider*, www.alleyinsider.com/ 2008/3; Peter Kafka (2008). "How are those DRM-free MP3s selling?" *Silicon Alley Insider*, www.alleyinsider.com/2008/3.

Figuring out how iTunes has come to dominate the music download industry and what competitors can do about it will go a long way in determining a firm's performance in this industry. The process by which these kinds of questions are answered is the strategic management process; the answer a firm develops for these questions is a firm's strategy.

Strategy and the Strategic Management Process

Although most can agree that a firm's ability to survive and prosper depends on choosing and implementing a good strategy, there is less agreement about what a strategy is, and even less agreement about what constitutes a good strategy. Indeed, there are almost as many different definitions of these concepts as there are books written about them.

Defining Strategy

In this book, a firm's **strategy** is defined as its theory about how to gain competitive advantages.[1] A good strategy is a strategy that actually generates such advantages. Apple's *theory* of how to gain a competitive advantage in the music download-for-a-fee business is to link the music download business with particular MP3 players. Amazon's eMusic's and Sony BMG's theory is that users will want to have no restrictions on the use of downloaded music.

Each of these theories of how to gain competitive advantages in the music download-for-a-fee business—like all theories—is based on a set of assumptions and hypotheses about the way competition in this industry is likely to evolve, and how that evolution can be exploited to earn a profit. The greater the extent to which these assumptions and hypotheses accurately reflect how competition in this industry actually evolves, the more likely it is that a firm will gain a competitive advantage from implementing its strategies. If these assumptions and hypotheses turn out not to be accurate, then a firm's strategies are not likely to be a source of competitive advantage.

But here is the challenge. It is usually very difficult to predict how competition in an industry will evolve, and so it is rarely possible to know for sure that a firm is choosing the right strategy. This is why a firm's strategy is almost always a theory: It's a firm's best bet about how competition is going to evolve, and how that evolution can be exploited for competitive advantage.

The Strategic Management Process

Although it is usually difficult to know for sure that a firm is pursuing the best strategy, it is possible to reduce the likelihood that mistakes are being made. The best way to do this is for a firm to choose its strategy carefully and systematically and to follow the strategic management process. The **strategic management process** is a sequential set of analyses and choices that can increase the likelihood that a firm will choose a good strategy; that is, a strategy that generates competitive advantages. An example of the strategic management process is presented in Figure 1.

A Firm's Mission
The strategic management process begins when a firm defines its mission. A firm's **mission** is its long-term purpose. Missions define both what a firm aspires to be in

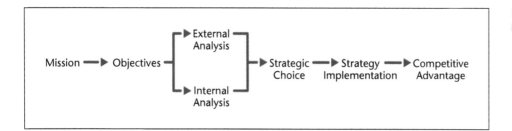

Figure 1 The Strategic Management Process

the long run and what it wants to avoid in the meantime. Missions are often written down in the form of **mission statements**. Table 1 contains examples of several mission statements taken from well-known firms.

Some Missions May Not Affect Firm Performance. As shown in Table 1, most mission statements incorporate common elements. For example, many define the businesses within which a firm will operate—automobiles for Ford; computer hardware, software, and services for IBM. Some define how a firm will compete in those businesses—doing everything direct at Dell, and just winning at the Oakland Raiders. Many even define the core values that a firm espouses—the "soul of Dell" and Anheuser-Busch's values, for examples.

Indeed, mission statements often contain so many common elements that some have questioned whether having a mission statement even creates value for a firm.[2] Moreover, even if a mission statement does say something unique about a company, if that mission statement does not influence behavior throughout an organization, it is unlikely to have much impact on a firm's actions. After all, Enron's 1999 annual report includes the following statement of values:

> *Integrity: We work with customers and prospects openly, honestly, and sincerely. When we say we will do something, we will do it; when we say we cannot or will not do something, then we won't do it.*[3]

This statement was published at exactly the same time that senior management at Enron was engaging in activities that ultimately defrauded investors, partners, and Enron's own employees, and that landed some Enron executives in jail.[4]

Some Missions Can Improve Firm Performance. Despite these caveats, research has identified some firms whose sense of purpose and mission permeates all that they do. Some of these **visionary firms**, or firms whose mission is central to all they do, have been compiled by Jim Collins and Jerry I. Porras in their book *Built to Last*, and are presented in Table 2.[5] One interesting thing to note about visionary firms is their long-term profitability. From 1926 through 1995, an investment of $1 in one of these firms would have increased in value to $6,536. That same dollar invested in an average firm over this same time period would have been worth $415 in 1995.

These visionary firms earned substantially higher returns than average firms even though many of their mission statements suggest that profit maximizing, although an important corporate objective, is not their primary reason for existence. Consider what Jim Burke, a former Chief Executive Officer (CEO) at Johnson & Johnson (J&J; one of the visionary firms identified in Table 2), says about the relationship between profits and his firm's mission and mission statement:

> *All our management is geared to profit on a day-to-day basis. That's part of the business of being in business. But too often, in this and other businesses, people are inclined to think, "We'd better do this because if we don't, it's going to show up on*

Johnson & Johnson

Our Credo

We believe our first responsibility is to the doctors, nurses and patients, to mothers and fathers and all others who use our products and services. In meeting their needs everything we do must be of high quality. We must constantly strive to reduce our costs in order to maintain reasonable prices. Customers' orders must be serviced promptly and accurately. Our suppliers and distributors must have an opportunity to make a fair profit.

We are responsible to our employees, the men and women who work with us through-out the world. Everyone must be considered as an individual. We must respect their dignity and recognize their merit. They must have a sense of security in their jobs. Compensation must be fair and adequate, and working conditions clean, orderly and safe. We must be mindful of ways to help our employees fulfill their family responsibil-ities. Employees must feel free to make suggestions and complaints. There must be equal opportunity for employment, development and advancement for those qualified. We must provide competent management, and their actions must be just and ethical.

We are responsible to the communities in which we live and work and to the world community as well. We must be good citizens—support good works and charities and bear our fair share of taxes. We must encourage civic improve-ments and better health and education. We must maintain in good order the prop-erty we are privileged to use, protecting the environment and natural resources.

Our final responsibility is to our stockholders. Business must make a sound profit. We must experiment with new ideas. Research must be carried on, innovative pro-grams developed and mistakes paid for. New equipment must be purchased, new facilities provided and new products launched. Reserves must be created to provide for adverse times. When we operate according to these principles, the stockholders should realize a fair return.

Dell

Dell is building its technology, its business, and its communities through direct rela-tionships with our customers, our employees, and our neighbors. Through this process, we are committed to bringing value to customers and adding value to our company, our neighborhoods, our communities, and our world through diversity, environmental and global citizenship initiatives.

The core elements of the "soul of Dell":

Customers: We believe in creating loyal customers by providing a superior expe-rience at a great value.

The Dell Team: We believe our continued success lies in teamwork and in the opportunity each team member has to learn, develop, and grow.

Direct Relationships: We believe in being direct in all we do.

Global Citizenship: We believe in participating responsibly in the global marketplace.

Winning: We have a passion for winning in everything we do.

IBM

At IBM, we strive to lead in the invention, development, and manufacture of the industry's most advanced information technologies, including computer systems, software, storage systems, and microelectronics. We translate these advanced technologies into value for customers through our professional solutions, services, and consulting businesses worldwide.

The Oakland Raiders

Just Win Baby!

Sources: © Johnson & Johnson; Used with permission of Dell Computer Corporation; Used with permission of IBM; Used with permission of the Oakland Raiders.

the figures over the short-term." [Our mission] allows them to say, "Wait a minute. I don't have to do that." The management has told me that they're ... interested in me operating under this set of principles.[6]

Some Missions Can Hurt Firm Performance. Although some firms have used their missions to develop strategies that create significant competitive advantages, missions can hurt a firm's performance as well. For example, sometimes a firm's mission will be very inwardly focused and defined only with reference to the personal values and priorities of its founders or top managers, independent of whether those values and priorities are consistent with the economic realities facing a firm. Strategies derived from such missions or visions are not likely to be a source of competitive advantage.

For example, Ben & Jerry's Ice Cream was founded in 1977 by Ben Cohen and Jerry Greenfield, both as a way to produce super-premium ice cream and as a way to create an organization based on the values of the 1960s' counterculture. This strong sense of mission led Ben & Jerry's to adopt some very unusual human resource and other policies. Among these policies, the company adopted a compensation system whereby the highest paid firm employee could earn no more than five times the income of the lowest paid firm employee. Later, this ratio was adjusted to seven to one. However, even at this level, such a compensation policy made it very difficult to acquire the senior management talent needed to ensure the growth and profitability of the firm without grossly overpaying the lowest paid employees in the firm. When a new CEO was appointed to the firm in 1995, his $250,000 salary violated this compensation policy.

Indeed, though the frozen dessert market rapidly consolidated through the late 1990s, Ben & Jerry's Ice Cream remained an independent firm, partly because of Cohen's and Greenfield's commitment to maintaining the social values that their firm embodied. Lacking access to the broad distribution network and managerial talent that would have been available if Ben & Jerry's had merged with another firm, the company's growth and profitability lagged. Finally, in April 2000, Ben & Jerry's Ice Cream was acquired by Unilever. The 66 percent premium finally earned by Ben & Jerry's stockholders in April 2000 had been delayed for

TABLE 2 A Sample of Visionary Firms

3M	Hewlett-Packard	Nordstrom
American Express	IBM	Philip Morris
Boeing	Johnson & Johnson	Procter & Gamble
Citicorp	Marriott	Sony
Ford	Merck	Wal-Mart
General Electric	Motorola	Walt Disney

Source: J. C. Collins and J. I. Porras. *Built to last: successful habits of visionary companies.* New York: Harper Collins Publishers, Inc. ©1994 James C. Collins and Jerry I. Porras. Reprinted with permission by Jim Collins.

several years. In this sense, Cohen's and Greenfield's commitment to a set of personal values and priorities was at least partly inconsistent with the economic realities of the frozen dessert market in the United States.[7]

Obviously, because a firm's mission can help, hurt, or have no impact on its performance, missions by themselves do not necessarily lead a firm to choose and implement strategies that generate competitive advantages. Indeed, as suggested in Figure 1, while defining a firm's mission is an important step in the strategic management process, it is only the first step in that process.

Objectives

Whereas a firm's mission is a broad statement of its purpose and values, its **objectives** are specific measurable targets a firm can use to evaluate the extent to which it is realizing its mission. Consider, for example, 3M's mission statement in Table 3. This statement emphasizes the importance of finding innovative products and producing high returns for shareholders. However, it is also possible to link specific objectives to each of the elements of this mission statement. This is also done in Table 3. For example, for the Investor Mission, possible objectives might include: growth in earnings per share averaging 10 percent or better per year, a return on employed capital of 27 percent or better, at least 30 percent of sales from products that are no more than four years old, and so forth.

High-quality objectives are tightly connected to elements of a firm's mission and are relatively easy to measure and track over time. Low-quality objectives either do not exist or are not connected to elements of a firm's mission, are not quantitative, or are difficult to measure or difficult to track over time. Obviously, low-quality objectives cannot be used by management to evaluate how well a mission is being realized. Indeed, one indication that a firm is not that serious about realizing part of its mission statement is when there are no objectives, or only low-quality objectives, associated with that part of the mission.

External and Internal Analysis

The next two phases of the strategic management process—external analysis and internal analysis—occur more or less simultaneously. By conducting an **external analysis**, a firm identifies the critical threats and opportunities in its competitive environment. It also examines how competition in this environment is likely to evolve and what implications that evolution has for the threats and opportunities a firm is facing. A considerable literature on techniques for and approaches to conducting external analysis has evolved over the past several years.

Whereas external analysis focuses on the environmental threats and opportunities facing a firm, **internal analysis** helps a firm identify its organizational strengths and weaknesses. It also helps a firm understand which of its resources and capabilities are likely to be sources of competitive advantage and which are less likely to be sources of such advantages. Finally, internal analysis can be used by firms to identify those areas of its organization that require improvement and change. As with external analysis, a considerable literature on techniques for and approaches to conducting internal analysis has evolved over the past several years.

Strategic Choice

Armed with a mission, objectives, and completed external and internal analyses, a firm is ready to make its strategic choices. That is, a firm is ready to choose its "theory of how to gain competitive advantage."

TABLE 3 3M's Value Statement

Our Values:

Act with uncompromising honesty and integrity in everything we do.

Satisfy our customers with innovative technology and superior quality, value and service.

Provide our investors with an attractive return through sustainable, global growth.

Respect our social and physical environment around the world.

Value and develop our employees' diverse talents, initiative and leadership.

Earn the admiration of all those associated with 3M worldwide.

Source: Courtesy of 3M Company.

As suggested in Abrahams (1995), these values could be expanded to include specific objectives:

Satisfy our customers with superior quality and value:

- Providing the highest quality products and services consistent with our customers' requirements and preferences.
- Making every aspect of every transaction a satisfying experience for our customers.
- Finding innovative ways to make life easier and better for our customers.

Providing investors an attractive return through sustained, high-quality growth:

Our goals are:

- Growth in earnings per share averaging 10 percent a year or better.
- A return on capital employed of 27 percent or better.
- A return on stockholders' equity of between 20 and 25 percent.
- At least 30 percent of our sales each year from products new in the last four years.

Respecting our social and physical environment:

- Complying with all laws and meeting or exceeding regulations.
- Keeping customers, employees, investors and the public informed about our operations.
- Developing products and processes that have a minimal impact on the environment.
- Staying attuned to the changing needs and preferences of our customers, employees and society.
- Uncompromising honesty and integrity in every aspect of our operations.

Being a company that employees are proud to be a part of:

- Respecting the dignity and worth of individuals.
- Encouraging individual initiative and innovation in an atmosphere characterized by flexibility, cooperation and trust.
- Challenging individual capabilities.
- Valuing human diversity and providing equal opportunity for development.

Source: J. Abrahams (1995). *The mission statement book.* Berkeley, CA: TenSpeedPress, pp. 400–402.

The strategic choices available to firms fall into two large categories: business-level strategies and corporate-level strategies. **Business-level strategies** are actions firms take to gain competitive advantages in a single market or industry. The two most common business-level strategies are cost leadership and product differentiation.

Corporate-level strategies are actions firms take to gain competitive advantages by operating in multiple markets or industries simultaneously.

Common corporate-level strategies include vertical integration strategies, diversification strategies, strategic alliance strategies, merger and acquisition strategies, and global strategies.

Obviously, the details of choosing specific strategies can be quite complex. However, the underlying logic of strategic choice is not complex. Based on the strategic management process, the objective when making a strategic choice is to choose a strategy that (1) supports the firm's mission, (2) is consistent with a firm's objectives, (3) exploits opportunities in a firm's environment with a firm's strengths, and (4) neutralizes threats in a firm's environment while avoiding a firm's weaknesses. Assuming that this strategy is implemented—the last step of the strategic management process—a strategy that meets these four criteria is very likely to be a source of competitive advantage for a firm.

Strategy Implementation

Of course, simply choosing a strategy means nothing if that strategy is not implemented. **Strategy implementation** occurs when a firm adopts organizational policies and practices that are consistent with its strategy. Three specific organizational policies and practices are particularly important in implementing a strategy: a firm's formal organizational structure, its formal and informal management control systems, and its employee compensation policies. A firm that adopts an organizational structure, management controls, and compensation policy that are consistent with and reinforce its strategies is more likely to be able to implement those strategies than a firm that adopts an organizational structure, management controls, and compensation policy that are inconsistent with its strategies.

What Is Competitive Advantage?

Of course, the ultimate objective of the strategic management process is to enable a firm to choose and implement a strategy that generates a competitive advantage. But what is a competitive advantage? In general, a firm has a **competitive advantage** when it is able to create more economic value than rival firms. **Economic value** is simply the difference between the perceived benefits gained by a customer that purchases a firm's products or services and the full economic cost of these products or services. Thus, the size of a firm's competitive advantage is the difference between the economic value a firm is able to create and the economic value its rivals are able to create.[8]

Consider the two firms presented in Figure 2. Both these firms compete in the same market for the same customers. However, Firm I generates $180 of economic value each time it sells a product or service, whereas Firm II generates $150 of economic value each time it sells a product or service. Because Firm I generates more economic value each time it sells a product or service, it has a competitive advantage

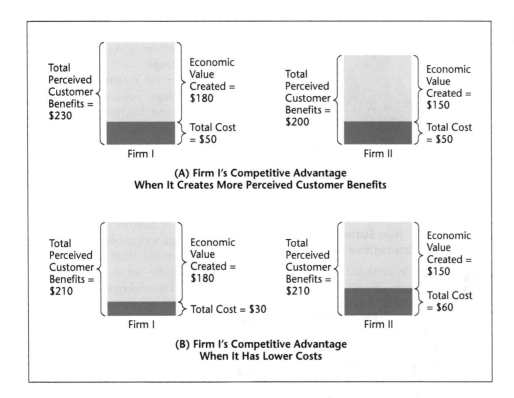

Figure 2 The Sources of a Firm's Competitive Advantage

over Firm II. The size of this competitive advantage is equal to the difference in the economic value these two firms create, in this case, $30 ($180 − $150 = $30).

However, as shown in the figure, Firm I's advantage may come from different sources. For example, it might be the case that Firm I creates greater perceived benefits for its customers than Firm II. In panel A of the figure, Firm I creates perceived customer benefits worth $230, whereas Firm II creates perceived customer benefits worth only $200. Thus, even though both firms' costs are the same (equal to $50 per unit sold), Firm I creates more economic value ($230 − $50 = $180) than Firm II ($200 − $50 = $150). Indeed, it is possible for Firm I, in this situation, to have higher costs than Firm II and still create more economic value than Firm II if these higher costs are offset by Firm I's ability to create greater perceived benefits for its customers.

Alternatively, as shown in panel B of the figure, these two firms may create the same level of perceived customer benefit (equal to $210 in this example) but have different costs. If Firm I's costs per unit are only $30, it will generate $180 worth of economic value ($210 − $30 = $180). If Firm II's costs are $60, it will generate only $150 of economic value ($210 − $60 = $150). Indeed, it might be possible for Firm I to create a lower level of perceived benefits for its customers than Firm II and still create more economic value than Firm II, as long as its disadvantage in perceived customer benefits is more than offset by its cost advantage.

A firm's competitive advantage can be temporary or sustained. As summarized in Figure 3, a **temporary competitive advantage** is a competitive advantage that lasts for a very short period of time. A **sustained competitive advantage**, in contrast, can last much longer. How long sustained competitive advantages can last is discussed in the Research Made Relevant feature. Firms that create the same economic value as their rivals experience **competitive parity**. Finally, firms that generate less economic value than their rivals have a **competitive disadvantage**. Not surprisingly, competitive disadvantages can be either temporary or sustained, depending on the duration of the disadvantage.

For some time, economists have been interested in how long firms are able to sustain competitive advantages. Traditional economic theory predicts that such advantages should be short-lived in highly competitive markets. This theory suggests that any competitive advantages gained by a particular firm will quickly be identified and imitated by other firms, ensuring competitive parity in the long run. However, in real life, competitive advantages often last longer than traditional economic theory predicts.

One of the first scholars to examine this issue was Dennis Mueller. Mueller divided a sample of 472 firms into eight categories, depending on their level of performance in 1949. He then examined the impact of a firm's initial performance on its subsequent performance. The traditional economic hypothesis was that all firms in the sample would converge on an average level of performance. This did not occur. Indeed, firms that were performing well in an earlier time period tended to perform well in later time periods, and firms that performed poorly in an earlier time period tended to perform poorly in later time periods as well.

Geoffrey Waring followed up on Mueller's work by explaining why competitive advantages seem to persist

How Sustainable Are Competitive Advantages?

longer in some industries than in others. Waring found that, among other factors, firms that operate in industries that (1) are informationally complex, (2) require customers to know a great deal in order to use an industry's products, (3) require a great deal of research and development, and (4) have significant economies of scale are more likely to have sustained competitive advantages compared to firms that operate in industries without these attributes.

Peter Roberts studied the persistence of profitability in one particular industry—the U.S. pharmaceutical industry. Roberts found that not only can firms sustain competitive advantages in this industry, but that the ability to do so is almost entirely

attributable to the firms' capacity to innovate by bringing out new and powerful drugs.

The most recent work in this tradition was published by Anita McGahan and Michael Porter. They showed that both high and low performance can persist for some time. Persistent high performance is related to attributes of the industry within which a firm operates and the corporation within which a business unit functions. In contrast, persistent low performance was caused by attributes of a business unit itself.

In many ways, the difference between traditional economics research and strategic management research is that the former attempts to explain why competitive advantages should not persist, whereas the latter attempts to explain when they can. Thus far, most empirical research suggests that firms, in at least some settings, can sustain competitive advantages.

Sources: D. C. Mueller (1977). "The persistence of profits above the norm." *Economica*, 44, pp. 369–380; P. W. Roberts (1999). "Product innovation, product-market competition, and persistent profitability in the U.S. pharmaceutical industry." *Strategic Management Journal*, 20, pp. 655–670; G. F. Waring (1996). "Industry differences in the persistence of firm-specific returns." *The American Economic Review*, 86, pp. 1253–1265; A. McGahan and M. Porter (2003). "The emergence and sustainability of abnormal profits." *Strategic Organization*, 1(1), pp. 79–108.

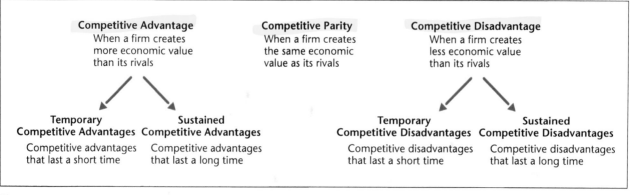

Figure 3 Types of Competitive Advantage

The Strategic Management Process, Revisited

With this description of the strategic management process now complete, it is possible to redraw the process, as depicted in Figure 1, to incorporate the various options a firm faces as it chooses and implements its strategy. This is done in Figure 4.

Measuring Competitive Advantage

A firm has a *competitive advantage* when it creates more economic value than its rivals. *Economic value* is the difference between the perceived customer benefits associated with buying a firm's products or services and the cost of producing and selling these products or services. These are deceptively simple definitions. However, these concepts are not always easy to measure directly. For example, the benefits of a firm's products or services are always a matter of customer perception, and perceptions are not easy to measure. Also, the total costs associated with producing a particular product or service may not always be easy to identify or associate with a particular product or service. Despite the very real challenges associated with measuring a firm's competitive advantage, two approaches have emerged. The first estimates a firm's competitive advantage by examining its accounting performance; the second examines the firm's economic performance. These approaches are discussed in the following sections.

Accounting Measures of Competitive Advantage

A firm's **accounting performance** is a measure of its competitive advantage calculated by using information from a firm's published profit and loss and balance sheet statements. A firm's profit and loss and balance sheet statements, in turn, are typically created using widely accepted accounting standards and principles. The application of these standards and principles makes it possible to compare the accounting performance of one firm to the accounting performance of other firms, even if those firms are not in the same industry. However, to the extent that these

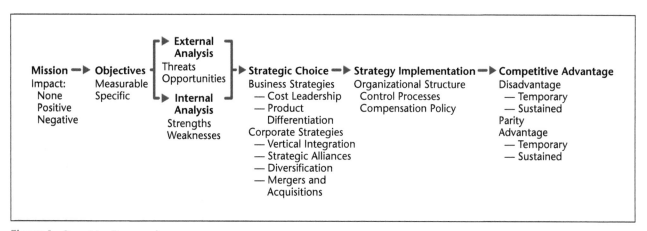

Figure 4   Organizing Framework

TABLE 4 Common Ratios to Measure a Firm's Accounting Performance

Ratio	Calculation	Interpretation
Profitability Ratios		
1. ROA	$\dfrac{\text{profit after taxes}}{\text{total assets}}$	A measure of return on total investment in a firm. Larger is usually better.
2. ROE	$\dfrac{\text{profit after taxes}}{\text{total stockholder's equity}}$	A measure of return on total equity investment in a firm. Larger is usually better.
3. Gross profit margin	$\dfrac{\text{sales} - \text{cost of goods sold}}{\text{sales}}$	A measure of sales available to cover operating expenses and still generate a profit. Larger is usually better.
4. Earnings per share (EPS)	$\dfrac{\text{profits (after taxes)} - \text{preferred stock dividends}}{\text{number of shares of common stock outstanding}}$	A measure of profit available to owners of common stock. Larger is usually better.
5. Price earnings ratio (p/e)	$\dfrac{\text{current market price/share}}{\text{after-tax earnings/share}}$	A measure of anticipated firm performance—a high p/e ratio tends to indicate that the stock market anticipates strong future performance. Larger is usually better.
6. Cash flow per share	$\dfrac{\text{after-tax profit} + \text{depreciation}}{\text{number of common shares stock outstanding}}$	A measure of funds available to fund activities above current level of costs. Larger is usually better.
Liquidity Ratios		
1. Current ratio	$\dfrac{\text{current assets}}{\text{current liabilities}}$	A measure of the ability of a firm to cover its current liabilities with assets that can be converted into cash in the short term. Recommended in the range of 2 to 3.
2. Quick ratio	$\dfrac{\text{current assets} - \text{inventory}}{\text{current liabilities}}$	A measure of the ability of a firm to meet its short-term obligations without selling off its current inventory. A ratio of 1 is thought to be acceptable in many industries.
Leverage Ratios		
1. Debt to assets	$\dfrac{\text{total debt}}{\text{total assets}}$	A measure of the extent to which debt has financed a firm's business activities. The higher, the greater the risk of bankruptcy.
2. Debt to equity	$\dfrac{\text{total debt}}{\text{total equity}}$	A measure of the use of debt versus equity to finance a firm's business activities. Generally recommended less than 1.
3. Times interest earned	$\dfrac{\text{profit before interest and taxes}}{\text{total interest charges}}$	A measure of how much a firm's profits can decline and still meet its interest obligations. Should be well above 1.

Activity Ratios

1. Inventory turnover	$\dfrac{\text{sales}}{\text{inventory}}$	A measure of the speed with which a firm's inventory is turning over.
2. Accounts receivable turnover	$\dfrac{\text{annual credit sales}}{\text{accounts receivable}}$	A measure of the average time it takes a firm to collect on credit sales.
3. Average collection period	$\dfrac{\text{accounts receivable}}{\text{average daily sales}}$	A measure of the time it takes a firm to receive payment after a sale has been made.

standards and principles are not applied in generating a firm's accounting statements, or to the extent that different firms use different accounting standards and principles in generating their statements, it can be difficult to compare the accounting performance of firms. As described in the Global Perspectives feature, these issues can be particularly challenging when comparing the performance of firms in different countries around the world.

One way to use a firm's accounting statements to measure its competitive advantage is through the use of accounting ratios. **Accounting ratios** are simply numbers taken from a firm's financial statements that are manipulated in ways that describe various aspects of a firm's performance. Some of the most common accounting ratios that can be used to characterize a firm's performance are presented in Table 4. These measures of firm accounting performance can be grouped into four categories: (1) **profitability ratios**, or ratios with some measure of profit in the numerator and some measure of firm size or assets in the denominator; (2) **liquidity ratios**, or ratios that focus on the ability of a firm to meet its short-term financial obligations; (3) **leverage ratios**, or ratios that focus on the level of a firm's financial flexibility, including its ability to obtain more debt; and (4) **activity ratios**, or ratios that focus on the level of activity in a firm's business.

Of course, these ratios, by themselves, say very little about a firm. To determine how a firm is performing, its accounting ratios must be compared with some standard. In general, that standard is the average of accounting ratios of other firms in the same industry. Using ratio analysis, a firm earns **above average accounting performance** when its performance is greater than the industry average. Such firms typically have competitive advantages, sustained or otherwise. A firm earns **average accounting performance** when its performance is equal to the industry average. These firms generally enjoy only competitive parity. A firm earns **below average accounting performance** when its performance is less than the industry average. These firms generally experience competitive disadvantages.

Consider, for example, the performance of Apple Computer. Apple's financial statements for 2007 and 2008 are presented in Table 5. Losses in this table would be presented in parentheses. Several ratio measures of accounting performance are calculated for Apple in these two years in Table 6.

Apple's sales increased dramatically from 2007 to 2008, from just over $24 billion to just under $32.5 billion. However, some profitability accounting ratios suggest that its profitability dropped somewhat during this same time period, from a return on total assets (ROA) of 0.138 to 0.122, and from a return on equity (ROE) of 0.241 to 0.230. On the other hand, Apple's gross profit margin increased from 0.340 to 0.343. So its sales went up, its overall profitability went

TABLE 5 Apple Computer's Financial Statements for 2007 and 2008 (numbers in millions of dollars)

	2007	2008
Net sales	24,006	32,479
Cost of goods sold	15,852	21,334
Gross margin	8,154	11,145
Selling, general and administrative expenses	2,963	3,761
Research and development expenses	782	1,109
Total operating expenses	3,745	4,870
Operating income (loss)	4,409	6,275
Total income (loss), before taxes	5,008	6,895
Provision for (benefit from) income taxes	1,512	2,061
Net income, after taxes	3,496	4,834
Inventories	346	509
Total current assets	21,956	34,690
Total assets	25,347	39,572
Total current liabilities	9,280	14,092
Total debt	10,815	18,542
Total shareholders' equity	14,532	21,030

down a little, but its gross profit margin went up a little. This pattern could reflect several changes in Apple's business. For example, perhaps Apple was selling more products, but at lower margins, in 2008 compared to 2007. This would explain the lower ROA and ROE, but would not explain the increased gross profit margin. Alternatively, maybe some of Apple's operating expenses increased at a rate greater than the increase in its sales revenues. However, a quick look at Table 5 suggests that Apple's operating expenses increased at about the same rate as its sales. The explanation of the slightly lower ROA and ROE numbers in 2008 doesn't have to do with revenues and costs, but rather has to do with increases in Apple's total assets and its total shareholders' equity. Both of these balance sheet numbers increased at a rate faster than Apple's sales increased, leading to slightly lower ROA and ROE numbers for 2008 compared to 2007.

On the other hand, Apple's liquidity and leverage ratios remain largely unchanged over these two years. With current and quick ratios well over two, it's pretty clear that Apple has enough cash on hand to respond to any short-term financial needs. And its leverage ratios suggest that it still has some opportunities to borrow money for long-term investments should the need arise.

Overall, the information in Tables 5 and 6 suggests that Apple Computer, in 2007 and 2008, is, financially speaking, very healthy.

TABLE 6 Some Accounting Ratios for Apple Computer in 2007 and 2008

	2007	2008
ROA	0.138	0.122
ROE	0.241	0.230
Gross profit margin	0.340	0.343
Current ratio	2.37	2.46
Quick ratio	2.33	2.43
Debt to assets	0.427	0.469
Debt to equity	0.744	0.882

Economic Measures of Competitive Advantage

The great advantage of accounting measures of competitive advantage is that they are relatively easy to compute. All publicly traded firms must make their accounting statements available to the public. Even privately owned firms will typically release some information about their accounting performance. From these statements, it is quite easy to calculate various accounting ratios. One can learn a lot about a firm's competitive position by comparing these ratios to industry averages.

However, accounting measures of competitive advantage have at least one significant limitation. Earlier, economic profit was defined as the difference between the perceived benefit associated with purchasing a firm's products or services and the cost of producing and selling that product or service. However, one important component of cost typically is not included in most accounting measures of competitive advantage—the cost of the capital a firm employs to produce and sell its products. The **cost of capital** is the rate of return that a firm promises to pay its suppliers of capital to induce them to invest in the firm. Once these investments are made, a firm can use this capital to produce and sell products and services. However, a firm must provide the promised return to its sources of capital if it expects to obtain more investment capital in the future. **Economic measures of competitive advantage** compare a firm's level of return to its cost of capital instead of to the average level of return in the industry.

Generally, there are two broad categories of sources of capital: **debt** (capital from banks and bondholders) and **equity** (capital from individuals and institutions that purchase a firm's stock). The **cost of debt** is equal to the interest that a firm must pay its debt holders (adjusted for taxes) in order to induce those debt holders to lend money to a firm. The **cost of equity** is equal to the rate of return a firm must promise its equity holders in order to induce these individuals and institutions to invest in a firm. A firm's **weighted average cost of capital (WACC)** is simply the percentage of a firm's total capital, which is debt times the cost of debt, plus the percentage of a firm's total capital; that is, equity times the cost of equity. A simple approach to measuring a firm's WACC is described in the Strategy in Depth feature.

Conceptually, a firm's cost of capital is the level of performance a firm must attain if it is to satisfy the economic objectives of two of its critical stakeholders: debt holders and equity holders. A firm that earns above its cost of capital is likely to be able to attract additional capital, because debt holders and equity holders will scramble to make additional funds available for this firm. Such a firm is said to be earning **above normal economic performance** and will be able to use its access to cheap capital to grow and expand its business. A firm that earns its cost of capital is said to have **normal economic performance**. This level of performance is said to be "normal" because this is the level of performance that most of a firm's equity and debt holders expect. Firms that have normal economic performance are able to gain access to the capital they need to survive, although they are not prospering. Growth opportunities may be somewhat limited for these firms. In general, firms with competitive parity usually have normal economic performance. A firm that earns less than its cost of capital is in the process of liquidating. **Below normal economic performance** implies that a firm's debt and equity holders will be looking for alternative ways to invest their money, someplace where they can earn at least what they expect to

Strategy in Depth

A firm's WACC can be an important benchmark against which to compare a firm's performance. However, calculating this number can sometimes be tricky. Fortunately, it is possible to obtain all the information needed to calculate a firm's WACC—at least for publicly traded firms—from information published in outlets such as Moody's, Standard and Poor's, Dun and Bradstreet, and Value Line. These publications are in every major business school library in the world and are also available online.

To calculate a firm's WACC, five pieces of information are required: (1) a firm's debt rating, (2) its marginal tax rate, (3) its Beta, (4) the risk-free and market rates of return in the years a firm's WACC is being calculated, and (5) information about a firm's capital structure.

Typically, a firm's debt rating will be presented in the form of a series of letters—for example, AA or BBB+. Think of these ratings as grades for a firm's riskiness: an "A" is less risky than an "AA," which is less risky than a "BBB+," and so forth. At any given point in time, a firm with a given debt rating has a market-determined interest. Suppose that the market-determined interest rate for a firm with a BBB debt rating is 7.5 percent. This is a firm's before-tax cost of debt. However, because interest payments are tax deductible in the United States, this before-tax cost of debt has to be adjusted for the tax savings a firm has from using debt. If a firm is reasonably large, then it will almost certainly have to pay the

Estimating a Firm's Weighted Average Cost of Capital

largest marginal tax rate, which in the United States has been 39 percent. So, the after-tax cost of debt in this example is $(1 - 0.39)(7.5)$, or 4.58 percent.

A firm's *Beta* is a measure of how highly correlated the price of a firm's equity is to the overall stock market. Betas are published for most publicly traded firms. The *risk-free rate of return* is the rate the U.S. federal government has to pay on its long-term bonds to get investors to buy these bonds, and the market rate of return is the return investors would obtain if they purchased one share of each of the stocks traded on public exchanges. Historically, this risk-free rate of return has been low—around 3 percent. The *market rate of return* has averaged around 8.5 percent in the United States. Using these numbers, and assuming that a firm's Beta is equal to 1.2, the cost of a firm's equity capital can be estimated using the Capital Asset Pricing Model (CAPM) as follows:

Cost of Equity = Risk Free Rate of Return + (Market Rate of Return − Risk Free Rate of Return) Beta

For our example, this equation is:

$$9.6 = 3.0 + (8.5 - 3.0)1.2$$

Because firms do not gain tax advantages from using equity capital, the before- and after-tax cost of equity is the same.

To calculate a firm's WACC, simply multiple the percentage of a firm's total capital; that is, debt times the after-tax cost of debt, and add it to the percentage of a firm's total capital; that is, equity times the cost of equity. If a firm has total assets of $5 million and stockholders' equity of $4 million, then it must have debt with a market value of $1 million. The WACC for this hypothetical firm thus becomes:

WACC = (Stockholders' Equity/Total Assets) Cost of Equity + (Debt/Total Assets) After-Tax Cost of Debt

$$= 4/5(9.6) + 1/5(4.58)$$
$$= 7.68 + 0.916$$
$$= 8.59$$

Obviously, firms can have a much more complicated capital structure than this hypothetical example. Moreover, the taxes a firm pays can be quite complicated to calculate. There are also some problems in using the CAPM to calculate a firm's cost of equity. However, even with these caveats, this approach usually gives a reasonable approximation to a firm's weighted average cost of capital.

earn; that is, normal economic performance. Unless a firm with below normal performance changes, its long-term viability will come into question. Obviously, firms that have a competitive disadvantage generally have below normal economic performance.

Measuring a firm's performance relative to its cost of capital has several advantages for strategic analysis. Foremost among these is the notion that a firm that earns at least its cost of capital is satisfying two of its most important stakeholders—debt holders and equity holders. Despite the advantages of comparing a firm's performance to its cost of capital, this approach has some important limitations as well.

For example, it can sometimes be difficult to calculate a firm's cost of capital. This is especially true if a firm is **privately held**—that is, if it has stock that is not traded on public stock markets or if it is a division of a larger company. In these situations, it may be necessary to use accounting ratios to measure a firm's performance.

Moreover, some have suggested that although accounting measures of competitive advantage understate the importance of a firm's equity and debt holders in evaluating a firm's performance, economic measures of competitive advantage exaggerate the importance of these two particular stakeholders, often to the disadvantage of other stakeholders in a firm. These issues are discussed in more detail in the Ethics and Strategy feature.

The Relationship Between Economic and Accounting Performance Measures

The correlation between economic and accounting measures of competitive advantage is high. That is, firms that perform well using one of these measures usually perform well using the other. Conversely, firms that do poorly using one of these measures normally do poorly using the other. Thus, the relationships among competitive advantage, accounting performance, and economic performance depicted in Figure 5 generally hold.

However, it is possible for a firm to have above average accounting performance and simultaneously have below normal economic performance. This could happen, for example, when a firm is not earning its cost of capital but has above industry average accounting performance. Also, it is possible for a firm to have below average accounting performance and above normal economic performance. This could happen when a firm has a very low cost of capital and is earning at a rate in excess of this cost, but still below the industry average.

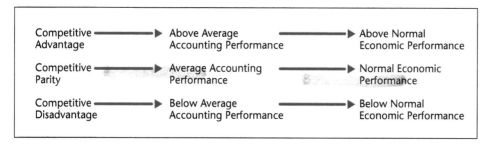

Figure 5 Competitive Advantage and Firm Performance

Emergent Versus Intended Strategies

The simplest way of thinking about a firm's strategy is to assume that firms choose and implement their strategies exactly as described by the strategic management process in Figure 1. That is, they begin with a well-defined mission and objectives, they engage in external and internal analyses, they make their strategic choices, and then they implement their strategies. And there is no doubt that this describes the process for choosing and implementing a strategy in many firms.

For example, FedEx, the world leader in the overnight delivery business, entered this industry with a very well-developed theory about how to gain competitive advantages in this business. Indeed, Fred Smith, the founder of FedEx (originally known as Federal Express), first articulated this theory as a student in a term paper for an undergraduate business class at Yale University. Legend has it that he received only a "C" on the paper, but the company that was founded on the theory of competitive advantage in the overnight delivery business developed in that paper has done extremely well. Founded in 1971, FedEx had 2008 sales just under $38 billion and profits of over $1.125 billion.[9]

Other firms have also begun operations with a well-defined, well-formed strategy, but have found it necessary to modify this strategy so much once it is actually implemented in the marketplace that it bears little resemblance to the theory with which the firm started. Emergent strategies are theories of how to gain competitive advantage in an industry that emerge over time or that have been radically reshaped once they are initially implemented.[10] The relationship between a firm's intended and emergent strategies is depicted in Figure 6.

Several well-known firms have strategies that are at least partly emergent. For example, J&J was originally a supplier of antiseptic gauze and medical plasters. It had no consumer business at all. Then, in response to complaints about irritation caused by some of its medical plasters, J&J began enclosing a small packet of talcum powder with each of the medical plasters it sold. Soon customers were asking to purchase the talcum powder by itself, and the company introduced "Johnson's Toilet and Baby Powder." Later, an employee invented a ready-to-use bandage for his wife. It seems she often cut herself while using knives in the

Figure 6 Mintzberg's Analysis of the Relationship Between Intended and Realized Strategies

Source: Reprinted from "Strategy formation in an adhocracy," by H. Mintzberg and A. McHugh, published in *Administrative Science Quarterly, 30*, No. 2, June 1985, by permission of Administrative Science Quarterly. Copyright © 1985 by Administrative Science Quarterly.

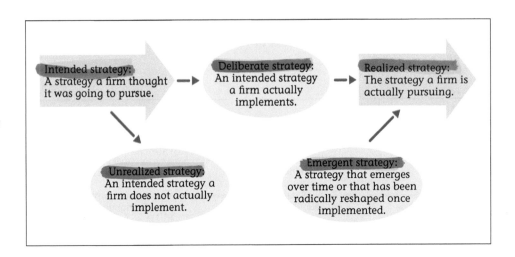

Ethics and Strategy

Considerable debate exists about the role of a firm's equity and debt holders versus its other stakeholders in defining and measuring a firm's performance. These other stakeholders include a firm's suppliers, its customers, its employees, and the communities within which it does business. Like equity and debt holders, these other stakeholders make investments in a firm. They, too, expect some compensation for making these investments.

On the one hand, some argue that if a firm maximizes the wealth of its equity holders, it will automatically satisfy all of its other stakeholders. This view of the firm depends on what is called the *residual claimants* view of equity holders. This view is that equity holders only receive payment on their investment in a firm after all legitimate claims by a firm's other stakeholders are satisfied. Thus, a firm's equity holders, in this view, only receive payment on their investments after the firm's employees are compensated, its suppliers are paid, its customers are satisfied, and its obligations to the communities within which it does business have been met. By maximizing returns to its equity holders, a firm is ensuring that its other stakeholders are fully compensated for investing in a firm.

Stockholders Versus Stakeholders

On the other hand, some argue that the interests of equity holders and a firm's other stakeholders often collide, and that a firm that maximizes the wealth of its equity holders does not necessarily satisfy its other stakeholders. For example, whereas a firm's customers may want it to sell higher-quality products at lower prices, a firm's equity holders may want it to sell low-quality products at higher prices; this obviously would increase the amount of money left over to pay off a firm's equity holders. Also, whereas a firm's employees may want it to adopt policies that lead to steady performance over long periods of time—because this will lead to stable employment—a firm's

equity holders may be more interested in its maximizing its short-term profitability, even if this hurts employment stability. The interests of equity holders and the broader community may also clash, especially when it is very costly for a firm to engage in environmentally friendly behaviors that could reduce its short-term performance.

This debate manifests itself in a variety of ways. For example, many groups that oppose the globalization of the U.S. economy do so on the basis that firms make production, marketing, and other strategic choices in ways that maximize profits for equity holders, often to the detriment of a firm's other stakeholders. These people are concerned about the effects of globalization on workers, on the environment, and on the cultures in the developing economies where global firms sometimes locate their manufacturing and other operations. Managers in global firms respond by saying that they have a responsibility to maximize the wealth of their equity holders. Given the passions that surround this debate, it is unlikely that these issues will be resolved soon.

Sources: T. Copeland, T. Koller, and J. Murrin (1995). *Valuation: Measuring and managing the value of companies.* New York: Wiley; L. Donaldson (1990). "The ethereal hand: Organizational economics and management theory." *Academy of Review,* 15, pp. 369–381.

kitchen. When J&J marketing managers learned of this invention, they decided to introduce it into the marketplace. J&J's Band-Aid products have since become the largest selling brand category at J&J. Overall, J&J's intended strategy was to compete in the medical products market, but its emergent consumer products strategies now generate over 40 percent of total corporate sales.

Another firm with what turns out to be an emergent strategy is the Marriott Corporation. Marriott was originally in the restaurant business. In the late 1930s, Marriott owned and operated eight restaurants. However, one of these restaurants was close to a Washington, D.C., airport. Managers at this restaurant noticed that airline passengers would come into the restaurant to purchase food to eat on their

Strategy in the Emerging Enterprise

Every entrepreneur—and would-be entrepreneur—is familiar with the drill: If you want to receive financial support for your idea, you need to write a business plan. Business plans are typically 25 to 30 pages long. Most begin with an Executive Summary; then move quickly to describing an entrepreneur's business idea, why customers will be interested in this idea, how much it will cost to realize this idea; and usually end with a series of charts that project a firm's cash flows over the next five years.

Of course, because these business ideas are often new and untried, no one—including the entrepreneur— really knows if customers will like the idea well enough to buy from this firm. No one really knows how much it will cost to build these products or produce these services—they've never been built or produced before. And, certainly, no one really knows what a firm's cash flows will look like over the next five years or so. Indeed, it is not unusual for entrepreneurs to constantly revise their business plan to reflect new information they have obtained about their business idea and its viability. It is not even unusual for entrepreneurs to fundamentally revise their central business idea as they begin to pursue it in earnest.

Emergent Strategies and Entrepreneurship

The truth is, most decisions about whether to create an entrepreneurial firm take place under conditions of high uncertainty and high unpredictability. In this setting, the ability to adjust on the fly, to be flexible, and to recast a business idea in ways that are more consistent with customer interests may be a central determinant of a firm's ultimate success. This, of course, suggests that emergent strategies are likely to be very important for entrepreneurial firms.

This view of entrepreneurship is different from the popular stereotype. In the popular view, entrepreneurs are assumed to be hit by a "blinding rush of insight" about a previously unexploited market opportunity. In reality, entrepreneurs are more likely to experience a series of smaller insights about market opportunities. But typically, these periods of insight will be preceded by periods of disappointment, as an entrepreneur discovers that what he or she thought was a new and complete business model is, in fact, either not new or not complete or both. In the popular view, entrepreneurship is all about creativity, about being able to see opportunities others cannot see. In reality, entrepreneurship may be more about tenacity than creativity, because entrepreneurs build their firms step-by-step out of the uncertainty and unpredictability that plague their decision making. In the popular view, entrepreneurs can envision their success well before it occurs. In reality, although entrepreneurs may dream about financial and other forms of success, they usually do not know the exact path they will take, nor what success will actually look like, until after they have arrived.

Sources: S. Alvarez and J. Barney (2005). "How do entrepreneurs organize firms under conditions of uncertainty?" *Journal of Management*, 31 (5), pp. 776–793; S. Alvarez and J. Barney (2004). "Organizing rent generation and appropriation: Toward a theory of the entrepreneurial firm," *Journal of Business Venturing*, 19, pp. 621–636; W. Gartner (1988). "Who is the entrepreneur? is the wrong question." *American Journal of Small Business*, 12, pp. 11–32; S. Sarasvathy (2001). "Causation and effectuation: Toward a theoretical shift from economic inevitability to entrepreneurial contingency." *Academy of Management Review*, 26, pp. 243–264.

trip. J. Willard Marriott, the founder of the Marriott Corporation, noticed this trend and negotiated a deal with Eastern Airlines whereby Marriott's restaurant would deliver prepackaged lunches directly to Eastern's planes. This arrangement was later extended to include American Airlines. Over time, providing food service to airlines became a major business segment for Marriott. Although Marriott's initial intended strategy was to operate in the restaurant business, it became engaged in the emergent food service business at over 100 airports throughout the world.[11]

Some firms have almost entirely emergent strategies. PEZ Candy, Inc., for example, manufactures and sells small plastic candy dispensers with cartoon and movie character heads, along with candy refills. This privately held firm has made few efforts to speed its growth, yet demand for current and older PEZ products continues to grow. In the 1990s, PEZ doubled the size of its manufacturing operation to keep up with demand. Old PEZ dispensers have become something of a collector's item. Several national conferences on PEZ collecting have been held, and some rare PEZ dispensers were once auctioned at Christie's. This demand has enabled PEZ to raise its prices without increases in advertising, sales personnel, and movie tie-ins so typical in the candy industry.[12]

Of course, one might argue that emergent strategies are only important when a firm fails to implement the strategic management process effectively. After all, if this process is implemented effectively, then would it ever be necessary to fundamentally alter the strategies that a firm has chosen?

In reality, it will often be the case that at the time a firm chooses its strategies, some of the information needed to complete the strategic management process may simply not be available. As suggested earlier, in this setting a firm simply has to make its "best bet" about how competition in an industry is likely to emerge. In such a situation, a firm's ability to change its strategies quickly to respond to emergent trends in an industry may be as important a source of competitive advantage as the ability to complete the strategic management process. For all these reasons, emergent strategies may be particularly important for entrepreneurial firms, as described in the Strategy in the Emerging Enterprise feature.

Why You Need to Know About Strategy

At first glance, it may not be obvious why students would need to know about strategy and the strategic management process. After all, the process of choosing and implementing a strategy is normally the responsibility of senior managers in a firm, and most students are unlikely to be senior managers in large corporations until many years after graduation. Why study strategy and the strategic management process now?

In fact, there are at least three very compelling reasons why it is important to study strategy and the strategic management process now. First, it can give you the tools you need to evaluate the strategies of firms that may employ you. We have already seen how a firm's strategy can have a huge impact on its competitive advantage. Your career opportunities in a firm are largely determined by that firm's competitive advantage. Thus, in choosing a place to begin or continue your career, understanding a firm's theory of how it is going to gain a competitive advantage can be essential in evaluating the career opportunities in a firm. Firms with strategies that are unlikely to be a source of competitive advantage will rarely provide the same career opportunities as firms with strategies that do generate such advantages. Being able to distinguish between these types of strategies can be very important in your career choices.

Second, once you are working for a firm, understanding that firm's strategies, and your role in implementing those strategies, can be very important for your personal success. It will often be the case that expectations of how you perform your function in a firm will change, depending on the strategies a firm is pursuing. For example, the accounting function plays a very different role in a firm pursuing a cost leadership strategy versus a product differentiation strategy. Marketing and manufacturing also play very different roles in these two types of strategies. Your effectiveness in a firm can be reduced by doing accounting, marketing, and manufacturing as if your firm were pursuing a cost leadership strategy when it is actually pursuing a product differentiation strategy.

Finally, although it is true that strategic choices are generally limited to very experienced senior managers in large organizations, in smaller and entrepreneurial firms many employees end up being involved in the strategic management process. If you choose to work for one of these smaller or entrepreneurial firms—even if it is not right after graduation—you could very easily find yourself to be part of the strategic management team, implementing the strategic management process and choosing which strategies this firm should implement. In this setting, a familiarity with the essential concepts that underlie the choice and implementation of a strategy may turn out to be very helpful.

Summary

A firm's strategy is its theory of how to gain competitive advantages. These theories, like all theories, are based on assumptions and hypotheses about how competition in an industry is likely to evolve. When those assumptions and hypotheses are consistent with the actual evolution of competition in an industry, a firm's strategy is more likely to be able to generate a competitive advantage.

One way that a firm can choose its strategies is through the strategic management process. This process is a set of analyses and decisions that increase the likelihood that a firm will be able to choose a "good" strategy, that is, a strategy that will lead to a competitive advantage.

The strategic management process begins when a firm identifies its mission, or its long-term purpose. This mission is often written down in the form of a mission statement. Mission statements, by themselves, can have no impact on performance, enhance a firm's performance, or hurt a firm's performance. Objectives are measurable milestones firms use to evaluate whether they are accomplishing their missions. External and internal analyses are the processes through which a firm identifies its environmental threats and opportunities and organizational strengths and weaknesses. Armed with these analyses, it is possible for a firm to engage in strategic choice. Strategies can be classified into two categories: business-level strategies (including cost leadership and product differentiation) and corporate-level strategies (including vertical integration, strategic alliances, diversification, and mergers and acquisitions). Strategy implementation follows strategic choice and involves choosing organizational structures, management control policies, and compensation schemes that support a firm's strategies.

The ultimate objective of the strategic management process is the realization of competitive advantage. A firm has a competitive advantage if it is creating more economic value than its rivals. Economic value is defined as the difference between the perceived customer benefits from purchasing a product or service from a firm and the total economic cost of developing and selling that product or service. Competitive advantages can be temporary or sustained. Competitive parity exists when a firm creates the same economic value as its rivals. A competitive disadvantage exists when a firm creates less economic value than its rivals, and it can be either temporary or sustained.

Two popular measures of a firm's competitive advantage are accounting performance and economic performance. Accounting performance measures competitive advantage using various ratios calculated from a firm's profit and loss and balance sheet statements. A firm's accounting performance is compared with the average level of accounting performance in a firm's industry. Economic performance compares a firm's level of return to its cost of capital. A firm's cost of capital is the rate of return it had to promise to pay to its debt and equity investors to induce them to invest in the firm.

Although many firms use the strategic management process to choose and implement strategies, not all strategies are chosen this way. Some strategies emerge over time, as firms respond to unanticipated changes in the structure of competition in an industry.

Students need to understand strategy and the strategic management process for at least three reasons. First, it can help in deciding where to work. Second, once you have a job it can help you to be successful in that job. Finally, if you have a job in a small or entrepreneurial firm you may become involved in strategy and the strategic management process from the very beginning.

Challenge Questions

1. Some firms publicize their corporate mission statements by including them in annual reports, on company letterheads, and in corporate advertising. What, if anything, does this practice say about the ability of these mission statements to be sources of sustained competitive advantage for a firm? Why?

2. Little empirical evidence indicates that having a formal, written mission statement improves a firm's performance. Yet many firms spend a great deal of time and money developing mission statements. Why?

3. Is it possible to distinguish between an emergent strategy and an ad hoc rationalization of a firm's past decisions? Explain.

4. Both external and internal analyses are important in the strategic management process. Is the order in which these analyses are conducted important? If yes, which should come first: external analysis or internal analysis? If the order is not important, why not?

5. Will a firm that has a sustained competitive disadvantage necessarily go out of business? What about a firm with below average accounting performance over a long period of time? Or a firm with below normal economic performance over a long period of time?

6. Can more than one firm have a competitive advantage in an industry at the same time? Is it possible for a firm to simultaneously have a competitive advantage and a competitive disadvantage?

Problem Set

1. Write objectives for each of the following mission statements.
   (a) We will be a leader in pharmaceutical innovation.
   (b) Customer satisfaction is our primary goal.
   (c) We promise on-time delivery.
   (d) Product quality is our first priority.

2. Rewrite each of the following objectives to make them more helpful in guiding a firm's strategic management process.
   (a) We will introduce five new drugs.
   (b) We will understand our customers' needs.
   (c) Almost all of our products will be delivered on time.
   (d) The number of defects in our products will fall.

3. Do firms with the following financial results have below normal, normal, or above normal economic performance?
   (a) ROA = 14.3%, WACC = 12.8%
   (b) ROA = 4.3%, WACC = 6.7%
   (c) ROA = 6.5%, WACC = 9.2%
   (d) ROA = 8.3%, WACC = 8.3%

4. Do these same firms have below average, average, or above average accounting performance?
   (a) ROA = 14.3%, Industry Avg. ROA = 15.2%
   (b) ROA = 4.3%, Industry Avg. ROA = 4.1%
   (c) ROA = 6.5%, Industry Avg. ROA = 6.1%
   (d) ROA = 8.3%, Industry Avg. ROA = 9.4%

5. Is it possible for a firm to simultaneously earn above normal economic returns and below average accounting returns? What about below normal economic returns and above average accounting returns? Why or why not? If this can occur, which measure of performance is more reliable: economic performance or accounting performance? Explain.

6. Examine the following corporate Web sites and determine if the strategies pursued by these firms were emergent, deliberate, or both emergent and deliberate. Justify your answer with facts from the Web sites.

(a) www.walmart.com

(b) www.ibm.com

(c) www.homedepot.com

(d) www.cardinal.com

7. Using the information provided, calculate this firm's ROA, ROE, gross profit margin, and quick ratio. If this firm's WACC is 6.6 percent and the average firm in its industry has an ROA of 8 percent, is this firm earning above or below normal economic performance and above or below average accounting performance?

Net sales	6,134	Operating cash	3,226	Net other operating assets	916
Cost of goods sold	(4,438)	Accounts receivable	681	Total assets	5,161
Selling, general administrative		Inventories	20	Net current liabilities	1,549
expenses	(996)	Other current assets	0	Long-term debt	300
Other expenses	(341)	Total current assets	3,927	Deferred income taxes	208
Interest income	72	Gross properties, plant,		Preferred stock	0
Interest expense	(47)	equipment	729	Retained earnings	0
Provision for taxes	(75)	Accumulated depreciation	(411)	Common stock	3,104
Other income	245	Book value of fixed assets	318	Other liabilities	0
Net income	554	Goodwill	0	Total liabilities and equity	5,161

End Notes

1. This approach to defining strategy was first suggested in Drucker, P. (1994). "The theory of business." *Harvard Business Review, 75,* September–October, pp. 95–105.
2. This approach to defining strategy was first suggested in Drucker, P. (1994). "The theory of business." *Harvard Business Review, 75,* September–October, pp. 95–105.
3. See www.enron.com.
4. See Emshwiller, J., D. Solomon, and R. Smith. (2004). "Lay is indicted for his role in Enron collapse." *The Wall Street Journal,* July 8, pp. A1+; Gilmartin, R. (2005). "They fought the law." *BusinessWeek,* January 10, pp. 82–83.
5. These performance results were presented originally in Collins, J. C., and J. I. Porras. (1997). *Built to last: successful habits of visionary companies.* New York: HarperCollins.
6. Quoted in Collins, J. C., and J. I. Porras. (1997). *Built to last: successful habits of visionary companies,* New York: HarperCollins.
7. See Theroux, J., and J. Hurstak. (1993). "Ben & Jerry's Homemade Ice Cream Inc.: keeping the mission(s) alive." Harvard Business School Case No. 9-392-025; Applebaum, A. (2000). "Smartmoney.com: Unilever feels hungry, buys Ben & Jerry's." *The Wall Street Journal,* April 13, pp. B1+.
8. This definition of competitive advantage has a long history in the field of strategic management. For example, it is closely related to the definitions provided in Barney (1986, 1991) and Porter (1985). It is also consistent with the value-based approach described in Peteraf (2001), Brandenburger, and Stuart (1999), and Besanko, Dranove, and Shanley (2000). For more discussion on this definition, see Peteraf and Barney (2004).
9. FedEx's history is described in Trimble, V. (1993). *Overnight success: Federal Express and Frederick Smith, its renegade creator.* New York: Crown.
10. Mintzberg, H. (1978). "Patterns in strategy formulation." *Management Science,* 24(9), pp. 934–948; and Mintzberg, H. (1985). "Of strategies, deliberate and emergent." *Strategic Management Journal,* 6(3), pp. 257–272. Mintzberg has been most influential in expanding the study of strategy to include emergent strategies.
11. The J&J and Marriott emergent strategy stories can be found in Collins, J. C., and J. I. Porras. (1997). *Built to last: successful habits of visionary companies.* New York: HarperCollins.
12. See McCarthy, M. J. (1993). "The PEZ fancy is hard to explain, let alone justify." *The Wall Street Journal,* March 10, p. A1, for a discussion of PEZ's surprising emergent strategy.

Evaluating a Firm's External Environment

From Chapter 2 of *Strategic Management and Competitive Advantage: Concepts and Cases*, 3/e. Jay B. Barney. William S. Hesterly. Copyright © 2010 by Pearson Education. Published by Prentice Hall. All rights reserved.

Evaluating a Firm's External Environment

Competing College?

On August 1, 2006, a new athletic stadium in Glendale, Arizona, opened. With 63,400 permanent seats, expandable to 73,000, this stadium was the first to have both a retractable roof and a retractable grass field. Weighing 18.9 billion pounds, the grass field is transported 741 feet at 1/8 mile per hour outside the stadium's wall so that it can soak up the Arizona sunshine and provide a healthy and safe playing surface for professional and college football players. Since opening, the stadium has hosted numerous NFL and college games, including a BCS National Championship game and Super Bowl XLII. An impressive architectural sight—described by many as an alien space ship landing on the desert—the stadium is the state of the art in providing fans and players a great sporting venue. Indeed, there is only one thing unusual about this stadium—its name. It is called the University of Phoenix Stadium.[1]

Now, having a football stadium associated with a university is not that unusual in the United States. Many large and small colleges and universities in the United States have football stadiums on campus, and some of them bear the name of the school or the state within which the school resides—Ohio State University has, for example, the 105,000-seat Ohio Stadium; the University of Michigan has

the 110,000-seat Michigan Stadium; the University of Texas has the 94,000-seat Texas Memorial Stadium.

However, unlike these other universities, the University of Phoenix has no football team. It has no cheerleaders, no mascot, no overpaid coach. Indeed, it has no campus, in the traditional sense of a single location where most of its students attend class. Instead, the University of Phoenix is a private university, founded in 1976, with more than 330,000 students attending classes in 194 locations in 39 U.S. states, Puerto Rico, District of Columbia, Netherlands, Canada, and Mexico. Its students can major in over 100 different degree programs, many of which can be completed entirely online. Just like United Airline's investment in the United Center in Chicago, and Chase's investment in Chase Ball Park in Arizona, the University of Phoenix signed on as a sponsor to the new stadium in Glendale to advertise its brand to potential consumers.

The University of Phoenix is one of an increasing number of new entrants into higher education. According to its founder, Dr. John Sperling, the University of Phoenix entered into this industry to meet the growing demand for higher education opportunities for working adults. Committed to removing the barriers that have prevented working adults from completing their education, the University of Phoenix

has been the fastest growing university in the United States virtually from its founding.[2]

Competition seems to have come to the higher education industry. And it's not just restricted to new entrants like the University of Phoenix. After almost two centuries of gentle competition among universities confined almost entirely to the athletic field, universities and colleges now find themselves competing for the best students with attractive financial packages, luxurious on-campus health clubs, and state-of-the-art computing facilities. Universities now compete to hire the best-known, most widely published professors, who then compete with each other for research grants from the government and various nongovernmental organizations. University and college development officers compete to gain the favor of potential donors—people who can help build a university or college's endowment, which, in turn, can be used to fund programs for faculty, staff, and students.

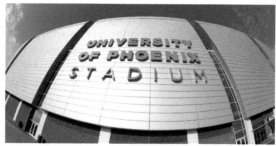

UPI Photo/Art Foxall/Landov Media

Indeed, competition in the higher education industry has never been more intense. University presidents are now held responsible to the Trustees, for the development and implementation of strategies designed to give their schools a competitive advantage. This is the case even though most colleges and universities in the United States are not-for-profit organizations. But, just because these organizations are not trying to maximize their economic profit does not mean that they are not competing in a very competitive industry.[3]

The strategic management process suggests that one of the critical determinants of a firm's strategies is the threats and opportunities in its competitive environment. If a firm understands these threats and opportunities, it is one step closer to being able to choose and implement a "good strategy"; that is, a strategy that leads to competitive advantage.

There are clearly both new threats—like new entrants including the University of Phoenix—and new opportunities in higher education.

However, it is not enough to recognize that it is important to understand the threats and opportunities in a firm's competitive environment. A set of tools that managers can apply to systematically complete this external analysis as part of the strategic management process is also required. These tools must be rooted in a strong theoretical base, so that managers know that they have not been developed in an arbitrary way. Fortunately, such tools exist and will be described in this chapter.

Understanding a Firm's General Environment

Any analysis of the threats and opportunities facing a firm must begin with an understanding of the general environment within which a firm operates. This general environment consists of broad trends in the context within which a firm operates that can have an impact on a firm's strategic choices. As depicted in Figure 1, the general environment consists of six interrelated elements: technological change, demographic trends, cultural trends, the economic climate, legal and political conditions, and specific international events. Each of these elements of the general environment is discussed in this section.

In 1899, Charles H. Duell, commissioner of the U.S. patent office, said, "Everything that can be invented has been invented."[4] He was wrong. Technological changes over the past few years have had significant impacts on the ways firms do business and on the products and services they sell. These impacts

Figure 1 The General Environment Facing Firms

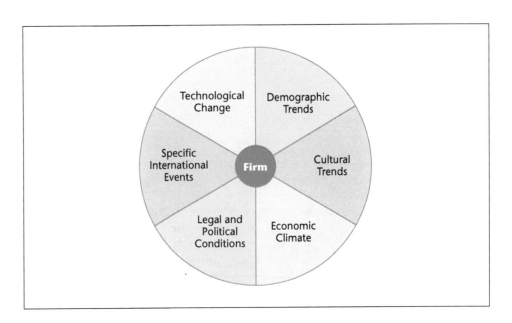

have been most obvious for technologies that build on digital information—computers, the Internet, cell phones, and so forth. Many of us routinely use digital products or services that did not exist just a few years ago—including TiVo. However, rapid technological innovation has not been restricted to digital technologies. Biotechnology has also made rapid progress over the past 10 years. New kinds of medicines are now being created. As important, biotechnology holds the promise of developing entirely new ways of both preventing and treating disease.[5]

Technological change creates both opportunity, as firms begin to explore how to use technology to create new products and services, and threats, as technological change forces firms to rethink their technological strategies. Indeed, one technological innovation—such as downloading digital music from the Internet—has changed competition in the music industry.

A second element of the general environment facing firms is demographic trends. **Demographics** is the distribution of individuals in a society in terms of age, sex, marital status, income, ethnicity, and other personal attributes that may determine buying patterns. Understanding this basic information about a population can help a firm determine whether its products or services will appeal to customers and how many potential customers for these products or services it might have.

Some demographic trends are very well known. For example, everyone has heard of the "baby boomers"—those who were born shortly after World War II. This large population has had an impact on the strategies of many firms, especially as the boomers have grown older and have had more disposable income. However, other demographic groups have also had an impact on firm strategies. This is especially true in the automobile industry. For example, minivans were invented to meet the demands of "soccer moms"—women who live in the suburbs and have young children. The 3-series BMW seems to have been designed for "Yuppies"—the young, urban, and upwardly mobile adults of the 1970s and 1980s—whereas the Jeep Liberty and Nissan Xterra seem to have been designed for the so-called Generation Y—young men and women currently in their twenties and either just out of college or anticipating graduation shortly.

In the United States, an important demographic trend over the past 20 years has been the growth of the Hispanic population. In 1990, the percentage of the U.S. population that was African American was greater than the percentage that was Hispanic. However, by 2000, people of Latin descent outnumbered African Americans. By 2010, it is expected that Hispanics will constitute almost 15 percent of the U.S. population, whereas the percentage of African Americans will remain constant at less than 8 percent. These trends are particularly notable in the South and Southwest. For example, 36 percent of children under 18 in Houston are Hispanic, 39 percent in Miami and San Diego, 53 percent in Los Angeles, and 61 percent in San Antonio.[6]

Of course, firms are aware of this growing population and its buying power. Indeed, Hispanic disposable income in the United States jumped 29 percent, to $652 billion, from 2001 to 2003. In response, firms have begun marketing directly to the U.S. Hispanic population. In one year, Procter & Gamble spent $90 million marketing directly to Spanish-speaking customers. Procter & Gamble has also formed a 65-person bilingual team to manage the marketing of products to Hispanics. Indeed, Procter & Gamble expects that the Hispanic population will be the cornerstone of its sales growth in North America.[7]

Firms can try to exploit their understanding of a particular demographic segment of the population to create a competitive advantage—as Procter &

Gamble is doing with the U.S. Hispanic population—but focusing on too narrow a demographic segment can limit demand for a firm's products. The WB, the alternative television network created by Time Warner in 1995, faced this dilemma. Initially, the WB found success in producing shows for teens—classics such as *Dawson's Creek* and *Buffy the Vampire Slayer*. However, in 2003, the WB saw an 11 percent drop in viewership and a $25 million drop in advertising revenues. Although it did not leave its traditional demographic behind, the WB began producing some programs intended to appeal to older viewers. Ultimately, the WB merged with UPN to form a new network, the CW network. CW is a joint venture between CBS (owner of UPN) and Time Warner (owner of the WB).[8]

A third element of a firm's general environment is cultural trends. **Culture** is the values, beliefs, and norms that guide behavior in a society. These values, beliefs, and norms define what is "right and wrong" in a society, what is acceptable and unacceptable, what is fashionable and unfashionable. Failure to understand changes in culture, or differences between cultures, can have a very large impact on the ability of a firm to gain a competitive advantage.

This becomes most obvious when firms operate in multiple countries simultaneously. Even seemingly small differences in culture can have an impact. For example, advertisements in the United States that end with a person putting their index finger and thumb together mean that a product is "okay"; in Brazil, the same symbol is vulgar and offensive. Ads in the United States that have a bride dressed in white may be very confusing to the Chinese, because in China, white is the traditional color worn at funerals. In Germany, women typically purchase their own engagement rings, whereas in the United States, men purchase engagement rings for their fiancées. And what might be appropriate ways to treat women colleagues in Japan or France would land most men in U.S. firms in serious trouble. Understanding the cultural context within which a firm operates is important in evaluating the ability of a firm to generate competitive advantages.[9]

A fourth element of a firm's general environment is the current economic climate. The **economic climate** is the overall health of the economic systems within which a firm operates. The health of the economy varies over time in a distinct pattern: Periods of relative prosperity, when demand for goods and services is high and unemployment is low, are followed by periods of relatively low prosperity, when demand for goods and services is low and unemployment is high. When activity in an economy is relatively low, the economy is said to be in **recession**. A severe recession that lasts for several years is known as a **depression**. This alternating pattern of prosperity followed by recession, followed by prosperity, is called the **business cycle**.

Throughout the 1990s, the world, and especially the United States, enjoyed a period of sustained economic growth. Some observers even speculated that the government had become so skilled at managing demand in the economy through adjusting interest rates that a period of recession did not necessarily have to follow a period of sustained economic growth. Of course, the business cycle has reared its ugly head twice since the 1990s—first with the technology bubble-burst around 2001 and, more recently, in the credit crunch in 2008. Most observers now agree that although government policy can have a significant impact on the frequency and size of economic downturns, these policies are unlikely to be able prevent these downturns altogether.

A fifth element of a firm's general environment is **legal and political conditions**. The legal and political dimensions of an organization's general environment are the laws and the legal system's impact on business, together with the general nature of the relationship between government and business. These laws and the relationship between business and government can vary significantly around the world. For example, in Japan, business and the government are generally seen as having a consistently close and cooperative relationship. Indeed, some have observed that one reason that the Japanese economy has been growing so slowly over the last decade has been the government's reluctance to impose economic restructuring that would hurt the performance of some Japanese firms—especially the largest Japanese banks. In the United States, however, the quality of the relationship between business and the government tends to vary over time. In some administrations, rigorous antitrust regulation and tough environmental standards—both seen as inconsistent with the interests of business—dominate. In other administrations, antitrust regulation is less rigorous and the imposition of environmental standards is delayed, suggesting a more business-friendly perspective.

A final attribute of a firm's general environment is **specific international events**. These include events such as civil wars, political coups, terrorism, wars between countries, famines, and country or regional economic recessions. All of these specific events can have an enormous impact on the ability of a firm's strategies to generate competitive advantage.

Of course, one of the most important of these specific events to have occurred over the past several decades was the terrorist attacks on New York City and Washington, D.C., on September 11, 2001. Beyond the tragic loss of life, these attacks had important business implications as well. For example, it took over five years for airline demand to return to pre–September 11 levels. Insurance companies had to pay out billions of dollars in unanticipated claims as a result of the attacks. Defense contractors saw demand for their products soar as the United States and some of its allies began waging war in Afghanistan and then Iraq.

A firm's general environment defines the broad contextual background within which it operates. Understanding this general environment can help a firm identify some of the threats and opportunities it faces. However, this general environment often has an impact on a firm's threats and opportunities through its impact on a firm's more local environment. Thus, while analyzing a firm's general environment is an important step in any application of the strategic management process, this general analysis must be accompanied by an analysis of a firm's more local environment if the threats and opportunities facing a firm are to be fully understood. The next section discusses specific tools for analyzing a firm's local environment and the theoretical perspectives from which these tools have been derived.

The Structure-Conduct-Performance Model of Firm Performance

In the 1930s, a group of economists began developing an approach for understanding the relationship among a firm's environment, behavior, and performance. The original objective of this work was to describe conditions under which competition in an industry would *not* develop. Understanding when competition was not developing in an industry assisted government regulators in identifying industries where competition-enhancing regulations should be implemented.[10]

Ethics and Strategy

One of the basic tenets of economic theory is that society is better off when industries are very competitive. Industries are very competitive when there are large numbers of firms operating in an industry, when the products and services that these firms sell are similar to each other, and when it is not very costly for firms to enter into or exit these industries. Indeed, as is described in more detail in the Strategy in Depth feature, these industries are said to be *perfectly competitive.*

The reasons that society is better off when industries are perfectly competitive are well known. In such industries, firms must constantly strive to keep their costs low, their quality high, and, when appropriate, innovate if they are to even survive. Low costs, high quality, and appropriate innovation are generally consistent with the interests of a firm's customers, and thus consistent with society's overall welfare.

Indeed, concern for **social welfare**, or the overall good of society, is the primary reason the S-C-P model was developed. This model was to be used to identify industries where perfect competition was not occurring, and thus where social welfare was not being maximized. With these industries identified, the government could then engage in activities to increase the

Is a Firm Gaining a Competitive Advantage Good for Society?

competitiveness of these industries, thereby increasing social welfare.

Strategic management scholars turned the S-C-P model upside down by using it to describe industries where firms could gain competitive advantages and attain above-average performance. However, some have asked that if strategic management is all about creating and exploiting competitive imperfections in industries, is strategic management also all about reducing the overall good of society for advantages to be gained by a few firms? It is not surprising that individuals who are more interested in improving society than improving the

performance of a few firms question the moral legitimacy of the field of strategic management.

However, there is another view about strategic management and social welfare. The S-C-P model assumes that any competitive advantages a firm has in an industry must hurt society. The alternative view is that at least some of the competitive advantages exist because a firm addresses customer needs more effectively than its competitors. From this perspective, competitive advantages are not bad for social welfare; they are actually good for social welfare.

Of course, both perspectives can be true. For example, a firm such as Microsoft has engaged in activities that at least some courts have concluded are inconsistent with social welfare. However, Microsoft also sells applications software that is routinely ranked among the best in the industry, an action that is consistent with meeting customer needs in ways that maximize social welfare.

Sources: J. B. Barney (1986). "Types of competition and the theory of strategy." *Academy of Management Review,* 11, pp. 791–800; H. Demsetz (1973). "Industry structure, market rivalry, and public policy." *Journal of Law and Economics,* 16, pp. 1–9; M. Porter (1981). "The contribution of industrial organization to strategic management." *Academy of Management Review,* 6, pp. 609–620.

The theoretical framework that developed out of this effort became known as the **structure-conduct-performance (S-C-P) model**; it is summarized in Figure 2. The term **structure** in this model refers to industry structure, measured by such factors as the number of competitors in an industry, the heterogeneity of products in an industry, the cost of entry and exit in an industry, and so forth. **Conduct** refers to the strategies that firms in an industry implement. **Performance** in the S-C-P model has two meanings: (1) the performance of individual firms and (2) the performance of the economy as a whole. Although both definitions of performance in the S-C-P model are important, the strategic management process is much more focused on the performance of individual firms than on the performance of the economy as a whole. That said, the

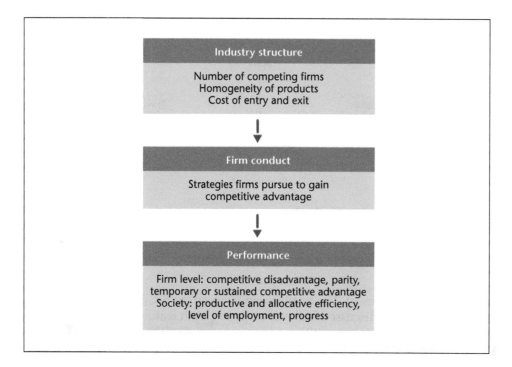

Figure 2 The Structure-Conduct-Performance Model

relationship between these two types of performance can sometimes be complex, as described in the Ethics and Strategy feature.

The logic that links industry structure to conduct and performance is well known. Attributes of the industry structure within which a firm operates define the range of options and constraints facing a firm. In some industries, firms have very few options and face many constraints. In general, firms in these industries can only gain competitive parity. In this setting, industry structure completely determines both firm conduct and long-run firm performance.

However, in other, less competitive industries, firms face fewer constraints and a greater range of conduct options. Some of these options may enable them to obtain competitive advantages. However, even when firms have more conduct options, industry structure still constrains the range of options. Moreover, as will be shown in more detail later in this chapter, industry structure also has an impact on how long firms can expect to maintain their competitive advantages in the face of increased competition.

The Five Forces Model of Environmental Threats

As a theoretical framework, the S-C-P model has proven to be very useful in informing both research and government policy. However, the model can sometimes be awkward to use to identify threats in a firm's local environment. Fortunately, several scholars have developed models of environmental threats based on the S-C-P model that are highly applicable in identifying threats facing a particular firm. The most influential of these models was developed by Professor Michael Porter and is known as the "five forces framework."[11] The **five forces framework** identifies the five most common threats faced by firms in their local competitive environments and the conditions under which these threats are more

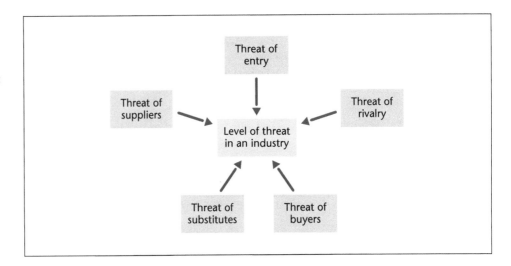

or less likely to be present. The relationship between the S-C-P model and the five forces framework is discussed in the Strategy in Depth feature.

To a firm seeking competitive advantages, an **environmental threat** is any individual, group, or organization outside a firm that seeks to reduce the level of that firm's performance. Threats increase a firm's costs, decrease a firm's revenues, or in other ways reduce a firm's performance. In S-C-P terms, environmental threats are forces that tend to increase the competitiveness of an industry and force firm performance to competitive parity level. The five common environmental threats identified in the five forces framework are: (1) the threat of entry, (2) the threat of rivalry, (3) the threat of substitutes, (4) the threat of suppliers, and (5) the threat of buyers. The five forces framework is summarized in Figure 3.

The Threat of Entry

The first environmental threat identified in the five forces framework is the threat of new entry. **New entrants** are firms that have either recently started operating in an industry or that threaten to begin operations in an industry soon. For Amazon.com, Barnes & Noble.com and Borders.com are new entrants to the online book-ordering business. Amazon largely invented this way of selling books, and both Barnes & Noble and Borders later followed with their entry into this market, even though both these firms already operated in the traditional book sales industry. For ESPN in the television sports industry, the Fox Sports Regional Network is a new entrant. The Fox Sports Regional Network consists of several regional sports channels that broadcast both national and regional sporting events, sports news shows, and sports entertainment shows—including *The Best Damn Sports Show Period*.[12]

According to the S-C-P model, new entrants are motivated to enter into an industry by the superior profits that some incumbent firms in that industry may be earning. Firms seeking these high profits enter the industry, thereby increasing the level of industry competition and reducing the performance of incumbent firms. With the absence of any barriers, entry will continue as long as any firms in the industry are earning competitive advantages, and entry will cease when all incumbent firms are earning competitive parity.

The extent to which new entry acts as a threat to an incumbent firm's performance depends on the cost of entry. If the cost of entry into an industry is

The relationship between the five forces framework and the S-C-P model turns on the relationship between the threats identified in the framework and the nature of competition in an industry. When all five threats are very high, competition in an industry begins to approach what economists call *perfect competition*. When all five threats are very low, competition in an industry begins to approach what economists call a *monopoly*. Between perfect competition and monopoly, economists have identified two other types of competition in an industry—*monopolistic competition* and *oligopoly*—where the five threats identified in the framework are moderately high. These four types of competition, and the expected performance of firms in these different industries, are summarized in the table below.

Industries are **perfectly competitive** when there are large numbers of competing firms, the products being sold are homogeneous with respect to cost and product attributes, and entry and exit costs are very low. An example of a perfectly competitive industry is the spot market for crude oil. Firms

The Five Forces Framework and the S-C-P Model

in perfectly competitive industries can expect to earn only competitive parity.

In **monopolistically competitive industries**, there are large numbers of competing firms and low-cost entry into and exit from the industry. However, unlike the case of perfect competition, products in these industries are not homogeneous with respect to costs or product attributes. Examples of monopolistically competitive industries include toothpaste, shampoo, golf balls, and automobiles. Firms in such industries can earn competitive advantages.

Oligopolies are characterized by a small number of competing firms, by homogeneous products, and by high entry and exit costs. Examples of oligopolistic industries include the U.S. automobile and steel industries in the 1950s and the U.S. breakfast cereal market today. Currently, the top four producers of breakfast cereal account for about 90 percent of the breakfast cereal sold in the United States. Firms in such industries can earn competitive advantages.

Finally, **monopolistic industries** consist of only a single firm. Entry into this type of industry is very costly. There are few examples of purely monopolistic industries. Historically, for example, the U.S. Post Office had a monopoly on home mail delivery. However, this monopoly has been challenged in small-package delivery by FedEx, larger-package delivery by UPS, and in mail delivery by e-mail. Monopolists can generate competitive advantages—although they are sometimes managed very inefficiently.

Source: J. Barney (2007). *Gaining and sustaining competitive advantage,* 3rd ed. Upper Saddle River, NJ: Pearson Higher Education.

Types of Competition and Expected Firm Performance

Type of Competition	Attributes	Examples	Expected Firm Performance
Perfect competition	Large number of firms Homogeneous products Low-cost entry and exit	Stock market Crude oil	Competitive parity
Monopolistic competition	Large number of firms Heterogeneous products Low-cost entry and exit	Toothpaste Shampoo Golf balls Automobiles	Competitive advantage
Oligopoly	Small number of firms Homogenous products Costly entry and exit	U.S. steel and autos in the 1950s U.S. breakfast cereal	Competitive advantage
Monopoly	One firm Costly entry	Home mail delivery	Competitive advantage

TABLE 1 Barriers to Entry into an Industry

1. Economies of scale
2. Product differentiation
3. Cost advantages independent of scale
4. Government regulation of entry

greater than the potential profits a new entrant could obtain by entering, then entry will not be forthcoming, and new entrants are not a threat to incumbent firms. However, if the cost of entry is lower than the return from entry, entry will occur until the profits derived from entry are less than the costs of entry.

The threat of entry depends on the cost of entry, and the cost of entry, in turn, depends on the existence and "height" of barriers to entry. **Barriers to entry** are attributes of an industry's structure that increase the cost of entry. The greater the cost of entry, the greater the height of these barriers. When there are significant barriers to entry, potential entrants will not enter into an industry even if incumbent firms are earning competitive advantages.

Four important barriers to entry have been identified in the S-C-P and strategy literatures. These four barriers, listed in Table 1, are (1) economies of scale, (2) product differentiation, (3) cost advantages independent of scale, and (4) government regulation of entry.[13]

Economies of Scale as a Barrier to Entry

Economies of scale exist in an industry when a firm's costs fall as a function of its volume of production. **Diseconomies of scale** exist when a firm's costs rise as a function of its volume of production. The relationship among economies of scale, diseconomies of scale, and a firm's volume of production is summarized in Figure 4. As a firm's volume of production increases, its costs begin to fall. This is a manifestation of economies of scale. However, at some point a firm's volume of production becomes too large and its costs begin to rise. This is a manifestation of diseconomies of scale. For economies of scale to act as a barrier to entry, the relationship between the volume of production and firm costs must have the shape of

Figure 4 Economies of Scale and the Cost of Production

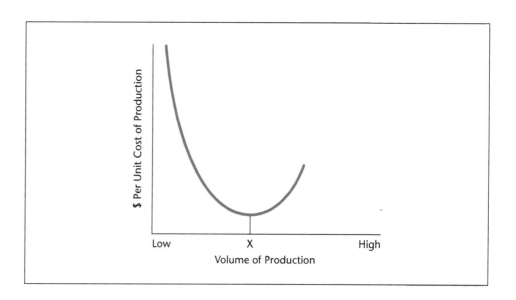

40

the line in Figure 4. This curve suggests that any deviation, positive or negative, from an optimal level of production (point X in Figure 4) will lead a firm to experience much higher costs of production.

To see how economies of scale can act as a barrier to entry, consider the following scenario. Imagine an industry with the following attributes: The industry has five incumbent firms (each firm has only one plant); the optimal level of production in each of these plants is 4,000 units (X = 4,000 units); total demand for the output of this industry is fixed at 22,000 units; the economies-of-scale curve is as depicted in Figure 4; and products in this industry are very homogeneous. Total demand in this industry (22,000 units) is greater than total supply (5 × 4,000 units = 20,000). Everyone knows that, when demand is greater than supply, prices go up. This means that the five incumbent firms in this industry will have high levels of profit. The S-C-P model suggests that, absent barriers, these superior profits should motivate entry.

However, look at the entry decision from the point of view of potential entrants. Certainly, incumbent firms are earning superior profits, but potential entrants face an unsavory choice. On the one hand, new entrants could enter the industry with an optimally efficient plant and produce 4,000 units. However, this form of entry will lead industry supply to rise to 24,000 units (20,000 + 4,000). Suddenly, supply will be greater than demand (24,000 > 22,000), and all the firms in the industry, including the new entrant, will earn negative profits. On the other hand, the new entrant might enter the industry with a plant of smaller-than-optimal size (e.g., 1,000 units). This kind of entry leaves total industry demand larger than industry supply (22,000 > 21,000). However, the new entrant faces a serious cost disadvantage in this case because it does not produce at the low-cost position on the economies-of-scale curve. Faced with these bleak alternatives, the potential entrant simply does not enter even though incumbent firms are earning positive profits.

Of course, potential entrants have other options besides entering at the efficient scale and losing money or entering at an inefficient scale and losing money. For example, potential entrants can attempt to expand the total size of the market (i.e., increase total demand from 22,000 to 24,000 units or more) and enter at the optimal size. Potential entrants can also attempt to develop new production technology, shift the economies-of-scale curve to the left (thereby reducing the optimal plant size), and enter. Or, potential entrants may try to make their products seem very special to their customers, enabling them to charge higher prices to offset higher production costs associated with a smaller-than-optimal plant.[14]

Any of these actions may enable a firm to enter an industry. However, these actions are costly. If the cost of engaging in these "barrier-busting" activities is greater than the return from entry, entry will not occur, even if incumbent firms are earning positive profits.

Historically, economies of scale acted as a barrier to entry into the worldwide steel market. To fully exploit economies of scale, traditional steel plants had to be very large. If new entrants into the steel market had built these efficient and large steel-manufacturing plants, they would have had the effect of increasing the steel supply over the demand for steel, and the outcome would have been reduced profits for both new entrants and incumbent firms. This discouraged new entry. However, in the 1970s, the development of alternative mini-mill technology shifted the economies-of-scale curve to the left by making smaller plants very efficient in addressing some segments of the steel market. This shift had the effect of decreasing barriers to entry into the steel industry. Recent entrants, including Nucor Steel and Chaparral Steel, now have significant cost advantages over firms still using outdated, less efficient production technology.[15]

Product Differentiation as a Barrier to Entry

Product differentiation means that incumbent firms possess brand identification and customer loyalty that potential entrants do not. Brand identification and customer loyalty serve as entry barriers because new entrants not only have to absorb the standard costs associated with starting production in a new industry; they also have to absorb the costs associated with overcoming incumbent firms' differentiation advantages. If the cost of overcoming these advantages is greater than the potential return from entering an industry, entry will not occur, even if incumbent firms are earning positive profits.

Numerous examples exist of industries in which product differentiation tends to act as a barrier to entry. In the brewing industry, for example, substantial investments by Budweiser, Miller, and Coors (among other incumbent firms) in advertising (will we ever forget the Budweiser frogs?) and brand recognition have made large-scale entry into the U.S. brewing industry very costly.[16] Indeed, rather than attempting to enter the U.S. market, InBev, a large brewer headquartered in Belgium, decided to purchase Anheuser Busch.[17]

E. & J. Gallo Winery, a U.S. winemaker, faced product differentiation barriers to entry in its efforts to sell Gallo wine in the French market. The market for wine in France is huge—the French consume 16.1 gallons of wine per person per year, for a total consumption of over 400 million cases of wine, whereas U.S. consumers drink only 1.8 gallons of wine per person per year, for a total consumption of less than 200 million cases. Despite this difference, intense loyalties to local French vineyards have made it very difficult for Gallo to break into the huge French market—a market where American wines are still given as "gag gifts" and only American theme restaurants carry U.S. wines on their menus. Gallo is attempting to overcome this product differentiation advantage of French wineries by emphasizing its California roots—roots that many French consider to be exotic—and downplaying the fact that it is a U.S. company, corporate origins that are less attractive to many French consumers.[18]

Cost Advantages Independent of Scale as Barriers to Entry

In addition to the barriers that have been cited, incumbent firms may have a whole range of cost advantages, independent of economies of scale, compared to new entrants. These cost advantages can act to deter entry, because new entrants will find themselves at a cost disadvantage vis-à-vis incumbent firms with these cost advantages. New entrants can engage in activities to overcome the cost advantages of incumbent firms, but as the cost of overcoming them increases, the economic profit potential from entry is reduced. In some settings, incumbent firms enjoying cost advantages, independent of scale, can earn superior profits and still not be threatened by new entry because the cost of overcoming those advantages can be prohibitive. Examples of these cost advantages, independent of scale, are presented in Table 2; they include (1) proprietary technology, (2) managerial know-how, (3) favorable access to raw materials, and (4) learning-curve cost advantages.

Proprietary Technology. In some industries, **proprietary** (i.e., secret or patented) **technology** gives incumbent firms important cost advantages over potential entrants. To enter these industries, potential entrants must develop their own substitute technologies or run the risks of copying another firm's patented technologies. Both of these activities can be costly. Numerous firms in a wide variety of industries have discovered the sometimes substantial economic costs associated with violating another firm's patented proprietary technology. For

Proprietary technology. When incumbent firms have secret or patented technology that reduces their costs below the costs of potential entrants, potential entrants must develop substitute technologies to compete. The cost of developing this technology can act as a barrier to entry.

Managerial know-how. When incumbent firms have taken-for-granted knowledge, skills, and information that take years to develop and that is not possessed by potential entrants. The cost of developing this know-how can act as a barrier to entry.

Favorable access to raw materials. When incumbent firms have low-cost access to critical raw materials not enjoyed by potential entrants. The cost of gaining similar access can act as a barrier to entry.

Learning-curve cost advantages. When the cumulative volume of production of incumbent firms gives them cost advantages not enjoyed by potential entrants. These cost disadvantages of potential entrants can act as a barrier to entry.

example, in the 1990s Eastman Kodak had to pay Polaroid $910 million and Intel had to pay Digital $700 million for violating patents. More recently, Roche Holding had to pay Igen International $505 million and Genentech had to pay City of Hope National Medical Center $500 million for violating patents. Eolas had to pay $521 million for infringing a Microsoft patent, and Gateway had to pay $250 million for violating an Intergraph patent.

Indeed, in the United States at least 20 firms have had to pay some other firm over $100 million for violating the other firm's patents. And this does not include the numerous patent infringement suits that are settled out of court, suits that involve literally billions of dollars exchanging hands. Obviously, if an industry has several firms with proprietary technologies, these technologies can substantially increase the cost of entry into that industry.[19]

The number of patent infringement suits filed in the United States has increased every year for the past 15 years. The number of such suits in 1991 was 1,171; the number in 2004 (the last year for which complete data are available) was 3,075. Since 1994, the median damage award in a patent infringement suit has been $8 million. Currently, 60 percent of the patent infringement suits filed lead to financial compensation. Patent suits are distributed across numerous industries, including electronic equipment (14.6 percent), chemicals (14 percent), measuring instruments (13.4 percent), computer equipment (12 percent), and business services (9.8 percent).[20]

Managerial Know-How. Even more important than technology per se as a barrier to entry is the managerial know-how built up by incumbent firms over their history.[21] **Managerial know-how** is the often-taken-for-granted knowledge and information that are needed to compete in an industry on a day-to-day basis.[22] Know-how includes information that it has taken years, sometimes decades, for a firm to accumulate that enables it to interact with customers and suppliers, to be innovative and creative, to manufacture quality products, and so forth. Typically, new entrants will not have access to this know-now, and it will often be costly for them to build it quickly.

One industry where this kind of know-how is a very important barrier to entry is the pharmaceutical industry. Success in this industry depends on having high-quality research and development skills. The development of world-class research and development skills—the know-how—takes decades to accumulate. New entrants face enormous cost disadvantages for decades as they attempt to develop these abilities, and thus entry into the pharmaceutical industry has been quite limited.[23]

Favorable Access to Raw Materials.   Incumbent firms may also have cost advantages, compared to new entrants, based on favorable access to raw materials. If, for example, only a few sources of high-quality iron ore are available in a specific geographic region, steel firms that have access to these sources may have a cost advantage over those that must ship their ore in from distant sources.[24]

Learning-Curve Cost Advantages.   It has been shown that in certain industries (such as airplane manufacturing) the cost of production falls with the cumulative volume of production. Over time, as incumbent firms gain experience in manufacturing, their costs fall below those of potential entrants. Potential entrants, in this context, must endure substantially higher costs while they gain experience, and thus they may not enter the industry despite the superior profits being earned by incumbent firms.

Government Policy as a Barrier to Entry

Governments, for their own reasons, may decide to increase the cost of entry into an industry. This occurs most frequently when a firm operates as a government-regulated monopoly. In this setting, the government has concluded that it is in a better position to ensure that specific products or services are made available to the population at reasonable prices than competitive market forces. Industries such as electric power generation and elementary and secondary education have been (and to some extent, continue to be) protected from competitive entry by government restrictions on entry.

Although the government has acted to restrict competitive entry in many industries in the past, the number of such industries and the level of this entry restriction have both fallen dramatically over the past several years. Indeed, in the United States, deregulation in the electric power generation industry has been occurring at a rapid pace. And although the bankruptcy of Enron may delay the relaxing of government-imposed barriers to entry into the power generation industry, most observers agree that these restrictions will continue to be less important in the future. Entry is even occurring in the primary and secondary school industry with the creation of "charter schools"—schools that provide educational alternatives to traditional public school systems.

The Threat of Rivalry

New entrants are an important threat to the ability of firms to maintain or improve their level of performance, but they are not the only threat in a firm's environment. A second environmental threat in the five forces framework is **rivalry**—the intensity of competition among a firm's direct competitors. Both Barnes & Noble.com and Borders.com have become rivals of Amazon.com. CBS, NBC, Fox, USA Networks, and TNN—to name a few—are all rivals of ESPN.

Rivalry threatens firms by reducing their economic profits. High levels of rivalry are indicated by such actions as frequent price cutting by firms in an

TABLE 3 Attributes of an Industry That Increase the Threat of Rivalry

1. Large number of competing firms that are roughly the same size
2. Slow industry growth
3. Lack of product differentiation
4. Capacity added in large increments

industry (e.g., price discounts in the airline industry), frequent introduction of new products by firms in an industry (e.g., continuous product introductions in consumer electronics), intense advertising campaigns (e.g., Pepsi versus Coke advertising), and rapid competitive actions and reactions in an industry (e.g., competing airlines quickly matching the discounts of other airlines).

Some of the attributes of an industry that are likely to generate high levels of rivalry are listed in Table 3. First, rivalry tends to be high when there are numerous firms in an industry and these firms tend to be roughly the same size. Such is the case in the laptop personal computer industry. Worldwide, over 120 firms have entered the laptop computer market, and no one firm dominates in market share. Since the early 1990s, prices in the laptop market have been declining 25 to 30 percent a year. Profit margins for laptop personal computer firms that used to be in the 10 to 13 percent range have rapidly fallen to 3 to 4 percent.[25]

Second, rivalry tends to be high when industry growth is slow. When industry growth is slow, firms seeking to increase their sales must acquire market share from established competitors. This tends to increase rivalry. Intense price rivalry emerged in the U.S. fast-food industry—with 99-cent Whoppers at Burger King and "dollar menus" at Wendy's and McDonald's—when the growth in this industry declined.[26]

Third, rivalry tends to be high when firms are unable to differentiate their products in an industry. When product differentiation is not a viable strategic option, firms are often forced to compete only on the basis of price. Intense price competition is typical of high-rivalry industries. In the airline industry, for example, intense competition on longer routes—such as between Los Angeles and New York and Los Angeles and Chicago—has kept prices on these routes down. These routes have relatively few product differentiation options. However, by creating hub-and-spoke systems, certain airlines (American, United, Delta) have been able to develop regions of the United States where they are the dominant carrier. These hub-and-spoke systems enable airlines to partially differentiate their products geographically, thus reducing the level of rivalry in segments of this industry.[27]

Finally, rivalry tends to be high when production capacity is added in large increments. If, in order to obtain economies of scale, production capacity must be added in large increments, an industry is likely to experience periods of oversupply after new capacity comes on line. This overcapacity often leads to price cuts. Much of the growing rivalry in the commercial jet industry between Boeing and AirBus can be traced to the large manufacturing capacity additions made by AirBus when it entered the industry.[28]

The Threat of Substitutes

A third environmental threat in the five forces framework is substitutes. The products or services provided by a firm's rivals meet approximately the same customer needs in the same ways as the products or services provided by the firm itself. **Substitutes** meet approximately the same customer needs, but do so in different ways. Close substitutes for Amazon.com include Barnes & Noble and Borders bookstores. Television is a somewhat more distant substitute for Amazon, because the popularity of television comedies, dramas, and documentaries dampens demand for books. Substitutes for ESPN include sports magazines, sports pages in the newspapers, and actually attending sporting events.

Substitutes place a ceiling on the prices firms in an industry can charge and on the profits firms in an industry can earn. In the extreme, substitutes can ultimately replace an industry's products and services. This happens when a substitute is clearly superior to previous products. Examples include electronic calculators as substitutes for slide rules and mechanical calculators, electronic watch movements as substitutes for pin–lever mechanical watch movements, and compact discs as substitutes for long-playing (LP) records (although some audiophiles continue to argue for the sonic superiority of LPs). An open question remains about the extent to which online downloading of music will replace compact discs.

Substitutes are playing an increasingly important role in reducing the profit potential in a variety of industries. For example, in the legal profession private mediation and arbitration services are becoming viable substitutes for lawyers. Computerized texts are becoming viable substitutes for printed books in the publishing industry. Television news programs, especially services such as CNN, are very threatening substitutes for weekly newsmagazines, including *Time* and *Newsweek*. In Europe, so-called superstores are threatening smaller food shops. Minor league baseball teams are partial substitutes for major league teams. Cable television is a substitute for broadcast television. Groups of "Big Box" retailers are substitutes for traditional shopping centers. Private mail delivery systems (such as those in the Netherlands and Australia) are substitutes for government postal services. Home financial planning software is a partial substitute for professional financial planners.[29]

The Threat of Powerful Suppliers

A fourth environmental threat in the five forces framework is suppliers. **Suppliers** make a wide variety of raw materials, labor, and other critical assets available to firms. Suppliers can threaten the performance of firms in an industry by increasing the price of their supplies or by reducing the quality of those supplies. Any profits that were being earned in an industry can be transferred to suppliers in this way. For Amazon, book publishers and, more recently, book authors are critical suppliers, along with the employees that provide programming and logistics capabilities to Amazon. Critical suppliers for ESPN include sports leagues—such as the NFL and the NHL—as well as the TV personalities that staff ESPN television shows.

Some supplier attributes that can lead to high levels of threat are listed in Table 4. First, a firm's suppliers are a greater threat if the *suppliers'* industry is

TABLE 4 Indicators of the Threat of Suppliers in an Industry

1. Suppliers' industry is dominated by small number of firms.
2. Suppliers sell unique or highly differentiated products.
3. Suppliers are *not* threatened by substitutes.
4. Suppliers threaten forward vertical integration.
5. Firms are *not* important customers for suppliers.

dominated by a small number of firms. In this setting, a firm has little choice but to purchase supplies from these firms. These few firms thus have enormous flexibility to charge high prices, to reduce quality, or in other ways to squeeze the profits of the firms to which they sell. Much of Microsoft's power in the software industry reflects its dominance in the operating system market, where Windows Vista remains the de facto standard for most personal computers. For now, at least, if a company wants to sell personal computers, it is going to need to interact with Microsoft. It will be interesting to see if Linux-based PCs become more powerful, thereby limiting some of Microsoft's power as a supplier.

Conversely, when a firm has the option of purchasing from a large number of suppliers, suppliers have less power to threaten a firm's profits. For example, as the number of lawyers in the United States has increased over the years (up 40 percent since 1981, currently over 1 million), lawyers and law firms have been forced to begin competing for work. Some corporate clients have forced law firms to reduce their hourly fees and to handle repetitive simple legal tasks for low flat fees.[30]

Second, suppliers are a greater threat when what they supply is unique or highly differentiated. There was only one Michael Jordan, as a basketball player, as a spokesperson, and as a celebrity (but *not* as a baseball player). Jordan's unique status gave him enormous bargaining power as a supplier and enabled him to extract much of the economic profit that would otherwise have been earned by the Chicago Bulls and Nike. Currently, there is only one LeBron James. In the same way, Intel's unique ability to develop, manufacture, and sell microprocessors gives it significant bargaining power as a supplier in the personal computer industry.

The uniqueness of suppliers can operate in almost any industry. For example, in the highly competitive world of television talk shows, some guests, as suppliers, can gain surprising fame for their unique characteristics. For example, one woman was a guest on eight talk shows. Her claim to fame: She was the tenth wife of a gay, con-man bigamist. Talk show hosts can also exercise significant power as suppliers. King World, the distributor of the *Oprah* talk show, has depended on *Oprah* for as much as 40 percent of its revenues. This, of course, has given the show's host, Oprah Winfrey, significant leverage in negotiating with King World.[31]

Third, suppliers are a greater threat to firms in an industry when suppliers are *not* threatened by substitutes. When there are no effective substitutes, suppliers can take advantage of their position to extract economic profits from firms they supply. Both Intel (in microprocessors) and Microsoft (in PC operating systems) have been accused of exploiting their unique product positions to extract profits from customers.

When there are substitutes for supplies, supplier power is checked. In the metal can industry, for example, steel cans are threatened by aluminum and plastic containers as substitutes. In order to continue to sell to can manufacturers, steel companies have had to keep their prices lower than would otherwise have been the case. In this way, the potential power of the steel companies is checked by the existence of substitute products.[32]

Fourth, suppliers are a greater threat to firms when they can credibly threaten to enter into and begin competing in a firm's industry. This is called **forward vertical integration**; in this situation, suppliers cease to be suppliers only and become suppliers *and* rivals. The threat of forward vertical integration is partially a function of barriers to entry into an industry. When an industry has high barriers to entry, suppliers face significant costs of forward vertical integration, and thus forward integration is not as serious a threat to the profits of incumbent firms.

Finally, suppliers are a threat to firms when firms are *not* an important part of suppliers' business. Steel companies, for example, are not too concerned with losing the business of a sculptor or of a small construction company. However, they are very concerned about losing the business of the major can manufacturers, major white-goods manufacturers (i.e., manufacturers of refrigerators, washing machines, dryers, and so forth), and automobile companies. Steel companies, as suppliers, are likely to be very accommodating and willing to reduce prices and increase quality for can manufacturers, white-goods manufacturers, and auto companies. Smaller, "less important" customers, however, are likely to be subject to greater price increases, lower-quality service, and lower-quality products.

The Threat of Powerful Buyers

The final environmental threat in the five forces framework is buyers. **Buyers** purchase a firm's products or services. Whereas powerful suppliers act to increase a firm's costs, powerful buyers act to decrease a firm's revenues. Amazon.com's buyers include all those who purchase books online as well as those who purchase advertising space on Amazon's Web site. ESPN's buyers include all those who watch sports on television as well as those who purchase advertising space on the network. Some of the important indicators of the threat of buyers are listed in Table 5.

First, if a firm has only one buyer, or a small number of buyers, these buyers can be very threatening. Firms that sell a significant amount of their output to the U.S. Department of Defense recognize the influence of this buyer on their operations. Reductions in defense spending have forced defense companies to try even harder to reduce costs and increase quality to satisfy government demands. All these actions reduce the economic profits of these defense-oriented companies.[33] Firms that sell to large retail chains have also found it difficult to maintain high levels of profitability. Powerful retail firms—such as Wal-Mart and Home Depot—can make significant and complex logistical and other demands on their suppliers and, if suppliers fail to meet these demands, buyers can "fire" their suppliers. These demands can have the effect of reducing the profits of suppliers.

Second, if the products or services that are being sold to buyers are standard and not differentiated, then the threat of buyers can be greater. For example, farmers sell a very standard product. It is very difficult to differentiate products such as wheat, corn, or tomatoes (although this can be done to some extent through the development of new strains of crops, the timing of harvests, pesticide-free crops, and so forth). In general, wholesale grocers and food brokers can always find alternative suppliers of basic food products. These numerous alternative suppliers increase the threat of buyers and force farmers to keep their prices and profits low. If any one farmer attempts to raise prices, wholesale grocers and food brokers simply purchase their supplies from some other farmer.

TABLE 5 Indicators of the Threat of Buyers in an Industry

1. Number of buyers is small.
2. Products sold to buyers are undifferentiated and standard.
3. Products sold to buyers are a significant percentage of a buyer's final costs.
4. Buyers are *not* earning significant economic profits.
5. Buyers threaten backward vertical integration.

Third, buyers are likely to be more of a threat when the supplies they purchase are a significant portion of the costs of their final products. In this context, buyers are likely to be very concerned about the costs of their supplies and constantly on the lookout for cheaper alternatives. For example, in the canned food industry, the cost of the can itself can constitute up to 40 percent of a product's final price. Not surprisingly, firms such as Campbell Soup Company are very concerned about keeping the price of the cans they purchase as low as possible.[34]

Fourth, buyers are likely to be more of a threat when they are *not* earning significant economic profits. In these circumstances, buyers are likely to be very sensitive to costs and insist on the lowest possible cost and the highest possible quality from suppliers. This effect can be exacerbated when the profits suppliers earn are greater than the profits buyers earn. In this setting, a buyer would have a strong incentive to enter into its supplier's business to capture some of the economic profits being earned by the supplier.

Finally, buyers are more of a threat to firms in an industry when they have the ability to vertically integrate backward. In this case, buyers become both buyers and rivals and lock in a certain percentage of an industry's sales. The extent to which buyers represent a threat to vertically integrate, in turn, depends on the barriers to entry that are not in place in an industry. If there are significant barriers to entry, buyers may not be able to engage in backward vertical integration, and their threat to firms is reduced.

The Five Forces Model and Average Industry Performance

The five forces model has three important implications for managers seeking to choose and implement strategies. First, this model describes the most common sources of local environmental threat in industries. These are the threat of entry, the threat of rivalry, the threat of substitutes, the threat of suppliers, and the threat of buyers. Second, this model can be used to characterize the overall level of threat in an industry. Finally, because the overall level of threat in an industry is, according to S-C-P logic, related to the average level of performance of a firm in an industry, the five forces model can also be used to anticipate the average level of performance of firms in an industry.

Of course, it will rarely be the case that all five forces in an industry will be equally threatening at the same time. This can sometimes complicate the anticipation of the average level of firm performance in an industry. Consider, for example, the four industries in Table 6. It is easy to anticipate the average level of performance of firms in the first two industries: In Industry I, this performance will be

	Industry I	Industry II	Industry III	Industry IV
Threat of entry	High	Low	High	Low
Threat of rivalry	High	Low	Low	High
Threat of substitutes	High	Low	High	Low
Threat of powerful suppliers	High	Low	Low	High
Threat of powerful buyers	High	Low	High	Low
Expected average firm performance	Low	High	Mixed	Mixed

TABLE 6 Estimating the Level of Average Performance in an Industry

low; in Industry II, this performance will be high; however, in Industries III and IV it is somewhat more complicated. In these mixed situations, the real question to ask in anticipating the average performance of firms in an industry is, "Are one or more threats in this industry powerful enough to appropriate most of the profits that firms in this industry might generate?" If the answer to this question is yes, then the anticipated average level of performance will be low. If the answer is no, then the anticipated performance will be high.

Even more fundamentally, the five forces framework can be used only to anticipate the average level of firm performance in an industry. This is acceptable if a firm's industry is the primary determinant of its overall performance. However, as described in the Research Made Relevant feature, research suggests that the industry a firm operates in is far from the only determinant of its performance.

Another Environmental Force: Complementors

Recently, Professors Adam Brandenburger and Barry Nalebuff have suggested that another force needs to be added to Porter's five forces framework.[35] These authors distinguish between competitors and what they call a firm's *complementors*. If you were the Chief Executive Officer of a firm, the following is how you could tell the difference between your competitors and your complementors: Another firm is a **competitor** if your customers value your product less when they have the other firm's product than when they have your product alone. Rivals, new entrants, and substitutes are all examples of competitors. In contrast, another firm is a **complementor** if your customers value your product more when they have this other firm's product than when they have your product alone.

Consider, for example, the relationship between producers of television programming and cable television companies. The value of these firms' products partially depends on the existence of one another. Television producers need outlets for their programming. The growth in the number of channels on cable television provides more of these outlets and thus increases the value of these production firms. Cable television companies can continue to add channels, but those channels need content. So, the value of cable television companies depends partly on the existence of television production firms. Because the value of program-producing companies is greater when cable television firms exist and because the value of cable television companies is greater when program-producing companies exist, these types of firms are complements.

Brandenburger and Nalebuff go on to argue that an important difference between complementors and competitors is that a firm's complementors help to increase the size of a firm's market, whereas a firm's competitors divide this market among a set of firms. Based on this logic, these authors suggest that, although it is usually the case that a firm will want to discourage the entry of competitors into its market, it will usually want to encourage the entry of complementors. Returning to the television producers/cable television example, television producers will actually want cable television companies to grow and prosper and constantly add new channels, and cable television firms will want television show producers to grow and constantly create new and innovative programming. If the growth of either of these businesses slows, it hurts the growth of the other.

Of course, the same firm can be a complementor for one firm and a competitor for another. For example, the invention of satellite television and increased popularity of DirecTV and the Dish Network represent a competitive challenge to cable television companies. That is, DirecTV and, say, Time Warner Cable are

Research Made Relevant

For some time now, scholars have been interested in the relative impact of the attributes of the industry within which a firm operates and the attributes of the firm itself on its performance. The first work in this area was published by Richard Schmalansee. Using a single year's worth of data, Schmalansee estimated the variance in the performance of firms that was attributable to the industries within which firms operated versus other sources of performance variance. Schmalansee's conclusion was that approximately 20 percent of the variance in firm performance was explained by the industry within which a firm operated—a conclusion consistent with the S-C-P model and its emphasis on industry as a primary determinant of a firm's performance.

Richard Rumelt identified some weaknesses in Schmalansee's research. Most important of these was that Schmalansee had only one year's worth of data with which to examine the effects of industry and firm attributes on firm performance. Rumelt was able to use four years' worth of data, which allowed him to distinguish between stable and transient industry and firm effects on firm performance.

The Impact of Industry and Firm Characteristics on Firm Performance

Rumelt's results were consistent with Schmalansee's in one sense: Rumelt also found that about 16 percent of the variance in firm performance was due to industry effects, versus Schmalansee's 20 percent. However, only about half of this industry effect was stable. The rest represented year-to-year fluctuations in the business conditions in an industry. This result is broadly inconsistent with the S-C-P model.

Rumelt also examined the impact of firm attributes on firm performance and found that over 80 percent of the variance in firm performance was due

to these firm attributes, but that over half of this 80 percent (46.38 percent) was due to stable firm effects. The importance of stable firm differences in explaining differences in firm performance is also inconsistent with the S-C-P framework. These results are consistent with another model of firm performance called the *Resource-Based View*.

Since Rumelt's research, efforts to identify the factors that explain variance in firm performance have accelerated. At least nine articles addressing this issue have been published in the literature. One of the most recent of these suggests that, while the impact of the industry, the corporation, and the business on business unit performance can vary across industries and across corporations, overall, business unit effects are larger than either corporate or industry effects.

Sources: R. P. Rumelt (1991). "How much does industry matter?" *Strategic Management Journal*, 12, pp. 167–185; R. Schmalansee (1985). "Do markets differ much?" *American Economic Review*, 75, pp. 341–351; V. F. Misangyi, H. Elms, T. Greckhamer, and J. A. Lepine (2006). "A new perspective on a fundamental debate: A multi-level approach to industry, corporate, and business unit effects." *Strategic Management Journal*, 27(6), pp. 571–590.

competitors. However, DirecTV and television production companies are complementors to each other. In deciding whether to encourage the entry of new complementors, a firm has to weigh the extra value these new complementors will create against the competitive impact of this entry on a firm's current complementors.

It is also the case that a single firm can be both a competitor and a complementor to the same firm. This is very common in industries where it is important to create technological standards. Without standards for, say, the size of a CD, how information on a CD will be stored, how this information will be read, and so forth, consumers will often be unwilling to purchase a CD player. With standards in place, however, sales of a particular technology can soar. To develop technology standards, firms must be willing to cooperate. This cooperation means that, with respect to the technology standard, these firms are complementors. And indeed, when these firms act as complementors, their actions have the effect of increasing the total size of the market. However, once these firms cooperate to establish standards, they begin to compete to try to obtain as much of the market they jointly created as possible. In this sense, these firms are also competitors.

Understanding when firms in an industry should behave as complementors and when they should behave as competitors is sometimes very difficult. It is even more difficult for a firm that has interacted with other firms in its industry as a competitor to change its organizational structure, formal and informal control systems, and compensation policy and start interacting with these firms as a complementor, at least for some purposes. Learning to manage what Brandenburger and Nalebuff call the "Jekyll and Hyde" dilemma associated with competitors and complementors can distinguish excellent from average firms.

Industry Structure and Environmental Opportunities

Identifying environmental threats is only half the task in accomplishing an external analysis. Such an analysis must also identify opportunities. Fortunately, the same S-C-P logic that made it possible to develop tools for the analysis of environmental threats can also be used to develop tools for the analysis of environmental opportunities. However, instead of identifying the threats that are common in most industries, opportunity analysis begins by identifying several generic industry structures and then describing the strategic opportunities that are available in each of these different kinds of industries.[36]

Of course, there are many different generic industry structures. However, four are very common: (1) fragmented industries, (2) emerging industries, (3) mature industries, and (4) declining industries. A fifth industry structure—international industries—will be discussed later in the chapter. The kinds of opportunities typically associated with these industry structures are presented in Table 7.

Opportunities in Fragmented Industries: Consolidation

Fragmented industries are industries in which a large number of small or medium-sized firms operate and no small set of firms has dominant market share or creates dominant technologies. Most service industries, including retailing, fabrics, and commercial printing, to name just a few, are fragmented industries.

TABLE 7 Industry Structure and Environmental Opportunities

Industry Structure	Opportunities
Fragmented industry	Consolidation
Emerging industry	First-mover advantages
Mature industry	Product refinement
	Investment in service quality
	Process innovation
Declining industry	Leadership
	Niche
	Harvest
	Divestment

Industries can be fragmented for a wide variety of reasons. For example, the fragmented industry may have few barriers to entry, thereby encouraging numerous small firms to enter. The industry may have few, if any, economies of scale, and even some important diseconomies of scale, thus encouraging firms to remain small. Also, close local control over enterprises in an industry may be necessary—for example, local movie houses and local restaurants—to ensure quality and to minimize losses from theft.

The major opportunity facing firms in fragmented industries is the implementation of strategies that begin to consolidate the industry into a smaller number of firms. Firms that are successful in implementing this **consolidation strategy** can become industry leaders and obtain benefits from this kind of effort, if they exist.

Consolidation can occur in several ways. For example, an incumbent firm may discover new economies of scale in an industry. In the highly fragmented funeral home industry, Service Corporation International (SCI) found that the development of a chain of funeral homes gave it advantages in acquiring key supplies (coffins) and in the allocation of scarce resources (morticians and hearses). By acquiring numerous previously independent funeral homes, SCI was able to substantially reduce its costs and gain higher levels of economic performance.[37]

Incumbent firms sometimes adopt new ownership structures to help consolidate an industry. Kampgrounds of America (KOA) uses franchise agreements with local operators to provide camping facilities to travelers in the fragmented private campgrounds industry. KOA provides local operators with professional training, technical skills, and access to its brand-name reputation. Local operators, in return, provide KOA with local managers who are intensely interested in the financial and operational success of their campgrounds. Similar franchise agreements have been instrumental in the consolidation of other fragmented industries, including fast food (McDonald's), muffler repair (Midas), and motels (La Quinta, Holiday Inn, Howard Johnson's).[38]

The benefits of implementing a consolidation strategy in a fragmented industry turn on the advantages larger firms in such industries gain from their larger market share. Firms with large market share can have important cost advantages. Large market share can also help a firm differentiate its products.

Opportunities in Emerging Industries: First-Mover Advantages

Emerging industries are newly created or newly re-created industries formed by technological innovations, changes in demand, the emergence of new customer needs, and so forth. Over the past 30 years, the world economy has been flooded by emerging industries, including the microprocessor industry, the personal computer industry, the medical imaging industry, and the biotechnology industry, to name a few. Firms in emerging industries face a unique set of opportunities, the exploitation of which can be a source of superior performance for some time for some firms.

The opportunities that face firms in emerging industries fall into the general category of first-mover advantages. **First-mover advantages** are advantages that come to firms that make important strategic and technological decisions early in the development of an industry. In emerging industries, many of the rules of the game and standard operating procedures for competing and succeeding have yet to be established. First-moving firms can sometimes help establish the rules of the game and create an industry's structure in ways that are uniquely beneficial to them.

In general, first-mover advantages can arise from three primary sources: (1) technological leadership, (2) preemption of strategically valuable assets, and (3) the creation of customer-switching costs.[39]

First-Mover Advantages and Technological Leadership

Firms that make early investments in particular technologies in an industry are implementing a **technological leadership strategy**. Such strategies can generate two advantages in emerging industries. First, firms that have implemented these strategies may obtain a low-cost position based on their greater cumulative volume of production with a particular technology. These cost advantages have had important competitive implications in such diverse industries as the manufacture of titanium dioxide by DuPont and Procter & Gamble's competitive advantage in disposable diapers.[40]

Second, firms that make early investments in a technology may obtain patent protections that enhance their performance.[41] Xerox's patents on the xerography process and General Electric's patent on Edison's original lightbulb design were important for these firms' success when these two industries were emerging.[42] However, although there are some exceptions (e.g., the pharmaceutical industry and specialty chemicals), patents, per se, seem to provide relatively small profit opportunities for first-moving firms in most emerging industries. One group of researchers found that imitators can duplicate first movers' patent-based advantages for about 65 percent of the first mover's costs.[43] These researchers also found that 60 percent of all patents are imitated within four years of being granted—without legally violating patent rights obtained by first movers. Patents are rarely a source of sustained competitive advantage for firms, even in emerging industries.

First-Mover Advantages and Preemption of Strategically Valuable Assets

First movers that invest only in technology usually do not obtain sustained competitive advantages. However, first movers that move to tie up strategically valuable resources in an industry before their full value is widely understood can gain sustained competitive advantages. **Strategically valuable assets** are resources required to successfully compete in an industry. Firms that are able to acquire these resources have, in effect, erected formidable barriers to imitation in an industry. Some strategically valuable assets that can be acquired in this way include access to raw materials, particularly favorable geographic locations, and particularly valuable product market positions.

When an oil company such as Royal Dutch Shell (because of its superior exploration skills) acquires leases with greater development potential than was expected by its competition, the company is gaining access to raw materials in a way that is likely to generate sustained competitive advantages. When Wal-Mart opens stores in medium-sized cities before the arrival of its competition, Wal-Mart is making it difficult for the competition to enter into this market. And, when breakfast cereal companies expand their product lines to include all possible combinations of wheat, oats, bran, corn, and sugar, they, too, are using a first-mover advantage to deter entry.[44]

First-Mover Advantages and Creating Customer-Switching Costs

Firms can also gain first-mover advantages in an emerging industry by creating customer-switching costs. **Customer-switching costs** exist when customers make investments in order to use a firm's particular products or services. These investments tie customers to a particular firm and make it more difficult for customers to begin purchasing from other firms.[45] Such switching costs are important factors in industries as diverse as applications software for personal computers, prescription pharmaceuticals, and groceries.[46]

In applications software for personal computers, users make significant investments to learn how to use a particular software package. Once computer users have learned how to operate particular software, they are unlikely to switch to new software, even if that new software system is superior to what they currently use. Such a switch would require learning the new software and determining how it is similar to and different from the old software. For these reasons, some computer users will continue to use outdated software, even though new software performs much better.

Similar switching costs can exist in some segments of the prescription pharmaceutical industry. Once medical doctors become familiar with a particular drug, its applications, and side effects, they are sometimes reluctant to change to a new drug, even if that new drug promises to be more effective than the older, more familiar one. Trying the new drug requires learning about its properties and side effects. Even if the new drug has received government approvals, its use requires doctors to be willing to "experiment" with the health of their patients. Given these issues, many physicians are unwilling to rapidly adopt new drug therapies. This is one reason that pharmaceutical firms spend so much time and money using their sales forces to educate their physician customers. This kind of education is necessary if a doctor is going to be willing to switch from an old drug to a new one.

Customer-switching costs can even play a role in the grocery store industry. Each grocery store has a particular layout of products. Once customers learn where different products in a particular store are located, they are not likely to change stores, because they would then have to relearn the location of products. Many customers want to avoid the time and frustration associated with wandering around a new store looking for some obscure product. Indeed, the cost of switching stores may be large enough to enable some grocery stores to charge higher prices than would be the case without customer-switching costs.

First-Mover Disadvantages

Of course, the advantages of first moving in emerging industries must be balanced against the risks associated with exploiting this opportunity. Emerging industries are characterized by a great deal of uncertainty. When first-moving firms are making critical strategic decisions, it may not be at all clear what the right decisions are. In such highly uncertain settings, a reasonable strategic alternative to first moving may be retaining flexibility. Where first-moving firms attempt to resolve the uncertainty they face by making decisions early and then trying to influence the evolution of an emerging industry, they use flexibility to resolve this uncertainty by delaying decisions until the economically correct path is clear and then moving quickly to take advantage of that path.

Opportunities in Mature Industries: Product Refinement, Service, and Process Innovation

Emerging industries are often formed by the creation of new products or technologies that radically alter the rules of the game in an industry. However, over time, as these new ways of doing business become widely understood, as technologies diffuse through competitors, and as the rate of innovation in new products and technologies drops, an industry begins to enter the mature phase of its development. As described in the Strategy in the Emerging Enterprise feature, this change in the nature of a firm's industry can be difficult to recognize and can create both strategic and operational problems for a firm.

Common characteristics of **mature industries** include (1) slowing growth in total industry demand, (2) the development of experienced repeat customers, (3) a slowdown in increases in production capacity, (4) a slowdown in the introduction of new products or services, (5) an increase in the amount of international competition, and (6) an overall reduction in the profitability of firms in the industry.[47]

The fast-food industry in the United States has matured over the past 10 to 15 years. In the 1960s, the United States had only three large national fast-food chains: McDonald's, Burger King, and Dairy Queen. Through the 1980s, all three of these chains grew rapidly, although the rate of growth at McDonald's outstripped the growth rate of the other two firms. During this time period, however, other fast-food chains also entered the market. These included some national chains, such as Kentucky Fried Chicken, Wendy's, and Taco Bell, and some strong regional chains, such as Jack in the Box and In and Out Burger. By the early 1990s, growth in this industry had slowed considerably. McDonald's announced that it was having difficulty finding locations for new McDonald's that did not impinge on the sales of already existing McDonald's. Except for non–U.S. operations, where competition in the fast-food industry is not as mature, the profitability of most U.S. fast-food companies did not grow as much in the 1990s as it did in the 1960s through the 1980s. Indeed, by 2002, all the major fast-food chains were either not making very much money, or, like McDonald's, actually losing money.[48]

Opportunities for firms in mature industries typically shift from the development of new technologies and products in an emerging industry to a greater emphasis on refining a firm's current products, an emphasis on increasing the quality of service, and a focus on reducing manufacturing costs and increased quality through process innovations.

Refining Current Products

In mature industries, such as home detergents, motor oil, and kitchen appliances, few, if any, major technological breakthroughs are likely. However, this does not mean that innovation is not occurring in these industries. Innovation in these industries focuses on extending and improving current products and technologies. In home detergents, innovation recently has focused on changes in packaging and on selling more highly concentrated detergents. In motor oil, packaging changes (from fiber foil cans to plastic containers), additives that keep oil cleaner longer, and oil formulated to operate in four-cylinder engines are recent examples of this kind of innovation. In kitchen appliances, recent improvements include the availability of refrigerators with crushed ice and water through the door, commercial-grade stoves for home use, and dishwashers that automatically adjust the cleaning cycle depending on how dirty the dishes are.[49]

Emphasis on Service

When firms in an industry have only limited ability to invest in radical new technologies and products, efforts to differentiate products often turn toward the quality of customer service. A firm that is able to develop a reputation for high-quality customer service may be able to obtain superior performance even though its products are not highly differentiated.

Strategy in the Emerging Enterprise

It began with a 5,000-word e-mail sent by Steve Balmer, CEO of Microsoft, to all 57,000 employees. Whereas previous e-mails from Microsoft founder Bill Gates—including one in 1995 calling on the firm to learn how to "ride the wave of the Internet"—inspired the firm to move on to conquer more technological challenges, Balmer's e-mail focused on Microsoft's current state and called on the firm to become more focused and efficient. Balmer also announced that Microsoft would cut its costs by $1 billion during the next fiscal year. One observer described it as the kind of e-mail you would expect to read at Procter & Gamble, not at Microsoft.

Then the other shoe dropped. In a surprise move, Balmer announced that Microsoft would distribute a large portion of its $56 billion cash reserve in the form of a special dividend to stockholders. In what is believed to be the largest such cash dispersion ever, Microsoft distributed $32 billion to its stockholders and used an additional $30 billion to buy back stock. Bill Gates received a $3.2 billion cash dividend. These changes meant that Microsoft's capital structure was more similar to, say, Procter & Gamble's than to an entrepreneurial, high-flying software company.

What happened at Microsoft? Did Microsoft's management conclude that the PC software industry was no longer emerging, but had matured to the point that Microsoft

Microsoft Grows Up

would have to alter some of its traditional strategies? Most observers believe that Balmer's e-mail, and the decision to reduce its cash reserves, signaled that Microsoft had come to this conclusion. In fact, although most of Microsoft's core businesses—its Windows operating systems, its PC applications software, and its server software—are still growing at the rate of about $3 billion a year, if they were growing at historical rates these businesses would be generating $7 billion in new revenues each year. Moreover, Microsoft's new businesses— video games, Internet services, business software, and software for phones and handheld computers—are adding less than $1 billion in new revenues each year. That is, growth in Microsoft's new businesses is not offsetting slower growth in its traditional businesses.

Other indicators of the growing maturity of the PC software industry,

and Microsoft's strategic changes, also exist. For example, during 2003 and 2004, Microsoft resolved most of the outstanding antitrust litigation it was facing, abandoned its employee stock option plan in favor of a stock-based compensation scheme popular with slower-growth firms, improved its systems for receiving and acting on feedback from customers, and improved the quality of its relationships with some of its major rivals, including Sun Microsystems, Inc. These are all the actions of a firm that recognizes that the rapid growth opportunities that existed in the software industry when Microsoft was a new company do not exist anymore.

At this point, Microsoft has to choose whether it is going to jump-start its growth through a series of large acquisitions or accept the lower growth rates in its core markets. It made a significant, but ultimately unsuccessful, effort to acquire Yahoo in an attempt to jump-start its growth in online services, a strong indicator that Microsoft, while acknowledging slower growth in its core, has not completely abandoned the idea of growing quickly in some parts of its business.

Sources: J. Greene (2004). "Microsoft's midlife crisis." *BusinessWeek*, April 19, 2004, pp. 88 +; R. Guth and S. Thurm (2004). "Microsoft to dole out its cash hoard." *The Wall Street Journal*, Wednesday, July 21, 2004, pp. A1 +; S. Hamm (2004). "Microsoft's worst enemy: Success." *BusinessWeek*, July 19, 2004, p. 33; www.microsoft.com/billgates/speeches/2006/00-15transition.asp.

This emphasis on service has become very important in a wide variety of industries. For example, in the convenience food industry, one of the major reasons for slower growth in the fast-food segment has been growth in the so-called "casual dining" segment. This segment includes restaurants such as Chili's and Applebee's. The food sold at fast-food restaurants and casual dining restaurants overlaps—they both sell burgers, soft drinks, salads, chicken, desserts, and so forth—although many consumers believe that the quality of food is superior in the casual dining restaurants. In addition to any perceived differences in the food, however, the level of service in the two kinds of establishments varies significantly. At fast-food restaurants, food is handed to consumers on a tray; in casual dining restaurants, wait staff actually bring food to consumers on a plate. This level of service is one reason that casual dining is growing in popularity.[50]

Process Innovation

A firm's **processes** are the activities it engages in to design, produce, and sell its products or services. **Process innovation**, then, is a firm's effort to refine and improve its current processes. Several authors have studied the relationship between process innovation, product innovation, and the maturity of an industry.[51] This work, summarized in Figure 5, suggests that, in the early stages of industry development, product innovation is very important. However, over time product innovation becomes less important, and process innovations designed to reduce manufacturing costs, increase product quality, and streamline management become more important. In mature industries, firms can often gain an advantage by manufacturing the same product as competitors, but at a lower cost. Alternatively, firms can manufacture a product that is perceived to be of higher quality and do so at a competitive cost. Process innovations facilitate both the reduction of costs and the increase in quality.

The role of process innovation in more mature industries is perhaps best exemplified by the improvement in quality in U.S. automobiles. In the 1980s, Japanese firms such as Nissan, Toyota, and Honda sold cars that were of significantly higher quality than those produced by U.S. firms General Motors, Ford, and Chrysler. In the face of that competitive disadvantage, the U.S. firms engaged in numerous process reforms to improve the quality of their cars. In the 1980s, U.S. manufacturers were cited for car body panels that did not fit well, bumpers that were hung crookedly on cars, and the wrong engines being placed in cars. Today, the differences in quality between newly manufactured U.S. and Japanese automobiles are very small. Indeed, one well-known judge of initial manufacturing quality—J. D. Powers—now focuses on items such as the quality of a car's cup

Figure 5 Process and Product Innovation and Industry Structure

Source: Taken from Hayes and Wheelwright, "The dynamics of process-product life cycles." *Harvard Business Review,* March–April, pp. 127–136.

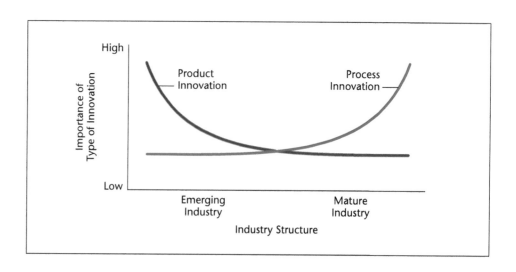

holders and the maximum distance at which a car's keyless entry system still works to establish quality rankings. The really significant quality issues of the 1980s are virtually gone.[52]

Opportunities in Declining Industries: Leadership, Niche, Harvest, and Divestment

A **declining industry** is an industry that has experienced an absolute decline in unit sales over a sustained period of time.[53] Obviously, firms in a declining industry face more threats than opportunities. Rivalry in a declining industry is likely to be very high, as is the threat of buyers, suppliers, and substitutes. However, even though threats are significant, firms do have opportunities they can exploit. The major strategic opportunities that firms in this kind of industry face are leadership, niche, harvest, and divestment.

Market Leadership

An industry in decline is often characterized by overcapacity in manufacturing, distribution, and so forth. Reduced demand often means that firms in a declining industry will have to endure a significant shakeout period until overcapacity is reduced and capacity is brought in line with demand. After the shakeout, a smaller number of lean and focused firms may enjoy a relatively benign environment with few threats and several opportunities. If the industry structure that is likely to exist after a shakeout is quite attractive, firms in an industry before the shakeout may have an incentive to weather the storm of decline—to survive until the situation improves to the point that they can begin to earn higher profits.

If a firm has decided to wait out the storm of decline in hopes of better environmental conditions in the future, it should consider various steps to increase its chances of survival. Most important of these is that a firm must establish itself as a **market leader** in the pre-shakeout industry, most typically by becoming the firm with the largest market share in that industry. The purpose of becoming a market leader is *not* to facilitate tacit collusion or to obtain lower costs from economies of scale. Rather, in a declining industry the leader's objective should be to try to facilitate the exit of firms that are not likely to survive a shakeout, thereby obtaining a more favorable competitive environment as quickly as possible.

Market leaders in declining industries can facilitate exit in a variety of ways, including purchasing and then deemphasizing competitors' product lines, purchasing and retiring competitors' manufacturing capacity, manufacturing spare parts for competitors' product lines, and sending unambiguous signals of their intention to stay in an industry and remain a dominant firm. For example, overcapacity problems in the European petrochemical industry were partially resolved when Imperial Chemical Industries (ICI) traded its polyethylene plants to British Petroleum for BP's polyvinylchloride (PVC) plants. In this case, both firms were able to close some excess capacity in specific markets (polyethylene and PVC), while sending clear signals of their intention to remain in these markets.[54]

Market Niche

A firm in a declining industry following a leadership strategy attempts to facilitate exit by other firms, but a firm following a **niche strategy** in a declining industry reduces its scope of operations and focuses on narrow segments of the declining industry. If only a few firms choose a particular niche, then these firms may have a favorable competitive setting, even though the industry as a whole is facing shrinking demand.

Two firms that used the niche approach in a declining market are GTE Sylvania and General Electric (GE) in the vacuum tube industry. The invention of the transistor followed by the semiconductor just about destroyed demand for vacuum tubes in new products. GTE Sylvania and GE rapidly recognized that new product sales in vacuum tubes were drying up. In response, these firms began specializing in supplying *replacement* vacuum tubes to the consumer and military markets. To earn high profits, these firms had to refocus their sales efforts and scale down their sales and manufacturing staffs. Over time, as fewer and fewer firms manufactured vacuum tubes, GTE Sylvania and GE were able to charge very high prices for replacement parts.[55]

Harvest

Leadership and niche strategies, though differing along several dimensions, have one attribute in common: Firms that implement these strategies intend to remain in the industry despite its decline. Firms pursuing a **harvest strategy** in a declining industry do not expect to remain in the industry over the long term. Instead, they engage in a long, systematic, phased withdrawal, extracting as much value as possible during the withdrawal period.

The extraction of value during the implementation of a harvest strategy presumes that there is some value to harvest. Thus, firms that implement this strategy must ordinarily have enjoyed at least some profits at some time in their history, before the industry began declining. Firms can implement a harvest strategy by reducing the range of products they sell, reducing their distribution network, eliminating less profitable customers, reducing product quality, reducing service quality, deferring maintenance and equipment repair, and so forth. In the end, after a period of harvesting in a declining industry, firms can either sell their operations (to a market leader) or simply cease operations.

In principle, the harvest opportunity sounds simple, but in practice it presents some significant management challenges. The movement toward a harvest strategy often means that some of the characteristics of a business that have long been a source of pride to managers may have to be abandoned. Thus, where prior to harvest a firm may have specialized in high-quality service, quality products, and excellent customer value, during the harvest period service quality may fall, product quality may deteriorate, and prices may rise. These changes may be difficult for managers to accept, and higher turnover may be the result. It is also difficult to hire quality managers into a harvesting business, because such individuals are likely to seek greater opportunities elsewhere.

For these reasons, few firms explicitly announce a harvest strategy. However, examples can be found. GE seems to be following a harvest strategy in the electric turbine business. Also, United States Steel and the International Steel Group seem to be following this strategy in certain segments of the steel market.[56]

Divestment

The final opportunity facing firms in a declining industry is divestment. Like a harvest strategy, the objective of **divestment** is to extract a firm from a declining industry. However, unlike harvest, divestment occurs quickly, often soon after a pattern of decline has been established. Firms without established competitive advantages may find divestment a superior option to harvest, because they have few competitive advantages they can exploit through harvesting.

In the 1980s, GE used this rapid divestment approach to virtually abandon the consumer electronics business. Total demand in this business was more or less stable during the 1980s, but competition (mainly from Asian manufacturers) increased substantially. Rather than remain in this business, GE sold most of its consumer electronics operations and used the capital to enter into the medical imaging industry, where this firm has found an environment more conducive to superior performance.[57]

In the defense business, divestment is the stated strategy of General Dynamics, at least in some of its business segments. General Dynamics' managers recognized early on that the changing defense industry could not support all the incumbent firms. When General Dynamics concluded that it could not remain a leader in some of its businesses, it decided to divest those and concentrate on a few remaining businesses. Since 1991, General Dynamics has sold businesses worth over $2.83 billion, including its missile systems business, its Cessna aircraft division, and its tactical aircraft division (maker of the very successful F-16 aircraft and partner in the development of the next generation of fighter aircraft, the F-22). These divestitures have left General Dynamics in just three businesses: armored tanks, nuclear submarines, and space launch vehicles. During this time, the market price of General Dynamics stock has returned almost $4.5 billion to its investors, has seen its stock go from $25 per share to a high of $110 per share, and has provided a total return to stockholders of 555 percent.[58]

Of course, not all divestments are caused by industry decline. Sometimes firms divest certain operations to focus their efforts on remaining operations, sometimes they divest to raise capital, and sometimes they divest to simplify operations. These types of divestments reflect a firm's diversification strategy.

Summary

The strategic management process requires that a firm engage in an analysis of threats and opportunities in its competitive environment before a strategic choice can be made. This analysis begins with an understanding of the firm's general environment. This general environment has six components: technological change, demographic trends, cultural trends, economic climate, legal and political conditions, and specific international events. Although some of these components of the general environment can affect a firm directly, more frequently they affect a firm through their impact on its local environment.

The S-C-P model is a theoretical framework that enables the analysis of a firm's local environment and that links the structure of the industry within which a firm operates, its strategic alternatives, and firm performance. In this model, *structure* is defined as industry structure and includes those attributes of a firm's industry that constrain a firm's strategic alternatives and performance. *Conduct* is defined as a firm's strategies. *Performance* refers either to the performance of a firm in an industry or the performance of the entire economy—although the former definition of performance is more important for most strategic management purposes.

The S-C-P model can be used to develop tools for analyzing threats in a firm's competitive environment. The most influential of these tools is called the "five forces framework." The five forces are: the threat of entry, the threat of rivalry, the threat of substitutes, the threat of suppliers, and the threat of buyers. The threat of entry depends on the existence and "height" of barriers to entry. Common barriers to entry include economies of scale, product differentiation, cost advantages independent of scale, and government regulation. The threat of rivalry depends on the number and competitiveness of firms in an industry. The threat of rivalry is high in an industry when there are large numbers of competing firms, competing firms are roughly the same size and have the same influence, growth in an industry is slow, there is no product differentiation, and productive capacity is added in large increments. The threat of substitutes depends on how close substitute products and services are—in performance and cost—to products and services in an industry. Whereas rivals all meet the same customer needs in approximately the same way, substitutes meet the same customer needs, but do so in very different ways. The threat of suppliers in an industry depends on the number and distinctiveness of the products suppliers provide to an industry. The threat of suppliers increases when a supplier's industry is dominated by a few firms, when suppliers sell unique or highly differentiated products, when suppliers are not threatened by substitutes, when suppliers threaten forward vertical integration, and when firms are not important customers for suppliers. Finally, the threat of buyers depends on the number and size of an industry's customers. The threat of buyers is greater when the number of buyers is small, products sold to buyers are undifferentiated and standard, products sold to buyers are a significant percentage of a buyer's final costs, buyers are not earning significant profits, and buyers threaten backward vertical integration. Taken together, the level of these threats in an industry can be used to determine the expected average performance of firms in an industry.

One force in a firm's environment not included within the five forces framework is complementors. Where competitors (including rivals, new entrants, and substitutes) compete with a firm to divide profits in a market, complementors increase the total size of the market. If you are a CEO of a firm, you know that another firm is a complementor when the value of your products to your customers is higher in combination with this other firm's products than when customers use your products alone. Where firms have strong incentives to reduce the entry of competitors, they can sometimes have strong incentives to increase the entry of complementors.

The S-C-P model can also be used to develop tools for analyzing strategic opportunities in an industry. This is done by identifying generic industry structures and the strategic opportunities available in these different kinds of industries. Four common industry structures are fragmented industries, emerging industries, mature industries, and declining industries. The primary opportunity in fragmented industries is consolidation. In emerging industries, the most important opportunity is first-mover advantages from technological leadership, preemption of strategically valuable assets, or creation of customer-switching costs. In mature industries, the primary opportunities are product refinement, service, and process innovation. In declining industries, opportunities include market leadership, niche, harvest, and divestment.

Challenge Questions

1. Your former college roommate calls you and asks to borrow $10,000 so that he can open a pizza restaurant in his hometown. In justifying this request, he argues that there must be significant demand for pizza and other fast food in his hometown because there are lots of such restaurants already there and three or four new ones are opening each month. He also argues that demand for convenience food will continue to increase, and he points to the large number of firms that now sell frozen dinners in grocery stores. Will you lend him the money? Why or why not?

2. According to the five forces model, one potential threat in an industry is buyers. Yet unless buyers are satisfied, they are likely to look for satisfaction elsewhere. Can the fact that buyers can be threats be reconciled with the need to satisfy buyers?

3. Government policies can have a significant impact on the average profitability of firms in an industry. Government, however, is not included as a potential threat in the five forces model. Should the model be expanded to include government (to make a "six forces" model)? Why or why not?

4. How would you add complementors to the five forces model? In particular, if an industry has large numbers of complementors, does that make it more attractive, less attractive, or does it have no impact on the industry's attractiveness? Justify your answer.

5. Opportunities analysis seems to suggest that strategic opportunities are available in almost any industry, including declining ones. If that is true, is it fair to say that there is really no such thing as an unattractive industry? If yes, what implications does this have for the five forces model? If no, describe an industry that has no opportunities.

6. Is the evolution of industry structure from an emerging industry to a mature industry to a declining industry inevitable? Why or why not?

Problem Set

1. Perform a five forces analysis on the following two industries:

The Pharmaceutical Industry

The pharmaceutical industry consists of firms that develop, patent, and distribute drugs. Although this industry does not have significant production economies, it does have important economies in research and development. Product differentiation exists as well, because firms often sell branded products. Firms compete in research and development. However, once a product is developed and patented, competition is significantly reduced. Recently, the increased availability of generic, nonbranded drugs has threatened the profitability of some drug lines. Once an effective drug is developed, few, if any, alternatives to that drug usually are available. Drugs are manufactured from commodity chemicals that are available from numerous suppliers. Major customers include doctors and patients. Recently, increased costs have led the federal government and insurance companies to pressure drug companies to reduce their prices.

The Textile Industry

The textile industry consists of firms that manufacture and distribute fabrics for use in clothing, furniture, carpeting, and so forth. Several firms have invested heavily in sophisticated manufacturing technology, and many lower-cost firms located in Asia have begun fabric production. Textiles are not branded products. Recently, tariffs on some imported textiles have been implemented. The industry has numerous firms; the largest have less than 10 percent market share. Traditional fabric materials (such as cotton and wool) have recently been threatened by the development of alternative chemical-based materials (such as nylon and rayon), although many textile companies have begun manufacturing with these new materials as well. Most raw materials are widely available, although some synthetic products periodically may be in short supply. There are numerous textile customers, but textile costs are usually a large percentage of their final product's total costs. Many users shop around the world for the lowest textile prices.

2. Perform an opportunities analysis on the following industries:

(a) The U.S. airline industry

(b) The U.S. beer industry

(c) The U.S. property and casualty insurance industry

(d) The worldwide portable digital media (e.g., flash drives) industry

(e) The worldwide small package overnight delivery industry

3. For each of the following firms identify at least two competitors (rivals, new entrants, or substitutes) and two complementors.

(a) Yahoo!

(b) Microsoft

(c) Dell

(d) Boeing

(e) McDonald's

End Notes

1. www.universityofphoenixstadium.com. Accessed June 17, 2009.
2. www.upxnewsroom.com/facts. Accessed June 17, 2009.
3. DeFraja, G., and E. Iossa (2002). "Competition among universities and the emergence of the elite institution." *Bulletin of Economic Research*, 54(3), pp. 275–293; Gate, Denise S. (2001). *The competition for top undergraduates by America's colleges and universities.* The Center. http://the center.ufl.edu.
4. See (2003). *The big book of business quotations.* New York: Basic Books, p. 209.
5. See Weintraub, A. (2004). "Repairing the engines of life." *BusinessWeek*, May 24, 2004, pp. 99 + for a discussion of recent developments in biotechnology research and the business challenges they have created.
6. Grow, B. (2004). "Hispanic nation." *BusinessWeek*, March 15, 2004, pp. 59 +.
7. Ibid.
8. Barnes, B. (2004). "The WB grows up." *The Wall Street Journal*, July 19, 2004, pp. B1 +; money.cnn.com/2006/01/24/news/companies/cbs_warner. Accessed February 2007.
9. These and other cultural differences are described in Rugman, A., and R. Hodgetts (1995). *International business.* New York: McGraw-Hill. A discussion of the dimensions along which country cultures can vary is presented in a later chapter.
10. Early contributors to the structure-conduct-performance model include Mason, E. S. (1939). "Price and production policies of large scale enterprises." *American Economic Review*, 29, pp. 61–74; and Bain, J. S. (1956). *Barriers to new competition.* Cambridge, MA: Harvard University Press. The major developments in this framework are summarized in Bain, J. S. (1968). *Industrial organization.* New York: John Wiley & Sons, Inc.; and Scherer, F. M. (1980). *Industrial market structure and economic performance.* Boston: Houghton Mifflin. The links between this framework and work in strategic management are discussed by Porter, M. E. (1981a). "The contribution of industrial organization to strategic management." *Academy of Management Review*, 6, pp. 609–620; and Barney, J. B. (1986c). "Types of competition and the theory of strategy: Toward an integrative framework." *Academy of Management Review*, 1, pp. 791–800.
11. The five forces framework is described in detail in Porter, M. E. (1979). "How competitive forces shape strategy." *Harvard Business Review*, March–April, pp. 137–156; and Porter, M. E. (1980). *Competitive strategy.* New York: Free Press.
12. In 2005, ESPN also entered the college sports cable business with the introduction of the ESPN-U channel. See http://sports.espn.go.com/espntv.
13. These barriers were originally proposed by Bain, J. S. (1968). *Industrial organization.* New York: John Wiley & Sons, Inc.; and Porter, M. E. (1980). *Competitive strategy.* New York: Free Press. It is actually possible to estimate the "height" of barriers to entry in an industry by comparing the cost of entry into an industry with barriers and the cost of entry into that industry if barriers did not exist. The difference between these costs is the "height" of the barriers to entry.
14. Another alternative would be for a firm to own and operate more than one plant. If there are economies of scope in this industry, a firm might be able to enter and earn above-normal profits. An economy of scope exists when the value of operating in two businesses simultaneously is greater than the value of operating in these two businesses separately.
15. See Ghemawat, P., and H. J. Stander III (1992). "Nucor at a crossroads." Harvard Business School Case No. 9-793-039.
16. See Montgomery, C. A., and B. Wernerfelt (1991). "Sources of superior performance: Market share versus industry effects in the U.S. brewing industry." *Management Science*, 37, pp. 954–959.
17. A. R. Sorkin and M. Merced (2008). "Brewer bids $46 billion for Anheuser-Busch." *New York Times*, June 12, 2008.
18. Stecklow, S. (1999). "Gallo woos French, but don't expect Bordeaux by the jug." *The Wall Street Journal*, March 26, pp. A1 +.
19. See www.bustpatents.com/awards.html. Accessed February 2007.
20. See www.pwc.com/images/us/eng/about/svcs/advisor for a very informative report written by PWC about patents and patent violators. Accessed February 2007.
21. See Kogut, B., and U. Zander. (1992). "Knowledge of the firm, combinative capabilities, and the replication of technology." *Organization Science*, 3, pp. 383–397; and Dierickx, I., and K. Cool. (1989). "Asset stock accumulation and sustainability of competitive advantage." *Management Science*, 35, pp. 1504–1511. Both emphasize the importance of know-how as a barrier to entry into an industry. More generally, intangible resources are seen as particularly important sources of sustained competitive advantage.
22. See Polanyi, M. (1962). *Personal knowledge: Towards a post-critical philosophy.* London: Routledge & Kegan Paul; and Itami, H. (1987). *Mobilizing invisible assets.* Cambridge, MA: Harvard University Press.

23. See Henderson, R., and I. Cockburn. (1994). "Measuring competence: Exploring firm effects in pharmaceutical research." *Strategic Management Journal*, 15, pp. 361–374.

24. See Scherer, F. M. (1980). *Industrial market structure and economic performance.* Boston: Houghton Mifflin.

25. See Saporito, B. (1992). "Why the price wars never end." *Fortune*, March 23, pp. 68–78; and Allen, M., and M. Siconolfi. (1993). "Dell Computer drops planned share offering." *The Wall Street Journal*, February 25, p. A3.

26. Chartier, John. (2002). "Burger battles." CNN/Money, http://money.cnn.com, December 11.

27. See Ghemawat, P., and A. McGahan. (1995). "The U.S. airline industry in 1995." Harvard Business School Case No. 9-795-113.

28. Labich, K. (1992). "Airbus takes off." *Fortune*, June 1, pp. 102–108.

29. See Pollock, E. J. (1993). "Mediation firms alter the legal landscape." *The Wall Street Journal*, March 22, p. B1; Cox, M. (1993). "Electronic campus: Technology threatens to shatter the world of college textbooks." *The Wall Street Journal*, June 1, p. A1; Reilly, P. M. (1993). "At a crossroads: The instant-new age leaves *Time* magazine searching for a mission." *The Wall Street Journal*, May 12, p. A1; Rohwedder, C. (1993). "Europe's smaller food shops face finis." *The Wall Street Journal*, May 12, p. B1; Fatsis, S. (1995). "Major leagues keep minors at a distance." *The Wall Street Journal*, November 8, pp. B1 +; Norton, E., and G. Stem. (1995). "Steel and aluminum vie over every ounce in a car's construction." *The Wall Street Journal*, May 9, pp. A1 +; Paré, T. P. (1995). "Why the banks lined up against Gates." *Fortune*, May 29, p. 18; "Hitting the mail on the head." *The Economist*, April 30, 1994, pp. 69–70; Pacelle, M. (1996). "'Big Boxes' by discounters are booming." *The Wall Street Journal*, January 17, p. A2; and Pope, K., and L. Cauley. (1998). "In battle for TV ads, cable is now the enemy." *The Wall Street Journal*, May 6, pp. B1 +.

30. Tully, S. (1992). "How to cut those #$%* legal costs." *Fortune*, September 21, pp. 119–124.

31. Jensen, E. (1993). "Tales are oft told as TV talk shows fill up airtime." *The Wall Street Journal*, May 25, p. A1; Jensen, E. (1995). "King World ponders life without Oprah." *The Wall Street Journal*, September 26, p. B1.

32. See DeWitt, W. (1997). "Crown Cork & Seal/Carnaud Metalbox." Harvard Business School Case No. 9-296-019.

33. Perry, N. J. (1993). "What's next for the defense industry." *Fortune*, February 22, pp. 94–100.

34. See "Crown Cork and Seal in 1989." Harvard Business School Case No. 5-395-224.

35. See Brandenburger, A., and B. Nalebuff (1996). *Co-opetition.* New York: Doubleday.

36. This approach to studying opportunities was also first suggested in Porter, M. E. (1980). *Competitive strategy.* New York: Free Press.

37. Jacob, R. (1992). "Service Corp. International: Acquisitions done the right way." *Fortune*, November 16, p. 96.

38. Porter, M. E. (1980). *Competitive strategy.* New York: Free Press.

39. For the definitive discussion of first-mover advantages, see Lieberman, M., and C. Montgomery. (1988). "First-mover advantages." *Strategic Management Journal*, 9, pp. 41–58.

40. See Ghemawat, P. (1991). *Commitment.* New York: Free Press.

41. See Gilbert, R. J., and D. M. Newbery. (1982). "Preemptive patenting and the persistence of monopoly." *American Economic Review*, 72(3), pp. 514–526.

42. See Bresnahan, T. F. (1985). "Post-entry competition in the plain paper copier market." *American Economic Review*, 85, pp. 15–19, for a discussion of Xerox's patents; and Bright, A. A. (1949). *The electric lamp industry.* New York: Macmillan, for a discussion of General Electric's patents.

43. See Mansfield, E., M. Schwartz, and S. Wagner. (1981). "Imitation costs and patents: An empirical study." *Economic Journal*, 91, pp. 907–918.

44. See Main, O. W. (1955). *The Canadian nickel industry.* Toronto: University of Toronto Press, for a discussion of asset preemption in the oil and gas industry; Ghemawat, P. (1986). "Wal-Mart store's discount operations." Harvard Business School Case No. 9-387-018, for Wal-Mart's preemption strategy; Schmalansee, R. (1978). "Entry deterrence in the ready-to-eat breakfast cereal industry." *Bell Journal of Economics*, 9(2), pp. 305–327; and Robinson, W. T., and C. Fornell. (1985). "Sources of market pioneer advantages in consumer goods industries." *Journal of Marketing Research*, 22(3), pp. 305–307, for a discussion of preemption in the breakfast cereal industry. In this latter case, the preempted valuable asset is shelf space in grocery stores.

45. Klemperer, P. (1986). "Markets with consumer switching costs." Doctoral thesis, Graduate School of Business, Stanford University; and Wernerfelt, B. (1986). "A special case of dynamic pricing policy." *Management Science*, 32, pp. 1562–1566.

46. See Gross, N. (1995). "The technology paradox." *BusinessWeek*, March 6, pp. 691–719; Bond, R. S., and D. F. Lean. (1977). *Sales, promotion, and product differentiation in two prescription drug markets.* Washington, D.C.: U.S. Federal Trade Commission; Montgomery, D. B. (1975). "New product distribution: An analysis of supermarket buyer decision." *Journal of Marketing Research*, 12, pp. 255–264; Ries, A., and J. Trout. (1986). *Marketing warfare.* New York: McGraw-Hill; and Davidson, J. H. (1976). "Why most new consumer brands fail." *Harvard Business Review*, 54, March–April, pp. 117–122, for a discussion of switching costs in these industries.

47. Porter, M. E. (1980). *Competitive strategy.* New York: Free Press.

48. Gibson, R. (1991). "McDonald's insiders increase their sales of company's stock." *The Wall Street Journal*, June 14, p. A1; and Chartier, J. (2002). "Burger Battles." CNN/Money, http://money.cnn.com, December 11. McDonald's lost money for only one quarter. It has since repositioned itself with nice upscale fast foods and has returned to profitability.

49. Descriptions of these product refinements can be found in Demetrakakes, P. (1994). "Household-chemical makers concentrate on downsizing." *Packaging*, 39(1), p. 41; Reda, S. (1995). "Motor oil: Hands-on approach." *Stores*, 77(5), pp. 48–49; and Quinn, J. (1995). "KitchenAid." *Incentive*, 169(5), pp. 46–47.

50. Chartier, J. (2002). "Burger Battles." CNN/Money, http://money.cnn.com, December 11.

51. See Hayes, R. H., and S. G. Wheelwright. (1979). "The Dynamics of process-product life cycles." *Harvard Business Review*, March–April, p. 127.

52. See www.jdpowers.com.

53. See Porter, M. E. (1980). *Competitive strategy.* New York: Free Press; and Harrigan, K. R. (1980). *Strategies for declining businesses.* Lexington, MA: Lexington Books.

54. See Aguilar, F. J., J. L. Bower, and B. Gomes-Casseres. (1985). "Restructuring European petrochemicals: Imperial Chemical Industries, P.L.C." Harvard Business School Case No. 9-385-203.

55. See Harrigan, K. R. (1980). *Strategies for declining businesses.* Lexington, MA: Lexington Books.

56. See Klebnikov, P. (1991). "The powerhouse." *Forbes*, September 2, pp. 46–52; and Rosenbloom, R. S., and C. Christenson. (1990). "Continuous casting investments at USX corporation." Harvard Business School Case No. 9-391-121.

57. Finn, E. A. (1987). "General Eclectic." *Forbes*, March 23, pp. 74–80.

58. See Smith, L. (1993). "Can defense pain be turned to gain?" *Fortune*, February 8, pp. 84–96; Perry, N. J. (1993). "What's next for the defense industry?" *Fortune*, February 22, pp. 94–100; and Dial, J., and K. J. Murphy. (1995). "Incentive, downsizing, and value creation at General Dynamics." *Journal of Financial Economics*, 37, pp. 261–314.

Evaluating a Firm's Internal Capabilities

From Chapter 3 of *Strategic Management and Competitive Advantage: Concepts and Cases*, 3/e. Jay B. Barney. William S. Hesterly.

Evaluating a Firm's Internal Capabilities

LEARNING OBJECTIVES

After reading this chapter, you should be able to:

1. Describe the critical assumptions of the resource-based view.

2. Describe four types of resources and capabilities.

3. Apply the VRIO framework to identify the competitive implications of a firm's resources and capabilities.

4. Apply value chain analysis to identify a firm's valuable resources and capabilities.

5. Describe the kinds of resources and capabilities that are likely to be costly to imitate.

6. Describe how a firm uses its structure, formal and informal control processes, and compensation policy to exploit its resources.

7. Discuss how the decision of whether to imitate a firm with a competitive advantage affects the competitive dynamics in an industry.

Has eBay Lost Its Way?

On January 23, 2008, Meg Whitman—the high-profile CEO of eBay—announced her retirement. During her 10 years as CEO, Whitman transformed eBay from a modestly profitable online auction site to a diversified e-commerce giant, with net income up 53 percent to $531 million on revenues that increased 27 percent to $2.2 billion in the fourth quarter of 2007. Not bad numbers to go out on for Whitman.

However, the story at eBay is actually a bit more complicated than these simple numbers suggest. Most of eBay's recent growth comes from businesses that eBay purchased—PayPal, the online payment system, and Skype, the free Internet telephone service. In fact, eBay's core online auction service has remained quite stable over the past few years. The number of active eBay users has remained constant for almost a year, at around 83 million. New product listings on the site have only increased 4 percent, and the number of companies selling products on eBay at fixed prices has actually declined.

What has happened to the core business at eBay? First, in an attempt to increase the firm's overall profitability, Whitman increased the fees that sellers are charged for using the auction service. This drove many sellers to look for alternative venues.

Second, competition emerged. For example, despite eBay's substantial head start, both in terms of auction software and its number of users, Amazon.com has become an increasingly attractive alternative to eBay for online auctions. Many users find Amazon's online auction system to be easier—and cheaper—to use. eBay only recently began upgrading is auction system to offer services currently available on Amazon—including new search software that enables shoppers to look at product photos instead of long lists of thumbnail product descriptions.

In addition to alternative online auction services like Yahoo, other Web sites that compete with eBay have also emerged—including the online classified ad site called Craig's List. Instead of trying to buy and sell products through an auction, many users prefer the simplicity of buying and selling on Craig's List.

Maybe part of eBay's challenge with its online auction business has been its efforts to expand beyond its core auction business. With two major acquisitions in three years—PayPal in October of 2002 and Skype in October of 2005—eBay's management has had to focus much of its effort on integrating these companies with

eBay. All this was complicated when, two years after acquiring Skype for $2.5 billion, eBay wrote off $1.43 billion of this investment—essentially acknowledging that it had significantly overpaid for Skype.

In any case, eBay's new CEO—John Donahoe—will have to find some way to revitalize eBay's core auction business. Once eBay's central product around which all of its other services were organized, the online auction service faces the real threat of becoming a mature, slow growth, and low-profit business for eBay.

Source: Catherin Holahan (2008). "eBay's new tough love CEO." *Business Week*, February 4, pp. 58–59.

Norbert Schewerin/The Image Works

Bay has historically been the leader in online auctions. But this position now seems to be at risk. Just how sustainable was eBay's original advantage in the auction market?

The Resource-Based View of the Firm

It is possible to take some theoretical models developed in economics—specifically the structure-conduct-performance (S-C-P) model—and apply them to develop tools for analyzing a firm's external threats and opportunities. The same is true for analyzing a firm's internal strengths and weaknesses. However, the tools described in this chapter are based on the **resource-based view (RBV)** of the firm. The RBV is a model of firm performance that focuses on the resources and capabilities controlled by a firm as sources of competitive advantage.[1]

What Are Resources and Capabilities?

Resources in the RBV are defined as the tangible and intangible assets that a firm controls that it can use to conceive and implement its strategies. Examples of resources include a firm's factories (a tangible asset), its products (a tangible asset), its reputation among customers (an intangible asset), and teamwork among its managers (an intangible asset). eBay's tangible assets include its Web site and associated software. Its intangible assets include its brand name in the auction business.

Capabilities are a subset of a firm's resources and are defined as the tangible and intangible assets that enable a firm to take full advantage of the other resources it controls. That is, capabilities alone do not enable a firm to conceive and implement its strategies, but they enable a firm to use other resources to conceive and implement such strategies. Examples of capabilities might include a firm's marketing skills and teamwork and cooperation among its managers. At eBay, the cooperation among software developers and marketing people that made it possible for eBay to dominate the online action market is an example of a capability.

A firm's resources and capabilities can be classified into four broad categories: financial resources, physical resources, individual resources, and organizational resources. **Financial resources** include all the money, from whatever source, that firms use to conceive and implement strategies. These financial resources include cash from entrepreneurs, equity holders, bondholders, and banks. **Retained earnings**, or the profit that a firm made earlier in its history and invests in itself, are also an important type of financial resource.

Physical resources include all the physical technology used in a firm. This includes a firm's plant and equipment, its geographic location, and its access to raw materials. Specific examples of plant and equipment that are part of a firm's physical resources are a firm's computer hardware and software technology, robots used in manufacturing, and automated warehouses. Geographic location, as a type of physical resource, is important for firms as diverse as Wal-Mart (with its operations in rural markets generating, on average, higher returns than its operations in more competitive urban markets) and L. L. Bean (a catalogue retail firm that believes that its rural Maine location helps its employees identify with the outdoor lifestyle of many of its customers).[2]

Human resources include the training, experience, judgment, intelligence, relationships, and insight of *individual* managers and workers in a firm.[3] The importance of the human resources of well-known entrepreneurs such as Bill Gates (Microsoft) and Steve Jobs (currently at Apple) is broadly understood. However, valuable human resources are not limited to just entrepreneurs or senior managers. Each employee at a firm like Southwest Airlines is seen as essential for the overall success of the firm. Whether it is the willingness of the gate agent to joke with the harried traveler, or a baggage handler hustling to get a passenger's bag into a plane, or even a pilot's decision to fly in a way that saves fuel—all of these human resources are part of the resource base that has enabled Southwest to gain competitive advantages in the very competitive U.S. airline industry.[4]

Whereas human resources are an attribute of single individuals, **organizational resources** are an attribute of groups of individuals. Organizational resources include a firm's formal reporting structure; its formal and informal planning, controlling, and coordinating systems; its culture and reputation; and informal relations among groups within a firm and between a firm and those in its environment. At Southwest Airlines, relationships among individual resources are an important organizational resource. For example, it is not unusual to see the pilots at Southwest helping to load the bags on an airplane to ensure that the plane leaves on time. This kind of cooperation and dedication shows up in an intense loyalty between Southwest employees and the firm—a loyalty that manifests itself in low employee turnover and high employee productivity, even though over 80 percent of Southwest's workforce is unionized.

Critical Assumptions of the Resource-Based View

The RBV rests on two fundamental assumptions about the resources and capabilities that firms may control. First, different firms may possess different bundles of resources and capabilities, even if they are competing in the same industry. This is the assumption of firm **resource heterogeneity**. Resource heterogeneity implies that for a given business activity, some firms may be more skilled in accomplishing this activity than other firms. In manufacturing, for example, Toyota continues to be more skilled than, say, General Motors. In product design, Apple continues to be more skilled than, say, IBM. In motorcycles, Harley Davidson's reputation for big, bad, and loud rides separates it from its competitors.

Second, some of these resource and capability differences among firms may be long lasting, because it may be very costly for firms without certain resources and capabilities to develop or acquire them. This is the assumption of **resource immobility**. For example, Toyota has had its advantage in manufacturing for at least 30 years. Apple has had product design advantages over IBM since Apple was founded in the 1980s. And eBay has been able to retain its brand reputation since the beginning of the online auction industry. It is not that GM, IBM, and eBay's competitors are unaware of their disadvantages. Indeed, some of these firms—notably GM and IBM—have made progress in addressing their disadvantages. However, despite these efforts, Toyota, Apple, and, to a lesser extent, eBay continue to enjoy advantages over their competition.

Taken together, these two assumptions make it possible to explain why some firms outperform other firms, even if these firms are all competing in the same industry. If a firm possesses valuable resources and capabilities that few other firms possess, and if these other firms find it too costly to imitate these resources and capabilities, the firm that possesses these tangible and intangible assets can gain a sustained competitive advantage. The economic logic that underlies the RBV is described in more detail in the Strategy in Depth feature.

The theoretical roots of the resource-based view can be traced to research done by David Ricardo in 1817. Interestingly, Ricardo was not even studying the profitability of firms; he was interested in the economic consequences of owning more or less fertile farm land.

Unlike many other inputs into the production process, the total supply of land is relatively fixed and cannot be significantly increased in response to higher demand and prices. Such inputs are said to be **inelastic in supply**, because their quantity of supply is fixed and does not respond to price increases. In these settings, it is possible for those who own higher-quality inputs to gain competitive advantages.

Ricardo's argument concerning land as a productive input is summarized in Figure 1. Imagine that there are many parcels of land suitable for growing wheat. Also, suppose that the fertility of these different parcels varies from high fertility (low costs of production) to low fertility (high costs of production). It seems obvious that when the market price for wheat is low, it will only pay farmers with the most fertile land to grow wheat. Only these farmers will have costs low enough to make money when the market price for wheat is low. As the market price for

Ricardian Economics and the Resource-Based View

wheat increases, then farmers with progressively less fertile land will be able to use it to grow wheat. These observations lead to the market supply curve in panel A of Figure 1: As prices (P) go up, supply (S) also goes up. At some point on this supply curve, supply will equal demand (D). This point determines the market price for wheat, given supply and demand. This price is called P^* in the figure.

Now consider the situation facing two different kinds of farmers. Ricardo assumed that both these farmers follow traditional economic logic by producing a quantity (q) such that their marginal cost (MC) equals their marginal revenue (MR); that is, they

produce enough wheat so that the cost of producing the last bushel of wheat equals the revenue they will get from selling that last bushel. However, this decision for the farm with less fertile land (in panel B of the figure) generates revenues that exactly equal the average total cost (ATC) of the only capital this farmer is assumed to employ, the cost of his land. In contrast, the farmer with more fertile land (in panel C of the figure) has an average total cost (ATC) less than the market-determined price, and thus is able to earn an above-normal economic profit. This is because at the market-determined price, P^*, MC equals ATC for the farmer with less fertile land, whereas MC is greater than ATC for the farmer with more fertile land.

In traditional economic analysis, the profit earned by the farmer with more fertile land should lead other farmers to enter into this market, that is, to obtain some land and produce wheat. However, all the land that can be used to produce wheat in a way that generates at least a normal return given the market price P^* is already in production. In particular, no more very fertile land is available, and fertile land (by assumption) cannot be created. This is what is meant by land being inelastic in supply. Thus, the farmer

The VRIO Framework

Armed with the RBV, it is possible to develop a set of tools for analyzing all the different resources and capabilities a firm might possess and the potential of each of these to generate competitive advantages. In this way, it will be possible to identify a firm's internal strengths and its internal weaknesses. The primary tool for accomplishing this internal analysis is called the VRIO framework.[5] The acronym, *VRIO*, in **VRIO framework** stands for four questions one must ask about a resource or capability to determine its competitive potential: the question

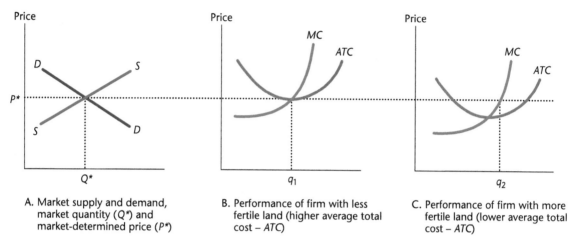

A. Market supply and demand, market quantity (Q^*) and market-determined price (P^*)

B. Performance of firm with less fertile land (higher average total cost – ATC)

C. Performance of firm with more fertile land (lower average total cost – ATC)

MC = marginal costs, ATC = average total costs, Q = aggregate quantity produced in the industry, q = quantity produced by each firm in the industry

Figure 1   The Economics of Land with Different Levels of Fertility

with more fertile land and lower production costs has a sustained competitive advantage over those farmers with less fertile land and higher production costs. Therefore, the farmer with the more fertile land is able to earn an above-normal economic profit.

Of course, at least two events can threaten this sustained competitive advantage. First, market demand may shift down and to the left. This would force farmers with less fertile land to cease production and would also reduce the profit of those with more fertile land. If demand shifted far enough, this profit might disappear altogether.

Second, farmers with less fertile land may discover low-cost ways of increasing their land's fertility, thereby reducing the competitive advantage of farmers with more fertile land. For example, farmers with less fertile land may be able to use inexpensive fertilizers to increase their land's fertility. The existence of such low-cost fertilizers suggests that, although *land* may be in fixed supply, *fertility* may not be. If enough farmers can increase the fertility of their land, then the profits originally earned by the farmers with the more fertile land will disappear.

Of course, what the RBV does is recognize that land is not the only productive input that is inelastic in supply, and that farmers are not the only firms that benefit from having such resources at their disposal.

Source: D. Ricardo (1817). *Principles of political economy and taxation.* London: J. Murray.

of **Value**, the question of **Rarity**, the question of **Imitability**, and the question of **Organization**. These four questions are summarized in Table 1.

The Question of Value

The **question of value** is: "Do resources and capabilities enable a firm to exploit an external opportunity or neutralize an external threat?" If a firm answers this question with a "yes," then its resources and capabilities are valuable and can be considered *strengths*. If a firm answers this question with a "no," its resources and

TABLE 1 Questions Needed to Conduct a Resource-Based Analysis of a Firm's Internal Strengths and Weaknesses

1. *The Question of Value.* Does a resource enable a firm to exploit an environmental opportunity and/or neutralize an environmental threat?
2. *The Question of Rarity.* Is a resource currently controlled by only a small number of competing firms?
3. *The Question of Imitability.* Do firms without a resource face a cost disadvantage in obtaining or developing it?
4. *The Question of Organization.* Are a firm's other policies and procedures organized to support the exploitation of its valuable, rare, and costly-to-imitate resources?

capabilities are *weaknesses*. There is nothing inherently valuable about a firm's resources and capabilities. Rather, they are only valuable to the extent that they enable a firm to enhance its competitive position. Sometimes, the same resources and capabilities can be strengths in one market and weaknesses in another. The Global Perspectives feature discusses this issue in more detail.

Valuable Resources and Firm Performance

Sometimes it is difficult to know for sure whether a firm's resources and capabilities really enable it to exploit its external opportunities or neutralize its external threats. Sometimes this requires detailed operational information that may not be readily available. Other times, the full impact of a firm's resources and capabilities on its external opportunities and threats may not be known for some time.

One way to track the impact of a firm's resources and capabilities on its opportunities and threats is to examine the impact of using these resources and capabilities on a firm's revenues and costs. In general, firms that use their resources and capabilities to exploit opportunities or neutralize threats will see an increase in their net revenues, or a decrease in their net costs, or both, compared to the situation in which they were not using these resources and capabilities to exploit opportunities or neutralize threats. That is, the value of these resources and capabilities will generally manifest itself in either higher revenues or lower costs or both, once a firm starts using them to exploit opportunities or neutralize threats.

Applying the Question of Value

For many firms, the answer to the question of value has been "yes." That is, many firms have resources and capabilities that are used to exploit opportunities and neutralize threats, and the use of these resources and capabilities enables these firms to increase their net revenues or decrease their net costs. For example, Sony has a great deal of experience in designing, manufacturing, and selling miniaturized electronic technology. Sony has used these resources and capabilities to exploit opportunities, including video games, digital cameras, computers and peripherals, handheld computers, home video and audio, portable audio, and car audio. 3M has used its resources and capabilities in substrates, coatings, and adhesives, along with an organizational culture that rewards risk-taking and creativity, to exploit opportunities in office products, including invisible tape and Post-It notes. Sony's and 3M's resources and capabilities—including their specific technological skills and their creative organizational cultures—have made it possible for these firms to respond to, and even create, new opportunities.[6]

Unfortunately, for other firms the answer to the question of value appears to be "no." The merger of AOL and Time Warner was supposed create a new kind of

Strategy in the Emerging Enterprise

Entrepreneurial firms, like all other firms, must be able to answer "yes" to the question of value. That is, decisions by entrepreneurs to organize a firm to exploit an opportunity must increase revenues or reduce costs beyond what would be the case if they did not choose to organize a firm to exploit an opportunity.

However, entrepreneurs often find it difficult to answer the question of value before they actually organize a firm and try to exploit an opportunity. This is because the impact of exploiting an opportunity on a firm's revenues and costs often cannot be known, with certainty, before that opportunity is exploited.

Despite these challenges, entrepreneurs often are required to not only estimate the value of any opportunities they are thinking about exploiting, but to do so in some detail and in a written form. Projections about how organizing a firm to exploit an opportunity will affect a firm's revenues and costs are often the centerpiece of an entrepreneur's **business plan**—a document that summarizes how an entrepreneur will organize a firm to exploit an opportunity, along with the economic implications of exploiting that opportunity.

Two schools of thought exist as to the value of entrepreneurs writing business plans. On the one hand, some authors argue that writing a business plan is likely to be helpful for entrepreneurs, because it forces them to be

Are Business Plans Good for Entrepreneurs?

explicit about their assumptions, exposes those assumptions to others for critique and analysis, and helps entrepreneurs focus their efforts on building a new organization and exploiting an opportunity. On the other hand, other authors argue that writing a business plan may actually hurt an entrepreneur's performance, because writing such a plan may divert an entrepreneur's attention from more important activities, may give entrepreneurs the illusion that they have more control of their business than they actually do, and may lead to decision-making errors.

Research supports both points of view. Scott Shane and Frederic Delmar have shown that writing a business plan significantly enhances the probability that an entrepreneurial firm will survive. In contrast, Amar Bhide shows that most entrepreneurs go through many different business plans before they land on one that describes a business opportunity that they actually support. For Bhide, writing the business plan is, at best, a means of helping to create a new opportunity. Because most business plans are abandoned soon after they are written, writing business plans has limited value.

One way to resolve the conflicts among these scholars is to accept that writing a business plan may be very useful in some settings and not so useful in others. In particular, when it is possible for entrepreneurs to collect sufficient information about a potential market opportunity so as to be able to describe the probability of different outcomes associated with exploiting that opportunity—a setting described as *risky* in the entrepreneurship literature—business planning can be very helpful. However, when such information cannot be collected—a setting described as *uncertain* in the entrepreneurship literature—then writing a business plan would be of only limited value, and its disadvantages might outweigh any advantages it might create.

Sources: S. Shane and F. Delmar (2004). "Planning for the market: Business planning before marketing and the continuation of organizing efforts." *Journal of Business Venturing,* 19, pp. 767–785; A. Bhide (2000). *The origin and evolution of new businesses.* New York: Oxford; R. H. Knight (1921). *Risk, uncertainty, and profit.* Chicago: University of Chicago Press; S. Alvarez and J. Barney (2006). "Discovery and creation: Alternative theories in the field of entrepreneurship." *Strategic Entrepreneurship Journal,* 1(1), pp. 11–26.

---

entertainment and media company; it is now widely recognized that Time Warner has been unable to marshal the resources necessary to create economic value. Time Warner wrote-off $90 billion in value in 2002; its stock price has been at record lows, and there have been rumors that it will be broken up. Ironically, many of the segments of this diverse media conglomerate continue to create value. However, the company as a whole has not realized the synergies that it was expected to generate when it was created. Put differently, these synergies—as resources and capabilities—are apparently not valuable.[7]

Using Value-Chain Analysis to Identify Potentially Valuable Resources and Capabilities

One way to identify potentially valuable resources and capabilities controlled by a firm is to study that firm's value chain. A firm's **value chain** is the set of business activities in which it engages to develop, produce, and market its products or services. Each step in a firm's value chain requires the application and integration of different resources and capabilities. Because different firms may make different choices about which value-chain activities they will engage in, they can end up developing different sets of resources and capabilities. This can be the case even if these firms are all operating in the same industry. These choices can have implications for a firm's strategies, and, as described in the Ethics and Strategy feature, they can also have implications for society more generally.

Consider, for example, the oil industry. Figure 2 provides a simplified list of all the business activities that must be completed if crude oil is to be turned into consumer products, such as gasoline. These activities include exploring for crude oil, drilling for crude oil, pumping crude oil, shipping crude oil, buying crude oil, refining crude oil, selling refined products to distributors, shipping refined products, and selling refined products to final customers.

Different firms may make different choices about which of these stages in the oil industry they want to operate. Thus, the firms in the oil industry may have very different resources and capabilities. For example, exploring for crude oil is very expensive and requires substantial financial resources. It also requires access to land (a physical resource), the application of substantial scientific and technical knowledge (individual resources), and an organizational commitment to risk-taking and exploration (organizational resources). Firms that operate in this stage of the oil business are likely to have very different resources and capabilities than those that,

Figure 2 A Simplified Value Chain of Activities of Oil-Based Refined Products such as Gasoline and Motor Oil

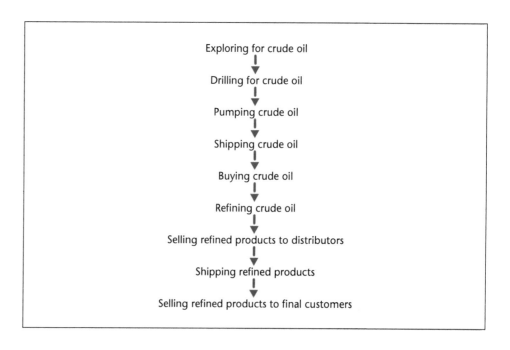

Ethics and Strategy

Strategic management adopts the perspective of a firm's owners in discussing how to gain and sustain competitive advantages. Even when adopting a stakeholder perspective, how a firm can improve its performance and increase the wealth of its owners still takes center stage.

However, an exclusive focus on the performance of a firm and the wealth of its owners can sometimes have broader effects—on society and on the environment—that are not fully recognized. Economists call these broader effects "externalities," because they are external to the core issue in economics and strategic management of how firms can maximize their performance. They are external to this issue because firms generally do not bear the full costs of the externalities their profit-maximizing behavior creates.

Externalities can take many forms. The most obvious of these has to do with pollution and the environment. If, for example, in the process of maximizing its performance a firm engages in activities that pollute the environment, the impact of that pollution is an externality. Such pollution reduces our quality of life and hurts the environment, but the firm creating this pollution often does not bear the full costs of doing so.

Other externalities have to do with a firm's impact on the public's health. For example, when tobacco companies maximize their profits by selling tobacco to children, they are also creating a public health externality. Getting children hooked on tobacco early on might be good for the

Externalities and the Broader Consequences of Profit Maximization

bottom line of a tobacco company, but it increases the chances of these children developing lung cancer, emphysema, heart disease, and the other ailments associated with tobacco. Obviously, these individuals absorb most of the adverse consequences of these diseases, but society suffers as well from the high health care costs that are engendered.

Put differently, while adopting a simple profit-maximizing perspective in choosing and implementing strategies can have positive impacts for a firm, its owners, and its stakeholders, it can also have negative consequences for society as a whole. Two broad solutions to this problem of externalities have been proposed. First, governments can take on the responsibility of directly monitoring and regulating the behavior of firms in areas where these kinds of externalities are likely to develop. Second, governments can use lawsuits and regulations to ensure that firms directly bear more

of the costs of any externalities their behavior might generate. Once these externalities are "internalized," it is then a matter of self-interest for firms not to engage in activities that generate negative externalities.

Consumers can sometimes also help internalize the externalities generated by a firm's behavior by adjusting their consumption patterns to buy products or services only from companies that do not generate negative externalities. Consumers can even be more proactive and let firms know which of their strategies are particularly troubling. For example, many consumers united to boycott firms with operations in South Africa when South Africa was still implementing a policy of apartheid. Ultimately, this pressure not only changed the strategies of many firms; it also helped change South Africa's domestic policies. More recently, consumer pressures on pharmaceutical companies forced these firms to make their AIDS drugs more accessible in less developed countries in Africa; similar pressures forced Nike to adjust the wages and working conditions of the individuals who manufacture Nike's shoes. To the extent that sufficient demand for "socially responsible firms" exists in the marketplace, it may make profit-maximizing sense for a firm to engage in socially responsible behavior by reducing the extent to which its actions generate negative externalities.

Sources: "AIDS in Africa." *British Medical Journal*, June 1, p. 456; J. S. Friedman (2003). "Paying for apartheid." *Nation*, June 6, pp. 7 +; L. Lee (2000). "Can Nike still do it?" *BusinessWeek*, February 21, pp. 121 +.

for example, sell refined oil products to final customers. To be successful in the retail stage of this industry, a firm needs retail outlets (such as stores and gas stations), which are costly to build and require both financial and physical resources. These outlets, in turn, need to be staffed by salespeople—individual resources—and marketing these products to customers through advertisements and other means can require a commitment to creativity—an organizational resource.

However, even firms that operate in the same set of value-chain activities in an industry may approach these activities very differently, and therefore may develop very different resources and capabilities associated with these activities. For example, two firms may sell refined oil products to final customers. However, one of these firms may sell only through retail outlets it owns, whereas the second may sell only through retail outlets it does not own. The first firm's financial and physical resources are likely to be very different from the second firm's, although these two firms may have similar individual and organizational resources.

Studying a firm's value chain forces us to think about firm resources and capabilities in a disaggregated way. Although it is possible to characterize a firm's resources and capabilities more broadly, it is usually more helpful to think about how each of the activities a firm engages in affects its financial, physical, individual, and organizational resources. With this understanding, it is possible to begin to recognize potential sources of competitive advantage for a firm in a much more detailed way.

Because this type of analysis can be so helpful in identifying the financial, physical, individual, and organizational resources and capabilities controlled by a firm, several generic value chains for identifying them have been developed. The first, proposed by the management-consulting firm McKinsey and Company, is presented in Figure 3.[8] This relatively simple model suggests that the creation of value almost always involves six distinct activities: technology development, product design, manufacturing, marketing, distribution, and service. Firms can develop distinctive capabilities in any one or any combination of these activities.

Michael E. Porter has developed a second generic value chain.[9] This value chain, presented in Figure 4, divides value-creating activities into two large categories: primary activities and support activities. Primary activities include inbound logistics (purchasing, inventory, and so forth), production, outbound logistics (warehousing and distribution), sales and marketing, and service (dealer support and customer service). Support activities include infrastructure (planning, finance, information services, legal), technology development (research and development, product design), and human resource management and development. Primary activities are directly associated with the manufacture and

Technology development	Product design	Manufacturing	Marketing	Distribution	Service
Source	Function	Integration	Prices	Channels	Warranty Speed
Sophistication	Physical	Raw materials	Advertising/	Integration	Captive/independent
Patents	characteristics	Capacity	promotion	Inventory	Prices
Product/process	Aesthetics	Location	Sales force	Warehousing	
choices	Quality	Procurement	Package	Transport	
		Parts production	Brand		
		Assembly			

Figure 3   The Generic Value Chain Developed by McKinsey and Company

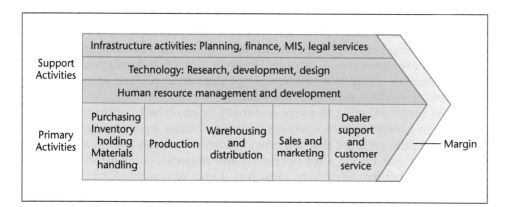

Figure 4 The Generic Value Chain Developed by Porter

Source: Reprinted with permission of The Free Press, a Division of Simon and Schuster Adult Publishing Group, from *Competitive Advantage: Creating and Sustaining Superior Performance* by Michael E. Porter. Copyright ©1985, 1998 by Michael E. Porter. All rights reserved.

distribution of a product. Support activities assist a firm in accomplishing its primary activities. As with the McKinsey value chain, a firm can develop strengths or weaknesses in any one or in any combination of the activities listed in Porter's value chain. These activities, and how they are linked to one another, point to the kinds of resources and capabilities a firm is likely to have developed.

The Question of Rarity

Understanding the value of a firm's resources and capabilities is an important first consideration in understanding a firm's internal strengths and weaknesses. However, if a particular resource or capability is controlled by numerous competing firms, then that resource is unlikely to be a source of competitive advantage for any one of them. Instead, valuable but common (i.e., not rare) resources and capabilities are sources of competitive parity. Only when a resource is not controlled by numerous other firms is it likely to be a source of competitive advantage. These observations lead to the **question of rarity**: "How many competing firms already possess particular valuable resources and capabilities?"

Consider, for example, competition among television sports channels. All the major networks broadcast sports. In addition, several sports-only cable channels are available, including the best-known all-sports channel, ESPN. Several years ago, ESPN began televising what were then called alternative sports—skateboarding, snowboarding, mountain biking, and so forth. The surprising popularity of these programs led ESPN to package them into an annual competition called the "X-Games." "X" stands for "extreme," and ESPN has definitely gone to the extreme in including sports in the X-Games. The X-Games now include sports such as sky-surfing, competitive high diving, competitive bungee cord jumping, and so forth. ESPN broadcasts both a summer X-Games and a winter X-Games. No other sports outlet has yet made such a commitment to so-called extreme sports, and it has paid handsome dividends for ESPN—extreme sports have very low-cost broadcast rights and draw a fairly large audience. This commitment to extreme sports has been a source of at least a temporary competitive advantage for ESPN.

Of course, not all of a firm's resources and capabilities have to be valuable and rare. Indeed, most firms have a resource base that is composed primarily of valuable but common resources and capabilities. These resources cannot be sources of even temporary competitive advantage, but are essential if a firm is to gain competitive parity. Under conditions of competitive parity, although no one firm gains a competitive advantage, firms do increase their probability of survival.

Consider, for example, a telephone system as a resource or capability. Because telephone systems are widely available, and because virtually all organizations have access to telephone systems, these systems are not rare, and thus are not a source of competitive advantage. However, firms that do not possess a telephone system are likely to give their competitors an important advantage and place themselves at a competitive disadvantage.

How rare a valuable resource or capability must be in order to have the potential for generating a competitive advantage varies from situation to situation. It is not difficult to see that, if a firm's valuable resources and capabilities are absolutely unique among a set of current and potential competitors, they can generate a competitive advantage. However, it may be possible for a small number of firms in an industry to possess a particular valuable resource or capability and still obtain a competitive advantage. In general, as long as the number of firms that possess a particular valuable resource or capability is less than the number of firms needed to generate perfect competition dynamics in an industry, that resource or capability can be considered rare and a potential source of competitive advantage.

The Question of Imitability

Firms with valuable and rare resources are often strategic innovators, because they are able to conceive and engage in strategies that other firms cannot because they lack the relevant resources and capabilities.

Valuable and rare organizational resources, however, can be sources of sustained competitive advantage only if firms that do not possess them face a cost disadvantage in obtaining or developing them, compared to firms that already possess them. These kinds of resources are **imperfectly imitable**.[10] These observations lead to the **question of imitability**: "Do firms without a resource or capability face a cost disadvantage in obtaining or developing it compared to firms that already possess it?"

Imagine an industry with five essentially identical firms. Each of these firms manufactures the same products, uses the same raw materials, and sells the products to the same customers through the same distribution channels. It is not hard to see that firms in this kind of industry will have normal economic performance. Now, suppose that one of these firms, for whatever reason, discovers or develops a heretofore unrecognized valuable resource and uses that resource either to exploit an external opportunity or to neutralize an external threat. Obviously, this firm will gain a competitive advantage over the others.

This firm's competitors can respond to this competitive advantage in at least two ways. First, they can ignore the success of this one firm and continue as before. This action, of course, will put them at a competitive disadvantage. Second, these firms can attempt to understand why this one firm is able to be successful and then duplicate its resources to implement a similar strategy. If competitors have no cost disadvantages in acquiring or developing the needed resources, then this imitative approach will generate competitive parity in the industry.

Sometimes, however, for reasons that will be discussed later, competing firms may face an important cost disadvantage in duplicating a successful firm's valuable resources. If this is the case, this one innovative firm may gain a **sustained competitive advantage**—an advantage that is not competed away through strategic imitation. Firms that possess and exploit costly-to-imitate, rare, and valuable resources in choosing and implementing their strategies may enjoy a period of sustained competitive advantage.

For example, other sports networks have observed the success of ESPN's X-Games and are beginning to broadcast similar competitions. NBC, for example, has developed its own version of the X-Games, called the "Gravity Games," and even the Olympics now include sports that were previously perceived as being "too extreme" for this mainline sports competition. Several Fox sports channels broadcast programs that feature extreme sports, and at least one new cable channel (Fuel) broadcasts only extreme sports. Whether these efforts will be able to attract the competitors that the X-Games attract, whether winners at these other competitions will gain as much status in their sports as do winners of the X-Games, and whether these other competitions and programs will gain the reputation among viewers enjoyed by ESPN will go a long way to determining whether ESPN's competitive advantage in extreme sports is temporary or sustained.[11]

Forms of Imitation: Direct Duplication and Substitution

In general, imitation occurs in one of two ways: **direct duplication** or **substitution**. Imitating firms can attempt to directly duplicate the resources possessed by the firm with a competitive advantage. Thus, NBC sponsoring an alternative extreme games competition can be thought of as an effort to directly duplicate the resources that enabled ESPN's X-Games to be successful. If the cost of this direct duplication is too high, then a firm with these resources and capabilities may obtain a sustained competitive advantage. If this cost is not too high, then any competitive advantages in this setting will be temporary.

Imitating firms can also attempt to substitute other resources for a costly to imitate resource possessed by a firm with a competitive advantage. Extreme sports shows and an extreme sports cable channel are potential substitutes for ESPN's X-Games strategy. These shows appeal to much the same audience as the X-Games, but they do not require the same resources as an X-Games strategy requires (i.e., because they are not competitions, they do not require the network to bring together a large number of athletes all at once). If substitute resources exist, and if imitating firms do not face a cost disadvantage in obtaining them, then the competitive advantage of other firms will be temporary. However, if these resources have no substitutes, or if the cost of acquiring these substitutes is greater than the cost of obtaining the original resources, then competitive advantages can be sustained.

Why Might It Be Costly to Imitate Another Firm's Resources or Capabilities?

A number of authors have studied why it might be costly for one firm to imitate the resources and capabilities of another. Four sources of costly imitation have been noted.[12] They are summarized in Table 2 and discussed in the following text.

Unique Historical Conditions. It may be the case that a firm was able to acquire or develop its resources and capabilities in a low-cost manner because of its unique historical conditions. The ability of firms to acquire, develop, and use resources often depends on their place in time and space. Once time and history pass, firms that do not have space-and-time-dependent resources face a significant cost disadvantage in obtaining and developing them, because doing so would require them to re-create history.[13]

81

TABLE 2 Sources of Costly Imitation

Unique Historical Conditions. When a firm gains low-cost access to resources because of its place in time and space, other firms may find these resources to be costly to imitate. Both first-mover advantages and path dependence can create unique historical conditions.

Causal Ambiguity. When competitors cannot tell, for sure, what enables a firm to gain an advantage, that advantage may be costly to imitate. Sources of causal ambiguity include when competitive advantages are based on "taken-for-granted" resources and capabilities, when multiple non-testable hypotheses exist about why a firm has a competitive advantage, and when a firm's advantages are based on complex sets of interrelated capabilities.

Social Complexity. When the resources and capabilities a firm uses to gain a competitive advantage involve interpersonal relationships, trust, culture, and other social resources that are costly to imitate in the short term.

Patents. Only a source of sustained competitive advantage in a few industries, including pharmaceuticals and specialty chemicals.

ESPN's early commitment to extreme sports is an example of these unique historical conditions. The status and reputation of the X-Games were created because ESPN happened to be the first major sports outlet that took these competitions seriously. The X-Games became the most important competition in many of these extreme sports. Indeed, for snowboarders, winning a gold medal in the X-Games is almost as important—if not more important—as winning a gold medal in the Winter Olympics. Other sports outlets that hope to be able to compete with the X-Games will have to overcome both the status of ESPN as "the worldwide leader in sports" and its historical advantage in extreme sports. Overcoming these advantages is likely to be very costly, making competitive threats from direct duplication, at least, less significant.

Of course, firms can also act to increase the costliness of imitating the resources and capabilities they control. ESPN is doing this by expanding its coverage of extreme sports and by engaging in a "grassroots" marketing campaign that engages young "extreme athletes" in local competitions. The purpose of these efforts is clear: to keep ESPN's status as the most important source of extreme sports competitions intact.[14]

Unique historical circumstances can give a firm a sustained competitive advantage in at least two ways. First, it may be that a particular firm was the first in an industry to recognize and exploit an opportunity, and being first gave the firm one or more of the first-mover advantages. Thus, although in principle other firms in an industry could have exploited an opportunity, that only one firm did so makes it more costly for other firms to imitate the original firm.

A second way that history can have an impact on a firm builds on the concept of **path dependence**.[15] A process is said to be path dependent when events early in the evolution of a process have significant effects on subsequent events. In the evolution of competitive advantage, path dependence suggests that a firm may gain a competitive advantage in the current period based on the acquisition and development of resources in earlier periods. In these earlier periods, it is often not clear what the full future value of particular resources will be. Because of this uncertainty, firms are able to acquire or develop these resources for less than what will turn out to be their full value. However, once the full value of these resources is revealed, other firms seeking to acquire or develop these resources will need to pay their full known value, which (in general) will be greater than the costs incurred by the firm that acquired or developed these resources in some earlier period. The cost of acquiring both duplicate and substitute resources would rise once their full value became known.

Consider, for example, a firm that purchased land for ranching some time ago and discovered a rich supply of oil on this land in the current period. The difference between the value of this land as a supplier of oil (high) and the value of this land for ranching (low) is a source of competitive advantage for this firm. Moreover, other firms attempting to acquire this or adjacent land will now have to pay for the full value of the land in its use as a supply of oil (high), and thus will be at a cost disadvantage compared to the firm that acquired it some time ago for ranching.

Causal Ambiguity. A second reason why a firm's resources and capabilities may be costly to imitate is that imitating firms may not understand the relationship between the resources and capabilities controlled by a firm and that firm's competitive advantage. In other words, the relationship between firm resources and capabilities and competitive advantage may be **causally ambiguous**.

At first, it seems unlikely that causal ambiguity about the sources of competitive advantage for a firm would ever exist. Managers in a firm seem likely to understand the sources of their own competitive advantage. If managers in one firm understand the relationship between resources and competitive advantage, then it seems likely that managers in other firms would also be able to discover these relationships and thus would have a clear understanding of which resources and capabilities they should duplicate or seek substitutes for. If there are no other sources of cost disadvantage for imitating firms, imitation should lead to competitive parity and normal economic performance.[16]

However, it is not always the case that managers in a particular firm will fully understand the relationship between the resources and capabilities they control and competitive advantage. This lack of understanding could occur for at least three reasons. First, it may be that the resources and capabilities that generate competitive advantage are so taken for granted, so much a part of the day-to-day experience of managers in a firm, that these managers are unaware of them.[17] Organizational resources and capabilities such as teamwork among top managers, organizational culture, relationships among other employees, and relationships with customers and suppliers may be almost "invisible" to managers in a firm.[18] If managers in firms that have such capabilities do not understand their relationship to competitive advantage, managers in other firms face significant challenges in understanding which resources they should imitate.

Second, managers may have multiple hypotheses about which resources and capabilities enable their firm to gain a competitive advantage, but they may be unable to evaluate which of these resources and capabilities, alone or in combination, actually create the competitive advantage. For example, if one asks successful entrepreneurs what enabled them to be successful, they are likely to reply with several hypotheses, such as "hard work, willingness to take risks, and a high-quality top management team." However, if one asks what happened to unsuccessful entrepreneurs, they, too, are likely to suggest that their firms were characterized by "hard work, willingness to take risks, and a high-quality top management team." It may be the case that "hard work, willingness to take risks, and a high-quality top management team" are important resources and capabilities for entrepreneurial firm success, but other factors may also play a role. Without rigorous experiments, it is difficult to establish which of these resources have a causal relationship with competitive advantage and which do not.

Finally, it may be that not just a few resources and capabilities enable a firm to gain a competitive advantage, but that literally thousands of these organizational attributes, bundled together, generate these advantages. When the resources and capabilities that generate competitive advantage are complex networks of relationships between individuals, groups, and technology, imitation can be costly.

Whenever the sources of competitive advantage are widely diffused across people, locations, and processes in a firm, those sources will be costly to imitate. Perhaps the best example of such a resource is knowledge itself. To the extent that valuable knowledge about a firm's products, processes, customers, and so on is widely diffused throughout an organization, competitors will have difficulty imitating that knowledge, and it can be a source of sustained competitive advantage.[19]

Social Complexity.   A third reason that a firm's resources and capabilities may be costly to imitate is that they may be socially complex phenomena, beyond the ability of firms to systematically manage and influence. When competitive advantages are based on such complex social phenomena, the ability of other firms to imitate these resources and capabilities, either through direct duplication or substitution, is significantly constrained. Efforts to influence these kinds of phenomena are likely to be much more costly than they would be if these phenomena developed in a natural way over time in a firm.[20]

A wide variety of firm resources and capabilities may be **socially complex**. Examples include the interpersonal relations among managers in a firm, a firm's culture, and a firm's reputation among suppliers and customers.[21] Notice that in most of these cases it is possible to specify how these socially complex resources add value to a firm. Thus, there is little or no causal ambiguity surrounding the link between these firm resources and capabilities and competitive advantage. However, understanding that an organizational culture with certain attributes or quality relations among managers can improve a firm's efficiency and effectiveness does not necessarily imply that firms lacking these attributes can engage in systematic efforts to create them, or that low-cost substitutes for them exist. For the time being, such social engineering may be beyond the abilities of most firms. At the very least, such social engineering is likely to be much more costly than it would be if socially complex resources evolved naturally within a firm.[22]

It is interesting to note that firms seeking to imitate complex physical technology often do not face the cost disadvantages of imitating complex social phenomena. A great deal of physical technology (machine tools, robots, and so forth) can be purchased in supply markets. Even when a firm develops its own unique physical technology, reverse engineering tends to diffuse this technology among competing firms in a low-cost manner. Indeed, the costs of imitating a successful physical technology are often lower than the costs of developing a new technology.[23]

Although physical technology is usually not costly to imitate, the application of this technology in a firm is likely to call for a wide variety of socially complex organizational resources and capabilities. These organizational resources may be costly to imitate, and, if they are valuable and rare, the combination of physical and socially complex resources may be a source of sustained competitive advantage.

The importance of socially complex resources and capabilities for firm performance has been studied in detail in the field of strategic human resource management, as described in the Research Made Relevant feature.

Patents.   At first glance, it might appear that a firm's patents would make it very costly for competitors to imitate its products.[24] Patents do have this effect in some industries. For example, patents in the pharmaceutical and specialty chemical industry effectively foreclose other firms from marketing the same products until a firm's patents expire. Patents can raise the cost of imitation in a variety of other industries as well.

However, from another point of view a firm's patents may decrease, rather than increase, the costs of imitation. When a firm files for patent protection, it is forced to reveal a significant amount of information about its product. Governments require this information to ensure that the technology in question is patentable. By obtaining a patent, a firm may provide important information to competitors about how to imitate its technology.

Moreover, most technological developments in an industry are diffused throughout firms in that industry in a relatively brief period of time, even if the technology in question is patented, because patented technology is not immune from low-cost imitation. Patents may restrict direct duplication for a time, but they may actually increase the chances of substitution by functionally equivalent technologies.[25]

The Question of Organization

A firm's potential for competitive advantage depends on the value, rarity, and imitability of its resources and capabilities. However, to fully realize this potential, a firm must be organized to exploit its resources and capabilities. These observations lead to the **question of organization**: "Is a firm organized to exploit the full competitive potential of its resources and capabilities?"

Numerous components of a firm's organization are relevant to the question of organization, including its formal reporting structure, its formal and informal management control systems, and its compensation policies. A firm's **formal reporting structure** is a description of whom in the organization reports to whom; it is often embodied in a firm's **organizational chart**. **Management control systems** include a range of formal and informal mechanisms to ensure that managers are behaving in ways consistent with a firm's strategies. **Formal management controls** include a firm's budgeting and reporting activities that keep people higher up in a firm's organizational chart informed about the actions taken by people lower down in a firm's organizational chart. **Informal management controls** might include a firm's culture and the willingness of employees to monitor each others' behavior. **Compensation policies** are the ways that firms pay employees. Such policies create incentives for employees to behave in certain ways.

These components of a firm's organization are often called **complementary resources and capabilities**, because they have limited ability to generate competitive advantage in isolation. However, in combination with other resources and capabilities they can enable a firm to realize its full potential for competitive advantage.[26]

For example, it has already been suggested that ESPN may have a sustained competitive advantage in the extreme sports segment of the sports broadcasting industry. However, if ESPN's management had not taken advantage of its

Research Made Relevant

Most empirical tests of the RBV have focused on the extent to which history, causal ambiguity, and social complexity have an impact on the ability of firms to gain and sustain competitive advantages. Among the most important of these tests has been research that examines the extent to which human resource practices that are likely to generate socially complex resources and capabilities are related to firm performance. This area of research is known as *strategic human resources management*.

The first of these tests was conducted as part of a larger study of efficient low-cost manufacturing in the worldwide automobile industry. A group of researchers from Massachusetts Institute of Technology developed rigorous measures of the cost and quality of over 70 manufacturing plants that assembled mid-size sedans around the world. They discovered that at the time of their study only six of these plants had simultaneous low costs and high-quality manufacturing—a position that obviously would give these plants a competitive advantage in the marketplace.

In trying to understand what distinguished these six plants from the

Strategic Human Resource Management Research

others in the sample, the researchers found that, not surprisingly, these six plants had the most modern and up-to-date manufacturing technology. However, so did many of the less effective plants. What distinguished these effective plants was not their manufacturing technology, per se, but their human resource (HR) practices. These six plants all implemented a bundle of such practices that included participative decision making, quality circles, and an emphasis on team production. One of the results of these efforts—and another distinguishing feature of these

six plants—was a high level of employee loyalty and commitment to a plant, as well as the belief that plant managers would treat employees fairly. These socially complex resources and capabilities are the types of resources that the RBV suggests should be sources of sustained competitive advantage.

Later work has followed up on this approach and has examined the impact of HR practices on firm performance outside the manufacturing arena. Using a variety of measures of firm performance and several different measures of HR practices, the results of this research continue to be very consistent with RBV logic. That is, firms that are able to use HR practices to develop socially complex human and organizational resources are able to gain competitive advantages over firms that do not engage in such practices.

Sources: J. P. Womack, D. I. Jones, and D. Roos (1990). *The machine that changed the world.* New York: Rawson; M. Huselid (1995). "The impact of human resource management practices on turnover, productivity, and corporate financial performance." *Academy of Management Journal*, 38, pp. 635–672; J. B. Barney and P. Wright (1998). "On becoming a strategic partner." *Human Resource Management*, 37, pp. 31–46.

opportunities in extreme sports by expanding coverage, ensuring that the best competitors come to ESPN competitions, adding additional competitions, and changing up older competitions, then its potential for competitive advantage would not have been fully realized. Of course, the reason that ESPN has done all these things is because it has an appropriate organizational structure, management controls, and employee compensation policies. By themselves, these attributes of ESPN's organization could not be a source of competitive advantage; however, they were essential for ESPN to realize its full competitive advantage potential.

Having an appropriate organization in place has enabled ESPN to realize the full competitive advantage potential of its other resources and capabilities. Having an inappropriate organization in place prevented Xerox from taking full advantage of some of its most critical valuable, rare, and costly-to-imitate resources and capabilities.

Through the 1960s and early 1970s, Xerox invested in a series of very innovative technology development research efforts. It managed these efforts by creating a stand-alone research center in Palo Alto, California (Palo Alto Research Center [PARC]), and staffing it with a large group of highly creative and innovative scientists and engineers. Left to their own devices, these scientists and engineers at Xerox PARC developed an amazing array of technological innovations: the personal computer, the "mouse," Windows-type software, the laser printer, the "paperless office," Ethernet, and so forth. In retrospect, it is clear that the market potential of these technologies was enormous. Moreover, because they were developed at Xerox PARC, they were rare. Xerox might have been able to gain some important first-mover advantages if the organization had been able to translate these technologies into products, thereby increasing the cost to other firms of imitating these technologies.

Xerox possessed the resources and capabilities, but it did not have an organization in place to take advantage of them. No structure existed whereby Xerox PARC innovations could become known to managers at Xerox. Indeed, most Xerox managers—even many senior managers—were unaware of these technological developments through the mid-1970s. Once they finally became aware of them, very few of the technologies survived Xerox's highly bureaucratic product development process, a process whereby product development projects were divided into hundreds of minute tasks and progress in each task was reviewed by dozens of large committees. Even innovations that survived the product development process were not exploited by Xerox managers, because management compensation at Xerox depended almost exclusively on maximizing current revenue. Short-term profitability was relatively less important in compensation calculations, and the development of markets for future sales and profitability was essentially irrelevant. Xerox's formal reporting structure, its explicit management control systems, and its compensation policies were all inconsistent with exploiting the valuable, rare, and costly-to-imitate resources it had developed. Not surprisingly, the company failed to exploit any of its potential sources of sustained competitive advantage.[27]

Applying the VRIO Framework

The questions of value, rarity, imitability, and organization can be brought together into a single framework to understand the return potential associated with exploiting any of a firm's resources or capabilities. This is done in Table 3. The relationship of the VRIO framework to strengths and weaknesses is presented in Table 4.

If a resource or capability controlled by a firm is not valuable, it will not enable a firm to choose or implement strategies that exploit environmental opportunities or neutralize environmental threats. Organizing to exploit this resource will increase a firm's costs or decrease its revenues. These types of resources are weaknesses. Firms will either have to fix these weaknesses or avoid using them when choosing and implementing strategies. If firms do exploit these kinds of resources and capabilities, they can expect to put themselves at a competitive disadvantage compared to those that either do not possess these nonvaluable resources or do not use them in conceiving and implementing strategies.

If a resource or capability is valuable but not rare, exploitation of this resource in conceiving and implementing strategies will generate competitive parity. Exploiting these types of resources will generally not create competitive

TABLE 3 The VRIO
Framework

Is a resource or capability:

Valuable?	Rare?	Costly to imitate?	Exploited by organization?	Competitive implications
No	—	—	No	Competitive disadvantage
Yes	No	—	↑	Competitive parity
Yes	Yes	No	↓	Temporary competitive advantage
Yes	Yes	Yes	Yes	Sustained competitive advantage

advantages, but failure to exploit them can put a firm at a competitive disadvantage. In this sense, valuable-but-not-rare resources can be thought of as organizational strengths.

If a resource or capability is valuable and rare but not costly to imitate, exploiting this resource will generate a temporary competitive advantage for a firm. A firm that exploits this kind of resource is, in an important sense, gaining a first-mover advantage, because it is the first firm that is able to exploit a particular resource. However, once competing firms observe this competitive advantage, they will be able to acquire or develop the resources needed to implement this strategy through direct duplication or substitution at no cost disadvantage, compared to the first-moving firm. Over time, any competitive advantage that the first mover obtained would be competed away as other firms imitate the resources needed to compete. Consequently, this type of resource or capability can be thought of as an organizational strength and as a **distinctive competence**.

If a resource or capability is valuable, rare, and costly to imitate, exploiting it will generate a sustained competitive advantage. In this case, competing firms face a significant cost disadvantage in imitating a successful firm's resources and capabilities. As suggested earlier, this competitive advantage may reflect the unique history of the successful firm, causal ambiguity about which resources to imitate, the socially complex nature of these resources and capabilities, or any patent advantages a firm might possess. In any case, attempts to compete away the advantages of firms that exploit these resources will not generate competitive advantage, or even

TABLE 4 The Relationship
Between the VRIO Framework
and Organizational Strengths
and Weaknesses

Is a resource or capability:

Valuable?	Rare?	Costly to imitate?	Exploited by organization?	Strength or weakness
No	—	—	No	Weakness
Yes	No	—	↑	Strength
Yes	Yes	No	↓	Strength and distinctive competence
Yes	Yes	Yes	Yes	Strength and sustainable distinctive competence

88

competitive parity, for imitating firms. Even if these firms are able to acquire or develop the resources or capabilities in question, the very high costs of doing so would put them at a competitive disadvantage. These kinds of resources and capabilities are organizational strengths and **sustainable distinctive competencies**.

The question of organization operates as an adjustment factor in the VRIO framework. For example, if a firm has a valuable, rare, and costly-to-imitate resource and capability but fails to organize itself to take full advantage of this resource, some of its potential competitive advantage could be lost (this is the Xerox example). Extremely poor organization, in this case, could actually lead a firm that has the potential for competitive advantage to gain only competitive parity or competitive disadvantages.

Applying the VRIO Framework to Southwest Airlines

To examine how the VRIO framework can be applied in analyzing real strategic situations, consider the competitive position of Southwest Airlines. Southwest Airlines has been the only consistently profitable airline in the United States over the past 30 years. While many U.S. airlines have gone in and out of bankruptcy, Southwest has remained profitable. How has it been able to gain this competitive advantage?

Potential sources of this competitive advantage fall into the two big categories: Operational choices Southwest has made and Southwest's approach to managing its people. On the operational side, Southwest has chosen to fly only a single type of aircraft (Boeing 737), only flies into smaller airports, has avoided complicated hub-and-spoke route systems, and, instead, flies a point-to-point system. On the people-management side, despite being highly unionized, Southwest has been able to develop a sense of commitment and loyalty among its employees. It is not unusual to see Southwest employees go well beyond their narrowly defined job responsibilities, helping out in whatever way is necessary to get a plane off the ground safely and on time. Which of these—operational choices or Southwest's approach to managing its people—are more likely to be a source of sustained competitive advantage?

Southwest's Operational Choices and Competitive Advantage

Consider first Southwest's operational choices. First, do these operational choices reduce Southwest's costs or increase the willingness of its customers to pay—that is, are these operational choices valuable? It can be shown most of Southwest's operational choices have the effect of reducing its costs. For example, by flying only one type of airliner, Southwest is able to reduce the cost of training its maintenance staff, reduce its spare parts inventory, and reduce the time its planes are being repaired. By flying into smaller airports, Southwest reduces the fees it would otherwise have to pay to land at larger airports. Its point-to-point system of routes avoids the costs associated with establishing large hub-and-spoke systems. Overall, these operational choices are valuable.

Second, are these operational choices rare? For most of its history, Southwest's operational choices have been rare. Only recently have large incumbent airlines and smaller new entrants begun to implement similar operational choices.

Third, are these operational choices costly to imitate? Several incumbent airline firms have set up subsidiaries designed to emulate most of Southwest's operational choices. For example, Continental created the Continental Lite division, United created the Ted division, and Delta created the Song division. All of these divisions chose a single type of airplane to fly, flew into smaller airports, adopted a point-to-point route structure, and so forth.

In addition to these incumbent airlines, many new entrants into the airline industry—both in the United States and elsewhere—have adopted similar operational choices as Southwest. In the United States, these new entrants include AirTran Airlines, Allegiant Airlines, JetBlue, Skybus Airlines, Spirit Airlines, and Virgin American Airlines.

Thus, while Southwest's operational choices are valuable and have been rare, they are apparently not costly to imitate. This is not surprising since these operational choices have few of the attributes of resources or capabilities that are costly to imitate. They do not derive from a firm's unique history, they are not path dependent, they are not causally ambiguous, and they are not socially complex.

Finally, is Southwest organized to fully exploit its operational choices? Most observers agree that Southwest's structure, management controls, and compensation policies are consistent with its operational choices.

Taken together, this analysis of Southwest's operational choices suggests that they are valuable, have been rare, but are not costly to imitate. While Southwest is organized to exploit these opportunities, they are likely to be only a source of temporary competitive advantage for Southwest.

Southwest's People-Management and Competitive Advantage

A similar VRIO analysis can be conducted for Southwest's approach to people management. First, is this approach valuable; that is, does it reduce Southwest's costs or increase the willingness of its customers to pay?

Employee commitment and loyalty at Southwest is one explanation of why Southwest is able to get higher levels of employee productivity than most other U.S. airlines. This increased productivity shows up in numerous ways. For example, the average turnaround time for Southwest flights is around 18 minutes. The average turnaround time for the average U.S. airline is 45 minutes. Southwest Airline employees are simply more effective in unloading and loading luggage, fueling, and catering their airplanes than employees in other airlines. This means that Southwest Airlines airplanes are on the ground for less time and in the air more time than its competitors. Of course, an airplane is only making money if it is in the air. This seemingly simple idea is worth hundreds of millions of dollars in lower costs to Southwest.

Has such loyalty and teamwork been rare in the U.S. airline industry? Over the past 15 years, the U.S. airline industry has been wracked by employment strife. Many airlines have had to cut employment, reduce wages, and in other ways strain their relationship with their employees. Overall, in comparison to incumbent airlines, the relationship that Southwest enjoys with its employees has been rare.

Is this relationship costly to imitate? Certainly, relationships between an airline and its employees have many of the attributes that should make them costly to imitate. They emerge over time; they are path dependent, causally ambiguous, and socially complex. It is reasonable to expect that incumbent airlines, airlines that already have strained relationships with their employees, would have difficulty imitating the relationship Southwest enjoys with its employees. Thus, in comparison to incumbent airlines, Southwest's approach to managing its people is probably valuable, rare, and costly to imitate. Assuming it is organized appropriately (and this seems to be the case), this would mean that—relative to incumbent airlines—Southwest has a sustained competitive advantage.

The situation may be somewhat different for new entrants into the U.S. airline industry. These airlines may not have a history of strained employee relationships. As new firms, they may be able to develop more valuable employee relationships from the very beginning. This suggests that, relative to new entrants, Southwest's approach to people management may be valuable and rare, but not costly to imitate. Again, assuming Southwest is organized appropriately, relative to new entrants into the U.S. airline industry, Southwest's people management capabilities may be a source of only a temporary competitive advantage.

Imitation and Competitive Dynamics in an Industry

Suppose a firm in an industry has conducted an analysis of its resources and capabilities, concludes that it possesses some valuable, rare, and costly-to-imitate resources and capabilities, and uses these to choose a strategy that it implements with the appropriate organizational structure, formal and informal management controls, and compensation policies. The RBV suggests that this firm will gain a competitive advantage even if it is operating in what a five forces analysis would suggest is a very unattractive industry. Examples of firms that have competitive advantages in unattractive industries include Southwest Airlines, Nucor Steel, Wal-Mart, and Dell, to name a few.

Given that a particular firm in an industry has a competitive advantage, how should other firms respond? Decisions made by other firms given the strategic choices of a particular firm define the nature of the **competitive dynamics** that exist in an industry. In general, other firms in an industry can respond to the advantages of a competitor in one of three ways. First, they can choose to limit their response. For example, when Airbus decided to build a super-jumbo airliner designed to dominate international travel for the next 30 years, Boeing limited its responses to redesigning some aspects of two of its existing planes, the 777 and the 747. Second, they can choose to alter some of their business tactics. For example, when Southwest Airlines began operating out of Philadelphia's airport and charged very low airfares, US Airways—the airline that used to dominate the Philadelphia market—lowered its fares as well. Finally, they can choose to alter their strategy—their theory of how to gain competitive advantage. For example, when Dell's direct and Internet-based approach to selling personal computers became dominant, Gateway decided to abandon its retail stores in favor of a direct and Internet-based approach.[28] A firm's responses determine the structure of the competitive dynamics in an industry.

Not Responding to Another Firm's Competitive Advantage

A firm might not respond to another firm's competitive advantage for at least three reasons. First, this firm might have its own competitive advantage. By responding to another firm's competitive advantage, it might destroy, or at least compromise, its own sources of competitive advantage. For example, digital timekeeping has made accurate watches available to most consumers at reasonable prices. Firms such as Casio have a competitive advantage in this market because of its miniaturization and electronic capabilities. Indeed, Casio's market share and performance in the watch business continue to climb. How should Rolex—a manufacturer of very expensive, non-electronic watches—respond to Casio? Rolex's decision has been: *Not at all.* Rolex appeals to a very different market segment than Casio. Should Rolex change its strategies—even if it replaced its mechanical self-winding design with the technologically superior digital design—it could easily compromise its competitive advantage in its own niche market.[29] In general, when a firm already possesses its own sources of competitive advantage, it will not respond to different sources of competitive advantage controlled by another firm.

Second, a firm may not respond to another firm's competitive advantage because it does not have the resources and capabilities to do so. A firm with insufficient or inappropriate resources and capabilities—be they physical, financial, human, or organizational—typically will not be able to imitate a successful firm's resources either through direct duplication or substitution. This may very well be the case with US Airways and Southwest Airlines. It may simply be beyond the ability of US Airways to imitate Southwest's managerial resources and capabilities. In this setting, US Airways is likely to find itself at a sustained competitive disadvantage.[30]

Finally, a firm may not respond to the advantages of a competitor because it is trying to reduce the level of rivalry in an industry. Any actions a firm takes that have the effect of reducing the level of rivalry in an industry and that also do not require firms in an industry to directly communicate or negotiate with each other can be thought of as **tacit cooperation**. Explicit cooperation is where firms do directly communicate and negotiate with each other.

Reducing the level of rivalry in an industry can benefit all firms operating in that industry. This decision can have the effect of reducing the quantity of goods and services provided in an industry to below the competitive level, actions that will have the effect of increasing the prices of these goods or services. When tacit cooperation has the effect of reducing supply and increasing prices, it is known as **tacit collusion**. Tacit collusion can be illegal in some settings. However, firms can also tacitly cooperate along other dimensions besides quantity and price. These actions can also benefit all the firms in an industry and typically are not illegal.[31]

For example, it may be that firms can tacitly agree not to invest in certain kinds of research and development. Some forms of research and development are very expensive, and although these investments might end up generating products or services that could benefit customers, firms might still prefer to avoid the expense and risk. Firms can also tacitly agree not to market their products in certain ways. For example, before regulations compelled them to do so, most tobacco companies had already decided not to put cigarette vending machines in locations usually frequented by children, even though these machines could have generated significant revenues. Also, firms can tacitly cooperate by agreeing not to engage in certain manufacturing practices, such as outsourcing to developing countries and engaging in environmentally unsound practices.

All of these actions can have the effect of reducing the level of rivalry in an industry. And reducing the level of rivalry can have the effect of increasing the average level of performance for a firm in an industry. However, tacit cooperative relationships among firms are sometimes difficult to maintain. Typically, in order for tacit cooperation to work, an industry must have the structural attributes described in Table 5. First, the industry must have relatively few firms. Informally communicating and coordinating strategies among a few firms is difficult enough; it is even more difficult when the industry has a large number of firms. For this reason, tacit cooperation is a viable strategy only when an industry is an oligopoly.

Second, firms in this industry must be homogeneous with respect to the products they sell and their cost structure. Having heterogeneous products makes it too easy for a firm to "cheat" on its tacitly cooperative agreements by modifying its products, and heterogeneous cost means that the optimal level of output for a particular firm may be very different from the level agreed to through tacit cooperation.

TABLE 5 Attributes of Industry Structure That Facilitate the Development of Tacit Cooperation

1. Small number of competing firms
2. Homogeneous products and costs
3. Market-share leader
4. High barriers to entry

In this setting, a firm might have a strong incentive to increase its output and upset cooperative agreements.

Third, an industry typically has to have at least one strong market-share leader if firms are going to tacitly cooperate. This would be a relatively large firm that has established an example of the kind of behavior that will be mutually beneficial in the industry, and other firms in the industry sometimes fall into line with this example. Indeed, it is often the market-share leader that will choose not to respond to the competitive actions of another firm in the industry in order to maintain cooperative relations.

Finally, the maintenance of tacit cooperation in an industry almost always requires the existence of high barriers to entry. If tacit cooperation is successful, the average performance of firms in an industry will improve. However, this higher level of performance can induce other firms to enter into this industry. Such entry will increase the number of firms in an industry and make it very difficult to maintain tacitly cooperative relationships. Thus, it must be very costly for new firms to enter into an industry for those in that industry to maintain their tacit cooperation. The higher these costs, the higher the barriers to entry.

Changing Tactics in Response to Another Firm's Competitive Advantage

Tactics are the specific actions a firm takes to implement its strategies. Examples of tactics include decisions firms make about various attributes of their products— including size, shape, color, and price—specific advertising approaches adopted by a firm, and specific sales and marketing efforts. Generally, firms change their tactics much more frequently than they change their strategies.[32]

When competing firms are pursuing approximately the same strategies, the competitive advantages that any one firm might enjoy at a given point in time are most likely due to the tactics that that firm is pursuing. In this setting, it is not unusual for competing firms to change their tactics by imitating the tactics of the firm with an advantage in order to reduce that firm's advantage. Although changing one's tactics in this manner will only generate competitive parity, this is usually better than the competitive disadvantage these firms were experiencing.

Several industries provide excellent examples of these kinds of tactical interactions. In consumer goods, for example, if one company increases its sales by adding a "lemon scent" to laundry detergent, then lemon scents start showing up in everyone's laundry detergent. If Coke starts selling a soft drink with half the sugar and half the carbs of regular Coke, can Pepsi's low-sugar/low-carb product be far behind? And when Delta Airlines cuts it airfares, can American and United be far behind? Not surprisingly, these kinds of tactical changes, because they initially may be valuable and rare, are seldom costly to imitate, and thus are typically only sources of temporary competitive advantage.

Sometimes, rather than simply imitating the tactics of a firm with a competitive advantage, a firm at a disadvantage may "leapfrog" its competitors by developing an entirely new set of tactics. Procter & Gamble engaged in this strategy when it introduced its laundry detergent, Tide, in a new, concentrated formula. This new formulation required new manufacturing and packaging equipment—the smaller box could not be filled in the current manufacturing lines in the industry—which meant that Tide's competitors had to take more time in imitating the concentrated laundry detergent tactic than other tactics pursued in this industry. Nevertheless, within just a few weeks other firms in this market were introducing their own versions of concentrated laundry detergent.

Indeed, some firms can become so skilled at innovating new products and other tactics that this innovative capability can be a source of sustained competitive advantage. Consider, for example, the performance of Sony. Most observers agree that Sony possesses some special management and coordination skills that enable it to conceive, design, and manufacture high-quality miniaturized consumer electronics. However, virtually every time Sony brings out a new miniaturized product several of its competitors quickly duplicate that product through reverse engineering, thereby reducing Sony's technological advantage. In what way can Sony's socially complex miniaturization resources and capabilities be a source of sustained competitive advantage when most of Sony's products are quickly imitated through direct duplication?

After Sony introduces each new product, it experiences a rapid increase in profits attributable to the new product's unique features. This increase, however, leads other firms to reverse-engineer the Sony product and introduce their own versions. Increased competition results in a reduction in the profits associated with a new product. Thus, at the level of individual products, Sony apparently enjoys only temporary competitive advantages. However, looking at the total returns earned by Sony across all of its new products over time makes clear the source of Sony's sustained competitive advantage: By exploiting its resources and capabilities in miniaturization, Sony is able to constantly introduce new and exciting personal electronics products. No single product generates a sustained competitive advantage, but, over time, across several such product introductions, Sony's resource and capability advantages lead to sustained competitive advantages.[33]

Changing Strategies in Response to Another Firm's Competitive Advantage

Finally, firms sometimes respond to another firm's competitive advantage by changing their strategies. Obviously, this does not occur very often, and it typically only occurs when another firm's strategies usurp a firm's competitive advantage. In this setting, a firm will not be able to gain even competitive parity if it maintains its strategy, even if it implements that strategy very effectively.

Changes in consumer tastes, in population demographics, and in the laws that govern a business can all have the effect of rendering what once was a valuable strategy as valueless. However, the most frequent impact is changes in technology. For example, no matter how well-made a mechanical calculator is, it is simply inferior to an electronic calculator. No matter how efficient the telegraph was in its day, it is an inferior technology to the telephone. And no matter how quickly one's fingers can move the beads on an abacus, an electronic cash register is a better way of keeping track of sales and making change in a store.

When firms change their strategies, they must proceed through the entire strategic management process. However, these firms will often have difficulty abandoning their traditional strategies. For most firms, their strategy helps define what they do and who they are. Changing its strategy often requires a firm to change its identity and its purposes. These are difficult changes to make, and many firms wait to change their strategy until absolutely forced to do so by disastrous financial results. By then, these firms not only have to change their strategy—with all that implies—they have to do so in the face of significant financial pressures.

The ability of virtually all strategies to generate competitive advantages typically expires, sooner or later. In general, it is much better for a firm to change its strategy before that strategy is no longer viable. In this way, a firm can make a planned move to a new strategy that maintains whatever resources and capabilities it still possesses while it develops the new resources and capabilities it will need to compete in the future.

Implications of the Resource-Based View

The RBV and the VRIO framework can be applied to individual firms to understand whether these firms will gain competitive advantages, how sustainable these competitive advantages are likely to be, and what the sources of these competitive advantages are. In this way, the RBV and the VRIO framework can be understood as important complements to the threats and opportunities analyses.

However, beyond what these frameworks can say about the competitive performance of a particular firm, the RBV has some broader implications for managers seeking to gain competitive advantages. Some of these broader implications are listed in Table 6 and discussed in the following section.

TABLE 6 Broader Implications of the Resource-Based View

1. The responsibility for competitive advantage in a firm:
   Competitive advantage is every employee's responsibility.
2. Competitive parity and competitive advantage:
   If all a firm does is what its competition does, it can gain only competitive parity. In gaining competitive advantage, it is better for a firm to exploit its own valuable, rare, and costly-to-imitate resources than to imitate the valuable and rare resources of a competitor.
3. Difficult to implement strategies:
   As long as the cost of strategy implementation is less than the value of strategy implementation, the relative cost of implementing a strategy is more important for competitive advantage than the absolute cost of implementing a strategy.
   Firms can systematically overestimate and underestimate their uniqueness.
4. Socially complex resources:
   Not only can employee empowerment, organizational culture, and teamwork be valuable; they can also be sources of sustained competitive advantage.
5. The role of the organization:
   Organization should support the use of valuable, rare, and costly-to-imitate resources. If conflicts between these attributes of a firm arise, change the organization.

Where Does the Responsibility for Competitive Advantage in a Firm Reside?

First, the RBV suggests that competitive advantages can be found in several of the different resources and capabilities controlled by the firm. These resources and capabilities are not limited to those that are controlled directly by a firm's senior managers. Thus, the responsibility for creating, nurturing, and exploiting valuable, rare, and costly-to-imitate resources and capabilities for competitive advantage is not restricted to senior managers, but falls on every employee in a firm. Therefore, employees should go beyond defining their jobs in functional terms and instead define their jobs in competitive and economic terms.

Consider a simple example. In a recent visit to a very successful automobile manufacturing plant, the plant manager was asked to describe his job responsibilities. He said, "My job is to manage this plant in order to help the firm make and sell the best cars in the world." In response to a similar question, the person in charge of the manufacturing line said, "My job is to manage this manufacturing line in order to help the firm make and sell the best cars in the world." A janitor was also asked to describe his job responsibilities. Although he had not been present in the two earlier interviews, the janitor responded, "My job is to keep this facility clean in order to help the firm make and sell the best cars in the world."

Which of these three employees is most likely to be a source of sustained competitive advantage for this firm? Certainly, the plant manager and the manufacturing line manager *should* define their jobs in terms of helping the firm make and sell the best cars in the world. However, it is unlikely that their responses to this question would be any different than the responses of other senior managers at other manufacturing plants around the world. Put differently, although the definition of these two managers' jobs in terms of enabling the firm to make and sell the best cars in the world is valuable, it is unlikely to be rare, and thus it is likely to be a source of competitive parity, not competitive advantage. However, a janitor who defines her job as helping the firm make and sell the best cars in the world instead of simply to clean the facility is, most would agree, quite unusual. Because it is rare, it might be a source of at least a temporary competitive advantage.[34]

The value created by one janitor defining her job in competitive terms rather than functional terms is not huge, but suppose that all the employees in this plant defined their jobs in these terms. Suddenly, the value that might be created could be substantial. Moreover, the organizational culture and tradition in a firm that would lead employees to define their jobs in this way is likely to be costly for other firms to imitate. Thus, if this approach to defining job responsibilities is broadly diffused in a particular plant, it seems likely to be valuable, rare, and costly to imitate, and thus a source of sustained competitive advantage, assuming the firm is organized to take advantage of this unusual resource.

In the end, it is clear that competitive advantage is too important to remain the sole property of senior management. To the extent that employees throughout an organization are empowered to develop and exploit valuable, rare, and costly-to-imitate resources and capabilities in the accomplishment of their job responsibilities, a firm may actually be able to gain sustained competitive advantages.

Competitive Parity and Competitive Advantage

Second, the RBV suggests that, if all a firm does is create value in the same way as its competitors, the best performance it can ever expect to gain is competitive parity. To do better than competitive parity, firms must engage in valuable and rare activities. They must do things to create economic value that other firms have not even thought of, let alone implemented.

This is especially critical for firms that find themselves at a competitive disadvantage. Such a firm certainly should examine its more successful competition, understand what has made this competition so successful, and, where imitation is very low cost, imitate the successful actions of its competitors. In this sense, benchmarking a firm's performance against the performance of its competitors can be extremely important.

However, if this is all that a firm does, it can only expect to gain competitive parity. Gaining competitive advantage depends on a firm discovering its own unique resources and capabilities and how they can be used in choosing and implementing strategies. For a firm seeking competitive advantage, it is better to be excellent in how it develops and exploits its own unique resources and capabilities than it is to be excellent in how it imitates the resources and capabilities of other firms.

This does not imply that firms must always be first movers to gain competitive advantages. Some firms develop valuable, rare, and costly-to-imitate resources and capabilities in being efficient second movers—that is, in rapidly imitating and improving on the product and technological innovations of other firms. Rather than suggesting that firms must always be first movers, the RBV suggests that, in order to gain competitive advantages, firms must implement strategies that rely on valuable, rare, and costly-to-imitate resources and capabilities, whatever those strategies or resources might be.

Difficult-to-Implement Strategies

Third, as firms contemplate different strategic options, they often ask how difficult and costly it will be to implement different strategies. As long as the cost of implementing a strategy is less than the value that a strategy creates, the RBV suggests that the critical question facing firms is not "Is a strategy easy to implement or not?" but rather "Is this strategy easier for us to implement than it is for our competitors to implement?" Firms that already possess the valuable, rare, and costly-to-imitate resources needed to implement a strategy will, in general, find it easier (i.e., less costly) to implement a strategy than firms that first have to develop the required resources and then implement the proposed strategy. For firms that already possess a resource, strategy implementation can be natural and swift.

In understanding the relative costs of implementing a strategy, firms can make two errors. First, they can overestimate the uniqueness of the resources they control. Although every firm's history is unique and no two management teams are exactly the same, this does not always mean that a firm's resources and capabilities will be rare. Firms with similar histories operating in similar industries will often develop similar capabilities. If a firm overestimates the rarity of its resources and capabilities, it can overestimate its ability to generate competitive advantages.

For example, when asked what their most critical sources of competitive advantage are, many firms will cite the quality of their top management team, the quality of their technology, and their commitment to excellence in all that they do. When pushed about their competitors, these same firms will admit that they too have high-quality top management teams, high-quality technology, and a commitment to excellence in all that they do. Although these three attributes can be sources of competitive parity, they cannot be sources of competitive advantage.

Second, firms can sometimes underestimate their uniqueness and thus underestimate the extent to which the strategies they pursue can be sources of sustained competitive advantage. When firms possess valuable, rare, and costly-to-imitate resources, strategy implementation can be relatively easy. In this context, it seems reasonable to expect that other firms will be able to quickly imitate this "easy-to-implement" strategy. Of course, this is not the case if these resources controlled by a firm are, in fact, rare and costly to imitate.

In general, firms must take great care not to overestimate or underestimate their uniqueness. An accurate assessment of the value, rarity, and imitability of a firm's resources is necessary to develop an accurate understanding of the relative costs of implementing a firm's strategies, and thus the ability of those strategies to generate competitive advantages. Often, firms must employ outside assistance in helping them describe the rarity and imitability of their resources, even though managers in firms will generally be much more familiar with the resources controlled by a firm than outsiders. However, outsiders can provide a measure of objectivity in evaluating the uniqueness of a firm.

Socially Complex Resources

Over the past several decades, much has been written about the importance of employee empowerment, organizational culture, and teamwork for firm performance. Most of this work suggests that firms that empower employees, that have an enabling culture, and that encourage teamwork will, on average, make better strategic choices and implement them more efficiently than firms without these organizational attributes. Using the language of the RBV, most of this work has suggested that employee empowerment, organizational culture, and teamwork, at least in some settings, are economically valuable.[35]

Resource-based logic acknowledges the importance of the value of these organizational attributes. However, it also suggests that these socially complex resources and capabilities can be rare and costly to imitate—and it is these attributes that make it possible for socially complex resources and capabilities to be sources of sustained competitive advantage. Put differently, the RBV actually extends and broadens traditional analyses of the socially complex attributes of firms. Not only can these attributes be valuable, but they can also be rare and costly to imitate, and thus sources of sustained competitive advantage.

The Role of Organization

Finally, resource-based logic suggests that an organization's structure, control systems, and compensation policies should support and enable a firm's efforts to fully exploit the valuable, rare, and costly-to-imitate resources and capabilities it controls. These attributes of organization, by themselves, are usually not sources of sustained competitive advantage.

These observations suggest that if there is a conflict between the resources a firm controls and that firm's organization, the organization should be changed. However, it is often the case that once a firm's structure, control systems, and compensation policies are put in place they tend to remain, regardless of whether they are consistent with a firm's underlying resources and capabilities. In such settings, a firm will not be able to realize the full competitive potential of its underlying resource base. To the extent that a firm's resources and capabilities are continuously evolving, its organizational structure, control systems, and compensation policies must also evolve. For these attributes of organization to evolve, managers must be aware of their link with a firm's resources and capabilities and of organizational alternatives.

Summary

The RBV is an economic theory that suggests that firm performance is a function of the types of resources and capabilities controlled by firms. Resources are the tangible and intangible assets a firm uses to conceive and implement its strategies. Capabilities are a subset of resources that enable a firm to take advantage of its other resources. Resources and capabilities can be categorized into financial, physical, human, and organizational resources categories.

The RBV makes two assumptions about resources and capabilities: the assumption of resource heterogeneity (that some resources and capabilities may be heterogeneously distributed across competing firms) and the assumption of resource immobility (that this heterogeneity may be long lasting). These two assumptions can be used to describe conditions under which firms will gain competitive advantages by exploiting their resources.

A tool for analyzing a firm's internal strengths and weaknesses can be derived from the RBV. Called the VRIO framework, this tool asks four questions about a firm's resources and capabilities in order to evaluate their competitive potential. These questions are the question of value, the question of rarity, the question of imitability, and the question of organization.

A firm's resources and capabilities are valuable when they enable it to exploit external opportunities or neutralize external threats. Such valuable resources and capabilities are a firm's strengths. Resources and capabilities that are not valuable are a firm's weaknesses. Using valuable resources to exploit external opportunities or neutralize external threats will have the effect of increasing a firm's net revenues or decreasing its net costs.

One way to identify a firm's valuable resources and capabilities is by examining its value chain. A firm's value chain is the list of business activities it engages in to develop, produce, and sell its products or services. Different stages in this value chain require different resources and capabilities, and differences in value-chain choices across firms can lead to important differences among the resources and capabilities controlled by different companies. Two generic value chains have been developed, one by McKinsey and Company and another by Michael Porter.

Valuable and common (i.e., not rare) resources and capabilities can be a source of competitive parity. Failure to invest in such resources can create a competitive disadvantage for a firm. Valuable and rare resources can be a source of at least a temporary competitive advantage. There are fewer firms able to control such a resource and still exploit it as a source of at least temporary competitive advantage than there are firms that will generate perfect competition dynamics in an industry.

Valuable, rare, and costly-to-imitate resources and capabilities can be a source of sustained competitive advantage. Imitation can occur through direct duplication or through substitution. A firm's resources and capabilities may be costly to imitate for at least four reasons: unique historical circumstances, causal ambiguity, socially complex resources and capabilities, and patents.

To take full advantage of the potential of its resources and capabilities, a firm must be appropriately organized. A firm's organization consists of its formal reporting structure, its formal and informal control processes, and its compensation policy. These are complementary resources in that they are rarely sources of competitive advantage on their own.

The VRIO framework can be used to identify the competitive implications of a firm's resources and capabilities—whether they are a source of competitive disadvantage, competitive parity, temporary competitive advantage, or sustained competitive advantage—and the extent to which these resources and capabilities are strengths or weaknesses.

When a firm faces a competitor that has a sustained competitive advantage, the firm's options are not to respond, to change its tactics, or to change its strategies. A firm may choose not to respond in this setting for at least three reasons. First, a response might weaken its own sources of sustained competitive advantage. Second, a firm may not have the resources required to respond. Third, a firm may be trying to create or maintain tacit cooperation within an industry.

The RBV has a series of broader managerial implications as well. For example, resource-based logic suggests that competitive advantage is every employee's responsibility. It also suggests that if all a firm does is what its competition does, it can gain only competitive parity, and that in gaining competitive advantage it is better for a firm to exploit its own valuable, rare, and costly-to-imitate resources than to imitate the valuable and rare resources of a competitor. Also, resource-based logic implies that as long as the cost of strategy implementation is less than the value of strategy implementation, the relative cost of implementing a strategy is more important for competitive advantage than the absolute cost of implementing a strategy. It also implies that firms can systematically overestimate and underestimate their uniqueness. With regard to a firm's resources and capabilities, resource-based logic suggests that not only can employee empowerment, organizational culture, and teamwork be valuable; they can also be sources of sustained competitive advantage. Also, if conflicts arise between a firm's valuable, rare, and costly-to-imitate resources and its organization, the organization should be changed.

Challenge Questions

1. Which of the following approaches to strategy formulation is more likely to generate economic profits: (a) evaluating external opportunities and threats and then developing resources and capabilities to exploit these opportunities and neutralize these threats or (b) evaluating internal resources and capabilities and then searching for industries where they can be exploited? Explain your answer.

2. Which firm will have a higher level of economic performance: (a) a firm with valuable, rare, and costly-to-imitate resources and capabilities operating in a very attractive industry or (b) a firm with valuable, rare, and costly-to-imitate resources and capabilities operating in a very unattractive industry? Assume both these firms are appropriately organized. Explain your answer.

3. Which is more critical to sustaining human life—water or diamonds? Why do firms that provide water to customers generally earn lower economic performance than firms that provide diamonds?

4. Will a firm currently experiencing competitive parity be able to gain sustained competitive advantages by studying another firm that is currently experiencing sustained competitive advantages? Why or why not?

5. Your former college roommate calls you and asks to borrow $10,000 so that he can open a pizza restaurant in his hometown. He acknowledges that there is a high degree of rivalry in this market, that the cost of entry is low, and that there are numerous substitutes for pizza, but he believes that his pizza restaurant will have some sustained competitive advantages. For example, he is going to have sawdust on his floor, a variety of imported beers, and a late-night delivery service. Will you lend him the money? Why or why not?

6. In the text, it is suggested that Boeing did not respond to Airbus's announcement of the development of a super-jumbo aircraft. Assuming this aircraft will give Airbus a competitive advantage in the segment of the airliner business that supplies airplanes for long international flights, why did Boeing not respond?

(a) Does it have its own competitive advantage that it does not want to abandon?

(b) Does it not have the resources and capabilities needed to respond?

(c) Is it trying to reduce the level of rivalry in this industry?

7. Which firm is more likely to be successful in exploiting its sources of sustained competitive advantage in its home market than in a highly competitive, nondomestic market: (a) a firm from a less competitive home country or (b) a firm from a more competitive home country? Why?

Problem Set

1. Apply the VRIO framework in the following settings. Will the actions described be a source of competitive disadvantage, parity, temporary advantage, or sustained competitive advantage? Explain your answers.

(a) Procter & Gamble introduces new, smaller packaging for its Tide laundry detergent.

(b) American Airlines announces a five percent across-the-board reduction in airfares.

(c) The Korean automobile firm Hyundai announces a 10-year, 100,000 mile warranty on its cars.

(d) Microsoft makes it easier to transfer data and information from Microsoft Word to Microsoft Excel.

(e) Merck is able to coordinate the work of its chemists and biologists in the development of new drugs.

(f) Ford patents a new kind of brake pad for its cars.

(g) Ashland Chemical, a specialty chemical company, patents a new chemical.

(h) The New York Yankees sign All-Star pitcher Randy Johnson to a long-term contract.

(i) Michael Dell uses the money he has made from Dell to purchase the Dallas Cowboys football team.

(j) Ted Turner uses the money he has made from his broadcasting empire to purchase the Atlanta Braves baseball team.

2. Identify three firms you might want to work for. Using the VRIO framework, evaluate the extent to which the resources and capabilities of these firms give them the potential to realize competitive disadvantages, parity, temporary advantages, or sustained advantages. What implications, if any, does this analysis have for the company you might want to work for?

3. You have been assigned to estimate the present value of a potential construction project for your company. How would you use the VRIO framework to construct the cash-flow analysis that is a part of any present-value calculation?

End Notes

1. The term *"the resource-based view"* was coined by Wernerfelt, B. (1984). "A resource-based view of the firm." *Strategic Management Journal*, 5, pp. 171–180. Some important early contributors to this theory include Rumelt, R. P. (1984). "Toward a strategic theory of the firm." In R. Lamb (ed.), *Competitive strategic management* (pp. 556–570). Upper Saddle River, NJ: Prentice Hall; and Barney, J. B. (1986). "Strategic factor markets: Expectations, luck and business strategy." *Management Science*, 32, pp. 1512–1514. A second wave of important early resource-based theoretical work includes Barney, J. B. (1991). "Firm resources and sustained competitive advantage." *Journal of Management*, 7, pp. 49–64; Dierickx, I., and K. Cool. (1989). "Asset stock accumulation and sustainability of competitive advantage." *Management Science*, 35, pp. 1504–1511; Conner, K. R. (1991). "A historical comparison of resource-based theory and five schools of thought within industrial organization economics: Do we have a new theory of the firm?" *Journal of Management*, 17(1), pp. 121–154; and Peteraf, M. A. (1993). "The cornerstones of competitive advantage: A resource-based view." *Strategic Management Journal*, 14, pp. 179–191. A review of much of this early theoretical literature can be found in Mahoney, J. T., and J. R. Pandian. (1992). "The resource-based view within the conversation of strategic management." *Strategic Management Journal*, 13, pp. 363–380. The theoretical perspective has also spawned a growing body of empirical work, including Brush, T. H., and K. W. Artz. (1999). "Toward a contingent resource-based theory." *Strategic Management Journal*, 20, pp. 223–250; A. Marcus and D. Geffen. (1998). "The dialectics of competency acquisition." *Strategic Management Journal*, 19, pp. 1145–1168; Brush, T. H., P. Bromiley, and M. Hendrickx. (1999). "The relative influence of industry and corporation on business segment performance." *Strategic Management Journal*, 20, pp. 519–547; Yeoh, P.-L., and K. Roth. (1999). "An empirical analysis of sustained advantage in the U.S. pharmaceutical industry." *Strategic Management Journal*, 20, pp. 637–653; Roberts, P. (1999). "Product innovation, product-market competition and persistent profitability in the U.S. pharmaceutical industry." *Strategic Management Journal*, 20, pp. 655–670; Gulati, R. (1999). "Network location and learning." *Strategic Management Journal*, 20, pp. 397–420; Lorenzoni, G., and A. Lipparini. (1999). "The leveraging of interfirm relationships as a distinctive organizational capability." *Strategic Management Journal*, 20, pp. 317–338; Majumdar, S. (1998). "On the utilization of resources." *Strategic Management Journal*, 19(9), pp. 809–831; Makadok, R. (1997). "Do inter-firm differences in capabilities affect strategic pricing dynamics?" *Academy of Management Proceedings '97*, pp. 30–34; Silverman, B. S., J. A. Nickerson, and J. Freeman. (1997). "Profitability, transactional alignment, and organizational mortality in the U.S. trucking industry." *Strategic Management Journal*, 18 (Summer special issue), pp. 31–52; Powell, T. C., and A. Dent-Micallef. (1997). "Information technology as competitive advantage." *Strategic Management Journal*, 18(5), pp. 375–405; Miller, D., and J. Shamsie. (1996). "The Resource-Based View of the firm in two environments." *Academy of Management Journal*, 39(3), pp. 519–543; and Maijoor, S., and A. Van Witteloostuijn. (1996). "An empirical test of the resource-based theory." *Strategic Management Journal*, 17, pp. 549–569; Barnett, W. P., H. R. Greve, and D. Y. Park. (1994). "An evolutionary model of organizational performance." *Strategic Management Journal*, 15 (Winter special issue), pp. 11–28; Levinthal, D., and J. Myatt. (1994). "Co-evolution of capabilities and industry: The evolution of mutual fund processing." *Strategic Management Journal*, 17, pp. 45–62; Henderson, R., and I. Cockburn. (1994). "Measuring competence? Exploring firm effects in pharmaceutical research." *Strategic Management Journal*, 15, pp. 63–84; Pisano, G. P. (1994). "Knowledge, integration, and the locus of learning: An empirical analysis of process development." *Strategic Management Journal*, 15, pp. 85–100; and Zajac, E. J., and J. D. Westphal. (1994). "The costs and benefits of managerial incentives and monitoring in large U.S. corporations: When is more not better?" *Strategic Management Journal*, 15, pp. 121–142.

2. Ghemawat, P. (1986). "Wal-Mart stores' discount operations." Harvard Business School Case No. 9-387-018, on Wal-Mart; Kupfer, A. (1991). "The champion of cheap clones." *Fortune*, September 23, pp. 115–120; and Holder, D. (1989). "L. L. Bean, Inc.—1974." Harvard Business School Case No. 9-676-014, on L. L. Bean. Some of Wal-Mart's more recent moves, especially its international acquisitions, are described in Laing, J. R. (1999). "Blimey! Wal-Mart." *Barron's*, 79, p. 14. L. L. Bean's lethargic performance in the 1990s, together with its turnaround plan, is described in Symonds, W. (1998). "Paddling harder at L. L. Bean." *BusinessWeek*, December 7, p. 72.

3. For an early discussion of the importance of human capital in firms, see Becker, G. S. (1964). *Human capital*. New York: Columbia University Press.

4. Heskett, J. L., and R. H. Hallowell. (1993). "Southwest Airlines: 1993 (A)." Harvard Business School Case No. 9-695-023.

5. See Barney, J. (1991). "Firm resources and sustained competitive advantage." *Journal of Management*, 17, pp. 99–120.

6. See Schlender, B. R. (1992). "How Sony keeps the magic going." *Fortune*, February 24, pp. 75–84; and (1999). "The weakling kicks back." *The Economist*, July 3, p. 46, for a discussion at Sony. See Krogh, L., J. Praeger, D. Sorenson, and J. Tomlinson. (1988). "How 3M evaluates its R&D programs." *Research Technology Management*, 31, pp. 10–14.

7. Anders, G. (2002). "AOL's true believers." *Fast Company*, July pp. 96 +. In a recent *The Wall Street Journal* article, managers of AOL Time Warner admitted they are no longer seeking synergies across their businesses. See Karnitschnig, M. (2006). "That's All, Folks: After years of pushing synergy, Time Warner, Inc. says enough." *The Wall Street Journal*, June 2, A1+.

8. See Grant, R. M. (1991). *Contemporary strategy analysis*. Cambridge, MA: Basil Blackwell.

9. Porter, M. E. (1987). *Competitive advantage*. New York: Free Press.

10. Lipman, S., and R. Rumelt. (1982). "Uncertain imitability: An analysis of interfirm differences in efficiency under competition." *Bell Journal of Economics*, 13, pp. 418–438; Barney, J. B. (1986). "Strategic factor markets: Expectations, luck and business strategy." *Management Science*, 32, pp. 1512–1514; and Barney, J. B. (1986). "Organizational culture: Can it be a source of sustained competitive advantage?" *Academy of Management Review*, 11, pp. 656–665.

11. See Breen, B. (2003). "What's selling in America." *Fast Company*, January, pp. 80 +.

12. These explanations of costly imitation were first developed by Dierickx, I., and K. Cool. (1989). "Asset stock accumulation and sustainability of competitive advantage." *Management Science*, 35, pp. 1504–1511; Barney, J. B. (1991). "Firm resources and sustained competitive advantage." *Journal of Management*, 7, pp. 49–64; Mahoney, J. T., and J. R. Pandian. (1992). "The resource-based view within the conversation of strategic management." *Strategic Management Journal*, 13, pp. 363–380; and Peteraf, M. A. (1993). "The cornerstones of competitive advantage: A resource-based view." *Strategic Management Journal*, 14, pp. 179–191.

13. Dierickx, I., and K. Cool. (1989). "Asset stock accumulation and sustainability of competitive advantage." *Management Science*, 35, pp. 1504–1511. In economics, the role of history in determining competitive outcomes was first examined by Arthur, W. B. (1989). "Competing technologies, increasing returns, and lock-in by historical events." *Economic Journal*, 99, pp. 116–131.

14. See Breen, B. (2003). "What's selling in America." *Fast Company*, January, pp. 80 +.

15. This term was first suggested by Arthur, W. B. (1989). "Competing technologies, increasing returns, and lock-in by historical events." *Economic Journal*, 99, pp. 116–131. A good example of path dependence is the development of Silicon Valley and the important role that Stanford University and a few early firms played in creating the network of organizations that has since become the center of much of the electronics business. See Alley, J. (1997). "The heart of Silicon Valley." *Fortune*, July 7, pp. 86 +.

16. Reed, R., and R. J. DeFillippi. (1990). "Causal ambiguity, barriers to imitation, and sustainable competitive advantage." *Academy of Management Review*, 15(1), pp. 88–102, suggest that causal ambiguity about the sources of a firm's competitive advantage need only exist among a firm's competitors for it to be a source of sustained competitive advantage. Managers in a firm, they argue, may fully understand the sources of their advantage. However, in a world where employees freely and frequently move from firm to firm, such special insights into the sources of a firm's competitive advantage would not remain proprietary for very long. For this reason, for causal ambiguity to be a source of sustained competitive advantage, both the firm trying to gain such an advantage and those trying to imitate it must face similar levels of causal ambiguity. Indeed, Wal-Mart recently sued Amazon for trying to steal some of its secrets by hiring employees away from Wal-Mart. See Nelson, E. (1998). "Wal-Mart accuses Amazon. com of stealing its secrets in lawsuit." *The Wall Street Journal*, October 19, p. B10. For a discussion of how difficult it is to maintain secrets, especially in a world of the World Wide Web, see Farnham, A. (1997). "How safe are your secrets?" *Fortune*, September 8, pp. 114 +. The international dimensions of the challenges associated with maintaining secrets are discussed in Robinson, E. (1998). "China spies target corporate America." *Fortune*, March 30, pp. 118 +.

17. Itami, H. (1987). *Mobilizing invisible assets*. Cambridge, MA: Harvard University Press.

18. See Barney, J. B., and B. Tyler. (1990). "The attributes of top management teams and sustained competitive advantage." In M. Lawless and L. Gomez-Mejia (eds.), *Managing the high technology firm* (pp. 33–48). Greenwich, CT: JAI Press, on teamwork in top management teams; Barney, J. B. (1986). "Organizational culture: Can it be a source of sustained competitive advantage?" *Academy of Management Review*, 11, pp. 656–665, on organizational culture; Henderson, R. M., and I. Cockburn. (1994). "Measuring competence? Exploring firm effects in pharmaceutical research." *Strategic Management Journal*, 15, pp. 63–84, on relationships among employees; and Dyer, J. H., and H. Singh. (1998). "The relational view: Cooperative strategy and sources of interorganizational competitive advantage." *Academy of Management Review*, 23(4), pp. 660–679, on relationships with suppliers and customers.

19. For a discussion of knowledge as a source of competitive advantage in the popular business press, see Stewart, T. (1995). "Getting real about brain power." *Fortune*, November 27, pp. 201 +; Stewart, T. (1995). "Mapping corporate knowledge." *Fortune*, October 30, pp. 209 +. For the academic version of this same issue, see Simonin, B. L. (1999). "Ambiguity and the process of knowledge transfer in strategic alliances." *Strategic Management Journal*, 20(7), pp. 595–623; Spender, J. C. (1996). "Making knowledge the basis of a dynamic theory of the firm." *Strategic Management Journal*, 17 (Winter special

issue), pp. 109–122; Hatfield, D. D., J. P. Liebeskind, and T. C. Opler. (1996). "The effects of corporate restructuring on aggregate industry specialization." *Strategic Management Journal*, 17, pp. 55–72; and Grant, R. M. (1996). "Toward a knowledge-based theory of the firm." *Strategic Management Journal*, 17 (Winter special issue), pp. 109–122.

20. Porras, J., and P. O. Berg. (1978). "The impact of organizational development." *Academy of Management Review*, 3, pp. 249–266, have done one of the few empirical studies on whether or not systematic efforts to change socially complex resources are effective. They found that such efforts are usually not effective. Although this study is getting older, it is unlikely that current change methods will be any more effective than the methods examined by these authors.

21. See Hambrick, D. (1987). "Top management teams: Key to strategic success." *California Management Review*, 30, pp. 88–108, on top management teams; Barney, J. B. (1986). "Organizational culture: Can it be a source of sustained competitive advantage?" *Academy of Management Review*, 11, pp. 656–665, on culture; Porter, M. E. (1980). *Competitive strategy*. New York: Free Press; and Klein, B., and K. Leffler. (1981). "The role of market forces in assuring contractual performance." *Journal of Political Economy*, 89, pp. 615–641, on relations with customers.

21. See Harris, L. C., and E. Ogbonna. (1999). "Developing a market oriented culture: A critical evaluation." *Journal of Management Studies*, 36(2), pp. 177–196.

23. Lieberman, M. B. (1987). "The learning curve, diffusion, and competitive strategy." *Strategic Management Journal*, 8, pp. 441–452, has a very good analysis of the cost of imitation in the chemical industry. See also Lieberman, M. B., and D. B. Montgomery. (1988). "First-mover advantages." *Strategic Management Journal*, 9, pp. 41–58.

24. Rumelt, R. P. (1984). "Toward a strategic theory of the firm." In R. Lamb (ed.), *Competitive strategic management* (pp. 556–570). Upper Saddle River, NJ: Prentice Hall, among others, cites patents as a source of costly imitation.

25. Significant debate surrounds the patentability of different kinds of products. For example, although typefaces are not patentable (and cannot be copyrighted), the process for displaying typefaces may be. See Thurm, S. (1998). "Copy this typeface? Court ruling counsels caution." *The Wall Street Journal*, July 15, pp. B1 +.

26. For an insightful discussion of these complementary resources, see Amit, R., and P. J. H. Schoemaker. (1993). "Strategic assets and organizational rent." *Strategic Management Journal*, 14(1), pp. 33–45.

27. See Kearns, D. T., and D. A. Nadler. (1992). *Prophets in the dark*. New York: HarperCollins; and Smith, D. K., and R. C. Alexander. (1988). *Fumbling the future*. New York: William Morrow.

28. (2004). "Gateway will close remaining retail stores." *The Wall Street Journal*, April 2, p. B2; Michaels, D. (2004). "AA Airbus, picturing huge jet was easy; building it was hard." *The Wall Street Journal*, May 27, pp. A1 +; Zeller, W., A. Michael, and L. Woellert. (2004). "The airline debate over cheap seats." *The Wall Street Journal*, May 24, pp. A1 +.

29. (2004). "Casio." *Marketing*, May 6, p. 95; Weisul, K. (2003). "When time is money—and art." *BusinessWeek*, July 21, p. 86.

30. That said, there have been some "cracks" in Southwest's capabilities armor lately. Its CEO suddenly resigned, and its level of profitability dropped precipitously in 2004. Whether these are indicators that Southwest's core strengths are being dissipated or there are short-term problems is not yet known. However, Southwest's stumbling would give US Airways some hope. Trottman, M., S. McCartney, and J. Lublin. (2004). "Southwest's CEO abruptly quits 'draining job.'" *The Wall Street Journal*, July 16, pp. A1 +.

31. One should consult a lawyer before getting involved in these forms of tacit cooperation.

32. This aspect of the competitive dynamics in an industry is discussed in Smith, K. G., C. M. Grimm, and M. J. Gannon. (1992). *Dynamics of competitive strategy*. Newberry Park, CA: Sage.

33. Schlender, B. R. (1992). "How Sony keeps the magic going." *Fortune*, February 24, pp. 75–84.

34. Personal communication.

35. See, for example, Peters, T., and R. Waterman. (1982). *In search of excellence*. New York: Harper Collins; Collins, J., and J. Porras. (1994). *Built to last*. New York: Harper Business; Collins, J. (2001). *Good to great*. New York: Harper Collins; and Bennis, W. G., and R. Townsend. (2006). *Reinventing leadership*. New York: Harper Collins.

Cost Leadership

From Chapter 4 of *Strategic Management and Competitive Advantage: Concepts and Cases*, 3/e. Jay B. Barney. William S. Hesterly. Copyright © 2010 by Pearson Education. Published by Prentice Hall. All rights reserved.

Cost Leadership

The World's Lowest-Cost Airline

Everyone's heard of low-cost airlines—Southwest, AirTran, and JetBlue, for example. But have you heard of the world's lowest-cost airline? This airline currently gives 25 percent of its seats away for free. Its goal is to double that within a couple of years. And yet, from 2007 to 2008, its revenues jumped 21 percent to €2.7 billion, while its net income increased 20 percent to €480.9 million. And this in spite of unprecedented increases in jet fuel prices during this same time period!

The name of this airline is Ryanair. Headquartered in Dublin, Ireland, Ryanair flies short flights throughout Western Europe. In 1985, Ryanair's founders started a small airline to fly between Ireland and England. For six years, this airline barely broke even. Then, in 1991, Michael O'Leary—current CEO at Ryanair—was brought on board. O'Leary traveled to the United States and studied the most successful low-cost airline in the world at that time—Southwest Airlines. O'Leary became convinced that, once European airspace was deregulated, an airline that adopted Southwest's model of quick turnarounds, no frills, no business class, flying into smaller regional airports, and using only a single kind of aircraft could be extremely successful. Prices in the European air market were fully deregulated in 1997.

Since then, Ryanair has become an even lower-cost airline than Southwest. For example, like Southwest, Ryanair only flies a single type of aircraft—a Boeing 737–800. However, to save on the cost of its airplanes, Ryanair orders them without window shades and with seats that do not recline. This saves several hundred thousand dollars per plane and also reduces ongoing maintenance costs. Both Southwest and Ryanair try to make it easy for consumers to order tickets online, thereby avoiding the costs of call centers and travel agents. However, just 59 percent of Southwest's tickets are sold online; 98 percent of Ryanair's tickets are sold online.

This focus on low costs allows Ryanair to have the lowest prices possible for a seat on its airplanes. The average fare on Southwest is $92; the average fare on Ryanair is $53. But, even at those low prices, Ryanair is still able to earn comfortable margins.

However, those net margins don't come just from Ryanair's low costs. They also reflect the fact that the fare you pay Ryanair includes only the seat and virtually no other services. If you want any other services, you have to pay extra for them. For example, you want to check bags? It will cost $9.95 per bag. You want a snack on the airplane? It will cost you $5.50. For that, you get a not-very-tasty hot dog. You want a bottle of water? It will cost you $3.50. You want a blanket or pillow—they cost $2.50 each.

In addition, flight attendants will sell you all sorts of extras to keep you occupied during your flight. These include scratch-card games, perfume, digital cameras ($137.50), and MP3 players ($165). During 2007, Ryanair began offering in-flight mobile telephone service. Not only did this enable passengers to call their friends and family, Ryanair also used this service to introduce mobile gambling on its planes. Now, on your way from London to Paris, you can play blackjack, poker, and slot machines.

Finally, to further increase revenues, Ryanair sells space on its planes to advertisers. When your seat tray is up, you may see an ad for a cell phone from Vodaphone. When the tray is down, you may see an ad from Hertz.

All of these actions enable Ryanair to keep its profits up while keeping its fares as low as possible. And the results of this strategy have been impressive—from near bankruptcy in 1991, Ryanair is now the largest international airline—transporting over 49 million passengers in 2008.

Of course, this success did not happen without some controversy. For example, in October 2006, Ryanair was chosen as the most disliked European airline in a poll of some 4,000 readers of TripAdvisor, a British Web site for frequent travelers. Ryanair's response:

Peter Frischmuth/Argus/Peter Arnold, Inc.

These frequent travelers usually have their companies pay for their travel. If they had to pay for their own tickets, they would prefer Ryanair. Also, Ryanair's strong anti-union stance has caused it political problems in many of the union-dominated countries where it flies. Finally, Ryanair has been criticized for some of its lax security and safety procedures, for how it treats disabled passengers, and for the cleanliness of its planes.

However, if you want to fly from London to Barcelona for $60 round trip, it's hard to beat Ryanair.

Source: K. Capell (2006). "Wal-Mart with wings." *BusinessWeek*, November 27, pp. 44–46; www//en.wikipedia.org/wiki/Ryanair; and Peter Arnold, Inc.

Ryanair has been profitable in an industry—the airline industry—that has historically been populated by bankrupt firms. It does this by implementing an aggressive low-cost strategy.

What Is Business-Level Strategy?

The basic tools required to conduct a strategic analysis are tools for analyzing external threats and opportunities and tools for analyzing internal strengths and weaknesses. Once you have completed these two analyses, it is possible to begin making strategic choices. Strategic choices fall into two large categories: business strategies and corporate strategies. **Business-level strategies** are actions firms take to gain competitive advantages in a single market or industry. **Corporate-level strategies** are actions firms take to gain competitive advantages by operating in multiple markets or industries simultaneously.

The two business-level strategies are cost leadership (this chapter) and product differentiation. The importance of these two business-level strategies is so widely recognized that they are often called **generic business strategies**.

What Is Cost Leadership?

A firm that chooses a **cost leadership business strategy** focuses on gaining advantages by reducing its costs to below those of all its competitors. This does not mean that this firm abandons other business or corporate strategies. Indeed, a single-minded focus on *just* reducing costs can lead a firm to make low-cost products that no one wants to buy. However, a firm pursuing a cost leadership strategy focuses much of its effort on keeping its costs low.

Numerous firms have pursued cost leadership strategies. Ryanair clearly follows this strategy in the airline industry, Timex and Casio in the watch industry, and BIC in the disposable pen and razor market. All these firms advertise their products. However, these advertisements tend to emphasize reliability and low prices—the kinds of product attributes that are usually emphasized by firms pursuing cost leadership strategies.

In automobiles, Hyundai has implemented a cost leadership strategy with its emphasis on low-priced cars for basic transportation. Like Ryanair, Timex, Casio, and BIC, Hyundai spends a significant amount of money advertising its products, but its advertisements tend to emphasize its sporty styling and high gas mileage. Hyundai is positioned as a fun and inexpensive car, not a high-performance sports car or a luxurious status symbol. Hyundai's ability to sell these fun and inexpensive automobiles depends on its design choices (keep it simple) and its low manufacturing costs.[1]

Sources of Cost Advantages

An individual firm may have a cost advantage over its competitors for a number of reasons. Cost advantages are possible even when competing firms produce similar products. Some of the most important of these sources of cost advantage are listed in Table 1 and discussed in this section.

1. Size differences and economies of scale
2. Size differences and diseconomies of scale
3. Experience differences and learning-curve economies
4. Differential low-cost access to productive inputs
5. Technological advantages independent of scale
6. Policy choices

TABLE 1 Important Sources of Cost Advantages for Firms

Size Differences and Economies of Scale

One of the most widely cited sources of cost advantages for a firm is its size. When there are significant economies of scale in manufacturing, marketing, distribution, service, or other functions of a business, larger firms (up to some point) have a cost advantage over smaller firms. **Economies of scale** are said to exist when the increase in firm size (measured in terms of volume of production) is associated with lower costs (measured in terms of average costs per unit of production), as depicted in Figure 1. As the volume of production in a firm increases, the average cost per unit decreases until some optimal volume of production (point X) is reached, after which the average costs per unit of production begin to rise because of **diseconomies of scale** (a concept discussed in more detail later in this chapter).

If the relationship between volume of production and average costs per unit of production depicted in Figure 1 holds, and if a firm in an industry has the largest volume of production (but not greater than the optimal level, X), then that firm will have a cost advantage in that industry. Increasing the volume of production can reduce a firm's costs for several reasons. Some of the most important of these reasons are summarized in Table 2 and discussed in the following text.

Volume of Production and Specialized Machines. When a firm has high levels of production, it is often able to purchase and use specialized manufacturing tools that cannot be kept in operation in small firms. Manufacturing managers at BIC

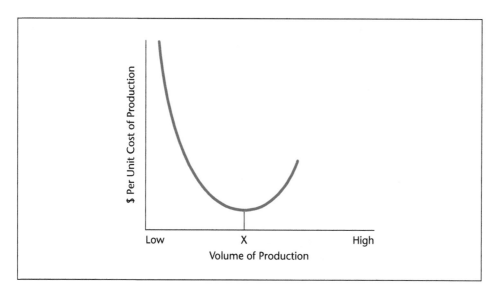

Figure 1 Economies of Scale

TABLE 2 Why Higher Volumes of Production in a Firm Can Lead to Lower Costs

With higher production volume . . .

1. firms can use specialized machines . . .
2. firms can build larger plants . . .
3. firms can increase employee specialization . . .
4. firms can spread overhead costs across more units produced . . .

. . . which can lower per-unit production costs.

Corporation, for example, have emphasized this important advantage of high volumes of production. A former director of manufacturing at BIC once observed:

> We are in the automation business. Because of our large volume, one tenth of 1 cent in savings turns out to be enormous. . . . One advantage of the high-volume business is that you can get the best equipment and amortize it entirely over a short period of time (4 to 5 months). I'm always looking for new equipment. If I see a cost-savings machine, I can buy it. I'm not constrained by money.[2]

Only firms with BIC's level of production in the pen industry have the ability to reduce their costs in this manner.

Volume of Production and the Cost of Plant and Equipment. High volumes of production may also enable a firm to build larger manufacturing operations. In some industries, the cost of building these manufacturing operations per unit of production is lower than the cost of building smaller manufacturing operations per unit of production. Thus, large-volume firms, other factors being equal, will be able to build lower-per-unit-cost manufacturing operations and will have lower average costs of production.

The link between volume of production and the cost of building manufacturing operations is particularly important in industries characterized by **process manufacturing**—chemical, oil refining, paper and pulp manufacturing, and so forth. Because of the physical geometry of process manufacturing facilities, the costs of constructing a processing plant with increased capacity can be expected to rise as the two-thirds power of a plant's capacity. This is because the area of the surface of some three-dimensional containers (such as spheres and cylinders) increases at a slower rate than the volume of these containers. Thus, larger containers hold greater volumes and require less material per unit volume for the outside skins of these containers. Up to some point, increases in capacity come at a less-than-proportionate rise in the cost of building this capacity.[3]

For example, it might cost a firm $100 to build a plant with a capacity of 1,000 units, for a per-unit average cost of $0.01. But, assuming that the "two-thirds rule" applies, it might cost a firm $465 to build a plant with a capacity of 10,000 units ($465 = 10,000^{2/3}$), for a per-unit average cost of $0.0046. The difference between $0.01 per unit and $0.0046 per unit represents a cost advantage for a large firm.

Volume of Production and Employee Specialization. High volumes of production are also associated with high levels of employee specialization. As workers specialize in accomplishing a narrow task, they can become more and more efficient at this task, thereby reducing their firm's costs. This reasoning applies both in specialized manufacturing tasks (such as the highly specialized manufacturing functions in an assembly line) and in specialized management functions (such as the highly specialized managerial functions of accounting, finance, and sales).

110

Smaller firms often do not possess the volume of production needed to justify this level of employee specialization. With smaller volumes of production, highly specialized employees may not have enough work to keep them busy an entire workday. This low volume of production is one reason why smaller firms often have employees that perform multiple business functions and often use outside contract employees and part-time workers to accomplish highly specialized functions, such as accounting, taxes, and human resource management.

Volume of Production and Overhead Costs. A firm with high volumes of production has the luxury of spreading its overhead costs over more units and thereby reducing the overhead costs per unit. Suppose, in a particular industry, that the operation of a variety of accounting, control, and research and development functions, regardless of a firm's size, is $100,000. Clearly, a firm that manufactures 1,000 units is imposing a cost of $100 per unit to cover overhead expenses. However, a firm that manufactures 10,000 units is imposing a cost of $10 per unit to cover overhead. Again, the larger-volume firm's average per-unit costs are lower than the small-volume firm's average per-unit cost.

Size Differences and Diseconomies of Scale

Just as economies of scale can generate cost advantages for larger firms, important diseconomies of scale can actually increase costs if firms grow too large. As Figure 1 shows, if the volume of production rises beyond some optimal point (point X in the figure), this can actually lead to an increase in per-unit costs. If other firms in an industry have grown beyond the optimal firm size, a smaller firm (with a level of production closer to the optimal) may obtain a cost advantage even when all firms in the industry are producing very similar products. Some important sources of diseconomies of scale for a firm are listed in Table 3 and discussed in this section.

Physical Limits to Efficient Size. Applying the two-thirds rule to the construction of manufacturing facilities seems to imply, for some industries at least, that larger is always better. However, there are some important physical limitations to the size of some manufacturing processes. Engineers have found, for example, that cement kilns develop unstable internal aerodynamics at capacities of above 7 million barrels per year. Others have suggested that scaling up nuclear reactors from small installations to huge facilities generates forces and physical processes that, though nondetectable in smaller facilities, can become significant in larger operations. These physical limitations on manufacturing processes reflect the underlying physics and engineering in a manufacturing process and suggest when the cost curve in Figure 1 will begin to rise.[4]

Managerial Diseconomies. Although the underlying physics and engineering in a manufacturing process have an important impact on a firm's costs, managerial diseconomies are perhaps an even more important cause of these cost increases.

When the volume of production gets too large . . .

1. physical limits to efficient size . . .
2. managerial diseconomies . . .
3. worker de-motivation . . .
4. distance to markets and suppliers . . .

. . . can increase per-unit costs.

TABLE 3 Major Sources of Diseconomies of Scale

As a firm increases in size, it often increases in complexity, and the ability of managers to control and operate it efficiently becomes limited.

One well-known example of a manufacturing plant that grew too large and thus became inefficient is Crown, Cork and Seal's can-manufacturing plant in Philadelphia. Through the early part of this century, this Philadelphia facility handled as many as 75 different can-manufacturing lines. The most efficient plants in the industry, however, were running from 10 to 15 lines simultaneously. The huge Philadelphia facility was simply too large to operate efficiently and was characterized by large numbers of breakdowns, a high percentage of idle lines, and poor-quality products.[5]

Worker De-Motivation.   A third source of diseconomies of scale depends on the relationship between firm size, employee specialization, and employee motivation. It has already been suggested that one of the advantages of increased volumes of production is that it allows workers to specialize in smaller and more narrowly defined production tasks. With specialization, workers become more and more efficient at the particular task facing them.

However, a significant stream of research suggests that these types of very specialized jobs can be unmotivating for employees. Based on motivational theories taken from social psychology, this work suggests that as workers are removed further from the complete product that is the end result of a manufacturing process, the role that a worker's job plays in the overall manufacturing process becomes more and more obscure. As workers become mere "cogs in a manufacturing machine," worker motivation wanes, and productivity and quality can both suffer.[6]

Distance to Markets and Suppliers.   A final source of diseconomies of scale can be the distance between a large manufacturing facility and where the goods in question are to be sold or where essential raw materials are purchased. Any reductions in cost attributable to the exploitation of economies of scale in manufacturing may be more than offset by large transportation costs associated with moving supplies and products to and from the manufacturing facility. Firms that build highly efficient plants without recognizing these significant transportation costs may put themselves at a competitive disadvantage compared to firms with slightly less efficient plants that are located closer to suppliers and key markets.

Experience Differences and Learning-Curve Economies

A third possible source of cost advantages for firms in a particular business depends on their different cumulative levels of production. In some circumstances, firms with the greatest experience in manufacturing a product or service will have the lowest costs in an industry and thus will have a cost-based advantage. The link between cumulative volumes of production and cost has been formalized in the concept of the **learning curve**. The relationship between cumulative volumes of production and per unit costs is graphically represented in Figure 2.

The Learning Curve and Economies of Scale.   As depicted in Figure 2, the learning curve is very similar to the concept of economies of scale. However, there are two important differences. First, whereas economies of scale focus on the relationship between the volume of production at a given point in time and average unit costs, the learning curve focuses on the relationship between the *cumulative* volume of production—that is, how much a firm has produced over time—and average unit costs. Second, where diseconomies of scale are presumed to exist if a firm gets too large, there is no corresponding increase in costs in the learning-curve model as

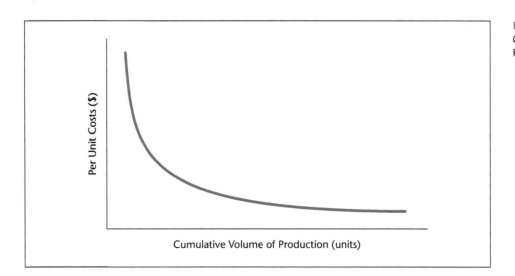

Per Unit Costs ($)

Cumulative Volume of Production (units)

Figure 2 The Learning Curve and the Cost of Production

the cumulative volume of production grows. Rather, costs continue to fall until they approach the lowest technologically possible cost.

The Learning Curve and Cost Advantages. The learning-curve model is based on the empirical observation that the costs of producing a unit of output fall as the cumulative volume of output increases. This relationship was first observed in the construction of aircraft before World War II. Research showed that the labor costs per aircraft fell by 20 percent each time the cumulative volume of production doubled.[7] A similar pattern has been observed in numerous industries, including the manufacture of ships, computers, spacecraft, and semiconductors. In all these cases, increases in cumulative production have been associated with detailed learning about how to make production as efficient as possible.

However, learning-curve cost advantages are not restricted to manufacturing. Learning can be associated with any business function, from purchasing raw materials to distribution and service. Service industries can also experience important learning effects. The learning curve applies whenever the cost of accomplishing a business activity falls as a function of the cumulative number of times a firm has engaged in that activity.[8]

The Learning Curve and Competitive Advantage. The learning-curve model summarized in Figure 2 has been used to develop a model of cost-based competitive advantage that links learning with market share and average production costs.[9]

The logic behind this application of the learning-curve model is straightforward: The first firm that successfully moves down the learning curve will obtain a cost advantage over rivals. To move a production process down the learning curve, a firm needs to have higher levels of cumulative volume of production. Of course, firms successful at producing high volumes of output need to sell that output to customers. In selling this output, firms are increasing their market share. Thus, to drive down the learning curve and obtain a cost advantage, firms must aggressively acquire market share.

This application of learning-curve logic has been criticized by a wide variety of authors.[10] Two criticisms are particularly salient. First, although the acquisition of market share is likely to allow a firm to reduce its production costs, the acquisition of share itself is expensive. Indeed, as described in the Research Made Relevant feature, sometimes the cost of acquiring share may rise to equal its value.

The second major criticism of this application of the learning-curve model is that there is, in this logic, no room for any other business or corporate strategies. In other words, this application of the learning curve implicitly assumes that firms can compete only on the basis of their low costs and that other strategies are not possible. Most industries, however, are characterized by opportunities for at least some of these other strategies, and thus this strict application of the learning-curve model can be misleading.[11]

These criticisms aside, it is still the case that in many industries firms with larger cumulative levels of production, other things being equal, will have lower average production costs. Thus, experience in all the facets of production can be a source of cost advantage even if the single-minded pursuit of market share to obtain these cost reductions may not give a firm above normal economic returns.

Differential Low-Cost Access to Productive Inputs

Besides economies of scale, diseconomies of scale, and learning-curve cost advantages, differential low-cost access to productive inputs may create cost differences among firms producing similar products in an industry. **Productive inputs** are any supplies used by a firm in conducting its business activities; they include, among other things, labor, capital, land, and raw materials. A firm that has differential low-cost access to one or more of these factors is likely to have lower economic costs compared to rivals.

Consider, for example, an oil company with fields in Saudi Arabia compared to an oil company with fields in the North Sea. The cost of obtaining crude oil for the first firm is considerably less than the cost of obtaining crude oil for the second. North Sea drilling involves the construction of giant offshore drilling platforms, housing workers on floating cities, and transporting oil across an often-stormy sea. Drilling in Saudi Arabia requires only the simplest drilling technologies, because the oil is found relatively close to the surface.

Of course, in order to create a cost advantage, the cost of acquiring low-cost productive inputs must be less than the cost savings generated by these factors. For example, even though it may be much less costly to drill for oil in Saudi Arabia than in the North Sea, if it is very expensive to purchase the rights to drill in Saudi Arabia compared to the costs of the rights to drill in the North Sea, the potential cost advantages of drilling in Saudi Arabia can be lost. As with all sources of cost advantages, firms must be careful to weigh the cost of acquiring that advantage against the value of that advantage for the firm.

Differential access to raw materials such as oil, coal, and copper ore can be important determinants of a cost advantage. However, differential access to other productive inputs can be just as important. For example, it may be easier (i.e., less costly) to recruit highly trained electronics engineers for firms located near where these engineers receive their schooling than for firms located some distance away. This lower cost of recruiting is a partial explanation of the development of geographic technology centers such as Silicon Valley in California, Route 128 in Massachusetts, and the Research Triangle in North Carolina. In all three cases, firms are located physically close to several universities that train the engineers that are the lifeblood of high-technology companies. The search for low-cost labor can create ethical dilemmas, as described in the Ethics and Strategy feature.

Research Made Relevant

Research on the relationship between market share and firm performance has continued over many decades. Early work identified market share as the primary determinant of firm performance. Indeed, one particularly influential article identified market share as being *the key* to firm profitability.

This initial conclusion about the relationship between market share and firm performance was based on the observed positive correlation between these two variables. That is, firms with large market share tend to be highly profitable; firms with low market share tend to be less profitable. The logical conclusion of this empirical finding seems to be that if a firm wants to increase its profitability, it should increase its market share.

Not so fast. It turns out that the relationship between market share and firm profits is not that simple. Consider the following scenario. Suppose that 10 companies all conclude that the key to their profitability is gaining market share. To acquire share from each other, each firm will probably increase its advertising and other marketing expenses as well as reduce its prices. This has the effect of putting a price on the market share that a firm seeks to acquire—that is, these competing firms are creating what might be called a "market-for-market share."

How Valuable Is Market Share—Really?

And because there are 10 firms competing for share in this market, this market is likely to be highly competitive. Returns to acquiring share in such competitive markets for market share should fall to a normal economic level.

All this analysis suggests that although there may be a cross-sectional positive correlation between market share and firm performance—that is, at a given point in time, market share and firm performance may be positively correlated—this correlation may not be positive over time, as firms seek to increase their market share. Several papers have examined this hypothesis. Two of the most influential of these papers—by Dick Rumelt and Robin Wensley and by Cynthia Montgomery and Birger Wernerfelt—have shown

that markets for market share often do emerge in industries, that these markets are often very competitive, and that acquiring market share in these competitive markets does not improve a firm's economic performance. Indeed, in their study of the consolidation of the beer industry Montgomery and Wernerfelt showed that firms such as Anheuser-Busch and Miller paid so much for the market share they acquired that it actually reduced their profitability.

The general consensus in the literature now seems to be that large market share is an outcome of a competitive process within an industry, not an appropriate objective of firm managers, per se. Thus, firms with particularly valuable strategies will naturally attract more customers, which, in turn, suggests that they will often have higher market share. That is, a firm's valuable strategies generate both high levels of firm performance and large market share. This, in turn, explains the positive correlation between market share and firm performance.

Sources: R. D. Buzzell, B. T. Gale, and R. M. Sultan (1975). "Market share—the key to profitability." *Harvard Business Review,* 53, pp. 97–106; R. Rumelt and R. Wensley (1981). "In search of the market share effect." *Proceedings of the Academy of Management Meetings, 1981,* pp. 2–6; C. Montgomery and B. Wernerfelt (1991). "Sources of superior performance: Market share versus industry effects in the U.S. brewing industry." *Management Science,* 37, pp. 954–959.

Technological Advantages Independent of Scale

Another possible source of cost advantage in an industry may be the different technologies that firms employ to manage their business. It has already been suggested that larger firms may have technology-based cost advantages that reflect their ability to exploit economies of scale (e.g., the two-thirds rule).

Traditionally, discussion of technology-based cost advantages has focused on the machines, computers, and other physical tools that firms use to manage their business. Clearly, in some industries, these physical technology differences between firms can create important cost differences—even when the firms in question are approximately the same size in terms of volume of production. In the steel industry, for example, technological advances can substantially reduce the cost of producing steel. Firms with the latest steel-manufacturing technology will typically enjoy some cost advantage compared to similar-sized firms that do not have the latest technology. The same applies in the manufacturing of semiconductors, automobiles, consumer electronics, and a wide variety of other products.[12]

These physical technology cost advantages apply in service firms as well as in manufacturing firms. For example, early in its history Charles Schwab, a leading discount brokerage, purchased a computer system that enabled it to complete customer transactions more rapidly and at a lower cost than its rivals.[13] Kaiser-Permanente, the largest HMO in the United States, has invested in information technology that doctors can use to avoid incorrect diagnoses and procedures that can adversely affect a patient's health. By avoiding these medical mistakes, Kaiser-Permanente can substantially reduce its costs of providing medical service.[14]

However, the concept of technology can be easily broadened to include not just the physical tools that firms use to manage their business, but any processes within a firm used in this way. This concept of firm technology includes not only the **technological hardware** of companies—the machines and robots—but also the **technological software** of firms—things such as the quality of relations between labor and management, an organization's culture, and the quality of managerial controls. All these characteristics of a firm can have an impact on a firm's economic costs.[15]

Policy Choices

Thus far, this discussion has focused on reasons why a firm can gain a cost advantage despite producing products that are similar to competing firms' products. When firms produce essentially the same outputs, differences in economies of scale, learning-curve advantages, differential access to productive inputs, and differences in technology can all create cost advantages (and disadvantages) for them. However, firms can also make choices about the kinds of products and services they will sell—choices that have an impact on their relative cost position. These choices are called **policy choices**.

In general, firms that are attempting to implement a cost leadership strategy will choose to produce relatively simple standardized products that sell for relatively low prices compared to the products and prices firms pursuing other business or corporate strategies choose. These kinds of products often tend to have high volumes of sales, which (if significant economies of scale exist) tend to reduce costs even further.

These kinds of choices in product and pricing tend to have a very broad impact on a cost leader's operations. In these firms, the task of reducing costs is not delegated to a single function or a special task force within the firm, but is the responsibility of every manager and employee. Cost reduction sometimes becomes the central objective of the firm. Indeed, in this setting management must be constantly alert to cost-cutting efforts that reduce the ability of the firm to meet customers' needs. This kind of cost-cutting culture is central to Ryanair's ability to implement its cost leadership strategy.

Ethics and Strategy

One of the most important productive inputs in almost all companies is labor. Getting differential low-cost access to labor can give a firm a cost advantage.

This search for low labor costs has led some firms to engage in an international "race to the bottom." It is well known that the wage rates of most U.S. and Western European workers are much higher than the wage rates of workers in other, less developed parts of the world. While a firm might have to pay its employees $20 per hour (in wages and benefits) to make sneakers and basketball shoes in the United States, that same firm may only have to pay an employee in the Philippines, or Malaysia, or China $1.00 per day to make the same sneakers and basketball shoes—shoes the firm might be able to sell for $150 a pair in the United States and Europe. Thus, many firms look to overseas manufacturing as a way to keep their labor cost low.

But this search for low labor cost has some important unintended consequences. First, the location of the lowest cost labor rates in the world changes over time. It used to be that Mexico had the lowest labor rates, then Korea and the Philippines, then Malaysia, then China. As the infrastructures of each of these countries evolve to the point that they can

The Race to the Bottom

support worldwide manufacturing, firms abandon their relationships with firms in prior countries in search of still lower costs in new countries. The only way former "low-cost centers" can compete is to drive their costs even lower.

This sometimes leads to a second unintended consequence of the "race to the bottom": horrendous working conditions and low wages in these low-cost manufacturing settings. Employees earning $1 for working a 10-hour day, six days a week may look good on the corporate bottom line, but many observers are deeply concerned about the moral and ethical issues associated with this strategy. Indeed, several companies—including Nike and Kmart—have been forced to

increase the wages and improve the working conditions of many of their overseas employees.

An even more horrific result of this "race to the bottom" has been the reemergence of what amounts to slavery in some Western European countries and some parts of the United States. In search of the promise of a better life, illegal immigrants are sometimes brought to Western European countries or the United States and forced to work in illegal, underground factories. These illegal immigrants are sometimes forced to work as many as 20 hours a day, for little or no pay—supposedly to "pay off" the price of bringing them out of their less developed countries. And because of their illegal status and language barriers, they often do not feel empowered to go to the local authorities.

Of course, the people who create and manage these facilities are criminals and deserve contempt. But what about the companies that purchase the services of these illegal and immoral manufacturing operations? Aren't they also culpable, both legally and morally?

Sources: R. DeGeorge (2000). "Ethics in international business—A contradiction in terms?" *Business Credit,* 102, pp. 50 +; G. Edmondson, K. Carlisle, I. Resch, K. Nickel Anhalt, and H. Dawley (2000). "Workers in bondage." *BusinessWeek,* November 27, pp. 146 +; D. Winter (2000). "Facing globalization." *Ward's Auto World,* 36, pp. 7 +.

The Value of Cost Leadership

There is little doubt that cost differences can exist among firms, even when those firms are selling very similar products. Policy choices about the kinds of products firms in an industry choose to produce can also create important cost differences. But under what conditions will these kinds of cost advantages actually create value for a firm?

One way to tell if a resource or capability—such as the ability of a firm to have a cost advantage—actually creates value for a firm is by whether that resource or capability enables a firm to neutralize its external threats or exploit its external opportunities. The ability of a cost leadership position to neutralize external threats will be examined here. The ability of such a position to enable a firm to exploit opportunities will be left as an exercise. The specific economic consequences of cost leadership are discussed in the Strategy in Depth feature.

Cost Leadership and the Threat of Entry

A cost leadership competitive strategy helps reduce the threat of new entrants by creating cost-based barriers to entry. Many of the barriers to entry, including economies of scale and cost advantages independent of scale, assume that incumbent firms have lower costs than potential entrants. If an incumbent firm is a cost leader, for any of the reasons just listed, then new entrants may have to invest heavily to reduce their costs prior to entry. Often, new entrants will enter using another business strategy (e.g., product differentiation) rather than attempting to compete on costs.

Cost Leadership and the Threat of Rivalry

Firms with a low-cost position also reduce the threat of rivalry. The threat of rivalry is reduced through pricing strategies that low-cost firms can engage in and through their relative impact on the performance of a low-cost firm and its higher-cost rivals.

Cost Leadership and the Threat of Substitutes

Substitutes become a threat to a firm when their cost and performance, relative to a firm's current products or services, become more attractive to customers. Thus, when the price of crude oil goes up, substitutes for crude oil become more attractive. When the cost and performance of electronic calculators improve, demand for mechanical adding machines disappears.

In this situation, cost leaders have the ability to keep their products and services attractive relative to substitutes. While high-cost firms may have to charge high prices to cover their costs, thus making substitutes more attractive, cost leaders can keep their prices low and still earn normal or above-normal economic profits.

Cost Leadership and the Threat of Powerful Suppliers

Suppliers can become a threat to a firm by charging higher prices for the goods or services they supply or by reducing the quality of those goods or services. However, when a supplier sells to a cost leader, that firm has greater flexibility in absorbing higher-cost supplies than does a high-cost firm. Higher supply costs may destroy any above-normal profits for high-cost firms but still allow a cost leader firm to earn an above-normal profit.

Cost leadership based on large volumes of production and economies of scale can also reduce the threat of suppliers. Large volumes of production imply large purchases of raw materials and other supplies. Suppliers are not likely to jeopardize these sales by threatening their customers. Indeed, as was suggested

Another way to demonstrate that cost leadership can be a source of economic value is to directly examine the economic profits generated by a firm with a cost advantage operating in an otherwise very competitive industry. This is done in Figure 3.

The firms depicted in this figure are **price takers**—that is, the price of the products or services they sell is determined by market conditions and not by individual decisions of firms. This implies that there is effectively no product differentiation in this market and that no one firm's sales constitute a large percentage of this market.

The price of goods or services in this type of market (P^*) is determined by aggregate industry supply and demand. This industry price determines the demand facing an individual firm in this market. Because these firms are price takers, the demand facing an individual firm is horizontal—that is, firm decisions about levels of output have a negligible impact on overall industry supply and thus a negligible impact on the market-determined price. A firm in this setting maximizes its economic performance by

The Economics of Cost Leadership

producing a quantity of output (Q) so that marginal revenue equals marginal cost (MC). The ability of firms to earn economic profits in this setting depends upon the relationship between the market-determined price (P^*) and the average total cost (ATC) of a firm at the quantity it chooses to produce.

Firms in the market depicted in Figure 3 fall into two categories. All but one firm have the average-total-cost curve ATC_2 and marginal-cost curve MC_2. However, one firm in this industry has the average-total-cost

curve ATC_1 and marginal-cost curve MC_1. Notice that ATC_1 is less than ATC_2 at the performance-maximizing quantities produced by these two kinds of firms (Q_1 and Q_2, respectively). In this particular example, firms with common average-total-cost curves are earning zero economic profits, while the low-cost firm is earning an economic profit (equal to the shaded area in the figure). A variety of other examples could also be constructed: The cost leader firm could be earning zero economic profits, while other firms in the market are incurring economic losses; the cost leader firm could be earning substantial economic profits, while other firms are earning smaller economic profits; the cost leader firm could be incurring small economic losses, while the other firms are incurring substantial economic losses; and so forth. However, in all these examples the cost leader's economic performance is greater than the economic performance of other firms in the industry. Thus, cost leadership can have an important impact on a firm's economic performance.

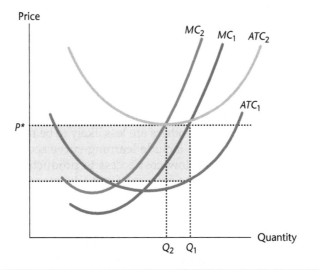

Figure 3 Cost Leadership and Economic Performance

earlier, buyers are often able to use their purchasing volume to extract volume discounts from suppliers.

Cost Leadership and the Threat of Powerful Buyers

Cost leadership can also reduce the threat of buyers. Powerful buyers are a threat to firms when they insist on low prices or higher quality and service from their suppliers. Lower prices threaten firm revenues; higher quality can increase a firm's costs. Cost leaders can have their revenues reduced by buyer threats and still have normal or above-normal performance. These firms can also absorb the greater costs of increased quality or service and still have a cost advantage over their competition.

Buyers can also be a threat through backward vertical integration. Being a cost leader deters backward vertical integration by buyers, because a buyer that vertically integrates backward will often not have costs as low as an incumbent cost leader. Rather than vertically integrating backward and increasing its cost of supplies, powerful buyers usually prefer to continue purchasing from their low-cost suppliers.

Finally, if cost leadership is based on large volumes of production, then the threat of buyers may be reduced, because buyers may depend on just a few firms for the goods or services they purchase. This dependence reduces the willingness of buyers to threaten a selling firm.

Cost Leadership and Sustained Competitive Advantage

Given that cost leadership can be valuable, an important question becomes "Under what conditions will firms implementing this business strategy be able to maintain that leadership to obtain a sustained competitive advantage?" If cost leadership strategies can be implemented by numerous firms in an industry, or if no firms face a cost disadvantage in imitating a cost leadership strategy, then being a cost leader will not generate a sustained competitive advantage for a firm. The ability of a valuable cost leadership competitive strategy to generate a sustained competitive advantage depends on that strategy being rare and costly to imitate, either through direct duplication or substitution. As suggested in Tables 4 and 5, the rarity and imitability of a cost leadership strategy depend, at least in part, on the sources of that cost advantage.

The Rarity of Sources of Cost Advantage

Some of the sources of cost advantage listed in Table 4 are likely to be rare among a set of competing firms; others are less likely to be rare. Sources of cost advantage that are likely to be rare include learning-curve economies (at least in emerging industries), differential low-cost access to productive inputs, and technological "software." The remaining sources of cost advantage are less likely to be rare.

Rare Sources of Cost Advantage

Early in the evolution of an industry, substantial differences in the cumulative volume of production of different firms are not unusual. Indeed, this is one of the major benefits associated with first-mover advantages These differences in cumulative volume of production, in combination with substantial

Likely-to-be-rare sources of cost advantage	Less-likely-to-be-rare sources of cost advantage
Learning-curve economies of scale (especially in emerging businesses)	Economies of scale (except when efficient plant size approximately equals total industry demand)
Differential low-cost access to productive inputs	Diseconomies of scale
Technological "software"	Technological hardware (unless a firm has proprietary hardware development skills)
	Policy choices

TABLE 4 The Rarity of Sources of Cost Advantage

learning-curve economies, suggest that, in some settings, learning-curve advantages may be rare and thus a source of at least temporary competitive advantage.

The definition of differential access to productive inputs implies that this access is often rare. Certainly, if large numbers of competing firms have this same access, then it cannot be a source of competitive advantage.

Technological software is also likely to be rare among a set of competing firms. These software attributes represent each firm's path through history. If these histories are unique, then the technological software they create may also be rare. Of course, if several competing firms experience similar paths through history, the technological software in these firms is less likely to be rare.

Less Rare Sources of Cost Advantage

When the efficient size of a firm or plant is significantly smaller than the total size of an industry, there will usually be numerous efficient firms or plants in that industry, and a cost leadership strategy based on economies of scale will not be rare. For example, if the efficient firm or plant size in an industry is 500 units, and the total size of the industry (measured in units produced) is 500,000 units, then there are likely to be numerous efficient firms or plants in this industry, and economies of scale are not likely to give any one firm a cost-based competitive advantage.

Cost advantages based on diseconomies of scale are also not likely to be rare. It is unusual for numerous firms to adopt levels of production in excess of optimal levels. If only a few firms are too large in this sense, then several competing firms in an industry that are *not* too large will have cost advantages over the firms that are too large. However, because several firms will enjoy these cost advantages, they are not rare.

One important exception to this generalization may be when changes in technology significantly reduce the most efficient scale of an operation. Given such changes in technology, several firms may be inefficiently large. If a small number of firms happen to be sized appropriately, then the cost advantages these firms obtain in this way may be rare. Such changes in technology have made large integrated steel producers "too big" relative to smaller mini-mills. Thus, mini-mills have a cost advantage over larger integrated steel firms.

Technological hardware is also not likely to be rare, especially if it is developed by suppliers and sold on the open market. However, if a firm has proprietary technology development skills, it may possess rare technological hardware that creates cost advantages.

TABLE 5 Direct Duplication
of Cost Leadership

		Basis for costly duplication		
	Source of Cost Advantage	History	Uncertainty	Social Complexity
Low-cost duplication possible	1. Economies of scale	—	—	—
	2. Diseconomies of scale	—	—	—
May be costly to duplicate	3. Learning-curve economies	*	—	—
	4. Technological "hardware"	—	*	*
	5. Policy choices	*	—	—
Usually costly to duplicate	6. Differential low-cost access to productive inputs	***	—	**
	7. Technological "software"	***	**	***

— = not a source of costly imitation, * = somewhat likely to be a source of costly imitation, ** = likely to be a source of costly imitation, *** = very likely to be a source of costly imitation

Finally, policy choices by themselves are not likely to be a rare source of cost advantage, particularly if the product or service attributes in question are easy to observe and describe.

The Imitability of Sources of Cost Advantage

Even when a particular source of cost advantage is rare, it must be costly to imitate in order to be a source of sustained competitive advantage. Both direct duplication and substitution, as forms of imitation, are important. Again, the imitability of a cost advantage depends, at least in part, on the source of that advantage.

Easy-to-Duplicate Sources of Cost Advantage

In general, economies of scale and diseconomies of scale are relatively easy-to-duplicate bases of cost leadership. As can be seen in Table 5, these sources of cost advantage do not build on history, uncertainty, or socially complex resources and capabilities and thus are not protected from duplication for these reasons.

For example, if a small number of firms obtain a cost advantage based on economies of scale, and if the relationship between production scale and costs is widely understood among competing firms, then firms at a cost disadvantage will rapidly adjust their production to exploit these economies of scale. This can be done by either growing a firm's current operations to the point that the firm exploits economies or by combining previously separate operations to obtain these economies. Both actions enable a firm at a cost disadvantage to begin using specialized machines, reduce the cost of plant and equipment, increase employee specialization, and spread overhead costs more effectively.

Indeed, perhaps the only time economies of scale are not subject to low-cost duplication is when the efficient size of operations is a significant percentage of total demand in an industry. For example, as suggested earlier, BIC

Corporation, with its dominant market share in the disposable pen market, has apparently been able to gain and retain an important cost advantage in that market based on economies of scale. BIC's ability to retain this advantage reflects the fact that the optimal plant size in the disposable pen market is a significant percentage of the pen market, and thus economies of scale act as a barrier to entry in that market.

Like economies of scale, in many settings diseconomies of scale will not be a source of sustained competitive advantage for firms that have *not* grown too large. In the short run, firms experiencing significant diseconomies can shrink the size of their operations to become more efficient. In the long run, firms that fail to adjust their size will earn below-normal economic performance and cease operations.

Although in many ways reducing the size of operations to improve efficiency seems like a simple problem for managers in firms or plants, in practice it is often a difficult change to implement. Because of uncertainty, managers in a firm or plant that is too large may not understand that diseconomies of scale have increased their costs. Sometimes, managers conclude that the problem is that employees are not working hard enough, that problems in production can be fixed, and so forth. These firms or plants may continue their inefficient operations for some time, despite costs that are higher than the industry average.[16]

Other psychological processes can also delay the abandonment of operations that are too large. One of these phenomena is known as **escalation of commitment**: Sometimes, managers committed to an incorrect (cost-increasing or revenue-reducing) course of action *increase* their commitment to this action as its limitations become manifest. For example, a manager who believes that the optimal firm size in an industry is larger than the actual optimal size may remain committed to large operations despite costs that are higher than the industry average.[17]

For all these reasons, firms suffering from diseconomies of scale must often turn to outside managers to assist in reducing costs. Outsiders bring a fresh view to the organization's problems and are not committed to the practices that generated the problems in the first place.[18]

Bases of Cost Leadership That May Be Costly to Duplicate

Although cost advantages based on learning-curve economies are rare (especially in emerging industries), they are usually not costly to duplicate. For learning-curve cost advantages to be a source of sustained competitive advantage the learning obtained by a firm must be proprietary. Most recent empirical work suggests that in most industries learning is not proprietary and thus can be rapidly duplicated as competing firms move down the learning curve by increasing their cumulative volume of production.[19]

However, the fact that learning is not costly to duplicate in *most* industries does not mean it is never costly to duplicate. In some industries, the ability of firms to learn from their production experience may vary significantly. For example, some firms treat production errors as failures and systematically punish employees who make those errors. These firms effectively reduce risk-taking among their production employees and thus reduce the chances of learning how to improve their production process. Alternatively, other firms treat production errors as opportunities to learn how to improve their production process. These firms are likely to move rapidly down the learning curve and retain cost advantages, despite the cumulative volume of production of competing firms. These different responses to production errors reflect the organizational cultures of these different firms. Because organizational cultures are socially complex, they can be very costly to duplicate.[20]

Because technological hardware can usually be purchased across supply markets, it is also not likely to be difficult to duplicate. Sometimes, however, technological hardware can be proprietary or closely bundled with other unique, costly-to-duplicate resources controlled by a firm. In this case, technological hardware *can* be costly to duplicate.

It is unusual, but not impossible, for policy choices, per se, to be a source of sustained competitive cost advantages for a firm. As suggested earlier, if the policies in question focus on easy to observe and easy to describe product characteristics, then duplication is likely, and cost advantages based on policy choices will be temporary. However, if policy choices reflect complex decision processes within a firm, teamwork among different parts of the design and manufacturing process, or any of the software commitments discussed previously, then policy choices can be a source of sustained competitive advantage, as long as only a few firms have the ability to make these choices.

Indeed, most of the successful firms that operate in unattractive industries make policy choices that are costly to imitate because they reflect historical, causally ambiguous, and socially complex firm processes. Thus, for example, Wal-Mart's supply chain management strategy—a policy with clear low-cost implications—actually reflects Wal-Mart's unique history, its socially complex relations with suppliers, and its unique organizational culture. And Ryanair's low-price pricing strategy—a strategy that reflects its low-cost position—is possible because of the kind of airplane fleet Ryanair has built over time, the commitment of its employees to Ryanair's success, a charismatic founder, and its unique organizational culture. Because these policies reflect costly-to-imitate attributes of these firms, they can be sources of sustained competitive advantage.

However, for these and other firms, it is not these policy choices, per se, that create sustainable cost leadership advantages. Rather, it is how these policies flow from the historical, causally ambiguous, and socially complex processes within a firm that makes them costly to duplicate. This has been the case for the Oakland A's baseball team, as described in the Strategy in the Emerging Enterprise feature.

Costly-to-Duplicate Sources of Cost Advantage

Differential access to low-cost productive inputs and technological software is usually a costly-to-duplicate basis of cost leadership. This is because these inputs often build on historical, uncertain, and socially complex resources and capabilities. As suggested earlier, differential access to productive inputs often depends on the location of a firm. Moreover, to be a source of economic profits, this valuable location must be obtained before its full value is widely understood. Both these attributes of differential access to productive inputs suggest that if, in fact, it is rare, it will often be costly to duplicate. First, some locations are unique and cannot be duplicated. For example, most private golf clubs would like to own courses with the spectacular beauty of Pebble Beach in Monterey, California, but there is only one Pebble Beach—a course that runs parallel to some of the most beautiful oceanfront scenery in the world. Although "scenery" is an important factor of production in running and managing a golf course, the re-creation of Pebble Beach's scenery at some other location is simply beyond our technology.

Second, even if a location is not unique, once its value is revealed, acquisition of that location is not likely to generate economic profits. Thus, for example, although being located in Silicon Valley provides access to some important low-cost productive inputs for electronics firms, firms that moved to this location after its value was revealed have substantially higher costs than firms that moved there before its full value was revealed. These higher costs effectively reduce the economic profit that otherwise could have been generated. These arguments suggest that gaining differential access to productive inputs in a way that generates economic profits may reflect a firm's unique path through history.

Technological software is also likely to be difficult to duplicate and often can be a source of sustained competitive advantage. The values, beliefs, culture, and teamwork that constitute this software are socially complex and may be immune from competitive duplication. Firms with cost advantages rooted in these socially complex resources incorporate cost savings in every aspect of their organization; they constantly focus on improving the quality and cost of their operations, and they have employees who are firmly committed to, and understand, what it takes to be a cost leader. Other firms may talk about low costs; these firms live cost leadership. Ryanair, Dell, Wal-Mart, and Southwest are all examples of such firms. If there are few firms in an industry with these kinds of beliefs and commitments, then they can gain a sustained competitive advantage from their cost advantage.

Substitutes for Sources of Cost Advantage

In an important sense, all of the sources of cost advantage listed in this chapter are at least partial substitutes for each other. Thus, for example, one firm may reduce its cost through exploiting economies of scale in large-scale production, and a competing firm may reduce its costs through exploiting learning-curve economies and large cumulative volume of production. If these different activities have similar effects on a firm's cost position, and if they are equally costly to implement, then they are strategic substitutes for each other.

Because of the substitute effects of different sources of cost advantage, it is not unusual for firms pursuing cost leadership to simultaneously pursue *all* the cost-reduction activities discussed in this chapter. Implementation of this *bundle* of cost-reducing activities may have few substitutes. If duplicating this bundle of activities is also rare and difficult, then a firm may be able to gain a sustained competitive advantage from doing so.

Several of the other strategies discussed in later chapters can also have the effect of reducing a firm's costs and thus may be substitutes for the sources of cost reduction discussed in this chapter. For example, one common motivation for firms implementing strategic alliance strategies is to exploit economies of scale in combination with other firms. Thus, a strategic alliance that reduces a firm's costs may be a substitute for a firm exploiting economies of scale on its own to reduce its costs. Many of the strategic alliances among aluminum mining and smelting companies are motivated by realizing economies of scale and cost reduction. Also, corporate diversification strategies often enable firms to exploit economies of scale across different businesses within which they operate. In this setting, each of these businesses—treated separately—may have scale disadvantages, but collectively their scale creates the same low-cost position as that of an individual firm that fully exploits economies of scale to reduce costs in a single business.

Baseball in the United States has a problem. Most observers agree that it is better for fans if there is competitive balance in the league—that is, if, at the beginning of the year, the fans of several teams believe that their team has a chance to go to the World Series and win it all. However, the economic reality of competition in baseball is that only a small number of financially successful teams in large cities—the New York Yankees, the Los Angeles Dodgers, the Chicago Cubs, the California Angels—have the resources necessary to compete for a spot in the World Series year after year. So-called "small-market teams," such as the Pittsburgh Pirates or the Milwaukee Brewers, may be able to compete every once in a while, but these exceptions prove the general rule—teams from large markets usually win the World Series.

And then there is Oakland and the Oakland A's. Oakland (with a population of just over 400,000) is the smallest—and least glamorous—of the three cities in the San Francisco Bay Area, the other two being San Francisco and San Jose. The A's play in an outdated stadium to an average crowd of 26,038 fans—ranking nineteenth among the 30 major league baseball teams in the United States. In 2008, the A's player payroll was $48 million, about one-fifth of the Yankees' player payroll.

Despite these liabilities, from 1999 to 2008, the A's either won their division or placed second in all but two years. Over this period, the A's won 57 percent of their games, second only to the Yankees, who won 60 percent of their games over this same period. And, the team made money!

What is the "secret" to the A's success? Their general manager, William Lamar Beane, says that it has to do with three factors: how players are evaluated, making sure that every personnel decision in the organization is consistent

The Oakland A's: Inventing a New Way to Play Competitive Baseball

with this approach to evaluation, and ensuring that all personnel decisions are thought of as business decisions.

The criteria used by the A's to evaluate players are easy enough to state. For batters, the A's focus on on-base percentage (i.e., how often a batter reaches base) and total bases (a measure of the ability of a batter to hit for power); that is, they focus on the ability of players to get on base and score. For pitchers, the A's focus on the percentage of first pitches that are strikes and the quality of a pitcher's fast ball. First-pitch strikes and throwing a good fast ball are correlated with keeping runners off base. Thus, not surprisingly, the A's criteria for evaluating pitchers are the reverse of their criteria for evaluating hitters.

Although these evaluation criteria are easy to state, getting the entire organization to apply them consistently in scouting, choosing, developing, and managing players is much more difficult. Almost every baseball player and fan has his or her own favorite way to evaluate players. However, if you want to work in the A's organization, you must be willing to let go of your personal favorite and evaluate players the A's way. The result is that players that come through the A's farm system—the minor leagues where younger players are developed

until they are ready to play in the major leagues—learn a single way of playing baseball instead of learning a new approach to the game every time they change managers or coaches. One of the implications of this consistency has been that the A's farm system has been among the most productive in baseball.

This consistent farm system enables the A's to treat personnel decisions—including decisions about whether they should re-sign a star player or let him go to another team—as business decisions. The A's simply do not have the resources necessary to play the personnel game the same way as the Los Angeles Dodgers or the New York Yankees. When these teams need a particular kind of player, they go and sign one. Oakland has to rely more on its farm system. But because its farm system performs so well, the A's can let so-called "superstars" go to other teams, knowing that they are likely to have a younger—and cheaper—player in the minor leagues, just waiting for the chance to play in "the show"—the players' nickname for the major leagues. This allows the A's to keep their payroll costs down and remain profitable, despite relatively small crowds, while still fielding a team that competes virtually every year for the right to play in the World Series.

Of course, an important question becomes: How sustainable is the A's competitive advantage? The evaluation criteria themselves are not a source of sustained competitive advantage. However, the socially complex nature of how these criteria are consistently applied throughout the A's organization may be a source of sustained competitive advantage in enabling the A's to gain the differential access to low-cost productive inputs—in this case, baseball players.

Sources: K. Hammonds (2003). "How to play Beane ball." *Fast Company*, May, pp. 84 +; M. Lewis (2003). *Moneyball*. New York: Norton; A. McGahan, J. F. McGuire, and J. Kou (1997). "The baseball strike." Harvard Business School Case No. 9-796-059.

Organizing to Implement Cost Leadership

As with all strategies, firms seeking to implement cost leadership strategies must adopt an organizational structure, management controls, and compensation policies that reinforce this strategy. Some key issues associated with using these organizing tools to implement cost leadership are summarized in Table 6.

Organizational Structure in Implementing Cost Leadership

As suggested in Table 6, firms implementing cost leadership strategies will generally adopt what is known as a **functional organizational structure**.[21] An example of a functional organization structure is presented in Figure 4. Indeed, this functional organizational structure is the structure used to implement all business-level strategies a firm might pursue, although this structure is modified when used to implement these different strategies.

In a functional structure, each of the major business functions is managed by a **functional manager**. For example, if manufacturing, marketing, finance, accounting, and sales are all included within a functional organization, then a manufacturing manager leads that function, a marketing manager leads that function, a finance manager leads that function, and so forth. In a functional organizational structure, all these functional managers report to one person. This person has many different titles—including *president, CEO, chair,* or *founder.* However, for purposes of this discussion, this person will be called the **chief executive officer (CEO)**.

The CEO in a functional organization has a unique status. Everyone else in this company is a functional specialist. The manufacturing people manufacture, the marketing people market, the finance people finance, and so forth. Indeed, only one person in the functional organization has to have a multifunctional perspective—the CEO. This role is so important that sometimes the functional organization is called a **U-form structure**, where the "U" stands for "unitary"—because there is only one person in this organization that has a broad, multifunctional corporate perspective.

When used to implement a cost leadership strategy, this U-form structure is kept as simple as possible. As suggested in Table 6, firms implementing cost leadership strategies will have relatively few layers in their reporting structure.

Organization structure: Functional structure with

1. Few layers in the reporting structure
2. Simple reporting relationships
3. Small corporate staff
4. Focus on narrow range of business functions

Management control systems

1. Tight cost control systems
2. Quantitative cost goals
3. Close supervision of labor, raw material, inventory, and other costs
4. A cost leadership philosophy

Compensation policies

1. Reward for cost reduction
2. Incentives for all employees to be involved in cost reduction

TABLE 6 Organizing to Realize the Full Potential of Cost Leadership Strategies

Figure 4   An Example of
the U-form Organizational
Structure

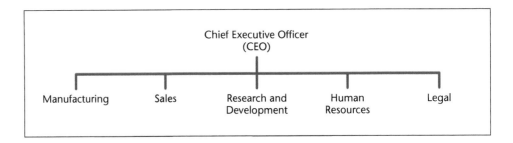

Complicated reporting structures, including **matrix structures** where one employee reports to two or more people, are usually avoided.[22] Corporate staff in these organizations is kept small. Such firms do not operate in a wide range of business functions, but instead operate only in those few business functions where they have valuable, rare, and costly-to-imitate resources and capabilities.

One excellent example of a firm pursuing a cost leadership strategy is Nucor Steel. A leader in the mini-mill industry, Nucor has only five layers in its reporting structure, compared to 12 to 15 in its major higher-cost competitors. Most operating decisions at Nucor are delegated to plant managers, who have full profit-and-loss responsibility for their operations. Corporate staff at Nucor is small and focuses its efforts on accounting for revenues and costs and on exploring new manufacturing processes to further reduce Nucor's operating expenses and expand its business opportunities. Nucor's former president, Ken Iverson, believed that Nucor does only two things well: build plants efficiently and run them effectively. Thus, Nucor focuses its efforts in these areas and subcontracts many of its other business functions, including the purchase of its raw materials, to outside vendors.[23]

Responsibilities of the CEO in a Functional Organization

The CEO in a U-form organization has two basic responsibilities: (1) to formulate the strategy of the firm and (2) to coordinate the activities of the functional specialists in the firm to facilitate the implementation of this strategy. In the special case of a cost leadership strategy, the CEO must decide on which bases such a strategy should be founded—including any of those listed in Table 1—and then coordinate functions within a firm to make sure that the economic potential of this strategy is fully realized.

Strategy Formulation.   The CEO in a U-form organization engages in strategy formulation by applying the strategic management process. A CEO establishes the firm's mission and associated objectives, evaluates environmental threats and opportunities, understands the firm's strengths and weaknesses, and then chooses one or more of the business and corporate strategies. In the case of a cost leadership strategy, the application of the strategic management process must lead a CEO to conclude that the best chance for achieving a firm's mission is for that firm to adopt a cost leadership business-level strategy.

Although the responsibility for strategy formulation in a U-form organization ultimately rests with the CEO, this individual needs to draw on the insights, analysis, and involvement of functional managers throughout the firm. CEOs who fail to involve functional managers in strategy formulation run several risks. First, strategic choices made in isolation from functional managers may be made without complete information. Second, limiting the involvement of functional managers in strategy formulation can limit their understanding of, and commitment to, the chosen strategy. This can severely limit their ability, and willingness, to implement any strategy—including cost leadership—that is chosen.[24]

Coordinating Functions for Strategy Implementation. Even the best formulated strategy is competitively irrelevant if it is not implemented. And the only way that strategies can be effectively implemented is if all the functions within a firm are aligned in a way consistent with this strategy.

For example, compare two firms pursuing a cost leadership strategy. All but one of the first firm's functions—marketing—are aligned with this cost leadership strategy. All of the second firm's functions—including marketing—are aligned with this cost leadership strategy. Because marketing is not aligned with the first firm's cost leadership strategy, this firm is likely to advertise products that it does not sell. That is, this firm might advertise its products on the basis of their style and performance, but sell products that are reliable (but not stylish) and inexpensive (but not high performers). A firm that markets products it does not actually sell is likely to disappoint its customers. In contrast, the second firm that has all of its functions—including marketing—aligned with its chosen strategy is more likely to advertise products it actually sells and thus is less likely to disappoint its customers. In the long run, it seems reasonable to expect this second firm to outperform the first, at least with respect to implementing a cost leadership strategy.

Of course, alignment is required of all of a firm's functional areas, not just marketing. Also, misalignment can emerge in any of a firm's functional areas. Some common misalignments between a firm's cost leadership strategy and its functional activities are listed in Table 7.

Management Controls in Implementing Cost Leadership

As suggested in Table 6, cost leadership firms are typically characterized by very tight cost-control systems; frequent and detailed cost-control reports; an emphasis on quantitative cost goals and targets; and close supervision of labor, raw materials, inventory, and other costs. Again, Nucor Steel is an example of a cost leadership firm that has implemented these kinds of control systems. At Nucor, groups of employees are given weekly cost and productivity improvement goals. Groups

	When Function Is *Aligned* with Cost Leadership Strategies	When Function Is *Misaligned* with Cost Leadership Strategies
Manufacturing	Lean, low cost, good quality	Inefficient, high cost, poor quality
Marketing	Emphasize value, reliability, and price	Emphasize style and performance
Research and Development	Focus on product extensions and process improvements	Focus on radical new technologies and products
Finance	Focus on low cost and stable financial structure	Focus on nontraditional financial instruments
Accounting	Collect cost data and adopt conservative accounting principles	Collect no-cost data and adopt very aggressive accounting principles
Sales	Focus on value, reliability, and low price	Focus on style and performance and high price

TABLE 7 Common Misalignments Between Business Functions and a Cost Leadership Strategy

that meet or exceed these goals receive extra compensation. Plant managers are held responsible for cost and profit performance. A plant manager who does not meet corporate performance expectations cannot expect a long career at Nucor. Similar group-oriented cost-reduction systems are in place at some of Nucor's major competitors, including Chaparral Steel.[25]

Less formal management control systems also drive a cost-reduction philosophy at cost leadership firms. For example, although Wal-Mart is one of the most successful retail operations in the world, its Arkansas headquarters is plain and simple. Indeed, some have suggested that Wal-Mart's headquarters looks like a warehouse. Its style of interior decoration was once described as "early bus station." Wal-Mart even involves its customers in reducing costs by asking them to "help keep your costs low" by returning shopping carts to the designated areas in Wal-Mart's parking lots.[26]

Compensation Policies and Implementing Cost Leadership Strategies

As suggested in Table 6, compensation in cost leadership firms is usually tied directly to cost-reducing efforts. Such firms often provide incentives for employees to work together to reduce costs and increase or maintain quality, and they expect *every* employee to take responsibility for both costs and quality. For example, an important expense for retail stores like Wal-Mart is "shrinkage"—a nice way of saying people steal stuff. About half the shrinkage in most stores comes from employees stealing their own companies' products.

Wal-Mart used to have a serious problem with shrinkage. Among other solutions (including hiring "greeters" whose real job is to discourage shoplifters), Wal-Mart developed a compensation scheme that took half the cost savings created by reduced shrinkage and shared it with employees in the form of a bonus. With this incentive in place, Wal-Mart's shrinkage problems dropped significantly.

Summary

Firms producing essentially the same products can have different costs for several reasons. Some of the most important of these are: (1) size differences and economies of scale, (2) size differences and diseconomies of scale, (3) experience differences and learning-curve economies, (4) differential access to productive inputs, and (5) technological advantages independent of scale. In addition, firms competing in the same industry can make policy choices about the kinds of products and services to sell that can have an important impact on their relative cost position. Cost leadership in an industry can be valuable by assisting a firm in reducing the threat of each of the five forces in an industry.

Each of the sources of cost advantage discussed in this chapter can be a source of sustained competitive advantage if it is rare and costly to imitate. Overall, learning-curve economies, differential access to productive inputs, and technological "software" are more likely to be rare than other sources of cost advantage. Differential access to productive inputs and technological "software" is more likely to be costly to imitate—either through direct duplication or through substitution—than the other sources of cost advantage. Thus, differential access to productive inputs and technological "software" will often be more likely to be a source of sustained competitive advantage than cost advantages based on other sources.

Of course, to realize the full potential of these competitive advantages, a firm must be organized appropriately. Organizing to implement a strategy always involves a firm's organizational structure, its management control systems, and its compensation policies. The organizational structure used to implement cost leadership—and other business strategies—is called a *functional,* or *U-form,* structure. The CEO is the only person in this structure who has a corporate perspective. The CEO has two responsibilities: to formulate a firm's strategy and to implement it by coordinating functions within a firm. Ensuring that a firm's functions are aligned with its strategy is essential to successful strategy implementation.

When used to implement a cost leadership strategy, the U-form structure generally has few layers, simple reporting relationships, and a small corporate staff. It focuses on a narrow range of business functions. The management control systems used to implement these strategies generally include tight cost controls; quantitative cost goals; close supervision of labor, raw materials, inventoray, and other costs; and a cost leadership culture and mentality. Finally, compensation policies in these firms typically reward cost reduction and provide incentives for everyone in the organization to be part of the cost-reduction effort.

Challenge Questions

1. Ryanair, Wal-Mart, Timex, Casio, and Hyundai are all cited as examples of firms pursuing cost leadership strategies, but these firms make substantial investments in advertising, which seems more likely to be associated with a product differentiation strategy. Are these firms really pursuing a cost leadership strategy, or are they pursuing a product differentiation strategy by emphasizing their lower costs?

2. When economies of scale exist, firms with large volumes of production will have lower costs than those with smaller volumes of production. The realization of these economies of scale, however, is far from automatic. What actions can firms take to ensure that they realize whatever economies of sale are created by their volume of production?

3. Firms engage in an activity called "forward pricing" when they establish, during the early stages of the learning curve, a price for their products that is lower than their actual costs, in anticipation of lower costs later on, after significant learning has occurred. Under what conditions, if any, does forward pricing make sense? What risks, if any, do firms engaging in forward pricing face?

4. One way of thinking about organizing to implement cost leadership strategies is that firms that pursue this strategy should be highly centralized, have high levels of direct supervision, and keep employee wages to an absolute minimum. Another approach is to decentralize decision-making authority—to ensure that individuals who know the most about reducing costs make decisions about how to reduce costs. This, in turn, would imply less direct supervision and somewhat higher levels of employee wages. Why is this? Which of these two approaches seems more reasonable? Under what conditions would these different approaches make more or less sense?

Problem Set

1. The economies of scale curve in Figure 1 can be represented algebraically in the following equation:

$$\text{Average costs} = a + bQ + cQ^2$$

where Q is the quantity produced by a firm and a, b, and c are coefficients that are estimated from industry data. For example, it has been shown that the economies of scale curve for U.S. savings and loans is:

$$\text{Average costs} = 2.38 - .615A + .54A^2$$

where A is a savings and loan's total assets. Using this equation, what is the optimal size of a savings and loan? (Hint: Plug in different values of A and calculate average costs. The lowest possible average cost is the optimal size for a savings and loan.)

2. The learning curve depicted in Figure 2 can be represented algebraically by the following equation:

$$\text{Average time to produce } x \text{ units} = ax^{-\beta}$$

where x is the total number of units produced by a firm in its history, a is the amount of time it took a firm to produce its first unit, and β is a coefficient that describes the rate of learning in a firm.

Suppose it takes a team of workers 45 hours to assemble its first product ($a = 45$) and 40.5 hours to assemble the second. When a firm doubles its production (in this case, from one to two units) and cuts its production time (in this case, from 45 hours to 40.5 hours), learning is said to have occurred (in this case, a 40.5/45, or 90 percent, learning curve). The β for a 90 percent learning curve is 0.3219. Thus, this firm's learning curve is:

$$\text{Average time to produce } x \text{ units} = 45x^{-0.3219}$$

What is the average amount of time it will take this firm to produce six products? (Hint: Simply plug "6" in for x in the equation and solve.) What is the total time it took this firm to produce these six products? (Hint: Simply multiply the number of units produced, 6, by the average time it will take to produce these six products.) What is the average time it will take this firm to produce five products? What is the total time it will take this firm to produce five products? So, what is the total time it will take this firm to produce its sixth product? (Hint: Subtract the total time needed to produce five products from the total time needed to produce six products.)

Suppose a new firm is going to start producing these same products. Assuming this new firm does not learn anything from established firms, what will its cost disadvantage be when it assembles its first product? (Hint: Compare the costs of the experienced firm's sixth product with the cost of the new firm's first product.)

End Notes

1. Weiner, S. (1987). "The road most traveled." *Forbes*, October 19, pp. 60–64.
2. Christensen, C. R., N. A. Berg, and M. S. Salter. (1980). *Policy formulation and administration: A casebook of senior management problems in business*, 8th ed. Homewood, IL: Irwin, p. 163.
3. Scherer, F. M. (1980). *Industrial market structure and economic performance*. Boston: Houghton Mifflin; Moore, F. T. (1959). "Economies of scale: Some statistical evidence." *Quarterly Journal of Economics*, 73, pp. 232–245; and Lau, L. J., and S. Tamura. (1972). "Economies of scale, technical progress, and the nonhomothetic leontief production function." *Journal of Political Economy*, 80, pp. 1167–1187.
4. Scherer, F. M. (1980). *Industrial market structure and economic performance*. Boston: Houghton Mifflin; and Perrow, C. (1984). *Normal accidents: Living with high-risk technologies*. New York: Basic Books.
5. Hamermesh, R. G., and R. S. Rosenbloom. (1989). "Crown Cork and Seal Co., Inc." Harvard Business School Case No. 9-388-096.
6. See Hackman, J. R., and G. R. Oldham. (1980). *Work redesign*. Reading, MA: Addison-Wesley.
7. This relationship was first noticed in 1925 by the commander of Wright-Patterson Air Force Base in Dayton, Ohio.
8. Learning curves have been estimated for numerous industries. Boston Consulting Group. (1970). "Perspectives on experience." Boston: BCG, presents learning curves for over 20 industries while Lieberman, M. (1984). "The learning curve and pricing in the chemical processing industries." *Rand Journal of Economics*, 15, pp. 213–228, estimates learning curves for 37 chemical products.
9. See Henderson, B. (1974). *The experience curve reviewed III—How does it work?* Boston: Boston Consulting Group; and Boston Consulting Group. (1970). "Perspectives on experience." Boston: BCG.
10. Hall, G., and S. Howell. (1985). "The experience curve from the economist's perspective." *Strategic Management Journal*, 6, pp. 197–212.
11. Hill, C. W. L. (1988). "Differentiation versus low-cost or differentiation and low-cost: A contingency framework." *Academy of Management Review*, 13(3), pp. 401–412.
12. See Ghemawat, P., and H. J. Stander III. (1992). "Nucor at a crossroads." Harvard Business School Case No. 9-793-039 on technology in steel manufacturing and cost advantages; Shaffer, R. A. (1995). "Intel as conquistador." *Forbes*, February 27, p. 130 on technology in semiconductor manufacturing and cost advantages; Monteverde, K., and D. Teece. (1982). "Supplier switching costs and vertical integration in the automobile industry." *Rand Journal of Economics*, 13(1), pp. 206–213; and McCormick, J., and N. Stone. (1990). "From national champion to

global competitor: An interview with Thomson's Alain Gomez." *Harvard Business Review*, May/June, pp. 126–135 on technology in consumer electronic manufacturing and cost advantages.
13. Schultz, E. (1989). "Climbing high with discount brokers." *Fortune*, Fall (special issue), pp. 219–223.
14. Schonfeld, E. (1998). "Can computers cure health care?" *Fortune*, March 30, pp. 111 +.
15. Ibid.
16. See Meyer, M. W., and L. B. Zucker. (1989). *Permanently failing organizations*. Newbury Park, CA: Sage.
17. Staw, B. M. (1981). "The escalation of commitment to a course of action." *Academy of Management Review*, 6, pp. 577–587.
18. Hesterly, W. S. (1989). *Top management succession as a determinant of firm performance and de-escalation: An agency problem*. Unpublished doctoral dissertation, University of California, Los Angeles.
19. Barney, J. B. (1986). "Organizational culture: Can it be a source of sustained competitive advantage?" *Academy of Management Review*, 11, pp. 656–665.
20. See Spence, A. M. (1981). "The learning curve and competition." *Bell Journal of Economics*, 12, pp. 49–70, on why learning needs to be proprietary; Mansfield, E. (1985). "How rapidly does new industrial technology leak out?" *Journal of Industrial Economics*, 34(2), pp. 217–223; Lieberman, M. B. (1982). *The learning-curve, pricing and market structure in the chemical processing industries*. Unpublished doctoral dissertation, Harvard University; Lieberman, M. B. (1987). "The learning curve, diffusion, and competitive strategy." *Strategic Management Journal*, 8, pp. 441–452 on why it usually is not proprietary.
21. Williamson, O. (1975). *Markets and hierarchies*. New York: Free Press.
22. Davis, S. M., and P. R. Lawrence. (1977). *Matrix*. Reading, MA: Addison-Wesley.
23. See Ghemawat, P., and H. J. Stander III. (1992). "Nucor at a crossroads." Harvard Business School Case No. 9-793-039.
24. See Floyd, S. W., and B. Woldridge. (1992). "Middle management involvement in strategy and its association with strategic type: A research note." *Strategic Management Journal*, 13, pp. 153–167.
25. Ibid.
26. Walton, S. (1992). *Sam Walton, Made in America: My story*. New York: Doubleday.

Product Differentiation

From Chapter 5 of *Strategic Management and Competitive Advantage: Concepts and Cases*, 3/e. Jay B. Barney.
William S. Hesterly.

Product Differentiation

After reading this chapter, you should be able to:

1. Define product differentiation.

2. Describe eleven bases of product differentiation and how they can be grouped into three categories.

3. Describe how product differentiation is ultimately limited only by managerial creativity.

4. Describe how product differentiation can be used to neutralize environmental threats and exploit environmental opportunities.

5. Describe those bases of product differentiation that are not likely to be costly to duplicate, those that may be costly to duplicate, and those that will often be costly to duplicate.

6. Describe the main substitutes for product differentiation strategies.

7. Describe how organizational structure, control processes, and compensation policies can be used to implement product differentiation strategies.

8. Discuss whether it is possible for a firm to implement cost leadership and product differentiation strategies simultaneously.

Who Is Victoria, and What Is Her Secret?

Sexy. Glamorous. Mysterious. Victoria's Secret is the world's leading specialty retailer of lingerie and beauty products. With 2007 sales of almost $6.1 billion, Victoria's Secret sells its mix of sexy lingerie, prestige fragrances, and fashion-inspired collections through over 1,000 retail stores and the almost 400 million catalogues it distributes each year.

But all this glamour and success leaves the two central questions about this firm unanswered: "Who is Victoria?" and "What is her secret?"

It turns out that Victoria is a retired fashion model who lives in an up-and-coming fashionable district in London. She has a committed relationship and is thinking about starting a family. However, these maternal instincts are balanced by Victoria's adventurous and sexy side. She loves good food, classical music, and great wine. She travels frequently and is as much at home in New York, Paris, and Los Angeles as she is in London. Her fashion tastes are edgy enough to never be boring, but practical enough to never be extreme. Her lingerie is an essential part of her wardrobe. Sexy and alluring, but never cheap, trashy, or vulgar, Victoria's lingerie is the perfect complement to her overall lifestyle. Most important, while Victoria knows she is beautiful and sexy, she also knows that it is her brains, not her looks, that have enabled her to succeed in life.

This is who Victoria is. This is the woman that Victoria's Secret's designers design for, the woman Victoria's Secret marketers create advertising for, and the woman to whom all Victoria's Secret sales associates are trained to sell.

And this is her secret—Victoria doesn't really exist. Or, more precisely, the number of real women in the entire world who are like Victoria is very small—no more than a handful. So why would a company like Victoria's Secret organize all of its design, marketing, and sales efforts around meeting the lingerie needs of a woman who, for all practical purposes, doesn't really exist?

Victoria's Secret knows how few of its actual customers are like Victoria. However, it is convinced that many of its customers would like to be treated as if they were Victoria, if only for a few hours, when they come into a Victoria's Secret store. Victoria's Secret is not just selling lingerie; it is selling an opportunity, almost a fantasy, to be like Victoria—to live in an exciting and sexy city, to travel the world, to have refined, yet edgy, tastes. To buy and wear Victoria's Secret lingerie is—if only for a moment or two—an opportunity to experience life as Victoria experiences it.

Practically speaking, building an entire company around meeting the needs of a customer who does not actually exist creates some interesting problems. You can't just call Victoria on the phone and ask her about trends in her lifestyle; you can't form a focus group of people like Victoria and ask them to evaluate new lines of lingerie. In a sense, not only has Victoria's Secret invented Victoria; it also had to invent Victoria's lifestyle—and the lingerie, fragrances, and accessories that go along with that lifestyle. And as long as the lifestyle that it invents for Victoria is desirable to but just beyond the reach of its actual customers, Victoria's Secret will continue to be able to sell a romantic fantasy—along with its bras and panties.

Corbis/Bettmann

Sources: www.limitedbrands.com; www.victoriassecret.com; and Corbis/Bettmann.

Victoria's Secret uses the fictional character "Victoria" to help implement its product differentiation strategy. As successful as this effort is, however, this is only one of many ways that firms can try to differentiate their products.

What is Product Differentiation?

Whereas Wal-Mart exemplifies a firm pursuing a cost leadership strategy, Victoria's Secret exemplifies a firm pursuing a product differentiation strategy. **Product differentiation** is a business strategy whereby firms attempt to gain a competitive advantage by increasing the perceived value of their products or services relative to the perceived value of other firms' products or services. These other firms can be rivals or firms that provide substitute products or services. By increasing the perceived value of its products or services, a firm will be able to charge a higher price than it would otherwise. This higher price can increase a firm's revenues and generate competitive advantages.

A firm's attempts to create differences in the relative perceived value of its products or services often are made by altering the objective properties of those products or services. Rolex attempts to differentiate its watches from Timex and Casio watches by manufacturing them with solid gold cases. Mercedes attempts to differentiate its cars from Hyundai's cars through sophisticated engineering and high performance. Victoria's Secret attempts to differentiate its shopping experience from Wal-Mart, and other retailers, through the merchandise it sells and the way it sells it.

Although firms often alter the objective properties of their products or services in order to implement a product differentiation strategy, the existence of product differentiation, in the end, is *always* a matter of customer perception. Products sold by two different firms may be very similar, but if customers believe the first is more valuable than the second, then the first product has a differentiation advantage.

In the world of "craft" or "microbrewery" beers, for example, the consumers' image of how a beer is brewed may be very different from how it is actually brewed. Boston Beer Company, for example, sells Samuel Adams Beer. Customers can tour the Boston Beer Company, where they will see a small row of fermenting tanks and two 10-barrel kettles being tended by a brewmaster wearing rubber boots. However, Samuel Adams Beer was not actually brewed in this small factory. Instead, it was, for much of its history, brewed—in 200-barrel steel tanks—in Cincinnati, Ohio, by the Hudepohl-Schoenling Brewing Company, a contract brewing firm that also manufactures Hudy Bold Beer and Little Kings Cream Ale. Maui Beer Company's Aloha Lager brand was brewed in Portland, Oregon, and Pete's Wicked Ale (a craft beer that claims it is brewed "one batch at a time. Carefully.") was brewed in batches of 400 barrels each by Stroh Brewery Company, makers of Old Milwaukee Beer. However, the more consumers believe there are important differences between these "craft" beers and more traditional brews—despite many of their common manufacturing methods—the more willing they will be to pay more for a craft beer. This willingness to pay more suggests that an important "perceptual" basis of product differentiation exists for these craft beers.[1] If products or services are *perceived* as being different in a way that is valued by consumers, then product differentiation exists.

Just as perceptions can create product differentiation between products that are essentially identical, the lack of perceived differences between products with very different characteristics can prevent product differentiation. For example, consumers with an untrained palate may not be able to distinguish between two different wines, even though expert wine tasters would be very much aware of their differences. Those who are not aware of these differences, even if they exist, will not be willing to pay more for one wine over the other. In this sense, for these consumers at least, these two wines, though different, are not differentiated.

Product differentiation is always a matter of customer perceptions, but firms can take a variety of actions to influence these perceptions. These actions can be thought of as different bases of product differentiation.

Bases of Product Differentiation

A large number of authors, drawing on both theory and empirical research, have developed lists of ways firms can differentiate their products or services.[2] Some of these are listed in Table 1. Although the purpose of all these bases of product differentiation is to create the perception that a firm's products or services are unusually valuable, different bases of product differentiation attempt to accomplish this objective in different ways. For example, the first four bases of product differentiation listed in Table 1 attempt to create this perception by focusing directly on the attributes of the products or services a firm sells. The second three attempt to create this perception by developing a relationship between a firm and its customers. The last five attempt to create this perception through linkages within and between firms. Of course, these bases of product differentiation are not mutually exclusive. Indeed, firms will often attempt to differentiate their products or services along multiple dimensions simultaneously. An empirical method for identifying ways that firms have differentiated their products is discussed in the Research Made Relevant feature.

Focusing on the Attributes of a Firm's Products or Services

The first group of bases of product differentiation identified in Table 1 focuses on the attributes of a firm's products or services.

TABLE 1 Ways Firms Can Differentiate Their Products

To differentiate its products, a firm can focus directly on the attributes of its products or services:

1. Product features
2. Product complexity
3. Timing of product introduction
4. Location

or, on relationships between itself and its customers:

5. Product customization
6. Consumer marketing
7. Product reputation

or, on linkages within or between firms:

8. Linkages among functions within a firm
9. Linkages with other firms
10. Product mix
11. Distribution channels
12. Service and support

Sources: M. E. Porter. (1980). *Competitive strategy.* New York: Free Press; R. E. Caves and P. Williamson. (1985). "What is product differentiation, really?" *Journal of Industrial Economics,* 34, pp. 113–132.

Product Features. The most obvious way that firms can try to differentiate their products is by altering the features of the products they sell. One industry in which firms are constantly modifying product features to attempt to differentiate their products is the automobile industry. Chrysler, for example, introduced the "cab forward" design to try to give its cars a distinctive look, whereas Audi went with a more radical flowing and curved design to differentiate its cars. For emergency situations, General Motors (GM) introduced the "On Star" system, which instantly connects drivers to GM operators 24 hours a day, while Mercedes-Benz continued to develop its "crumple zone" system to ensure passenger safety in a crash. In body construction, General Motors continues to develop its "uni-body" construction system, whereby different parts of a car are welded to each other rather than built on a single frame, while Jaguar introduced a 100 percent aluminum body to help differentiate its top-of-the-line model from other luxury cars. Mazda continues to tinker with the motor and suspension of its sporty Miata, while Nissan introduced the 370 Z—a continuation of the famous 240 Z line—and Porsche changed from air-cooled to water-cooled engines in its 911 series of sports cars. All these—and many more—changes in the attributes of automobiles are examples of firms trying to differentiate their products by altering product features.

Product Complexity. Product complexity can be thought of as a special case of altering a product's features to create product differentiation. In a given industry, product complexity can vary significantly. The BIC "crystal pen," for example, has only a handful of parts, whereas a Cross or a Mont Blanc pen has many more parts. To the extent that these differences in product complexity convince consumers that the products of some firms are more valuable than the products of other firms, product complexity can be a basis of product differentiation.

Timing of Product Introduction. Introducing a product at the right time can also help create product differentiation. In some industry settings (e.g., in emerging industries) *the* critical issue is to be a first mover—to introduce a new product before all other firms. Being first in emerging industries can enable a firm to set important technological standards, preempt strategically valuable assets, and develop customer-switching costs. These first-mover advantages can create a perception among customers that the products or services of the first-moving firm are somehow more valuable than the products or services of other firms.[3]

Timing-based product differentiation, however, does not depend only on being a first mover. Sometimes, a firm can be a later mover in an industry but introduce products or services at just the right time and thereby gain a competitive advantage. This can happen when the ultimate success of a product or service depends on the availability of complementary products or technologies. For example, the domination of Microsoft's MS-DOS operating system, and thus ultimately the domination of Windows, was only possible because IBM introduced its version of the personal computer. Without the IBM PC, it would have been difficult for any operating system—including MS-DOS—to have such a large market presence.[4]

Location. The physical location of a firm can also be a source of product differentiation.[5] Consider, for example, Disney's operations in Orlando, Florida. Beginning with The Magic Kingdom and EPCOT Center, Disney built a world-class destination resort in Orlando. Over the years, Disney has added numerous attractions to its core entertainment activities, including MGM Studios, over 11,000 Disney-owned hotel rooms, a $100 million sports center, an automobile racing track, an after-hours entertainment district, and most recently, a $1 billion

Of all the possible bases of product differentiation that might exist in a particular market, how does one pinpoint those that have actually been used? Research in strategic management and marketing has shown that the bases of product differentiation can be identified using multiple regression analysis to estimate what are called **hedonic prices**. A hedonic price is that part of the price of a product or service that is attributable to a particular characteristic of that product or service.

The logic behind hedonic prices is straightforward. If customers are willing to spend more for a product with a particular attribute than they are willing to spend for that same product without that attribute, then that attribute differentiates the first product from the second. That is, this attribute is a basis of product differentiation in this market.

Consider, for example, the price of used cars. The market price of a used car can be determined through the use of a variety of used car buying guides. These guides typically establish the base price of a used car. This base price typically includes product features that are common to almost all cars—a radio, a standard engine, a heater/defroster. Because these product attributes are

**Discovering the Bases
of Product Differentiation**

common to virtually all cars, they are not a basis for product differentiation.

However, in addition to these common features, the base price of an automobile is adjusted based on some less common features—a high-end stereo system, a larger engine, airconditioning. How much the base price of the car is adjusted when these features are added—$300 for a high-end stereo, $500 for a larger engine, $200 for air-conditioning—are the hedonic prices of these product attributes. These product attributes differentiate well-equipped cars from less-well-equipped cars and, because consumers are willing to pay more for

well-equipped cars, can be thought of as bases of product differentiation in this market.

Multiple regression techniques are used to estimate these hedonic prices in the following way. For our simple car example, the following regression equation is estimated:

$$Price = a_1 + b_1(Stereo) + b_2(Engine) + b_3(AC)$$

where *Price* is the retail price of cars, *Stereo* is a variable describing whether a car has a high-end stereo, *Engine* is a variable describing whether a car has a large engine, and *AC* is a variable describing whether or not a car has airconditioning. If the hedonic prices for these features are those suggested earlier, the results of running this regression analysis would be:

$$Price = \$7,800 + \$300(Stereo) + \$500(Engine) + \$200(AC)$$

where $7,800 is the base price of this type of used car.

Source: D. Hay and D. Morris. (1979). *Industrial economics: Theory and evidence.* Oxford: Oxford University Press; K. Cowling and J. Cubbin (1971). "Price, quality, and advertising competition." *Economica,* 38, pp. 378–394.

theme park called "The Animal Kingdom"—all in and around Orlando. Now, families can travel from around the world to Orlando, knowing that in a single location they can enjoy a full range of Disney adventures.[6]

Focusing on the Relationship Between a Firm and Its Customers

The second group of bases of product differentiation identified in Table 1 focuses on relationships between a firm and its customers.

Product Customization. Products can also be differentiated by the extent to which they are customized for particular customer applications. Product customization is an important basis for product differentiation in a wide variety of industries, from enterprise software to bicycles.

Enterprise software is software that is designed to support all of a firm's critical business functions, including human resources, payroll, customer service, sales, quality control, and so forth. Major competitors in this industry include Oracle and SAP. However, although these firms sell basic software packages, most firms find it necessary to customize these basic packages to meet their specific business needs. The ability to build complex software packages that can also be customized to meet the specific needs of a particular customer is an important basis of product differentiation in this marketplace.

In the bicycle industry, consumers can spend as little as $50 on a bicycle, and as much as—well, almost as much as they want on a bicycle, easily in excess of $10,000. High-end bicycles use, of course, the very best components, such as brakes and gears. But what really distinguishes these bicycles is their customized fit. Once a serious rider becomes accustomed to a particular bicycle, it is very difficult for that rider to switch to alternative suppliers.

Consumer Marketing. Differential emphasis on consumer marketing has been a basis for product differentiation in a wide variety of industries. Through advertising and other consumer marketing efforts, firms attempt to alter the perceptions of current and potential customers, whether or not specific attributes of a firm's products or services are actually altered.

For example, in the soft drink industry, Mountain Dew—a product of PepsiCo—was originally marketed as a fruity, lightly carbonated drink that tasted "as light as a morning dew in the mountains." However, beginning in the late 1990s Mountain Dew's marketing efforts changed dramatically. "As light as a morning dew in the mountains" became "Do the Dew," and Mountain Dew focused its marketing efforts on young, mostly male, extreme-sports–oriented consumers. Young men riding snowboards, roller blades, mountain bikes, and skateboards—mostly upside down—became central to most Mountain Dew commercials. Mountain Dew became a sponsor of a wide variety of extreme sports contests and an important sponsor of the X Games on ESPN. And will we ever forget the confrontation between the young Dew enthusiast and a big horn sheep over a can of Mountain Dew in a meadow? Note that this radical repositioning of Mountain Dew depended entirely on changes in consumer marketing. The features of the underlying product were not changed.

Reputation. Perhaps the most important relationship between a firm and its customers depends on a firm's reputation in its marketplace. Indeed, a firm's **reputation** is really no more than a socially complex relationship between a firm and its customers. Once developed, a firm's reputation can last a long time, even if the basis for that reputation no longer exists.[7]

A firm that has tried to exploit its reputation for cutting-edge entertainment is MTV, a division of Viacom, Inc. Although several well-known video artists—including Madonna—have had their videos banned from MTV, it has still been able to develop a reputation for risk-taking on television. MTV believes that its viewers have come to expect the unexpected in MTV programming. One of the first efforts to exploit, and reinforce, this reputation for risk-taking was *Beavis and Butthead*, an animated series starring two teenage boys with serious social and emotional development problems. More recently, MTV exploited its reputation by inventing an entirely new genre of television—"reality TV"—through its *Real World* and *House Rules* programs. Not only are these shows cheap to produce, they build on the reputation that MTV has for providing entertainment that is a little risky, a little sexy, and a little controversial. Indeed, MTV has been so successful in providing this kind of entertainment that it had to form an entirely new cable station—MTV 2—to actually show music videos.[8]

Focusing on Links Within and Between Firms

The third group of bases of product differentiation identified in Table 1 focuses on links within and between firms.

Linkages Between Functions. A less obvious but still important way in which a firm can attempt to differentiate its products is through linking different functions within the firm. For example, research in the pharmaceutical industry suggests that firms vary in the extent to which they are able to integrate different scientific specialties—such as genetics, biology, chemistry, and pharmacology—to develop new drugs. Firms that are able to form effective multidisciplinary teams to explore new drug categories have what some have called an **architectural competence**, that is, the ability to use organizational structure to facilitate coordination among scientific disciplines to conduct research. Firms that have this competence are able to more effectively pursue product differentiation strategies—by introducing new and powerful drugs—than those that do not have this competence. And in the pharmaceutical industry, where firms that introduce such drugs can experience very large positive returns, the ability to coordinate across functions is an important source of competitive advantage.[9]

Links with Other Firms. Another basis of product differentiation is linkages with other firms. Here, instead of differentiating products or services on the basis of linkages between functions within a single firm or linkages between different products, differentiation is based on explicit linkages between one firm's products and the products or services of other firms.

This form of product differentiation has increased in popularity over the last several years. For example, with the growth in popularity of stock car racing in the United States, more and more corporations are looking to link their products or services with famous names and cars in NASCAR. Firms such as Kodak, Gatorade, McDonald's, Home Depot, The Cartoon Network, True Value, and Pfizer (manufacturers of Viagra) have all been major sponsors of NASCAR teams. In one year, the Coca-Cola Corporation filled orders for over 200,000 NASCAR-themed vending machines. Visa struggled to keep up with demand for its NASCAR affinity cards, and over 1 million NASCAR Barbies were sold by Mattel—generating revenues of about $50 million. Notice that none of these firms sells products for automobiles. Rather, these firms seek to associate themselves with NASCAR because of the sport's popularity.[10]

In general, linkages between firms that differentiate their products are examples of cooperative strategic alliance strategies.

Product Mix. One of the outcomes of links among functions within a firm and links between firms can be changes in the mix of products a firm brings to the market. This mix of products or services can be a source of product differentiation, especially when (1) those products or services are technologically linked or (2) when a single set of customers purchases several of a firm's products or services.

For example, technological interconnectivity is an extremely important selling point in the information technology business, and thus an important basis of potential product differentiation. However, seamless interconnectivity—where Company A's computers talk to Company B's computers across Company C's data line merging a database created by Company D's software with a database created by Company E's software to be used in a calling center that operates with Company F's technology—has been extremely difficult to realize. For this reason, some information technology firms try to realize the goal of interconnectivity by adjusting their product mix, that is, by selling a bundle of products whose interconnectivity they can control and guarantee to customers. This goal of selling a bundle of interconnected technologies can influence a firm's research and development, strategic alliance, and merger and acquisition strategies, because all these activities can influence the set of products a firm brings to market.

Shopping malls are an example of the second kind of linkage among a mix of products—where products have a common set of customers. Many customers prefer to go to one location, to shop at several stores at once, rather than travel to a series of locations to shop. This one-stop shopping reduces travel time and helps turn shopping into a social experience. Mall development companies have recognized that the value of several stores brought together in a particular location is greater than the value of those stores if they were isolated, and they have invested to help create this mix of retail shopping opportunities.[11]

Distribution Channels. Linkages within and between firms can also have an impact on how a firm chooses to distribute its products, and distribution channels can be a basis of product differentiation. For example, in the soft drink industry Coca-Cola, PepsiCo, and 7-Up all distribute their drinks through a network of independent and company-owned bottlers. These firms manufacture key ingredients for their soft drinks and ship these ingredients to local bottlers, who add carbonated water, package the drinks in bottles or cans, and distribute the final product to soft drink outlets in a given geographic area. Each local bottler has exclusive rights to distribute a particular brand in a geographic location.

Canada Dry has adopted a completely different distribution network. Instead of relying on local bottlers, Canada Dry packages its soft drinks in several locations and then ships them directly to wholesale grocers, who distribute the product to local grocery stores, convenience stores, and other retail outlets.

One of the consequences of these alternative distribution strategies is that Canada Dry has a relatively strong presence in grocery stores but a relatively small presence in soft drink vending machines. The vending machine market is dominated by Coca-Cola and PepsiCo. These two firms have local distributors that maintain and stock vending machines. Canada Dry has no local distributors and is able to get its products into vending machines only when they are purchased by local Coca-Cola or Pepsi distributors. These local distributors are likely to purchase and stock Canada Dry products such as Canada Dry ginger ale, but they are contractually prohibited from purchasing Canada Dry's various cola products.[12]

Service and Support. Finally, products have been differentiated by the level of service and support associated with them. Some firms in the home appliance market, including General Electric, have not developed their own service and support network and instead rely on a network of independent service and support operations throughout the United States. Other firms in the same industry, including Sears, have developed their own service and support networks.[13]

Product Differentiation and Creativity

The bases of product differentiation listed in Table 1 indicate a broad range of ways in which firms can differentiate their products and services. In the end, however, any effort to list all possible ways to differentiate products and services is doomed to failure. Product differentiation is ultimately an expression of the creativity of individuals and groups within firms. It is limited only by the opportunities that exist, or that can be created, in a particular industry and by the willingness and ability of firms to creatively explore ways to take advantage of those opportunities. It is not unreasonable to expect that the day some academic researcher claims to have developed the definitive list of bases of product differentiation, some creative engineer, marketing specialist, or manager will think of yet another way to differentiate his or her product.

The Value of Product Differentiation

In order to have the potential for generating competitive advantages, the bases of product differentiation upon which a firm competes must be valuable. The market conditions under which product differentiation can be valuable are discussed in the Strategy in Depth feature. More generally, in order to be valuable, bases of product differentiation must enable a firm to neutralize its threats and/or exploit its opportunities.

Product Differentiation and Environmental Threats

Successful product differentiation helps a firm respond to each of the environmental threats identified in the five forces framework. For example, product differentiation helps reduce the threat of new entry by forcing potential entrants to an industry to absorb not only the standard costs of beginning business, but also the additional costs associated with overcoming incumbent firms' product differentiation advantages.

Product differentiation reduces the threat of rivalry, because each firm in an industry attempts to carve out its own unique product niche. Rivalry is not reduced to zero, because these products still compete with one another for a common set of customers, but it is somewhat attenuated because the customers each firm seeks are different. For example, both a Rolls Royce and a Hyundai satisfy the same basic consumer need—transportation—but it is unlikely that potential customers of Rolls Royce will also be interested in purchasing a Hyundai or vice versa.

Product differentiation also helps firms reduce the threat of substitutes by making a firm's current products appear more attractive than substitute products. For example, fresh food can be thought of as a substitute for frozen processed foods. In order to make its frozen processed foods more attractive than fresh foods, products such as Stouffer's and Swanson are marketed heavily through television advertisements, newspaper ads, point-of-purchase displays, and coupons.

Product differentiation can also reduce the threat of powerful suppliers. Powerful suppliers can raise the prices of the products or services they provide. Often, these increased supply costs must be passed on to a firm's customers in the form of higher prices if a firm's profit margin is not to deteriorate. A firm without a highly differentiated product may find it difficult to pass its increased costs on to customers, because these customers will have numerous other ways to purchase

The two classic treatments of the relationship between product differentiation and firm value, developed independently and published at approximately the same time, are by Edward Chamberlin and Joan Robinson.

Both Chamberlin and Robinson examine product differentiation and firm performance relative to perfect competition. Under perfect competition, it is assumed that there are numerous firms in an industry, each controlling a small proportion of the market, and the products or services sold by these firms are assumed to be identical. Under these conditions, firms face a horizontal demand curve (because they have no control over the price of the products they sell), and they maximize their economic performance by producing and selling output such that marginal revenue equals marginal costs. The maximum economic performance a firm in a perfectly competitive market can obtain, assuming no cost differences across firms, is normal economic performance.

When firms sell differentiated products, they gain some ability to adjust their prices. A firm can sell its output at very high prices and produce relatively smaller amounts of output, or it can sell its output at very low prices and produce relatively greater

The Economics of Product Differentiation

amounts of output. These trade-offs between price and quantity produced suggest that firms selling differentiated products face a downward-sloping demand curve, rather than the horizontal demand curve for firms in a perfectly competitive market. Firms selling differentiated products and facing a downward-sloping demand curve are in an industry structure described by Chamberlin as **monopolistic competition**. It is as if, within the market niche defined by a firm's differentiated product, a firm possesses a monopoly.

Firms in monopolistically competitive markets still maximize their economic profit by producing and selling a quantity of products such that

marginal revenue equals marginal cost. The price that firms can charge at this optimal point depends on the demand they face for their differentiated product. If demand is large, then the price that can be charged is greater; if demand is low, then the price that can be charged is lower. However, if a firm's average total cost is below the price it can charge (i.e., if average total cost is less than the demand-determined price), then a firm selling a differentiated product can earn an above-normal economic profit.

Consider the example presented in Figure 1. Several curves are relevant in this figure. First, note that a firm in this industry faces downward-sloping demand (D). This means that the industry is not perfectly competitive and that a firm has some control over the prices it will charge for its products. Also, the marginal-revenue curve (MR) is downward sloping and everywhere lower than the demand curve. Marginal revenue is downward sloping because in order to sell additional levels of output of a single product, a firm must be willing to lower its price. The marginal-revenue curve is lower than the demand curve because this lower price applies to all the products sold by a firm, not just to any additional products the firm sells. The marginal-cost curve (MC) is upward sloping,

similar products or services from a firm's competitors. However, a firm with a highly differentiated product may have loyal customers or customers who are unable to purchase similar products or services from other firms. These types of customers are more likely to accept increased prices. Thus, a powerful supplier may be able to raise its prices, but, up to some point, these increases will not reduce the profitability of a firm selling a highly differentiated product.

Finally, product differentiation can reduce the threat of powerful buyers. When a firm sells a highly differentiated product, it enjoys a "quasi-monopoly" in that segment of the market. Buyers interested in purchasing this particular product must buy it from a particular firm. Any potential buyer power is reduced by the ability of a firm to withhold highly valued products or services from a buyer.

indicating that in order to produce additional outputs a firm must accept additional costs. The average-total-cost curve (ATC) can have a variety of shapes, depending on the economies of scale, the cost of productive inputs, and other cost phenomena.

These four curves (demand, marginal revenue, marginal cost, and average total cost) can be used to determine the level of economic profit for a firm under monopolistic competition. To maximize profit, the firm produces an amount (Q_e) such that marginal costs equal marginal revenues. To determine the price of a firm's output at this level of production, a vertical line is drawn from the point where marginal costs equal marginal revenues. This line will intersect with the demand curve. Where this vertical line intersects demand, a horizontal line is drawn to the vertical (price) axis to determine the price a firm can charge. In the figure, this price is P_e. At the point P_e, average total cost is less than the price. The total revenue obtained by the firm in this situation (price × quantity) is indicated by the shaded area in the figure. The economic profit portion of this total revenue is indicated by the crosshatched section of the shaded portion of the figure. Because this crosshatched section is above average total costs in the figure, it represents a competitive advantage. If this section was below average total costs, it would represent a competitive disadvantage.

Chamberlin and Robinson go on to discuss the impact of entry into the market niche defined by a firm's differentiated product. A basic assumption of S-C-P models is that the existence of above-normal economic performance motivates entry into an industry or into a market niche within an industry. In monopolistically competitive industries, such entry means that the demand curve facing incumbent firms shifts downward and to the left. This implies that an incumbent firm's customers will buy less of its output if it maintains its prices or (equivalently) that a firm will have to lower its prices to maintain its current volume of sales. In the long run, entry into this market niche can lead to a situation where the price of goods or services sold when a firm produces output such that marginal cost equals marginal revenue is exactly equal to that firm's average total cost. At this point, a firm earns zero economic profits even if it still sells a differentiated product.

Sources: E. H. Chamberlin. (1933). *The economics of monopolistic competition.* Cambridge, MA: MIT Press; J. Robinson. (1934). "What is perfect competition?" *Quarterly Journal of Economics,* 49, pp. 104–120.

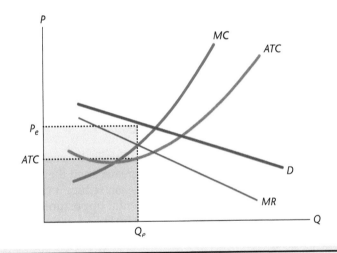

Figure 1 Product Differentiation and Firm Performance: The Analysis of Monopolistic Competition

Product Differentiation and Environmental Opportunities

Product differentiation can also help a firm take advantage of environmental opportunities. For example, in fragmented industries firms can use product differentiation strategies to help consolidate a market. In the office-paper industry, Xerox has used its brand name to become the leading seller of paper for office copy machines and printers. Arguing that its paper is specially manufactured to avoid jamming in its own copy machines, Xerox was able to brand what had been a commodity product and facilitate the consolidation of what had been a very fragmented industry.[14]

By being a first mover in these industries, firms can gain product differentiation advantages based on perceived technological leadership, preemption of strategically valuable assets, and buyer loyalty due to high switching costs.

In mature industries, product differentiation efforts often switch from attempts to introduce radically new technologies to product refinement as a basis of product differentiation. For example, in the mature retail gasoline market firms attempt to differentiate their products by selling slightly modified gasoline (cleaner-burning gasoline, gasoline that cleans fuel injectors, and so forth) and by altering the product mix (linking gasoline sales with convenience stores). In mature markets, it is sometimes difficult to find ways to actually refine a product or service. In such settings, firms can sometimes be tempted to exaggerate the extent to which they have refined and improved their products or services. The implications of these exaggerations are discussed in the Ethics and Strategy feature.

Product differentiation can also be an important strategic option in a declining industry. Product-differentiating firms may be able to become leaders in this kind of industry (based on their reputation, unique product attributes, or some other product differentiation basis). Alternatively, highly differentiated firms may be able to discover a viable market niche that will enable them to survive despite the overall decline in the market.

Finally, the decision to implement a product differentiation strategy can have a significant impact on how a firm acts in a global industry. For example, several firms in the retail clothing industry with important product differentiation advantages in their home markets are beginning to enter into the U.S. retail clothing market. These firms include Sweden's H & M Hennes & Mauritz AB, with its emphasis on "cheap chic"; the Dutch firm Mexx (a division of Liz Claiborne); the Spanish company Zara (a division of Inditex SA); and the French sportswear company Lacoste (a division of Devanlay SA).[15]

Product Differentiation and Sustained Competitive Advantage

Product differentiation strategies add value by enabling firms to charge prices for their products or services that are greater than their average total cost. Firms that implement this strategy successfully can reduce a variety of environmental threats and exploit a variety of environmental opportunities. However, the ability of a strategy to add value to a firm must be linked with rare and costly-to-imitate organizational strengths in order to generate a sustained competitive advantage. Each of the bases of product differentiation listed earlier in this chapter varies with respect to how likely it is to be rare and costly to imitate.

Rare Bases for Product Differentiation

The concept of product differentiation generally assumes that the number of firms that have been able to differentiate their products in a particular way is, at some point in time, smaller than the number of firms needed to generate perfect competition dynamics. Indeed, the reason that highly differentiated firms can charge a price for their product that is greater than average total cost is because these firms are using a basis for product differentiation that few competing firms are also using.

Ultimately, the rarity of a product differentiation strategy depends on the ability of individual firms to be creative in finding new ways to differentiate

Ethics and Strategy

One of the most common ways to try to differentiate a product is to make claims about that product's performance. In general, high-performance products command a price premium over low-performance products. However, the potential price advantages enjoyed by high-performance products can sometimes lead firms to make claims about their products that, at the least, strain credibility, and at the most, simply lie about what their products can do.

Some of these claims are easily dismissed as harmless exaggerations. Few people actually believe that using a particular type of whitening toothpaste is going to make your in-laws like you or that not wearing a particular type of deodorant is going to cause patrons in a bar to collapse when you lift your arms in victory after a foosball game. These exaggerations are harmless and present few ethical challenges.

However, in the field of health care, exaggerated product performance claims can have serious consequences. This can happen when a patient takes a medication with exaggerated performance claims in lieu of a medication with more modest, although accurate, performance claims. A history of false medical performance claims in the United States led to the formation of the Food and Drug Administration (FDA), a federal regulatory agency charged with evaluating the efficacy of drugs before they are marketed. Historically, the FDA has adopted the

Product Claims and the Ethical Dilemmas in Health Care

"gold standard" of drug approval—not only must a drug demonstrate that it does what it claims, it must also demonstrate that it does not do any significant harm to the patient. Patients can be confident that drugs that pass the FDA approval process meet the highest standards in the world.

However, this "gold standard" of approval creates important ethical dilemmas—mostly stemming from the time it takes a drug to pass FDA inspections. This process can take between five and seven years. During FDA trials, patients who might otherwise benefit from a drug are not allowed to use it because it has not yet received FDA approval. Thus, although the FDA approval process may work very well for people who may need a drug sometime in the future, it works less well for those who need a drug right now.

A growing suspicion among some consumers that the FDA process may prevent effective drugs from being marketed has helped feed the growth of alternative treatments—usually based on some herbal or more natural formula. Such treatments are careful to note that their claims—everything from regrowing hair to losing weight to enhancing athletic performance to quitting smoking—have not been tested by the FDA. And yet, these claims are still made.

Some of these performance claims seem at least reasonable. For example, it is now widely accepted that ephedra does behave as an amphetamine and thus is likely to enhance strength and athletic performance. Others—including those that claim that a mixture of herbs can actually increase the size of male genitals—seem far-fetched, at best. Indeed, a recent analysis of herbal treatments making this claim found no ingredients that could have this effect, but did find an unacceptably high concentration of bacteria from animal feces that can cause serious stomach disorders. Firms that sell products on the basis of exaggerated and unsubstantiated claims face their own ethical dilemmas. And, without the FDA to ensure product safety and efficacy, the adage *caveat emptor*—let the buyer beware—seems like good advice.

Sources: J. Angwin. (2003). "Some 'enlargement pills' pack impurities." *The Wall Street Journal,* April 8, p. B1; G. Pisano. (1991). "Nucleon, Inc." Harvard Business School Case No. 9-692-041.

their products. As suggested earlier, highly creative firms will be able to discover or create new ways to do this. These kinds of firms will always be one step ahead of the competition, because rival firms will often be trying to imitate these firms' last product differentiation moves while creative firms are working on their next one.

The Imitability of Product Differentiation

Valuable and rare bases of product differentiation must be costly to imitate if they are to be sources of sustained competitive advantage. Both direct duplication and substitution, as approaches to imitation, are important in understanding the ability of product differentiation to generate competitive advantages.

Direct Duplication of Product Differentiation

Firms that successfully implement a cost leadership strategy can choose whether they want to reveal this strategic choice to their competition by adjusting their prices. If they keep their prices high—despite their cost advantages—the existence of those cost advantages may not be revealed to competitors. Of course, other firms—such as Wal-Mart—that are confident that their cost advantages cannot be duplicated at low cost are willing to reveal their cost advantage through charging lower prices for their products or services.

Firms pursuing product differentiation strategies usually do not have this option. More often than not, the act of selling a highly differentiated product or service reveals the basis upon which a firm is trying to differentiate its products. In fact, most firms go to great lengths to let their customers know how they are differentiating their products, and in the process of informing potential customers they also inform their competitors. Indeed, if competitors are not sure how a firm is differentiating its product, all they need to do is purchase that product themselves. Their own experience with the product—its features and other attributes—will tell them all they need to know about this firm's product differentiation strategy.

Knowing how a firm is differentiating its products, however, does not necessarily mean that competitors will be able to duplicate the strategy at low cost. The ability to duplicate a valuable and rare product differentiation strategy depends on the basis upon which a firm is differentiating its products. As suggested in Table 2, some bases of product differentiation—including the use of product features—are almost always easy to duplicate. Others—including product mix, links with other firms, product customization, product complexity, and consumer marketing—can sometimes be costly to duplicate. Finally, still other bases of product differentiation—including links between functions, timing, location, reputation, distribution channels, and service and support—are usually costly to duplicate.

How costly it is to duplicate a particular basis of product differentiation depends on the kinds of resources and capabilities that basis uses. When those resources and capabilities are acquired in unique historical settings, when there is some uncertainty about how to build these resources and capabilities, or when these resources and capabilities are socially complex in nature, then product differentiation strategies that exploit these kinds of resources and capabilities will be costly to imitate. These strategies can be a source of sustained competitive advantage for a firm. However, when a product differentiation strategy exploits resources and capabilities that do not possess these attributes, then those strategies are likely to be less costly to duplicate, and even if they are valuable and rare, will only be sources of temporary competitive advantage.

Bases of Product Differentiation That Are Easy to Duplicate.   The one basis of product differentiation in Table 2 that is identified as almost always being easy to duplicate is product features. The irony is that product features are by far the most popular way for firms to try to differentiate their products. Rarely do product

	History	Uncertainty	Social Complexity
Low-cost duplication usually possible			
1. Product features	—	—	—
May be costly to duplicate			
2. Product mix	*	*	*
3. Links with other firms	*	—	**
4. Product customization	*	*	**
5. Product complexity	*	—	*
6. Consumer marketing		**	—
Usually costly to duplicate			
7. Links between functions	*	*	**
8. Timing	***	*	—
9. Location	***	—	—
10. Reputation	***	**	***
11. Distribution channels	**	*	**
12. Service and support	*	*	**

— = Not likely to be a source of costly duplication, * = Somewhat likely to be a source of costly duplication, ** = Likely to be a source of costly duplication, *** = Very likely to be a source of costly duplication

TABLE 2 Bases of Product Differentiation and the Cost of Duplication

features, by themselves, enable a firm to gain sustained competitive advantages from a product differentiation strategy.

For example, virtually every one of the product features used in the automobile industry to differentiate the products of different automobile companies has been duplicated. Chrysler's "cab forward" design has been incorporated into the design of many manufacturers. The curved, sporty styling of the Audi has surfaced in cars manufactured by Lexus and General Motors. GM's "On Star" system has been duplicated by Mercedes. Mercedes' crumple-zone technology has become the industry standard, as has GM's uni-body construction method. Indeed, only the Mazda Miata, Nissan 370 Z, and the Porsche 911 have remained unduplicated—and this has little to do with the product features of these cars and much more to do with their reputation.

The only time product features, per se, can be a source of sustained competitive advantage for a firm is when those features are protected by patents. However, even patents provide only limited protection from direct duplication, except in very unusual settings.

Although product features, by themselves, are usually not a source of sustained competitive advantage, they can be a source of a temporary competitive advantage. During the period of time when a firm has a temporary competitive advantage from implementing a product differentiation strategy based on product features, it may be able to attract new customers. Once these customers try the product, they may discover other features of a firm's products that make them attractive. If these other features are costly to duplicate, then they can be a source of sustained competitive advantage, even though the features that originally attracted a customer to a firm's products will often be rapidly duplicated by competitors.

Bases of Product Differentiation That May Be Costly to Duplicate. Some bases of product differentiation may be costly to duplicate, at least in some circumstances. The first of these, listed in Table 2, is product mix.

151

Duplicating the features of another firm's products is usually not difficult. However, if that firm brings a series of products to market, if each of these products has unique features, and most important, if the products are highly integrated with each other, then this mix of products may be costly to duplicate. Certainly, the technological integration of the mix of information technology products sold by IBM and other firms has been relatively difficult to duplicate for firms that do not manufacture all these products themselves.

However, when this basis of a product mix advantage is a common customer, then duplication is often less difficult. Thus, although having a mall that brings several stores together in a single place is a source of competitive advantage over stand-alone stores, it is not a competitive advantage over other malls that provide the same service. Because there continue to be opportunities to build such malls, the fact that malls make it easier for a common set of customers to shop does not give any one mall a sustained competitive advantage.

Links with other firms may also be costly to duplicate, especially when those links depend on socially complex relationships.

In the same way, product customization and product complexity are often easy-to-duplicate bases of product differentiation. However, sometimes the ability of a firm to customize its products for one of its customers depends on the close relationships it has developed with those customers. Product customization of this sort depends on the willingness of a firm to share often-proprietary details about its operations, products, research and development, or other characteristics with a supplying firm. Willingness to share this kind of information, in turn, depends on the ability of each firm to trust and rely on the other. The firm opening its operations to a supplier must trust that that supplier will not make this information broadly available to competing firms. The firm supplying customized products must trust that its customer will not take unfair advantage of it. If two firms have developed these kinds of socially complex relationships, and few other firms have them, then links with other firms will be costly to duplicate and a source of sustained competitive advantage.

The product customization seen in both enterprise software and in high-end customized bicycles has these socially complex features. In a real sense, when these products are purchased, a relationship with a supplier is being established—a relationship that is likely to last a long period of time. Once this relationship is established, partners are likely to be unwilling to abandon it, unless, of course, a party to the exchange tries to take unfair advantage of another party to that exchange.

Finally, consumer marketing, though a very common form of product differentiation, is often easy to duplicate. Thus, whereas Mountain Dew has established itself as the "extreme games" drink, other drinks, including Gatorade, have also begun to tap into this market segment. Of course, every once in a while an advertising campaign or slogan, a point-of-purchase display, or some other attribute of a consumer marketing campaign will unexpectedly catch on and create greater-than-expected product awareness. In beer, marketing campaigns such as "Tastes great, less filling," "Why ask why?," the "Budweiser Frogs," and "What's Up?" have had these unusual effects. If a firm, in relation with its various consumer marketing agencies, is systematically able to develop these superior consumer marketing campaigns, then it may be able to obtain a sustained competitive advantage. However, if such campaigns are unpredictable and largely a matter of a firm's good luck, they cannot be expected to be a source of sustained competitive advantage.

Bases of Product Differentiation That Are Usually Costly to Duplicate. The remaining bases of product differentiation listed in Table 2 are usually costly to duplicate. Firms that differentiate their products on these bases may be able to obtain sustained competitive advantages.

Linkages across functions within a single firm are usually a costly-to-duplicate basis of product differentiation. Whereas linkages with other firms can be either easy or costly to duplicate, depending on the nature of the relationship that exists between firms, linkages across functions within a single firm usually require socially complex, trusting relations. There are numerous built-in conflicts between functions and divisions within a single firm. Organizations that have a history and culture that support cooperative relations among conflicting divisions may be able to set aside functional and divisional conflicts to cooperate in delivering a differentiated product to the market. However, firms with a history of conflict across functional and divisional boundaries face a significant, and costly, challenge in altering these socially complex, historical patterns.

Indeed, the research on architectural competence in pharmaceutical firms suggests that not only do some firms possess this competence, but that other firms do not. Moreover, despite the significant advantages that accrue to firms with this competence, firms without this competence have, on average, been unable to develop it. All this suggests that such a competence, if it is also rare, is likely to be costly to duplicate and thus a source of sustained competitive advantage.

Timing is also a difficult-to-duplicate basis of product differentiation. It is difficult (if not impossible) to re-create a firm's unique history. If that history endows a firm with special resources and capabilities it can use to differentiate its products, this product differentiation strategy can be a source of sustained competitive advantage. Rivals of a firm with such a timing-based product differentiation advantage may need to seek alternative ways to differentiate their products. Thus, it is not surprising that universities that compete with the oldest universities in the country find alternative ways to differentiate themselves—through their size, the quality of the extramural sports, through their diversity—rather than relying on their age.

Location is often a difficult-to-duplicate basis of product differentiation. This is especially the case when a firm's location is unique. For example, research on the hotel preferences of business travelers suggests that location is a major determinant of the decision to stay in a hotel. Hotels that are convenient to both major transportation and commercial centers in a city are preferred, other things being equal, to hotels in other types of locations. Indeed, location has been shown to be a more important decision criterion for business travelers than price. If only a few hotels in a city have these prime locations, and if no further hotel development is possible, then hotels with these locations can gain sustained competitive advantages.

Of all the bases of product differentiation listed in this chapter, perhaps none is more difficult to duplicate than a firm's reputation. As suggested earlier, a firm's reputation is actually a socially complex relationship between a firm and its customers, based on years of experience, commitment, and trust. Reputations are not built quickly, nor can they be bought and sold. Rather, they can only be developed over time by consistent investment in the relationship between a firm and its customers. A firm with a positive reputation can enjoy a significant competitive advantage, whereas a firm with a negative reputation, or no reputation, may have to invest significant amounts over long periods of time to match the differentiated firm.

Distribution channels can also be a costly-to-duplicate basis of product differentiation, for at least two reasons. First, relations between a firm and its distribution channels are often socially complex and thus costly to duplicate. Second, the supply of distribution channels may be limited. Firms that already have access to these channels may be able to use them, but firms that do not have such access may be forced to create their own or develop new channels. Creating new channels, or developing entirely new means of distribution, can be difficult and costly undertakings.[16] These costs are one of the primary motivations underlying many international joint ventures.

Finally, level of service and support can be a costly-to-duplicate basis of product differentiation. In most industries, it is usually not too costly to provide a minimum level of service and support. In home electronics, this minimum level of service can be provided by a network of independent electronic repair shops. In automobiles, this level of service can be provided by service facilities associated with dealerships. In fast foods, this level of service can be provided by a minimum level of employee training.

However, moving beyond this minimum level of service and support can be difficult for at least two reasons. First, increasing the quality of service and support may involve substantial amounts of costly training. McDonald's has created a sophisticated training facility (Hamburger University) to maintain its unusually high level of service in fast foods. General Electric has invested heavily in training for service and support over the last several years. Many Japanese automakers spent millions on training employees to help support auto dealerships, before they opened U.S. manufacturing facilities.[17]

More important than the direct costs of the training needed to provide high-quality service and support, these bases of product differentiation often reflect the attitude of a firm and its employees toward customers. In many firms throughout the world, the customer has become "the bad guy." This is, in many ways, understandable. Employees tend to interact with their customers less frequently than they interact with other employees. When they do interact with customers, they are often the recipients of complaints directed at the firm. In these settings, hostility toward the customer can develop. Such hostility is, of course, inconsistent with a product differentiation strategy based on customer service and support.

In the end, high levels of customer service and support are based on socially complex relations between firms and customers. Firms that have conflicts with their customers may face some difficulty duplicating the high levels of service and support provided by competing firms.

Substitutes for Product Differentiation

The bases of product differentiation outlined in this chapter vary in how rare they are likely to be and in how difficult they are to duplicate. However, the ability of the bases of product differentiation to generate a sustained competitive advantage also depends on whether low-cost substitutes exist.

Substitutes for bases of product differentiation can take two forms. First, many of the bases of product differentiation listed in Table 1 can be partial substitutes for each other. For example, product features, product customization, and product complexity are all very similar bases of product differentiation and thus can act as substitutes for each other. A particular firm may try to develop a competitive advantage by differentiating its products on the basis of product customization only to find that its customization advantages are reduced as another firm alters the features of its products. In a similar way, linkages between functions, linkages between firms, and product mix, as bases of product differentiation, can also be substitutes for each other. IBM links its sales, service, and consulting functions to differentiate itself in the computer market. Other computer firms, however, may develop close relationships with computer service companies and consulting firms to close this product differentiation advantage. Given that different bases of product differentiation are often partial substitutes for each other, it is not surprising that firms pursue these multiple bases of product differentiation simultaneously.

Second, other strategies discussed throughout this book can be substitutes for many of the bases of product differentiation listed in Table 1. One firm may try to gain a competitive advantage through adjusting its product mix, and another firm may substitute strategic alliances to create the same type of product differentiation. For example, Southwest Airline's continued emphasis on friendly, on-time, low-cost service and United Airlines' emphasis on its links to Lufthansa and other worldwide airlines through the Star Alliance can both be seen as product differentiation efforts that are at least partial substitutes.[18]

In contrast, some of the other bases of product differentiation discussed in this chapter have few obvious close substitutes. These include timing, location, distribution channels, and service and support. To the extent that these bases of product differentiation are also valuable, rare, and difficult to duplicate, they may be sources of sustained competitive advantage.

Organizing to Implement Product Differentiation   V R I O

The ability to implement a strategy depends on the adjustment of a firm's structure, its management controls, and its compensation policies to be consistent with that strategy. Whereas strategy implementation for firms adopting a cost leadership strategy focuses on reducing a firm's costs and increasing its efficiency, strategy implementation for a firm adopting a product differentiation strategy must focus on innovation, creativity, and product performance. Whereas cost-leading firms are all about customer value, product-differentiating firms are all about style. How the need for style is reflected in a firm's structure, controls, and compensation policies is summarized in Table 3.

Organizational Structure:

1. Cross-divisional/cross-functional product development teams
2. Complex matrix structures
3. Isolated pockets of intense creative efforts: Skunk works

Management Control Systems:

1. Broad decision-making guidelines
2. Managerial freedom within guidelines
3. A policy of experimentation

Compensation Policies:

1. Rewards for risk-taking, not punishment for failures
2. Rewards for creative flair
3. Multidimensional performance measurement

TABLE 3 Organizing to Implement Product Differentiation Strategies

Organizational Structure and Implementing Product Differentiation

Both cost leadership and product differentiation strategies are implemented through the use of a functional, or U-form, organizational structure. However, whereas the U-form structure used to implement a cost leadership strategy has few layers, simple reporting relationships, a small corporate staff, and a focus on only a few business functions, the U-form structure for a firm implementing a product differentiation strategy can be somewhat more complex. For example, these firms often use temporary cross-divisional *and* cross-functional teams to manage the development and implementation of new, innovative, and highly differentiated products. These teams bring individuals from different businesses and different functional areas together to cooperate on a particular new product or service.

One firm that has used these cross-divisional and cross-functional teams effectively is the British advertising agency WPP. WPP owns several very large advertising agencies, several public relations firms, several market research companies, and so forth. Each of these businesses operates relatively independently in most areas. However, the corporation has identified a few markets where cross-divisional and cross-functional collaboration is important. One of these is the health care market. To exploit opportunities in the health care market, WPP, the corporation, forms teams of advertising specialists, market research specialists, public relations specialists, and so on, drawn from each of the businesses it owns. The resulting cross-divisional teams are given the responsibility of developing new and highly differentiated approaches to developing marketing strategies for their clients in the health care industry.[19]

The creation of cross-divisional or cross-functional teams often implies that a firm has implemented some form of matrix structure. A **matrix structure** exists when individuals in a firm have two or more "bosses" simultaneously. Thus, for example, if a person from one of WPP's advertising agencies is assigned temporarily to a cross-divisional team, that person has two bosses: the head of the temporary team and the boss back in the advertising agency. Managing two bosses simultaneously can be very challenging, especially when they have conflicting interests. The interests of these multiple bosses *will* often conflict.

A particularly important form of the cross-divisional or cross-functional team exists when this team is relieved of all other responsibilities in the firm and focuses all its attention on developing a new innovative product or service. The best-known example of this approach to developing a differentiated product occurred at the Lockheed Corporation during the 1950s and 1960s when small groups of engineers were put on very focused teams to develop sophisticated and top secret military aircraft. These teams would have a section of the Lockheed facility dedicated to their efforts and designated as off-limits to almost all other employees. The joke was that these intensive creative efforts were so engaging that members of these teams actually would forget to shower—hence, the name **"skunk works."** Skunk works have been used by numerous firms to focus the creative energy required to develop and introduce highly differentiated products.[20]

Management Controls and Implementing Product Differentiation

The first two management controls helpful for implementing product differentiation listed in Table 3—broad decision-making guidelines and managerial freedom within those guidelines—often go together, even though they sound somewhat contradictory. These potential contradictions are discussed in the Strategy in the

Strategy in the Emerging Enterprise

In the 1950s, a well-known economist named Joseph Schumpeter suggested that only very large and profitable companies have the resources necessary to invest in creating new and highly innovative products and services. His conclusion suggested that the social evils caused by economic power being concentrated in the hands of a relatively few large and powerful organizations was simply the price society had to pay for innovations that could benefit consumers.

The economic history of the past 30 years or so suggests that one of Schumpeter's key assumptions—that only large firms can afford to be innovative—is wrong. Indeed, over this time period it is clear that a great deal of innovation has occurred through the creation of entrepreneurial firms. Firms such as Dell, Microsoft, Intel, Apple, Home Depot, Cisco, Gateway, Sun, Office Depot, Nike, Oracle, PeopleSoft, Foot Locker, Amazon.com, and Starbucks have all been sources of major innovations in their industries, and all were begun as entrepreneurial ventures in the past 35 years. Indeed, given the impact of these and other entrepreneurial ventures on the worldwide economy during this time period, it is possible to call the past 30 years the "era of the entrepreneur."

What is it about entrepreneurial firms that enables them to develop

Can Only Small Firms Be Innovative?

innovations that sometimes come to dominate a market? Some scholars have suggested that the small size and lack of resources that characterize entrepreneurial start-ups, far from limiting their innovativeness, actually facilitate innovation.

For example, entrepreneurial firms have relatively little to lose when engaging in innovation. If the market accepts their innovation, great; if it doesn't, they can move on to the next innovation. Established firms, however, may have a significant stake in an older technology, an older distribution system, or an older type of customer. Established firms may be unwilling to cannibalize the sales of their current products for new and innovative products.

Moreover, small entrepreneurial firms have relatively few bureaucratic controls. Information and ideas flow freely in these organizations. Such information flow tends to facilitate innovation. Larger firms, in contrast, have usually installed numerous bureaucratic controls that impede cross-functional communication, and thus slow innovation.

Indeed, some have even argued that the types of people who are attracted to small entrepreneurial firms tend to be more innovative than those who are attracted to larger, more stable companies. People who are comfortable with risk-seeking and creativity may be attracted to an entrepreneurial firm, whereas those who are less comfortable with risk-seeking and creativity may be attracted to larger, more stable firms.

Whatever the reasons, many large firms have come to realize that they cannot afford to be "out-innovated" and "outmaneuvered" by entrepreneurial start-ups. In response, larger firms have begun to adopt policies and procedures that try to create the kind of innovativeness and creativity one often sees in entrepreneurial firms. Some firms—such as 3M (see Table 4)—have been quite successful in this effort. Others have been less successful.

Sources: C. Christensen. (1997). *The innovator's dilemma.* Boston: Harvard Business School Press; J. Schumpeter. (1942). *Capitalism, socialism, and democracy.* New York: Harper and Rowe; T. Zenger and E. Rasmusen. (1990). "Diseconomies of scale in employment contracts." *Journal of Law, Economics, and Organization,* 6, pp. 65–98.

Emerging Enterprise feature. Managing these contradictions is one of the central challenges of firms looking to implement product differentiation strategies.

Broad decision-making guidelines help bring order to what otherwise might be a chaotic decision-making process. When managers have no constraints in their decision making, they can make decisions that are disconnected from each other and inconsistent with a firm's overall mission and objectives. This results in decisions that are either not implemented or not implemented well.

TABLE 4 Guiding Innovative Principles at 3M*

1. **Vision.** Declare the importance of innovation; make it part of the company's self-image.

   "Our efforts to encourage and support innovation are proof that we really do intend to achieve our vision of ourselves . . . that we intend to become what we want to be . . . as a business and as creative individuals."

2. **Foresight.** Find out where technologies and markets are going. Identify articulated and unarticulated needs of customers.

   "If you are working on a next-generation medical imaging device, you'll probably talk to radiologists, but you might also sit down with people who enhance images from interplanetary space probes."

3. **Stretch goals.** Set goals that will make you and the organization stretch to make quantum improvements. Although many projects are pursued, place your biggest bets on those that change the basis of competition and redefine the industry.

   "We have a number of stretch goals at 3M. The first states that we will drive 30 percent of all sales from products introduced in the past 4 years. . . . To establish a sense of urgency, we've recently added another goal, which is that we want 10 percent of our sales to come from products that have been in the market for just 1 year. . . . Innovation is time sensitive . . . you need to move quickly."

4. **Empowerment.** Hire good people and trust them, delegate responsibilities, provide slack resources, and get out of the way. Be tolerant of initiative and the mistakes that occur because of that initiative.

   "William McKnight [a former chairman of 3M] came up with one way to institutionalize a tolerance of individual effort. He said that all technical employees could devote 15 percent of their time to a project of their own invention. In other words, they could manage themselves for 15 percent of the time. . . . The number is not so important as the message, which is this: The system has some slack in it. If you have a good idea, and the commitment to squirrel away time to work on it and the raw nerve to skirt your lab manager's expressed desires, then go for it.

   "Put another way, we want to institutionalize a bit of rebellion in our labs. We can't

have all our people off totally on their own . . . we do believe in discipline . . . but at the same time 3M management encourages a healthy disrespect for 3M management. This is not the sort of thing we publicize in our annual report, but the stories we tell—with relish—are frequently about 3Mers who have circumvented their supervisors and succeeded.

   "We also recognize that when you let people follow their own lead . . . everyone doesn't wind up at the same place. You can't ask people to have unique visions and march in lockstep. Some people are very precise, detail-oriented people . . . and others are fuzzy thinkers and visionaries . . . and this is exactly what we want."

5. **Communications.** Open, extensive exchanges according to ground rules in forums that are present for sharing ideas and where networking is each individual's responsibility. Multiple methods for sharing information are necessary.

   "When innovators communicate with each other, you can leverage their discoveries. This is critically important because it allows companies to get the maximum return on their substantial investments in new technologies. It also acts as a stimulus to further innovation. Indeed, we believe that the ability to combine and transfer technologies is as important as the original discovery of a technology."

6. **Rewards and recognition.** Emphasize individual recognition more than monetary rewards through peer recognition and by choice of managerial or technical promotion routes. "Innovation is an intensely human activity."

   "I've laid out six elements of 3M's corporate culture that contribute to a tradition of innovation: vision, foresight, stretch goals, empowerment, communication, and recognition. . . . The list is . . . too orderly. Innovation at 3M is anything but orderly. It is sensible, in that our efforts are directed at reaching our goals, but the organization . . . and the process . . . and sometimes the people can be chaotic. We are managing in chaos, and this is the right way to manage if you want innovation. It's been said that the competition never knows what we are going to come up with next. The fact is, neither do we."

*As expressed by W. Coyne. (1996). *Building a tradition of innovation.* The Fifth U.K. Innovation Lecture, Department of Trade and Industry, London. Cited in Van de Ven et al. (1999), pp. 198–200.

However, if these decision-making guidelines become too narrow, they can stifle creativity within a firm. As was suggested earlier, a firm's ability to differentiate its products is limited only by its creativity. Thus, decision guidelines must be narrow enough to ensure that the decisions made are consistent with a firm's mission and objectives. Yet, these guidelines also must be broad enough so that managerial creativity is not destroyed. In well-managed firms implementing product differentiation strategies, as long as managerial decisions fall within the broad decision-making guidelines in a firm, managers have the right—in fact, are expected—to make creative decisions.

A firm that has worked hard to reach this balance between chaos and control is 3M. In an effort to provide guiding principles that define the range of acceptable decisions at 3M, its senior managers have developed a set of innovating principles. These are presented in Table 4 and define the boundaries of innovative chaos at 3M. Within these boundaries, managers and engineers are expected to be creative and innovative in developing highly differentiated products and services.[21]

Another firm that has managed this tension well is British Airways (BA). BA has extensive training programs to teach its flight attendants how to provide world-class service, especially for its business-class customers. This training constitutes standard operating procedures that give purpose and structure to BA's efforts to provide a differentiated service in the highly competitive airline industry. Interestingly, however, BA also trains its flight attendants in when to violate these standard policies and procedures. By recognizing that no set of management controls can ever anticipate all the special situations that can occur when providing service to customers, BA empowers its employees to meet specific customer needs. This enables BA to have both a clearly defined product differentiation strategy and the flexibility to adjust this strategy as the situation dictates.[22]

Firms can also facilitate the implementation of a product differentiation strategy by adopting a **policy of experimentation**. Such a policy exists when firms are committed to engaging in several related product differentiation efforts simultaneously. That these product differentiation efforts are related suggests that a firm has some vision about how a particular market is likely to unfold over time. However, that there are several of these product differentiation efforts occurring simultaneously suggests that a firm is not overly committed to a particular narrow vision about how a market is going to evolve. Rather, several different experiments facilitate the exploration of different futures in a marketplace. Indeed, successful experiments can actually help define the future evolution of a marketplace.

Consider, for example, Charles Schwab, the innovative discount broker. In the face of increased competition from full-service and Internet-based brokerage firms, Schwab engaged in a series of experiments to discover the next generation of products it could offer to its customers and the different ways it could differentiate those products. Schwab investigated software for simplifying online mutual fund selection, online futures trading, and online company research. It also formed an exploratory alliance with Goldman Sachs to evaluate the possibility of enabling Schwab customers to trade in initial public offerings. Not all of Schwab's experiments led to the introduction of highly differentiated products. For example, based on some experimental investments, Schwab decided not to enter the credit card market. However, by experimenting with a range of possible product differentiation moves, it was able to develop a range of new products for the fast-changing financial services industry.[23]

Compensation Policies and Implementing Product Differentiation Strategies

The compensation policies used to implement product differentiation listed in Table 3 very much complement the organizational structure and managerial controls listed in that table. For example, a policy of experimentation has little impact on the ability of a firm to implement product differentiation strategies if every time an innovative experiment fails individuals are punished for taking risks. Thus, compensation policies that reward risk-taking and celebrate a creative flair help to enable a firm to implement its product differentiation strategy.

Consider, for example, Nordstrom. Nordstrom is a department store that celebrates the risk-taking and creative flair of its associates as they try to satisfy their customers' needs. The story is often told of a Nordstrom sales associate who allowed a customer to return a set of tires to the store because she wasn't satisfied with them. What makes this story interesting—whether or not it is true—is that Nordstrom doesn't sell tires. But this sales associate felt empowered to make what was obviously a risky decision, and this decision is celebrated within Nordstrom as an example of the kind of service that Nordstrom's customers should expect.

The last compensation policy listed in Table 3 is multidimensional performance measurement. In implementing a cost leadership strategy, compensation should focus on providing appropriate incentives for managers and employees to reduce costs. Various forms of cash payments, stock, and stock options can all be tied to the attainment of specific cost goals, and thus can be used to create incentives for realizing cost advantages. Similar techniques can be used to create incentives for helping a firm implement its product differentiation advantage. However, because the implementation of a product differentiation strategy generally involves the integration of multiple business functions, often through the use of product development teams, compensation schemes designed to help implement this strategy must generally recognize its multifunctional character.

Thus, rather than focusing only on a single dimension of performance, these firms often examine employee performance along multiple dimensions simultaneously. Examples of such dimensions include not only a product's sales and profitability, but customer satisfaction, an employee's willingness to cooperate with other businesses and functions within a firm, an employee's ability to effectively facilitate cross-divisional and cross-functional teams, and an employee's ability to engage in creative decision making.

Can Firms Implement Product Differentiation and Cost Leadership Simultaneously?

The arguments developed in this chapter suggest that cost leadership and product differentiation business strategies, under certain conditions, can both create sustained competitive advantages. Given the beneficial impact of both strategies on a firm's competitive position, an important question becomes: Can a single firm simultaneously implement both strategies? After all, if each separately can improve a firm's performance, wouldn't it be better for a firm to implement both?

No: These Strategies Cannot Be Implemented Simultaneously

A quick comparison of the organizational requirements for the successful implementation of cost leadership strategies and product differentiation strategies presented in Table 5 summarizes one perspective on the question of whether these strategies can be implemented simultaneously. In this view, the organizational requirements of these strategies are essentially contradictory. Cost leadership requires simple reporting relationships, whereas product differentiation requires cross-divisional/cross-functional linkages. Cost leadership requires intense labor supervision, whereas product differentiation requires less intense supervision of creative employees. Cost leadership requires rewards for cost reduction, whereas product differentiation requires rewards for creative flair. It is reasonable to ask "Can a single firm combine these multiple contradictory skills and abilities?"

Some have argued that firms attempting to implement both strategies will end up doing neither well. This logic leads to the curve pictured in Figure 2. This figure suggests that there are often only two ways to earn superior economic performance within a single industry: (1) by selling high-priced products and gaining small market share (product differentiation) or (2) by selling low-priced products and gaining large market share (cost leadership). Firms that do not make this choice of strategies (medium price, medium market share) or that attempt to implement both strategies will fail. These firms are said to be "stuck in the middle."[24]

TABLE 5 The Organizational Requirements for Implementing Cost Leadership and Product Differentiation Strategies

Cost leadership	Product differentiation
Organizational structure	**Organizational structure**
1. Few layers in the reporting structure	1. Cross-divisional/cross-functional product development teams
2. Simple reporting relationships	2. Willingness to explore new structures to exploit new opportunities
3. Small corporate staff	3. Isolated pockets of intense creative efforts
4. Focus on narrow range of business functions	
Management control systems	**Management control systems**
1. Tight cost-control systems	1. Broad decision-making guidelines
2. Quantitative cost goals	2. Managerial freedom within guidelines
3. Close supervision of labor, raw material, inventory, and other costs	3. Policy of experimentation
4. A cost leadership philosophy	
Compensation policies	**Compensation policies**
1. Reward for cost reduction	1. Rewards for risk-taking, not punishment for failures
2. Incentives for all employees to be involved in cost reduction	2. Rewards for creative flair
	3. Multidimensional performance measurement

Figure 2 Simultaneous Implementation of Cost Leadership and Product Differentiation Competitive Strategies: Being "Stuck in the Middle"

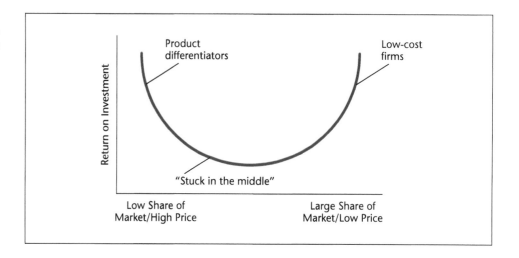

Yes: These Strategies Can Be Implemented Simultaneously

More recent work contradicts assertions about being "stuck in the middle." This work suggests that firms that are successful in both cost leadership and product differentiation can often expect to gain a sustained competitive advantage. This advantage reflects at least two processes.

Differentiation, Market Share, and Low-Cost Leadership

Firms able to successfully differentiate their products and services are likely to see an increase in their volume of sales. This is especially the case if the basis of product differentiation is attractive to a large number of potential customers. Thus, product differentiation can lead to increased volumes of sales. It has already been established that an increased volume of sales can lead to economies of scale, learning, and other forms of cost reduction. So, successful product differentiation can, in turn, lead to cost reductions and a cost leadership position.[25]

This is the situation that best describes McDonald's. McDonald's has traditionally followed a product differentiation strategy, emphasizing cleanliness, consistency, and fun in its fast-food outlets. Over time, McDonald's has used its differentiated product to become the market share leader in the fast-food industry. This market position has enabled it to reduce its costs, so that it is now the cost leader in fast foods as well. Thus, McDonald's level of profitability depends both on its product differentiation strategy and its low-cost strategy. Either one of these two strategies by itself would be difficult to overcome; together they give McDonald's a very costly-to-imitate competitive advantage.[26]

Managing Organizational Contradictions

Product differentiation can lead to high market share and low costs. It may also be the case that some firms develop special skills in managing the contradictions that are part of simultaneously implementing low-cost and product differentiation strategies. Some recent research on automobile manufacturing helps describe these special skills.[27] Traditional thinking in automotive manufacturing was that plants could either reduce manufacturing costs by speeding up the assembly line or increase the quality of the cars they made by slowing the line, emphasizing

162

team-based production, and so forth. In general, it was thought that plants could not simultaneously build low-cost/high-quality (i.e., low-cost *and* highly differentiated) automobiles.

Several researchers at the Massachusetts Institute of Technology examined this traditional wisdom. They began by developing rigorous measures of the cost and quality performance of automobile plants and then applied these measures to over 70 auto plants throughout the world that assembled mid-size sedans. What they discovered was six plants in the entire world that had, at the time this research was done, very low costs *and* very high quality.[28]

In examining what made these six plants different from other auto plants, the researchers focused on a broad range of manufacturing policies, management practices, and cultural variables. Three important findings emerged. First, these six plants had the best manufacturing technology hardware available—robots, laser-guided paint machines, and so forth. However, because many of the plants in the study had these same technologies, manufacturing technology by itself was not enough to make these six plants special. In addition, policies and procedures at these plants implemented a range of highly participative, group-oriented management techniques, including participative management, team production, and total quality management. As important, employees in these plants had a sense of loyalty and commitment toward the plant they worked for—a belief that they would be treated fairly by their plant managers.

What this research shows is that firms *can* simultaneously implement cost leadership and product differentiation strategies if they learn how to manage the contradictions inherent in these two strategies. The management of these contradictions, in turn, depends on socially complex relations among employees, between employees and the technology they use, and between employees and the firm for which they work. These relations are not only valuable (because they enable a firm to implement cost leadership and differentiation strategies) but also socially complex and thus likely to be costly to imitate and a source of sustained competitive advantage.

Recently, many scholars have backed away from the original "stuck in the middle" arguments and now suggest that low-cost firms must have competitive levels of product differentiation to survive, and that product differentiation firms must have competitive levels of cost to survive.[29] For example, the fashion design company Versace—the ultimate product differentiating firm—has recently hired a new CEO and controller to help control its costs.[30]

Summary

Product differentiation exists when customers perceive a particular firm's products to be more valuable than other firms' products. Although differentiation can have several bases, it is, in the end, always a matter of customer perception. Bases of product differentiation include: (1) attributes of the products or services a firm sells (including product features, product complexity, the timing of product introduction, and location); (2) relations between a firm and its customers (including product customization, consumer marketing, and reputation); and (3) links within and between firms (including links between functions, links with other firms, a firm's product mix, its distribution system, and its level of service and support). However, in the end, product differentiation is limited only by the creativity of a firm's managers.

Product differentiation is valuable to the extent that it enables a firm to set its prices higher than what it would otherwise be able to. Each of the bases of product differentiation identified can be used to neutralize environmental threats and exploit environmental opportunities. The rarity and imitability of bases of product differentiation vary. Highly imitable bases of product differentiation include product features. Somewhat imitable bases include product mix, links with other firms, product customization, and consumer marketing. Costly-to-imitate bases of product differentiation include linking business functions, timing, location, reputation, and service and support.

The implementation of a product differentiation strategy involves management of organizational structure, management controls, and compensation policies. Structurally, it is not unusual for firms implementing product differentiation strategies to use cross-divisional and cross-functional teams, together with teams that are focused exclusively on a particular product differentiation effort, so-called "skunk works." Managerial controls that provide free managerial decision making within broad decision-making guidelines can be helpful in implementing product differentiation strategies, as is a policy of experimentation. Finally, compensation policies that tolerate risk-taking and a creative flair and that measure employee performance along multiple dimensions simultaneously can also be helpful in implementing product differentiation strategies.

A variety of organizational attributes is required to successfully implement a product differentiation strategy. Some have argued that contradictions between these organizational characteristics and those required to implement a cost leadership strategy mean that firms that attempt to do both will perform poorly. More recent research has noted the relationship between product differentiation, market share, and low costs and has observed that some firms have learned to manage the contradictions between cost leadership and product differentiation.

Challenge Questions

1. Although cost leadership is perhaps less relevant for firms pursuing product differentiation, costs are not totally irrelevant. What advice about costs would you give a firm pursuing a product differentiation strategy?

2. Product features are often the focus of product differentiation efforts. Yet product features are among the easiest-to-imitate bases of product differentiation and thus among the least likely bases of product differentiation to be a source of sustained competitive advantage. Does this seem paradoxical to you? If no, why not? If yes, how can you resolve this paradox?

3. What are the strengths and weaknesses of using regression analysis and hedonic prices to describe the bases of product differentiation?

4. Chamberlin used the term "monopolistic competition" to describe firms pursuing a product differentiation strategy in a competitive industry. However, it is usually the case that firms that operate in monopolies are less efficient and less competitive than those that operate in more competitive settings. Does this same problem exist for firms operating in a "monopolistic competition" context? Why or why not?

5. Implementing a product differentiation strategy seems to require just the right mix of control and creativity. How do you know if a firm has the right mix? Is it possible to evaluate this mix before problems associated with being out of balance manifest themselves? If yes, how? If no, why not?

6. A firm with a highly differentiated product can increase the volume of its sales. Increased sales volumes can enable a firm to reduce its costs. High volumes with low costs can lead a firm to have very high profits, some of which the firm can use to invest in further differentiating its products. What advice would you give a firm whose competition is enjoying this product differentiation and cost leadership advantage?

Problem Set

1. For each of the listed products, describe at least two ways they are differentiated.
(a) Ben & Jerry's ice cream
(b) The Hummer H2
(c) The X-Games
(d) The Pussycat Dolls
(e) The movies *Animal House* and *Caddyshack*
(f) Frederick's of Hollywood
(g) Taco Bell

2. Which, if any, of the bases of product differentiation in question #1 are likely to be sources of sustained competitive advantage? Why?

3. Suppose you obtained the following regression results, where the starred (*) coefficients are statistically significant. What could you say about the bases of product differentiation in this market? (Hint: A regression coefficient is statistically significant when it is so large that its effect is very unlikely to have emerged by chance.)

$$\begin{aligned}
\text{House Price} = \ &\$125{,}000^* + \$15{,}000^* \,(\text{More than three bedrooms}) \\
&+ \$18{,}000^* \,(\text{More than 3,500 square feet}) \\
&+ \$150 \,(\text{Has plumbing}) + \$180 \,(\text{Has lawn}) \\
&+ \$17{,}000^* \,(\text{Lot larger than 1/2 acre})
\end{aligned}$$

How much would you expect to pay for a four-bedroom, 3,800-square-foot house on a one-acre lot? How much for a four-bedroom, 2,700-square-foot house on a quarter-acre lot?

Do these results say anything about the sustainability of competitive advantages in this market?

4. Which of the following management controls and compensation policies is consistent with implementing cost leadership? With product differentiation? With both cost leadership and product differentiation? With neither cost leadership nor product differentiation?

(a) Firm-wide stock options

(b) Compensation that rewards each function separately for meeting its own objectives

(c) A detailed financial budget plan

(d) A document that describes, in detail, how the innovation process will unfold in a firm

(e) A policy that reduces the compensation of a manager who introduces a product that fails in the market

(f) A policy that reduces the compensation of a manager who introduces several products that fail in the market

(g) The creation of a purchasing council to discuss how different business units can reduce their costs

5. Identify three industries or markets that have the volume–profit relationship described in Figure 2. Which firms in this industry are implementing cost leadership strategies? Which are implementing product differentiation strategies? Are any firms "stuck in the middle"? If yes, which ones? If no, why not? Are any firms implementing both cost leadership and product differentiation strategies? If yes, which ones? If no, why not?

End Notes

1. See Ono, Y. (1996). "Who really makes that cute little beer? You'd be surprised." *Wall Street Journal*, April 15, pp. A1 +. Since this 1996 article, some of these craft beer companies have changed the way they manufacture the beers to be more consistent with the image they are trying to project.
2. See Porter, M. E. (1980). *Competitive strategy*. New York: Free Press; and Caves, R. E., and P. Williamson. (1985). "What is product differentiation, really?" *Journal of Industrial Organization Economics*, 34, pp. 113–132.
3. Lieberman, M. B., and D. B. Montgomery. (1988). "First-mover advantages." *Strategic Management Journal*, 9, pp. 41–58.
4. Carroll, P. (1993). *Big blues: The unmaking of IBM*. New York: Crown Publishers.
5. These ideas were first developed in Hotelling, H. (1929). "Stability in competition." *Economic Journal*, 39, pp. 41–57; and Ricardo, D. (1817). *Principles of political economy and taxation*. London: J. Murray.
6. See Gunther, M. (1998). "Disney's Call of the Wild." *Fortune*, April 13, pp. 120–124.
7. The idea of reputation is explained in Klein, B., and K. Leffler. (1981). "The role of market forces in assuring contractual performance." *Journal of Political Economy*, 89, pp. 615–641.
8. See Robichaux M. (1995). "It's a book! A T-shirt! A toy! No, just MTV trying to be Disney." *Wall Street Journal*, February 8, pp. A1 +.
9. See Henderson, R., and I. Cockburn. (1994). "Measuring competence? Exploring firm effects in pharmaceutical research." *Strategic Management Journal*, 15, pp. 63–84.
10. See Johnson, R. (1999). "Speed sells." *Fortune*, April 12, pp. 56–70. In fact, NASCAR fans either love or hate Jeff Gordon.
11. Kotler, P. (1986). *Principles of marketing*. Upper Saddle River, NJ: Prentice Hall.
12. Porter, M. E., and R. Wayland. (1991). "Coca-Cola vs. Pepsi-Cola and the soft drink industry." Harvard Business School Case No. 9-391-179.
13. Ghemawat, P. (1993). "Sears, Roebuck and Company: The merchandise group." Harvard Business School Case No. 9-794-039.
14. Welsh, J. (1998). "Office-paper firms pursue elusive goal: Brand loyalty." *The Wall Street Journal*, September 21, p. B6.
15. See White, E., and K. Palmer. (2003). "U.S. retailing 101." *The Wall Street Journal*, August 12, pp. B1 +.
16. See Hennart, J. F. (1988). "A transaction cost theory of equity joint ventures." *Strategic Management Journal*, 9, pp. 361–374.
17. Deutsch, C. H. (1991). "How is it done? For a small fee. . ." *New York Times*, October 27, p. 25; and Armstrong, L. (1991). "Services: The customer as 'Honored Guest.'" *BusinessWeek*, October 25, p. 104.
18. See Yoffie, D. (1994). "Swissair's alliances (A)." Harvard Business School Case No. 9-794-152.
19. "WPP—Integrating icons." Harvard Business School Case No. 9-396-249.
20. Orosz, J. J. (2002). "Big funds need a 'Skunk Works' to stir ideas." *Chronicle of Philanthropy*, June 27, p. 47.
21. Van de Ven, A., D. Polley, R. Garud, and S. Venkatraman. (1999). *The innovation journey*. New York: Oxford, pp. 198–200.
22. Prokesch, S. (1995). "Competing on customer service: An interview with British Airways' Sir Colin Marshall." *Harvard Business Review*, November–December, p. 101. Now if they wouldn't lose our luggage at Heathrow, they would be a great airline.
23. Position, L. L. (1999). "David S. Pottruck." *BusinessWeek*, September 27, EB 51.
24. Porter, M. E. (1980). *Competitive strategy*. New York: Free Press.
25. Hill, C. W. L. (1988). "Differentiation versus low cost or differentiation and low cost: A contingency framework." *Academy of Management Review*, 13(3), pp. 401–412.
26. Gibson, R. (1995). "Food: At McDonald's, new recipes for buns, eggs." *The Wall Street Journal*, June 13, p. B1.
27. Originally discussed in the Research Made Relevant feature in Chapter 3.
28. Womack, J. P., D. I. Jones, and D. Roos. (1990). *The machine that changed the world*. New York: Rawson.
29. Porter, M. E. (1985). *Competitive advantage*. New York: Free Press.
30. Agins, T., and A. Galloni. (2003). "Facing a squeeze, Versace struggles to trim the fat." *The Wall Street Journal*, September 30, pp. A1 +.

Crafting Business Strategy for Dynamic Contexts

Crafting Business Strategy for Dynamic Contexts

In This Chapter We Challenge You To >>>

1. Distinguish the ways in which firms' strategies are related to dynamic contexts.

2. Identify, compare, and contrast the various routes to revolutionary strategies.

3. Evaluate the advantages and disadvantages of choosing a first-mover strategy.

4. Recognize when an incumbent is caught off guard by a revolutionary strategy and identify defensive tactics to reduce the effects of this competition.

5. Explain the difficulties and solutions to implementing revolutionary strategies.

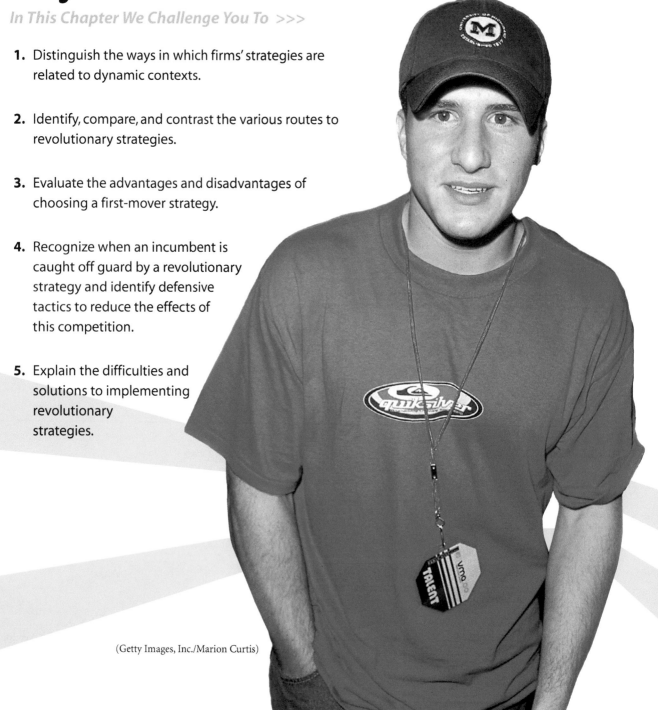

(Getty Images, Inc./Marion Curtis)

Roxio *and the* Resurrection *of* Napster

(NewsCom/PR Newswire Photo Service)

"Napster concludes our fiscal year 2007 with over 830,000 paid subscribers, which we believe makes us the largest on demand music subscription service in the industry," said Chris Gorog, Napster's chairman and chief executive officer.[1] "We have a paid subscriber base that is both larger than Rhapsody, as well as larger than all of the remaining subscription competitors combined." Napster was riding high again in April 2007, under the leadership of Chris Gorog, whose career spans virtually all aspects of the media and entertainment industry and its convergence with technology. In this dynamic industry, Gorog was the one to lead Napster, given his background. Gorog had been Chairman and CEO of Napster, the leader in CD recording and digital media, which he took public under the corporate name of Roxio in 2001. Before that, Gorog served as President of New Business Development and Executive Vice President of Group Operations for Universal Studios Recreations Group. Prior to Universal, Gorog was President and CEO of ITC Entertainment Group, a leading motion picture and television producer, and led a management buy-out of the group's global business. Before joining ITC, Gorog served as Vice President of Business Affairs for Motion Pictures and Television at The Walt Disney Company. Gorog was also a director of House of Blues, a leading North American concert producer and The Guitar Center, the nation's largest musical instrument retailer.

When someone draws up a conclusive list of the software that made the Internet what it is, somewhere among e-mail and Web browsers there will be a spot for Napster. Napster was really two pieces of software: freely available "client" software that ran on home computers, enabling individuals to copy music to their PCs and play it for free, and a central Napster-run server that dispensed information about music. When it arrived in late 1999, Napster showed how easily music could be distributed without a costly infrastructure (namely, recording-artist royalties, CD manufacturers, record distribution, and record stores). The timing was also right as consumer preferences were shifting to entertainment-on-demand, big players such as Sony and Samsung were providing stylish, miniaturized portable music systems, and there was little in terms of clear legal precedent against music sharing. By facilitating music sharing, Napster sent ripples of panic through the music industry, which depended on the traditional music-industry infrastructure to generate a considerable amount of revenue. In June 2002, after four years of legal battles with the Recording Industry Association of America (RIAA), which represents every major U.S. music label, Napster filed for bankruptcy. At the time, Napster had listed assets of $7.9 million and liabilities of more than $101 million.

Gorog led the acquisition of Napster after its bankruptcy through his software company, Roxio. This illustrates a common pattern in which a new CEO, such as Gorog, remakes his company to fit his prior experience. Under Gorog, with his media background, Roxio morphed from software company to a media company. In 2003, Gorog relaunched Napster as a legal download music provider site and took over as its CEO. Roxio itself had gone public in 2001 as a software-only firm specializing in the development and sale of CD-recording products to both original-equipment manufacturers (OEMs) of PCs and CD-recordable-drive manufacturers, integrators, and distributors. In preparation for the Napster launch, Roxio courted two tech-industry players once spurned by Napster—Microsoft and music producers. Why Microsoft? Roxio supplied the CD-burning software bundled with all new PCs operated by Microsoft XP. As for music producers, Roxio, unlike the original Napster, intended to keep them happy by abandoning the idea of free music sharing.

The question for Roxio was whether it would still be around in five years, after the online-music business had shaken out. It faced competition not only in its original software business, but in its new online-music business as well. Approaches to providing online music included the following:

■ The à la carte approach (employed by Roxio and Apple's iTunes). For 79 cents to $1.20, customers can buy any number of individual tracks (or albums for $9.99 and up). After downloading music onto their hard drives, they can burn it onto CDs, copy it to portable music players, or stream it through home-entertainment centers.

- The subscription model (used by emusic). Customers pay a monthly fee to download a specified number of songs. For $9.99 a month, emusic lets customers download 40 songs (65 for $14.99) and use them any way they want.

- The streaming model (favored by RealNetwork's Rhapsody). Music lovers pay a monthly fee to listen to as many songs as they can stand and, for a little extra (usually under a dollar a track), download their favorites.

The uncertainty created by the availability of competing technological standards was heightened by the fact that the idea of online-music consumption had only just begun to catch on.

Going forward, Roxio aimed to compete by keeping its hand in the turbulent online-music business while keeping a firm grip on its position as the number-one seller of CD- and DVD-burning software. This strategy meant that the company had to maintain strong ties with Microsoft as well as with other tech-industry heavyweights, such as RealNetworks, and the music industry—an array of stakeholders who view Roxio as everything from a partner to competitor. Moreover, Roxio would also need to keep close tabs on firms that manufacture CD and DVD burner/players. Why? Because they may enter the software business as a means of differentiating increasingly commoditized hardware products.

Perhaps the most telling factor in this story of dynamic strategy in dynamic contexts is the sale of Roxio's software business to competitor Sonic Solutions in January 2004 and the subsequent renaming of the surviving online-music company to Napster. This completed the remaking of the company to fit Gorog's background in media. In May 2005, Yahoo! entered the online-music fray with a service priced at half that of Napster's—now that's a dynamic context!

The dynamic nature of the Internet has made it challenging for Gorog to find a workable (that is, a legal and profitable) business model for Napster. Even as late as September 2006, Gorog was struggling. "Napster's still trying to find a working business model, which is bad from an operating standpoint," said Kit Spring, analyst with Stifel Nicolaus & Co Inc. Spring thought that Gorog would put Napster up for sale, based on Gorog's hints that "We do not have our heads in the sand regarding an M&A (merger and acquisition) transaction," In a call to analysts in September 2006, Gorog left all options on the table. "We continue to receive a lot of interest in the company. We will always carefully weigh any valuation alternative against the opportunity and risk associated with continuing as a stand-alone company," Gorog said.

In 2006, Napster was facing stiff competition from iTunes, which is not a subscription-based service. Gorog decided to go back to a model that had worked before: free. Gorog created a Web site where consumers could listen to as many as five tracks for free while watching ads. This time, though, the free music would be legal because Napster would pay the record labels from the ad revenues. New subscriber growth on Napster fell as Gorog focused on the new site, but Gorog believed that the new site would improve conversion from free users to paid users. In addition, Napster would get a new revenue stream from ads. Gorog's ad sales team worked with advertisers to create custom playlists to accompany the ads. Analysts remained skeptical, however. "It will be interesting to see how much revenue they can get from advertising," said Jupiter Research analyst David Card. "But they're still going to live and die by subscriptions."

Perhaps the greatest testimony to the competitiveness and dynamism of this market space is Napster's profitability: From the date of its spinoff from Adaptec through April 2007, Napster has never shown a profit. <<<

171

Strategy and Dynamic Contexts

In this chapter, we show you how firms can develop competitive advantage in the face of dynamic competition. Although the notion of the industry life cycle suggests that strategy should always be dynamic, because it must be externally oriented to be effective, the dynamic competition we refer to here requires that strategies also be dynamic by virtue of the rapid and sometimes unpredictable changes taking place in the firm's external environment. For most industries, certain features of the industry are dynamic. In some industries, these features are central to success in the largest and most lucrative parts of the industry. So, at a minimum, firms must know how to respond to dynamic competition. More important is figuring out how to be the instigator of successful and dynamic change; being an industry revolutionary can be the path to improved and dynamic competitive advantage. As you can see from our opening vignette about the on-line music business, dynamic strategies still require firms to make coherent tradeoffs between the economic logic of low cost and differentiation as the primary factors in any strategy for getting customers to buy their products. Dynamic competition, however, challenges a firm to improve its game continuously, and maybe even figure out how to rewrite the rules of competition.

This challenge is what differentiates the relatively stable context of strategies—even those that address one stage of the industry life cycle—from the *dynamic* context of strategy. Moreover, successful strategies increasingly require that they be revolutionary—that they change the rules of the game. These strategies, however, also necessitate the nearly seamless integration of formulation and implementation and tend to reward an appetite for experimentation and risk taking. This is why, after understanding what constitutes a dynamic context, you will also learn how to conceive of a revolutionary strategy and use tools designed to help formulate revolutionary strategies, such as the value-curve and real-options analysis.

Before introducing the strategies and tools for dealing with dynamic markets, let's start by reviewing the specific ways in which dynamic contexts can undermine competitive advantage.

THE CHALLENGES TO SUSTAINABLE COMPETITIVE ADVANTAGE

It's important to understand why dynamic conditions can undermine competitive advantage, whether with blinding speed or over an extended period of time. Indeed, as we saw in the opening vignette, even though it may seem that an industry has changed overnight, many of the seeds of that apparently dramatic change may have been sown and nourished over a fairly long period. For instance, changes in consumer preferences and portable music technologies evolved over an extended period of time. In addition, change often results from a combination of drivers, several of which you learned about in earlier chapters and which are reviewed further in this chapter.

Recall from prior chapters that competitive advantage is developed when a firm can create value in ways that rivals cannot. And the likelihood of developing a competitive advantage is facilitated by possessing resources and capabilities that fulfill the VRINE criteria. Firms with VRINE resources and capabilities are much more likely to be able to create strategic positions of low cost and differentiation than firms that lack such resources and capabilities. Challenges to sustained competitive advantage include anything that threatens VRINE resources and capabilities. Consequently, we need to examine the types of change that make valuable resources and capabilities lose their value; that make valuable and rare resources and capabilities become common; that make valuable and rare resources and capabilities easy to imitate or substitute; and that weaken a firm's ability to exploit resources and capabilities that satisfy the value, rarity, inimitability, and nonsubstitutability criteria of the VRINE model.

In addition, formulating strategies either to protect against threats from or to exploit the opportunities associated with dynamic environments generally encompass special cases of finding new ways to generate a low-cost or differentiation advantage. Because dynamic markets move at a much faster pace than stable markets, strategies for dealing with dynamic markets involve special attention to the *arenas* and *staging* elements of the strategy diamond.

Three dimensions of dynamic change are explored in this chapter: *Competitive interactions, industry evolution,* and *technological disruptions.* These categories are interrelated and are intended to help you think about the different facets of a changing competitive landscape. The relative speed of changes in these categories further complicates strategy in dynamic contexts.

Competitive Interaction   How do principles of dynamic context and change complement the principles of strategic decision making that we've already discussed in prior chapters? We know that managers can use tools such as the strategy diamond, the VRINE model, and industry structure analysis to formulate a strategy and hammer out a strategic position. We know, too, that the firm's strategy and strategic position should be consistent with its strengths and its ability to seize opportunities presented by its competitive environment. Finally, we know that strategic positioning decisions are supported by a wealth of tactical decisions made to implement and reinforce the firm's strategy.

Now consider the possible effects of all this decision making in a context of interactive competition. Competitive interactions are composed of two related factors: the interactions between incumbents and the interactions of new entrants and incumbents. The interactions caused by new entrants are a particularly severe source of dynamism when the entrants introduce a new business model—that is, a strategy that varies significantly from those used by incumbents. Research on competitive interaction has identified four underlying phases, summarized in Exhibit 1.[2]

To examine these phases, let's say that a regional title insurance company developed a strategy designed to help it grow into a premier national company. That strategy involves a sequence of activities: entry into adjacent regional markets, followed by increased focus on differentiators designed to build brand awareness, followed by more rapid expansion through acquisitions funded by an increasingly valuable stock price.[3] In its first phase, such an aggressive series of tactical moves may go unnoticed or ignored by competitors. Eventually, however, if customer reactions in phase 2 appear to be, or are anticipated to be, positive, then other firms will formulate responses to the first firm's competitive behavior, as shown in phase 3. In phase 4, competitors evaluate the results of their interactions, and the cycle may then recommence.

Competitive actions can generate a wide range of competitive responses.[4] *Competitive interaction theory* suggests that because competitive actions will generate reactions, a firm's managers should predict reactions to its actions and use that information to determine what would be the best course of action given competitors' likely reactions.[5] Competitive action can be initiated in phase 1 in essentially four ways: aggressiveness, complexity of the competitive action repertoire, unpredictability, and tactics that delay the leaders' competitive reaction. The responses to those various actions have been shown to play out differently in terms of the competitive advantage of the challenger and the challenged.

With regard to competitive aggressiveness, strategy research has shown that a challenger can erode the leadership position of another firm by rapidly launching many assaults on the leader in a short period of time. Such interaction explains how Nike overtook Reebok's dominant sports shoe position in the late 1980s and how, in 2005, SABMiller regained market-share-growth leadership from Anheuser Busch in the light beer segment. SABMiller did so through a combination of aggressive advertising that suggested that Anheuser Busch's beers lacked flavor and backed it up with consumer surveys saying that the SABMiller's beers had more and better taste.

Exhibit 1 Phases of
Competitive Interaction

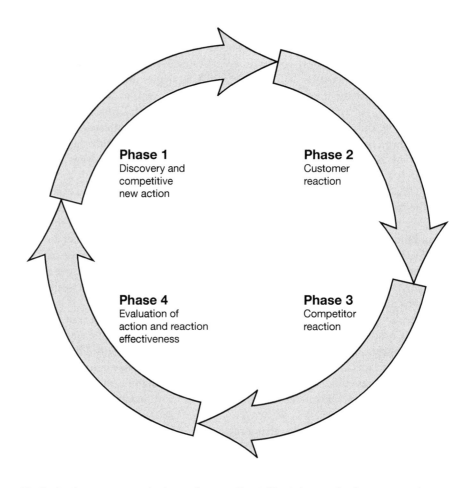

Phase 1
Discovery and
competitive
new action

Phase 2
Customer
reaction

Phase 4
Evaluation of
action and reaction
effectiveness

Phase 3
Competitor
reaction

Similarly, the more complexity and unpredictability inherent in these aggressive moves, the more likely the attacker will succeed in improving its market position. Complexity and unpredictability play to the attacker's advantage by confusing the industry leader and putting it on the defensive. As a result, the leader may also lose focus on the coherent execution of its strategy, as seen by the fragmentation of scarce resources to defending multiple competitive fronts. For example, Anheuser Busch was so thrown off by SABMiller's aggressive tactics that it responded by launching a new beer, Budweiser Select, and advertising it as a flavorful, high-quality beer. SABMiller turned around and pointed to the new product as further evidence that Anheuser Busch's products did not have taste.

Finally, to the extent that the challenger can engage in competitive moves that are difficult to respond to quickly or simply catch the leader unaware, the attacker can gain competitive market position. Strategy research has shown, for instance, that Nike's competitive success can be partially attributed to the fact that Nike initiated new competitive moves (e.g., promotions, new product launches, endorsements) and responded to Reebok's actions much faster than Reebok responded to Nike's.[6] This same research has shown such tactics to hold true in industries ranging from telecommunications and personal computers to airlines and brewing.

When leading companies face new competitors who utilize new business models that are disruptive—strategies that are both different from and in conflict with those of incumbents— they face vexing dilemmas. Should they respond to these new entrants with disruptive strategies and, if so, how? These types of innovations essentially result in a possible change in the rules of competition within the industry. Such disruptions have several common characteristics. First, compared to incumbents, these firms typically emphasize different product attributes. Second, they generally start out as rather low-margin businesses. Third, they can grow into significant companies that take away market share. However, because of tradeoffs with value-chain activities that are essential to the incumbents, these new firms' business models cannot be imitated in short order by incumbents. Examples of these types of disruptive entrants are found in many industries, such as rental cars (Enterprise), retailing (Amazon.com), retail brokerage (E*Trade and Charles Schwab), steel (Nucor), and airlines (Southwest, JetBlue, and RyanAir). Your opening vignette on the new Napster is another good example of a new business model. Devising appropriate strategies to deal with these types of competitive interactions is particularly difficult.

Industry Evolution   Rivalry and the nature of competition often change as a function of industry evolution—from differentiation to cost, or vice versa. Because a successful low-cost strategy requires different resources and capabilities than a differentiation strategy, a change in the basis of competitive advantage will cause advantage to shift over time from firms with the obsolete resources and capabilities to those favored by industry conditions. Because all industries evolve and mature, a firm's strategy must always anticipate the repercussions of change. Of course, the best case is where the firms can both be the cause of such change, and be positioned to benefit from it. For example, strategies may differ from one stage of the industry life cycle to another. The strategic management of industry evolution involves not only dealing with the industry life cycle but also strategies for changing arenas and strategies for responding to changes in a firm's environment. One particular challenge associated with industry evolution that goes beyond the industry life cycle challenges are the pressures of commoditization.

The Pressures of Commoditization   Managers must consider the pressure for change exerted by *commoditization,* which we define as the process by which industrywide sales come to depend less on unique product features and more on price. As industry products become perceived as undifferentiated, the ability of firms to generate premium pricing diminishes. Consequently, differentiation strategies are vulnerable to the pressures of commoditization.

Research suggests that firms can choose from among different tactics to deal with the pressures of commoditization.[7] The manager, however, must make difficult choices in terms of timing—for instance, if the firm changes its strategy too soon, it risks losing extra profits, but if it moves too late, it may never be able to regain the market lost to newcomers or incumbents who moved sooner. As you will see, all the tactics have clear implications for the five elements in the strategy diamond—namely, arenas, differentiators, vehicles, pacing, and economic logic.

Technological Change   Recall the concept of *technological disruptions*, which can cause leading firms to fall by the wayside. Industry decline is often forestalled by the introduction of a new technology that propels the industry into another growth phase. A *technological discontinuity* is an innovation that dramatically advances an industry's price-versus-performance frontier; it generally triggers a period of ferment that is closed by the emergence of a dominant design. A period of incremental technical change then follows, which is, in turn, broken by the next technological discontinuity.[8]

Keep in mind that *technology* is a very broad term. We tend to think of technology rather myopically, focusing only on pure technological innovations. However, technological disruptions may also be *process innovations* (such as Charles Schwab's migration to on-line trading or Toyota's adaptation of lean manufacturing), *application innovations* (such as GM's integration of Global Positioning Systems into vehicles through the OnStar system), and *business model innovations* (such as Amazon.com's move from online bookselling to becoming a logistics provider for countless retailers).[9]

175

Technological change is particularly disruptive when change is discontinuous, so that it does not sustain existing leaders' advantage. Additionally, technological change is particularly risky when it primarily affects business *processes*. The Progressive Direct on-line insurance market is an example of this. Progressive bypasses traditional and costly insurance agents and relies instead on direct sales through the Internet. In doing so, Progressive is able to offer some of the lowest-priced insurance products on the market. And to ensure that customers shop with Progressive first, the company provides quotes for competitors' policies, and will even sell them instead if a consumer prefers that. Progressive makes money both ways, through the sale of its own policies and through the commissions it receives from the sale of competitors' policies. Discontinuities that affect *product* technology often favor differentiation strategies. In the moderate to high-end segment of the photo industry, for instance, the current technological shift from chemical film to digital photography gives firms like Sony an opportunity to establish a competitive stronghold based on their electronic miniaturization capabilities in an industry that it might never have entered prior to the digital age. Similarly, Apple's pricey iPod portable music device takes advantage of the technological shift reviewed in the opening vignette on Napster.

If the new technology is introduced by an incumbent firm, it stands a good chance to continue its dominance. For instance, in the aircraft manufacture business, Boeing has long been an innovator in the development of new airframes and has persisted as a leading firm, though the technology of the most efficient design has changed numerous times. Some discontinuous technologies are introduced by new entrants, and because they change the face of the business landscape by altering who the leaders are, they are often referred to as *disruptive technologies*. When the new technology is developed by new entrants, incumbent firms face the very real possibility that they will be marginalized or eliminated. For instance, every leading firm in the minicomputer business was wiped out by firms that innovated and marketed the PC.

What can firms do to avoid or withstand a technological discontinuity? Research suggests that to withstand such technological changes, firms must either proactively create new opportunities for themselves or react defensively in ways to counteract the powerful forces of change.

Speed of Change Over and above any particular change driver, the speed of change is a critical factor in keeping up with the basis of competition in an industry. Speed tends to compound the effects of every change driver, whether industry evolution, technological discontinuities, or other causes. As the pace of change increases, so, too, must a firm's ability to react swiftly to (and even anticipate) changes in the basis of competitive advantage. In many cases, the most profitable avenue is availed to firms that have the ability to *lead* industry change.[10] *Reacting to change* means detecting and responding quickly to unexpected customer demands, new government regulations, or competitor's actions. *Anticipating change* means foreseeing the appearance of global markets, the development of new market segments, and emergence of the complementary or conflicting technologies.

Then we'll discuss the development of revolutionary strategies designed to help firms thrive in dynamic environments. We then examine when and why firms would want to be firm movers in introducing new strategies. Finally, we conclude by applying the five elements of the strategy diamond to strategies in dynamic contexts. When you're finished with this chapter, you should be able to formulate a strategy for managing the dynamic context and prepare a plan for implementing it.

Revolutionary Strategies That Lead Industry Change

Some fundamental theories and models of strategic management, like the model of industry structure and generic strategies, are frequently used in industry and have enormous analytical power. However, if used naively, these tools present a static picture of the world and suggest that there is a strategic position that a firm can assume to assure high levels of profitability. If you correctly identify the factors affecting industry profitability, and zero in on the key success factors in the industry, you can then use your resources and capabilities to position your firm with a well-developed strategy that results in a cost or differentiation advantage. But industry contexts are not usually stable; they are always changing (slowly or quickly, but inevitably) and this makes formulating a strategy that will have enduring profitable returns very problematic.

Consider a few industries that you are very familiar with; you will see several types of competitors. First, there are the large incumbents, usually some of the earliest and most successful entrants. Companies such as McDonald's in fast food, Hertz in rental cars, and Blockbuster in movie rentals are firms that originally established the "rules" of the industry; these "rules" are the norms that most firms follow in carving out their strategy. Each of these industries has a group of other firms that have imitated the leader and tried to carve out a subsistence through a similar, if somewhat differentiated, strategy. These are firms like Burger King, Avis, and Hollywood Video that all compete directly with the major leaders using strategies that are only slightly differentiated from their rival—they implicitly seem to follow the rules laid down by the market leaders. But, then there are the rule breakers. These are firms like Subway, Enterprise, and NetFlix. Each of these firms made fundamentally different assumptions about what consumers would pay for and introduced strategies that differed in some radical ways from the industry leaders.

In this section we outline five types of revolutionary strategies that can introduce dynamic change into an industry. Successfully implemented, such strategies can overturn an established industrial structure and rewrite the rules of competition. Research suggests that these five revolutionary strategies tend to fall into one of three categories: high-end disruptions, low-end disruptions, or hybrid.

High-End Disruption A new-market disruption that significantly changes the industry value curve by disrupting the expectations of customers by vastly improving product performance is referred to as **high-end disruption**. High-end disruption often results in huge new markets in which new players unseat the largest incumbents. Incumbents can also use new-market disruption strategies. To do so, they need to shift competitive focus from head-to-head competition to the task of redefining the business model for at least a part of the existing market. A new-market-creation strategy, for example, may enable a firm to avoid the pitfalls of commoditization and evolution, but pursuing it doesn't necessarily mean that the same firm will become, or even intends to become, the industry leader. Cirque du Soleil significantly disrupted the circus industry by incorporating many features more common in Broadway theater than in traditional circuses, generating significant new growth and higher profits than any other traditional circus.

high-end disruption Strategy that may result in huge new markets in which new players redefine industry rules to unseat the largest incumbents.

Low-End Disruption Recall the concept of *disruptive technologies*. Some disruptive technologies appear at the low end of industry offerings and are referred to as **low-end disruptions**. Incumbents tend to ignore such new entrants because they target the incumbents' least valuable customers. These low-end disruptions rarely offer features that satisfy the best customers in the industry. However, these low-end entrants often use such footholds as platforms to migrate into the more attractive space once their products or services improve. Indeed, by the time they do improve, these low-end disruptions often satisfy the needs of the center of the market better than incumbents' products do because incumbents have been busily making incremental improvements to satisfy their best clients' demands even while these improvements cause the firms to outshoot the needs of the center of the market. Southwest Airlines has been a very successful low-end disrupter, satisfying only the most basic travel needs and eliminating many services that had been taken for granted by established airlines.

low-end disruption Strategy that appears at the low end of industry offerings, targeting the least desirable of incumbents' customers.

Hybrid Disruption Strategies As you might expect, most newcomers adopt some combination of new-market and low-end disruption strategies. Today, it may look as if Amazon.com has pursued a single-minded low-end disruption strategy, but along the way, it also has created some new markets, mainly by bringing more buyers into the market for books. Many Amazon customers buy in the quantities they do because of the information that the Amazon site makes available. The strategies of such companies as JetBlue, Charles Schwab, and the University of Phoenix are also hybrids of new-market and low-cost disruption strategies.[11] JetBlue's focused low-cost strategy, for instance, has been able to achieve the lowest-cost position in the industry by eliminating many services (a business model it borrowed from Southwest) but also adding services that increased customer loyalty. In addition, they targeted overpriced but underserved markets, thereby stimulating new demand—both taking a portion of the existing market from incumbent competitors *and* creating a new market by attracting consumers who couldn't ordinarily afford air travel. Schwab pioneered discount brokerage as a new market but has since enticed legions of clients from full-service brokers such as Merrill-Lynch. The University of Phoenix is taking a strategic path much like the one blazed by Schwab.

We now turn to the five types of revolutionary strategies that can introduce major disruption into an industry by changing the rules of the game. In Exhibit 2, we categorize these five types as: *reconceiving a product/service, reconfiguring the value chain, redefining the arenas, rescaling the industry,* and *reconsidering the competitive mindset.*

Exhibit 2 Revolutionary Strategies

Type of Industry Disruption	Reconceiving a Product/Service	Reconfiguring the Value Chain	Redefining the Arenas	Rescaling the Industry	Reconsidering the Competitive Mindset
Definition	Breaking away from existing industry conceptions of what products and services look like	Changing elements of the industry value chain	Changing when and where you compete	Using a business model that relies on different economics relative to scale	Avoid direct competition
Example	• Creating a new value curve (e.g., Cirque du Soleil) • Separate function from form (e.g., electronic hotel keys)	• Use a new value chain (e.g., Amazon) • Compress the value chain (e.g., IKEA)	• Changing temporal and geographical availability (e.g., Redbox) • Total imagined market versus served market (e.g., disposable cameras)	• Increase scale for greater economies of scale (e.g., waste disposal) • Downscale in search of higher prices in niche markets (e.g., microbreweries)	• Look to make competitors complementors (e.g., American and Delta defraying costs from Boeing) • Avoid head-to-head competition by moving into areas where there is little competition (e.g., [yellow tail]®)

RECONCEIVE A PRODUCT OR SERVICE

Creating a New Value Curve   You are probably already familiar with Cirque du Soleil, a recent example of how a new value curve is created. Exhibit 3 summarizes Cirque's novelty. Cirque's value curve demonstrates that they dropped a number of features common in other circuses, but they added features completely unheard of before in the circus industry. Where did these ideas come from? They appear to have been borrowed from another form of entertainment—Broadway.

Most companies have no trouble focusing on their existing rivals and actively trying to match or beat their rivals' customer offerings. However, as a result of this focus on rivals' behaviors, strategies often converge. This convergence grows stronger according to the amount of conventional industry wisdom about how to compete. This type of convergence is often associated with incremental innovation. It will rarely result in breakthroughs that create new markets.

One way to create a revolutionary strategy that avoids the pitfall of strategic incrementalism is the creation of a new value curve. Creating a new value curve requires a different approach and a different way of thinking about innovation. Instead of looking for the next incremental improvement, new markets are often created when managers create innovations that build on the best of the existing industry, import ideas from other industries, and eliminate some features that industry incumbents take for granted but that are not critical to key customers. This style of new-market creation has been shown to work in both fast-paced industries and those that are seemingly stagnant—both conditions that are ripe for significant changes. Fast-paced industries are dynamic by definition. Stagnant industries are often ripe for change—through new technologies that will send the industry on a new growth trajectory, or through shakeout, which is a dynamic process but usually in a very negative sense for many incumbents.

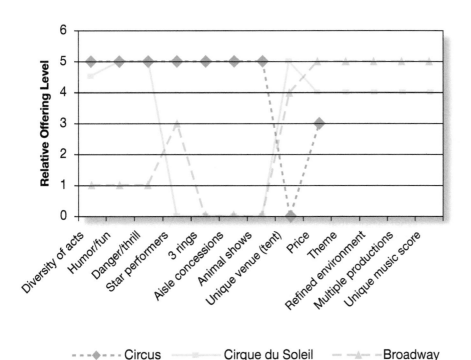

Exhibit 3 Cirque du Soleil at the Nexus of Circus and Broadway

The key to discovering a new-market space lies in asking four basic questions. These questions are illustrated in the Four-Actions Framework shown in Exhibit 4.[12] By answering these questions, you will be able to define a new value curve for an industry, or at least a segment of an industry.

First, what product or service attributes that rivals take for granted should be *reduced* well below the industry standard? Second, what factors that the industry has taken for granted should be *eliminated?* Third, what product or service attributes should be *raised* well above the industry standard? And fourth, are there any factors that the industry has never offered that should be *created?* By finding answers to these questions, managers could modify a firm's strategy either so that its products are further differentiated from competitors', so that its cost structure is driven significantly below that of competitors or, conceivably, both. In addition, by following this path, firms often generate new customers for the industry or industry segment; they actually grow the business by means other than, or in addition to, stealing customers from competitors. And while we introduce the four-actions framework in the context of new value curve creation, you will likely find that the framework translates well to all the revolutionary strategies covered in this section.

"How Would *You* Do That? 1" illustrates the application of the value-curve tool, in conjunction with the four-actions framework, to the wine industry using [yellow tail]®.[13] Previously you learned how to apply the value curve to help map existing competitors. Here, the purpose of the tool is extended to reveal how a firm might create a new value curve in ways that separate its strategy from those of incumbents.

As you will recall, a strategic group is a cluster of firms that pursue similar strategies within an industry. The curve for each strategic group visually represents how those firms present their products to customers along key buying criteria. It conceptually represents the underlying logic incumbents use in positioning their products. Being able to visualize how competitors perform along these differentiators helps reveal the assumptions being made by the industry. It also helps you to determine which assumptions might be tested. Along these dimensions, question whether some levels of delivery on the key success factors can be reduced or eliminated; likewise, question whether some can be increased or whether new points of differentiation can be added. As a re-

Exhibit 4 The Four-Actions Framework of New Market Creation

The key to discovering a new value curve lies in answering four basic questions.

Reduce
What factors should be reduced *well below* the industry standard?

Eliminate
What factors that the industry has taken for granted should be eliminated?

Creating New Markets: A new value curve

Create/Add
What factors that the industry has never offered should be created or added?

Raise
What factors should be raised *well above* the industry standard?

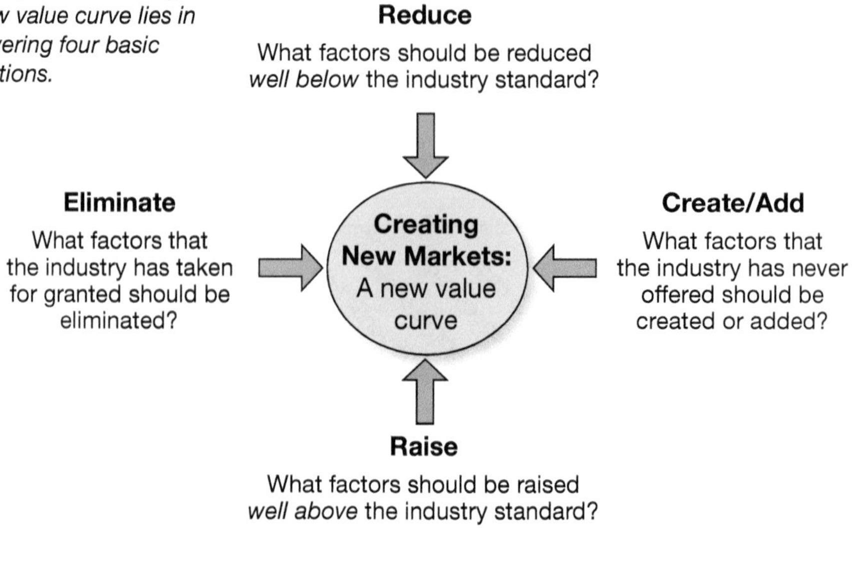

sult of using the value-curve tool, firms can develop strategies that challenge and change the rules of competition.

Separating Function and Form   Another way to create a revolutionary strategy is to look for ways to separate function and form. *Function* is the benefits of the product; *form* is the embodied product. Let's consider credit cards as an example. Credit cards first emerged at the beginning of the 20th century. Toward the end of the century, magnetic storage technology was used to make credit cards more secure and speed the payment to merchants by encoding cards with data about the customer and their account. When swiping the card through a reader, the transfer of funds from the purchaser to the merchant could be significantly accelerated.

So, let's think about the function and the form of the credit card. The function includes the identification of the cardholder and their account along with permission to charge a purchase. The form is a slim piece of plastic. How can permission and identification be used in ways other than the specific case of permission to make a charge at a merchant? Several uses have emerged: employment identification badges, which allow access to secured areas; hotel keys, which grant access to your hotel room but no others; student identification cards, which allow everything from library checkout privileges to payment for lunch; and membership and discount cards for establishments ranging from grocery stores to athletic gyms. In all of these cases, the credit card companies did not see the opportunity to apply the form of the encoded card to a new or related function—rather it was new entrants attempting to solve problems for customers that used existing technology from other industries to do so.

RECONFIGURE THE VALUE CHAIN

Recall that a value chain is the sequential steps of value-added activities that are necessary to create a product or service that is used by the end consumer. Some revolutionary strategies were created while reconfiguring the value chain in ways that others never thought of, or tried to do, before. Two related ways this can be done are to improve the customer's value equation by using a *new* value chain, and *compressing* the value chain.

Radically New Value Chain   Sometimes an industry can be revolutionized by making completely new assumptions about the value chain. When Jeff Bezos started Amazon.com as the world's largest bookstore, he actually started with the concept that the Internet would provide an opportunity to bring a radically new value chain to a number of industries. He settled on the book industry, but Amazon has now taken their radically new value chain into many products. Beyond eliminating the costly physical infrastructure of retail stores, the Amazon model also cuts other significant costs from the value chain. For instance, large book retailers return on average about 30 percent of their orders each year to wholesalers and publishers, but at Amazon, returns are a slim 3 percent.

Skype Technologies' popular Web-based phone service is another example of a radically new value chain. Indeed, there was virtually no overlap in Skype's value chain and that of traditional telephone companies. Skype uses software to allow users to make phone calls using the Internet. Initially, all calls had to be made PC-to-PC, but a new SkypeOut service allows PC-to-phone calling, and these calls are still at much lower rates than traditional phone service. After eBay purchased Skype in 2005, Skype added new services, including content distribution (users can send and receive pictures and ringtones, for example) and a call-forwarding service. To use Skype, customers download free software, and must have a PC with a microphone and speakers, or a USB phone. So, the only portion of the traditional telecommunications value chain that Skype kept was the local land line for customers who use dial-up Internet access.

Compress the Value Chain   A more conventional way to reconfigure the value chain is to simply compress it. Wal-Mart, Dell, and IKEA are all good examples of this. The typical compression involves eliminating a middle-man in the value chain. Often, the

181

[yellow tail]® Creates a New Value Curve in the Wine Industry[14]

When we map the intensely competitive wine industry based on the characteristics of the key players, we see that the industry is comprised of two dominant strategic groups—wineries competing in the budget segment or high-price segments, or both.

So what is a new entrant to do? [yellow tail]® arrived at its new value curve through a process of strategic steps taken over many years. It all began back in the 1820s, when the first Casellas began crafting wine in Italy, then moved to Australia in 1951 to pursue their hopes and dreams of a better life. After years of growing and selling grapes to local wineries in 1969, the Casellas decided it was time to put their own winemaking skills to use, and the Casella winery was born. A new generation of Casellas entered the family business in 1994 and embarked on an ambitious expansion to build a new winery with a vision of blending Old World heritage with New World technology. Today, Casella Wines is run by fifth- and sixth-generation Casella family members. In 2000, Casella Wines joined forces with another family-run company, W. J. Deutsch & Sons, to bring Casella wines and [yellow tail]® to the United States.

As shown in Exhibits 5 and 6, you can use the value-curve and four-actions framework to see how [yellow tail]® reconfigured the way it defined being a winery: offering wines at a moderate price; avoiding wine lingo; encouraging impulse purchases with its catchy labels; and targeting only two high-demand wines, Chardonnay and Shiraz. It also added new features that incumbents did not offer—easy drinking, ease of selection (again, only two varieties), and a spirit of fun and adventure.[15] [yellow tail]® used the four-actions framework to create a new value curve. It created alternatives instead of competing head-on with the major players. It converted noncustomers to customers by luring traditional beer and cocktail drinkers with its catchy labels and easy-drinking wines. Sold around $7 a bottle, the [yellow tail]® Shiraz is the top-selling imported red wine in the U.S., while the [yellow tail]® Merlot and Chardonnay are both number two in their respective categories. This year, the Australian brand could sell 15 million cases in the U.S., and [yellow tail]® accounted for 39 percent of the total imported Australian wine market in the U.S. food store segment in 2006.

Ultimately, the choice between new-market and low-end disruption strategies depends on a firm's resources and capabilities, and the ability to then execute the chosen strategy. [yellow tail]® conceived of a new way to approach the wine industry, but it did so with the knowledge that it possessed the resources and capabilities to do so.

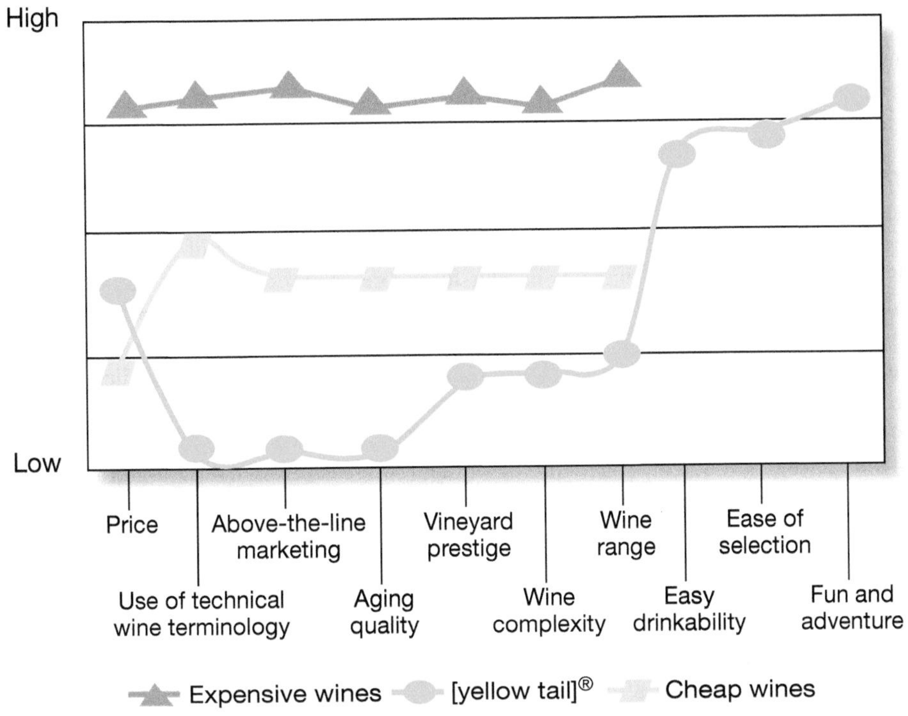

Exhibit 5 A Value Curve for [yellowtail]®

Value curve axis (left): High ... Low

Horizontal axis categories:
Price | Use of technical wine terminology | Above-the-line marketing | Aging quality | Vineyard prestige | Wine complexity | Wine range | Easy drinkability | Ease of selection | Fun and adventure

Legend: Expensive wines — [yellow tail]® — Cheap wines

Exhibit 6 The Four-Actions Framework and [yellowtail]®

Reduce	Eliminate	Create/Add	Raise
Wine complexity Wine range Vineyard prestige	Enological terminology and distinctions Aging qualities Above-the-line marketing	Easy drinking Ease of selection Fun and adventure	Price versus budget wines Retail store involvement

wholesaler or distributor is removed, though the compression need not be at this link in the value chain. Dell eliminated retail stores and manufacturing components (choosing to outsource all parts and simply oversee the assembly of computers). IKEA, one of the world's top furniture retailers, sells Scandinavian-style home furnishings and other housewares. IKEA lowers cost significantly by compressing several value chain activities. First, it cuts transportation costs by shipping unassembled furniture to its retail stores in flat packaging, allowing it to ship more product in much smaller spaces. But, it doesn't stop there; rather than incur the cost of assembly at the retail site, it shifts this step of the value chain to customers because customers buy the product in the box and assemble it at home. So, by designing furniture in pieces that can be easily assembled, it eliminates two costly steps from the value chain. This allows IKEA to pass some of the savings on to customers and keep some of the savings in the form of higher margins.

REDEFINE YOUR ARENAS

Managers generally have an idea of who their customers are and in what arenas they compete. Sometimes these conceptions act as blinders; they can obscure the vision of potential customers that don't traditionally purchase the company's products.

Changing the Temporal or Geographic Availability

New customers are often available at different times or places than those conventionally served. Fast food outlets inside large retailers like Wal-Mart and Target are obvious examples of finding new geographic availability without venturing into far-flung foreign markets. Similarly, most grocery stores now have bank branches located on the premises. Airlines, too, have a captive shopping audience during the flight. Of course, the Internet has opened up temporal and geographic accessibility for many businesses. McDonald's and Coinstar are partners in a radical innovation to the DVD rental industry by making DVDs available in vending machines located at McDonald's restaurants. After initial market tests were successful in the Denver market, the RedBox concept was quickly rolled out. Customers can select from a selection of recent releases and popular titles and rent a DVD for one night for one dollar. The concept was so popular, that it quickly expanded into other non-McDonald's locations such as grocery stores.

Imagining the Total Possible Market Rather than the Served Market

One way to redefine your arenas is to imagine the *possible* market rather than focusing on the *served* market. Consider the market for cameras. Today you can find inexpensive disposable cameras available at every grocery store checkout stand. These relatively new products opened up an entirely new market for filmmakers—children. Prior to these disposable cameras, no child was viewed as a likely customer for film.

New technologies can enable this reconceptualization of the total possible market as well. For instance, Copeland Corporation was considering the introduction of a new scroll compressor for residential air conditioning units. The compressor is to an air conditioner, what a computer processing chip is to a PC (the analogy would be "Intel Inside"). At low production volumes, this new and highly efficient and quiet scroll technology would cost too much for the average homeowner, and would therefore be attractive only to a small niche market. However, with higher production volumes, Copeland's costs for the scroll compressor dropped dramatically, to the point where it could actually be price-competitive with low-cost units. Copeland opted for the volume option, and actually helped move the technological standard in the industry to scroll.

Spearheading Industry Convergence

Industry convergence occurs when two distinct industries evolve toward a single point where old industry boundaries no longer exist. Convergence examples are numerous. Computing and entertainment have come together in the TiVo video digital recorder, which allows users to time-shift their TV viewing.

184

The convergence of entertainment and communications have created a mobile music revolution—the distribution of digital music over wireless networks. Your cell phone is a tangible illustration of multiple industries converging in a single product; at one moment you use it as a phone, later you click a photograph, it serves as your music and video player, and it may also be your personal organizer all rolled into one. For example, the PlayStation 2 is not only a games console, but also a CD player, DVD player, and Internet connector. Broadband Internet access, television, telephone, and mobile phone service by firms that traditionally only offered one or two of these services, is another example of leading industry convergence.

Industries will converge over time. A revolutionary firm is one that discovers and leads convergence. Opportunities to create significant value are often found at the convergence of two or more industries. For instance, Napster and Swedish telecommunications company Ericsson teamed up to offer a new digital music service aimed at mobile phone customers around the world. Ericsson's long-established relationships with carriers could help Napster gain ground in what is new territory for a primarily PC-focused company. As this example illustrates, convergence can be the driver behind bundling multiple products into a single offering, or it may lay the groundwork for entirely new products.

RESCALE THE INDUSTRY

Significant economic opportunities can be found by exploring whether industry conventions about minimum efficient scale are correct. Revolutionary strategies can be created by searching for industries that have opportunities to benefit from increases in economies of scale. However, there are also many opportunities available to create value by downscaling.

Increase Scale The financial services industry is currently in the middle of a major rescaling from local and regional, to national. Historically, regulation kept banks from seeking national economies of scale but deregulation opened the door for new business models. In this industry, rescaling has been accomplished mostly through mergers and acquisitions.

Service Corporation International (SCI) is a company whose strategy was almost entirely developed around the economic logic of seeking economies of scale through consolidating an industry. SCI is to death what McDonald's is to hamburgers; it is the largest funeral, cremation, and cemetery services company in the world. Historically, the funeral business was a local business with most operations owned and operated by local families. When SCI founder Robert Waltrip was 20 years old in the early 1950s, he inherited Houston's Heights Funeral Home, which his father and aunt founded in 1926. Waltrip noticed that national chains were emerging in several industries such as hotels (Holiday Inn) and fast food (McDonald's). As he examined the economics of running a funeral business, he determined that several of the cost drivers would indeed be sensitive to scale increases. Thus, Waltrip began his quest to achieve cost advantages through scale. SCI went public in 1969, and by 1975 it was the largest provider of funeral services in the United States.

Some revolutionary strategies used increases in scale that were unconventional at the time in their industries; examples include such disparate industries as waste management services and adult education. Many firms attempting to rescale an industry toward larger economies of scale do so through acquisitions (e.g., SCI, Waste Management), but others, such as the University of Phoenix in adult education, have done so primarily through internal growth.

Downscaling to Serve Narrow or Local Customers In some industries, there is an opportunity to generate significant margins by downscaling. Downscaling necessarily implies going after a smaller segment of the market. But, rather than just going after a small market, downscaling also implies attempting to add significant value to a niche of the market that is underserved.

185

Take the example of local microbreweries. The minimum efficient scale for breweries necessitates broad-based, national marketing. However, significantly smaller scale can be efficient if the market is local and the quality offered justifies a significant price premium. Examples of successful microbreweries can be found in almost every major city. Bed and breakfast inns (B&Bs) are another example of how one can compete against large national chains in the lodging industry. Bed and breakfast inns typically have only a few to a dozen rooms. At one level of analysis, the cost structure would seem very inefficient compared to the scale economies available to national chains. However, because the level of service is so personal at B&Bs, and because the properties are generally very unique and charming, B&Bs can charge prices that far exceed that of the chain hotel.

RECONSIDERING THE COMPETITIVE MINDSET

Creating Complementors Out of Suppliers, Buyers, and Competitors Recall Porter's Five-Forces model, which suggests that the attractiveness of an industry is a function of the power of *suppliers, buyers,* and *substitutes,* the *barriers to entry,* and the degree of *rivalry.* In essence, each of these forces competes for a share of industry profitability.

Note also that a new factor is often added to that model, the idea of *complementors.* Rather than compete for industry profitability, a complementor helps to increase the total profits that can be made in an industry. How does the idea of complementors relate to reconsidering the competitive mindset? Research suggests that most managers tend to view the parties they interact with as competitive threats. As summarized in Exhibit 7, the value net model is a framework that represents all the players in the market and the interdependencies between them.[16] It will help you think about how the competitive mindset might be changed.

Here is how you use the value net. Identify a player as a complementor if customers value your product more when they have the other player's product than when they have your

Exhibit 7
The Value Net

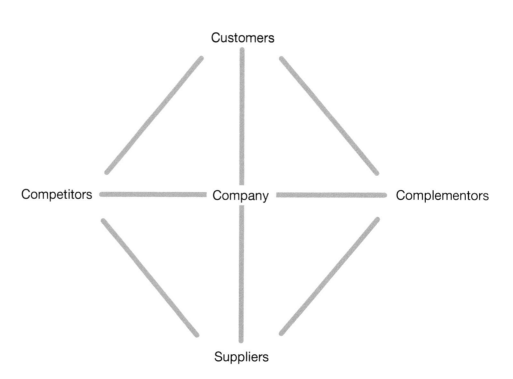

product alone. Alternatively, identify them as a competitor if customers value your product less when they have the other player's product than when they have your product alone. One complementor for GM would be any company providing auto loans. Most customers cannot afford to pay cash for a new car. Thus, more GM cars are sold when there are more firms involved in automobile financing. Similarly, FedEx and UPS are complementors for Land's End catalog. The ability to ship product quickly and reliably increases catalog sales, so they are complementors. Of course, novel software that is available to run on computers will increase PC sales.

An important insight from the value net model is that the same player might be a competitor in some interactions but a complementor in others. Let's illustrate this through a few simple relationships. Delta and American are fierce competitors in the airline business. Do Delta and American ever act as complementors? The answer is *yes*. Consider who the suppliers to Delta and American are. Both airlines buy many planes from Boeing, but they also have the option of buying from Airbus. In order for Boeing to make money on a new plane, they need many orders. If only Delta orders the new 787, Boeing's costs must all be passed on to Delta. Alternatively, if American also places an order for the 787, then Boeing can amortize its fixed costs of product development over a greater number of sales, which results in the ability to lower the price for both airlines. Boeing also will benefit from greater production scale economies, and some of the benefits of these economies will likely be passed on to buyers like Delta and American in the form of lower prices. Consequently, in trying to persuade travelers to fly on their airlines, Delta and American are competitors, but in dealing with one of their key suppliers, Delta and American are complementors.

This insight leads us to four observations about competitors and complementors.

- A firm is your *competitor* if customers value your product *less* when they have the other firm's product than when they have your product alone (e.g., Delta and American).

- A firm is your *complementor* if customers value your product *more* when they have the other firm's product than when they have your product alone (e.g., Delta and American Express).

- A firm is your *competitor* if it's *less* attractive for a supplier to provide resources to you when it's also supplying the other firm than when it's supplying you alone (e.g., Micron and Apple bidding for flash memory from Lexar when Lexar has capacity constraints).

- A firm is your *complementor* if it's *more* attractive for a supplier to provide resources to you when it's also supplying the other firm than when it's supplying you alone (e.g., Delta and American).

The opportunity to use this insight to create value, then, is to avoid the bias of looking at other players in your industry strictly from a competitive mindset; hunt for opportunities to cooperate as complementors as well. As the value net framework suggests, turning parties who compete with you for profits into partners who help you create value increases the size of the economic pie available in the industry.

A Shift in the Focus of Strategic Thinking

Several of the revolutionary strategies just reviewed suggest a shift in focus from conventional head-to-head rivalry to a different strategic mindset. Some of the fundamental differences in assumptions between viewing strategy as head-to-head competition and thinking instead about creating new markets through revolutionary strategies are summarized in Exhibit 8. Whereas the traditional view emphasizes actions and capabilities that are determined by competitors' moves, new-market creation emphasizes *actions and capabilities that eclipse the competition rather than meet it head-on* [yellow tail]®, the company discussed in the box entitled "How Would *You* Do That? 6.1," provides a nice example of such a strategy in dynamic contexts.

Exhibit 8 Creation of New Markets through Revolutionary Strategies

Dimensions of Competition	Head-to-Head Competition	New-Market Creation
Industry	Emphasizes rivalry	Emphasizes substitutes across industries
Strategic group and industry segments	Emphasizes competitive position within group and segments	Looks across groups and segments
Buyers	Emphasizes better buyer service	Emphasizes redefinition of the buyer and buyer's preferences
Product and service offerings	Emphasizes product or service value and offerings within industry definition	Emphasizes complementary products and services within and across industries and segments
Business model	Emphasizes efficient operation of the model	Emphasizes rethinking of the industry business model
Time	Emphasizes adaptation and capabilities that support competitive retaliation	Emphasizes strategic intent— seeking to shape the external environment over time

First Movers, Second Movers, and Fast Followers

First- versus second-mover categories are related to the principles of competitive interaction. In this chapter, we focus on the relative magnitude of the firm's actions. Specifically, here we are talking about the introduction of a new product or service that defines or redefines a new market segment as opposed to actions taken within a preexisting market segment. In particular, we need to know how each approach to technological discontinuities depends on a firm's resources and capabilities. The principle of dynamic strategy suggests that firms consider the relative strength of their resources and capabilities when they determine whether to lead or to respond to change.

first mover The firm that is first to offer a new product or service in a market.

second mover (often *fast follower*) Second significant company to move into a market, quickly following the first mover.

First movers are firms that choose to initiate a strategic action. This action may be the introduction of a new product or service or the development of a new process that improves quality, lowers price, or both. Consequently, you may see firms pursuing either differentiation or low-cost strategies here. **Second movers** are simply firms that aren't first movers, but their actions are important nonetheless.[17] A second mover, for instance, may simply imitate a first mover—that is, those aspects of its new product, service, or strategy that meet its needs—or it may introduce its own innovation.[18]

FIRST-MOVER STRATEGY AND THE INDUSTRY LIFE CYCLE

Being a second mover doesn't necessarily mean that a firm is a *late* mover; in fact, many effective second movers can legitimately be characterized as *fast followers*—even if the elapsed time between first and second moves is several years. Why isn't the lag necessarily detrimental? For one, new products don't always catch on right away. They may eventually generate rapid growth and huge sales increases, but this period—widely known as the takeoff period—starts, *on average*, at some point within six years of the new-product introduction.[19] Although the industry life cycle suggests that the drivers of industry demand evolve over time, it doesn't predict how *quickly* they'll evolve. Indeed, it may take some new products a decade or more to reach the growth stage, and only then will they attract competitors.

By the same token, of course, *habitually* late movers will eventually fall by the wayside. Typically, survivors are either first movers or relatively fast followers. Late movers usually survive only if they're protected by government regulation, monopolistic or oligopolistic industry positions, or extensive cash reserves. Increasingly, however, competitive advantage results from the ability to manage change and harness the resources and capabilities consistent with first- or second-mover strategies.

takeoff period Period during which a new product generates rapid growth and huge sales increases.

THE PROS AND CONS OF FIRST-MOVER POSITIONING

Intuitively, we tend to think of first movers as having a distinct advantage: After all, many races are won by the first contestant out of the starting blocks. The history of the Internet offers a wealth of first-mover success stories. The market dominance of Amazon.com, for instance, reflects a first-mover advantage—namely, the firm's ability to charge higher prices for books. According to a recent study, a 1-percent price increase reduced Amazon.com sales by 0.5 percent; at BarnesandNoble.com, however, the same price hike cut sales by a relatively whopping 4 percent.[20]

However, if you take a close look at Exhibit 9, you'll see that first-movers don't always attain dominant positions.[21] For instance, you are probably familiar with the Microsoft XBox, the Palm Pilot PDA, and the Boeing 747, but did you know that the first electronic games, PDA, and commercial jets were released by Atari, Apple (the Newton in 1993), and deHaviland, respectively? In some cases, a first-mover strategy can even be a liability, and in many others, the first mover isn't necessarily in a position to exploit the advantages of being first.

A first-mover advantage is valuable only under certain conditions:

- A firm achieves an absolute cost advantage in terms of scale or scope.

- A firm's image and reputation advantages are hard to imitate at a later date.

- First-time customers are locked into a firm's products or services because of preferences or design characteristics.

- The scale of a firm's first move makes imitation unlikely.[22]

First movers also bear significant risks, including the costs not only of designing, producing, and distributing new products, but of educating customers about them. Let's say, for example, that you're a midsized consumer products company with a promising new product. When you stop to consider the immense power wielded by a certain member of your distribution channel—say, Wal-Mart—you'll recall how dependent you are on one giant retailer to help you attract a market large enough to make your product profitable. Meanwhile, certain second movers (say, Unilever or Procter & Gamble) may take the time to evaluate your new product and decide to compete with it only when it's developed some traction in the market (at some point during the takeoff period). Sometimes, a patient (and sufficiently powerful) second mover simply acquires the first mover; sometimes, a second mover introduces a similar product, perhaps of higher quality or with added features.

In short, first-mover advantages diminish—and fast-follower advantages increase—under a variety of conditions, including the following:

- Rapid technological advances enable a second mover to leapfrog a first mover's new product or service.

189

Exhibit 9   A Gallery of First Movers and Fast Followers

Product	Pioneer(s)	Imitators/Fast Followers	Comments
Automated teller machines (ATMs)	DeLaRue (1967) Docutel (1969)	Diebold (1971) IBM (1973) NCR (1974)	The first movers were small entrepreneurial upstarts that faced two types of competitors: (1) larger firms with experience selling to banks and (2) the computer giants. The first movers did not survive.
Ballpoint pens	Reynolds (1945) Eversharp (1946)	Parker (1954) Bic (1960)	The pioneers disappeared when the fad first ended in the late 1940s. Parker entered 8 years later. Bic entered last and sold pens as cheap disposables.
Commercial jets	deHaviland (1952)	Boeing (1958) Douglas (1958)	The pioneer rushed to market with a jet that crashed frequently. Boeing and Douglas (later known as McDonnel-Douglas) followed with safer, larger, and more powerful jets unsullied by tragic crashes.
Credit cards	Diners Club (1950)	Visa/Mastercard (1966) American Express (1968)	The first mover was undercapitalized in a business in which money is the key resource. American Express entered last with funds and name recognition from its traveler's check business.
Diet soda	Kirsch's No-Cal (1952) Royal Crown's Diet Rite Cola (1962)	Pepsi's Patio Cola (1963) Coke's Tab (1964) Diet Pepsi (1964) Diet Coke (1982)	The first mover could not match the distribution advantages of Coke and Pepsi. Nor did it have the money or marketing expertise needed for massive promotional campaigns.
Light beer	Rheingold's & Gablinger's (1968) Meister Brau Lite (1967)	Miller Lite (1975) Natural Light (1977) Coors Light (1978) Bud Light (1982)	The first movers entered 9 years before Miller and 16 years before Budweiser, but financial problems drove both out of business. Marketing and distribution determined the outcome. Costly legal battles, again requiring access to capital, were commonplace.
PC operating systems	CP/M (1974)	Microsoft DOS (1981) Microsoft Windows (1985)	The first mover set the early industry standard but did not upgrade for the IBM PC. Microsoft bought an imitative upgrade and became the new standard. Windows entered later and borrowed heavily from predecessors (and competitor Apple), then emerged as the leading interface.
Video games	Magnavox's Odyssey (1972) Atari's Pong (1972)	Nintendo (1985) Sega (1989) Microsoft (1998)	The market went from boom to bust to boom. The bust occurred when home computers seemed likely to make video games obsolete. Kids lost interest when games lacked challenge. Price competition ruled. Nintendo rekindled interest with better games and restored market order with managed competition. Microsoft entered with its Xbox when they perceived gaming to be a possible component of its wired world.

- The first mover's product or service strikes a positive chord but is flawed.

- The first mover lacks a key complement, such as channel access, that a fast follower possesses.

- The first mover's costs outweigh the benefits of its first-mover position. (Fast followers, for example, can often enter markets more cheaply because they don't face the initial costs incurred by the first mover.)

Status of Complementary Assets

Exhibit 10 First-Mover Dependencies

	Freely available or unimportant	Tightly held and important
Weak protection from imitation	It is difficult for anyone to make money: Industry incumbents may simply give new product or service away as part of its larger bundle of offerings	Value-creation opportunities favor the holder of complementary assets, who will probably pursue a fast-follower strategy
Strong protection from imitation	First mover can do well depending on the execution of its strategy	Value will go either to first mover or to party with the most bargaining power

Bases of First Mover Advantages

FIRST MOVERS AND COMPLEMENTARY ASSETS

An additional framework for assessing whether a firm should pursue a first-mover or fast-follower strategy incorporates the factor of *complementary assets*. Exhibit 10, for example, provides a framework that explains why a number of notable first movers fared poorly despite apparently advantageous positions one would expect them to extract by virtue of being a first mover.[23] What's the moral of the lessons collected in Exhibit 10? Basically, they remind us that any firm contemplating a first-mover strategy should consider the inimitability of its new product, the switching costs holding together current customer relationships, and the strength of its complementary assets. It should, for example, consider its distribution channels as important complementary assets. Industry key success factors are also complementary assets, as is access to capital.

Let's say, for instance, that a firm makes a critical breakthrough in cancer therapy. Before putting any product on the market, it will need to conduct a decade's worth of animal and clinical trials, and if it doesn't have hundreds of millions of dollars in the bank, it won't be able to pay for such extensive preliminary testing. New PC-software applications often depend on Microsoft because its operating system and bundled software constitute a whole set of complements—a product, a channel, and a potential competitor. As you can see from the illustrations in Exhibit 9, in the context of the framework summarized in Exhibit 10, first-movers tend to succeed if their initial advantages are unique and defensible *and* if they're in a position to exploit the complementary assets needed to bring a new product to market.

Defensive Strategies for Incumbents Caught Off-Guard

Incumbents, such as Anheuser Busch, deserve special attention because they are increasingly viewed as Goliaths in the many David-and-Goliath competitive interactions unfolding around the world. In the mid-1990s, the front pages of the business press were littered with stories decrying the demise of the brick-and-mortar business and the rise of e-commerce and the dot-com. Inasmuch as most firms currently occupied real estate rather than cyberspace, the trend—or at least warnings about its repercussions—threatened most of them with extinction. Some, of course, did disappear, but most did not. As a matter of fact, the Internet phenomenon—and especially the breakneck speed with which it became a regular feature of the cultural landscape—underscored a number of strategies that incumbents can adopt to respond to rapid changes in the environment of an industry. As usual, the success of these strategies depends on a given firm's strengths and weaknesses. They are, however, particularly attractive to incumbent firms because they depend on—and can even reinforce—a firm's basic strengths. Each seeks a resource-based competitive advantage—that is, a position in which the exploitation of a resource makes that resource stronger and more resilient. Hopefully, the firm is organized per the VRINE framework to realize value from the stronger and more resilient resource.

Competitor-response strategies can be thought about in a number of different ways. Incumbent firms can respond to sources of industry dynamism through any of the following strategies: (1) containment, (2) neutralization, (3) shaping, (4) absorption, or (5) annulment. These responses typically vary in terms of the ease with which the external threat can be controlled and the corresponding level of action taken in response. We'll discuss and provide examples of each strategy in the following sections.

CONTAINMENT

The containment strategy works well when the firm has identified the threat at an early stage. (You may detect facets of this strategy in the bundling or process-innovation strategies encountered in the context of industry evolution.) Although firms sometimes select one of these strategies, they typically resort to a combination that aligns well with their particular resources and capabilities. American Airlines, for instance, can compete with Southwest not only by increasing the benefits of its frequent flier program but by using its bargaining power to secure more exclusive airport gates (thus effectively raising Southwest's distribution costs at airports where it used to share gates with American).

Similarly, a large consumer products company can release a copy-cat product that both leverages the new market created by a competitor and can be sold through its own existing channels. Consider, for example, the fact that retailers in industries from clothing to groceries typically charge *slotting fees*—fees that suppliers pay for access to retailers' shelf space. Because of this practice, any new product may bump an existing product from retail shelves, and if the one that gets bumped is a new entrant's only product, the containment strategy will have been highly effective.

NEUTRALIZATION

If containment does not work, then leaders will try to neutralize the threat. Incumbents who pursue a neutralization strategy aggressively often succeed in short-circuiting the moves of innovators or new entrants even *before* they make them—or at least in forcing them to seek out the incumbent as a partner or acquirer. Microsoft, for example, is so aggressive at adding free software features to its popular Windows platform that new software firms include partnership with Microsoft as part of their entry strategies.

A more common neutralization tactic, however, is the threat or use of legal action. For example, one reason for Napster's initial downfall was legal action taken by the recording industry. In fact, the Recording Industry Association of America (RIAA) launched such a fierce legal attack on Napster that it forced even smaller Napster-like firms to stay out of the fray.[24] The German media giant Bertelsmann AG later acquired the Napster name when it realized that the Internet upstart was trying to engage in a legitimate music-sharing business. (When Bertelsmann couldn't turn a profit in the music-sharing business, Roxio was later able to acquire Napster and its assets for only $5 million.) Meanwhile, the RIAA also attempted to neutralize the Napster model by setting up an industrywide sharing standard, but this initiative collapsed when the major record labels squabbled about intellectual property rights, technology, and pricing.

SHAPING

Sometimes, of course, it's simply not possible to contain or neutralize the growth of a new product, often due to antitrust laws. Moreover, in some cases, the new product may be attractive to the incumbent even if the incumbent can't gain full control of it. Today, for example, a state of peaceful coexistence prevails between the American Medical Association (AMA) and chiropractic medicine. For decades, however, the AMA characterized chiropractors as quacks. Eventually, the AMA used regulators and educators as part of a strategy to *shape* the evolution of chiropractic practice until chiropractics transformed itself into a complement to conventional healthcare, as defined by the AMA.

Large firms can also use funding to pursue shaping strategies. Intel, for example, maintains its Intel Capital unit as one of the world's largest corporate venture programs for investing in the technology segment. The concept is fairly simple: Each investment is aimed at helping businesses that, if successful, will need Intel products to grow. In many ways, then, Intel is not only creating future markets for its own products but discouraging demand for competing products and technology and co-opting potential future competitors at the same time.

ABSORPTION

The purpose of this strategy is to minimize the risks entailed by being either a first mover or an imitator. Sometimes, the approach is direct: The incumbent identifies and acquires the new entrant or establishes an alliance. In the late 1980s, for instance, Microsoft identified money-management software as a potentially attractive, high-growth market. It therefore entered into an agreement to acquire Intuit, the market leader, which offers such products as Quicken, QuickBooks, and TurboTax. However, antitrust action forced Microsoft to abandon the purchase, and it resorted to a containment strategy—namely, by developing its own product, Microsoft Money (although Intuit's Quicken still has an 80-percent market share). If it's difficult to acquire the new entrant, the incumbent may also try to leverage a buyout by taking control over industry suppliers or distribution channels.

ANNULMENT

Incumbents can annul the threat of new entrants by improving their own products. In many ways, for example, Kodak has so successfully improved the quality of film-based prints that they're superior to many digital-based alternatives. The annulment strategy, however, is less about quashing the competition than about making it irrelevant. Indeed, to excel at an annulment strategy a firm must often assume the role of first mover—a position that entails considerable risk. Kodak forestalled the advance of digital photography, but Kodak executives knew that in order to stay in the photo business, the company eventually had to shift to digital.[25] For this reason, firms usually resort to annulment only when the competition is otherwise unstoppable.

IBM provides another excellent example of a firm that annulled a competitive threat by sidestepping it.[26] In the early 1990s, IBM was faced with a flagging core business in PCs and minicomputers. Its first strategic shift catapulted IBM into second place behind Microsoft as a PC- and networking-software powerhouse. Its next move entrenched the company in the IT and Internet consulting markets, where it emerged as the largest firm among such competitors as Accenture. Next, IBM took on such companies as EDS to become the

193

market leader in outsourcing IT and service solutions. Throughout this transition process, IBM leveraged its resources, capabilities, and dynamic capabilities in services and software. In many ways, IBM, though ostensibly on the defensive, was also wielding the tools of offensive strategy, effectively combining improvisation and experimentation with deft staging and pacing. As a result of this complex strategy, IBM not only emerged as a leader in information technology but, at the same time, avoided the commoditization pressures that affected PC firms such as HP-Compaq. Most recently, it has completely exited its core PC manufacturing business by spinning off this part of its operations to China-based Lenovo.

THE PITFALLS OF THE RETALIATORY MINDSET

A word of warning about the five strategies covered in this section. Although they are certainly viable strategies for dynamic markets, many of the strategies are nonetheless purely defensive. If you rely on them exclusively, you'll soon stumble over an important pitfall of purely defensive strategizing: *Any firm that invests in resources and capabilities that support retaliation to the exclusion of innovation and change may only be prolonging its inevitable demise.*

Here's a good example. Ralston Purina was long considered one of the most efficient and competitively aggressive pet-food companies in the world. Every time a competitor made a move or a new entrant set foot in the market, Ralston responded with a twofold defensive strategy: undermining prices in the competitor's stronghold markets while simultaneously attacking its weaker markets. Although its defensive posture secured Ralston's market leadership for over 20 years, it also ensured that the company lagged behind the industry in terms of innovation. In 2003, Ralston sold out to Nestlé, whose constant attention to innovative products had positioned it to take over Ralston's slot as industry leader.

Taking an Option on Revolutionary Strategies Instead of retaliation, incumbent firms may strategically decide that waiting for uncertainty to clear is the best course of action. Rather than be an early mover in a new strategy, the firm might decide to make a small investment that will allow it to have an option on making a bolder move later. This type of investment is generally referred to as a **real option**. The idea behind real op-

For more than 20 years, Ralston Purina fiercely—and successfully—defended its position as top dog in the pet-food industry. Unfortunately, the company put so much energy into its defensive strategy that it had little left for innovation. Ralston sold out to Nestlé in 2003.

(Myrleen Ferguson Cate/PhotoEdit Inc.)

tions is to preserve flexibility so that the firm has an ability to be well-positioned in the future when the competitive environment shifts. A perfectly positioned firm can become ill-positioned as the industry evolves, as new competitors emerge, and as technology makes current core competencies obsolete. By making small investments that preserve the option of taking a new course of action in the future, a firm can maintain its advantage. As an example, Intel invests heavily in internal R&D; however, it determined that it was unlikely to be the source of most innovations that could change how processing technology is used. Consequently, Intel made a conscious decision to invest in startups. By being a partial owner of the startups, Intel would have inside information on many new technologies being developed elsewhere. Intel has no obligation to increase its investment in these operations or to buy the products or internalize these innovations. However, by making these small investments, it has the option of doing so in the future.

So, what are real options? Quite simply, a real option is *the opportunity (though by no means the obligation) to take action that will either maximize the upside or limit the downside of a capital investment.* Ironically, of course, the greater the uncertainty and flexibility in the project, the greater the potential value of having options in managing it. Increasingly, managers in industries characterized by large capital investments and high degrees of uncertainty and flexibility (such as oil and gas, mining, pharmaceuticals, and biotechnology) are beginning to think in terms of real options. These companies typically have plenty of the market and R&D data needed to make confident assumptions about uncertain outcomes. They also have the sort of engineering-oriented corporate culture that isn't averse to complex mathematical tools.

Although real-options analysis is not a cure-all for strategic uncertainty, the technique is getting much more attention not only in the fields of finance and strategic management but among other companies and industries as well. In addition to those industries cited earlier, the automotive, aerospace, consumer goods, industrial products, and high tech industries are also interested in real-options analysis. Intel, for example, now trains finance employees in real-options valuation and has used the technique to analyze a number of capital projects. As a starting point, we suggest that you introduce yourself to real options by considering the following five categories:[27]

- **Waiting-to-invest options.** The value of waiting to build a factory until better market information comes along may exceed the value of immediate expansion.

- **Growth options.** An entry investment may create opportunities to pursue valuable follow-up projects.

- **Flexibility options.** Serving markets on two continents by building two plants instead of one gives a firm the option of switching production from one plant to the other as conditions dictate.

- **Exit (or abandonment) options.** The option to walk away from a project in response to new information increases its value.

- **Learning options.** An initial investment may generate further information about a market opportunity and may help to determine whether the firm should add more capacity.

real-options Process of maximizing the upside or limiting the downside of an investment opportunity by uncovering and quantifying the options and discussion points embedded within it.

Formulating and Implementing Dynamic Strategies

In this final section we focus on the ways in which dynamic strategies should be reflected in your application of both the strategy diamond and the strategy implementation models.

The arenas and staging, in conjunction with the implementation levers, will be key decision areas as you move forward to put your strategy into place.

FOCUSING ON ARENAS AND STAGING

Let's look first at our model of strategy formulation, which is critical because it establishes a set of simple rules for describing the business and showing how it creates value. Of course, all five elements of strategy are important and must be managed in concert, but the *arenas* and *staging* diamonds are especially important. In addition to recognizing the need for dynamic capabilities, focusing on these facets of strategy is what differentiates a dynamic strategy from a strategy developed for more stable contexts.

 Arenas

The Role of Arenas

Arenas designate your choice of customers to be served and the products to be provided.◆ In each section of this chapter on dynamic strategy—sections dealing with industry and product evolution, technological discontinuity, and turbulence—we've tried to emphasize that the strategist is always making important and reasoned choices about the firm's mix of customers, noncustomers, products, and services. The remaining four diamonds of strategy—vehicles, differentiators, staging, and economic logic, will tell the strategist whether the mix of arenas is consistent with a *coherent* strategy.

Moreover, the role of arenas in the firm's strategy will vary according to the factor of the dynamic environment being considered. In the context of *industry evolution,* for example, arenas must fit with a firm's resources, capabilities, and dynamic capabilities. With regard to *technological discontinuities,* the role of arenas, though overlapping with its role in low-end disruption strategies, was broadened to include noncustomers, particularly when the strategy is designed to create new markets. *Globalization* adds yet another dimension to the role of arenas: If a firm is going global, managers need to apply what they have learned about competing in one geographic arena to the task of competing in others. Finally, in navigating *turbulent and hypercompetitive markets,* managers need to think of arenas as laboratories—sites in which to conduct experiments or launch probes into the possible future of the firm and its strategy.

 Staging & Pacing

The Role of Staging

Competing in turbulent environments requires finesse in addressing the staging element of the strategy diamond.◆ In many ways, strategies in this context require the regular deployment and testing of options—options with new growth initiatives, new businesses, and new ways of doing business. From the prior section you now have a sense of how you would evaluate these options, financially. In this section, we review the findings of recent research on how firms manage the staging of strategy in order to succeed in turbulent or hypercompetitive environments. Research on strategy in this particularly dynamic context is typically anchored in so-called *systems, chaos,* or *complexity theories.* They're peppered with such biological terms as *self-organizing systems* and *co-adaptation,* and they're concerned with the same phenomenon—adaptation to a changing external environment in which change may be rapid and its direction uncertain.[28] By and large, they all share a basic premise: Firms need some degree of ability to thrive in chaotic environments in order to survive. In one study of several firms competing on the edge of chaos, researchers encountered the following three levels of activity, summarized by the curves in Exhibit 11:[29]

- Activities designed to test today's competitive strategy (defending today's business)

- Activities designed to lead to tomorrow's competitive strategy (drive growth in emerging businesses)

- Activities designed to influence the pacing and timing of change (seeding options for future new businesses and growth initiatives)

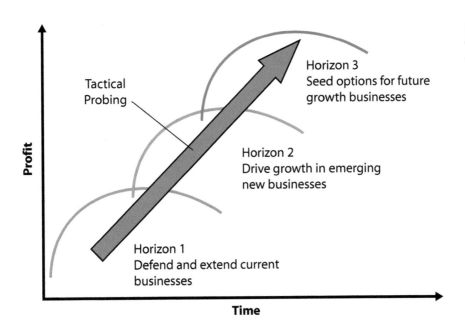

Exhibit 11 Creating Options for Future Competitive Advantage

The lower left-hand curve depicted in Exhibit 11 is the defense of existing businesses. The middle and upper right-hand curves represent activities focused on the future—the conditions toward which the change-oriented activities at the foundation of the strategy are aimed. At the same time, however, future products will embody indelible links to the past. In this model of business strategy, the bridge between past activities and future conditions is built on a substructure of experimentation and learning. For instance, S. C. Johnson found that one of its innovative home pesticide products in Europe could not pass U.S. regulatory hurdles, preventing its introduction in that country. However, through experimentation with its fragrances division, a key technology in the product was thought to be valuable and gave rise to the introduction of Glade PlugIns in 1993. S. C. Johnson effectively joined knowledge embedded in previously disconnected and geographically removed operating units (pesticides and fragrances divisions) to create an entirely new product category in the home air-freshener industry.

Successful new-business conditions are a reflection of those strategies that have been most successful. Ineffective strategies are jettisoned or marginalized as customers migrate toward firms with strategies that best meet their needs. Thus, managers use their understanding of the competitive environment to guide their selection and reconfiguration of portions of yesterday's business practices. Dell, for example, developed its direct-sales model for the consumer and small-business PC market, and when it entered the large-business computer-server market, it adapted its direct-sales model by providing on-site customer service. The model, however, had evolved: In this sector, while maintaining a very modest level of on-site staff for its largest corporate clients, most of Dell's consumer service is provided by a Web-based platform. With virtually a single stroke, Dell had changed the industry business model in a way that favored and further strengthened the model that had long been its fundamental source of competitive advantage. In other words, Dell's dynamic move forward into the server market was anchored in its past strengths in the PC market, and it has had a profound effect on the strategies of other firms as they've attempted to adapt to signals from the environment.

Tactical Probing A striking feature of this model of dynamic strategy is the close relationship between tactical moves and strategy evolution. A clear strategy enables the firm to excel in a given business, but it also gives rise to experimentation that leads to options on future businesses—horizons 2 and 3 in Exhibit 11. Often, we don't think of the operating decisions that we call tactics as *strategic* activities because, in and of themselves, they're fairly inconsequential in affecting cost or competitive impact. In dynamic markets, however, many tactical moves can be used as low-cost "probes" for experimentation—testing the current strategy and suggesting future changes.

Tactics, in other words, can be both tools for competing today and experiments in new ways of competing tomorrow. Consider the case of discount broker Charles Schwab. When the company found itself being squeezed on one side by deep-discount Internet startups such as E*Trade and discount initiatives by full-service brokers such as Merrill Lynch on the other, it experimented with new ways of reinforcing customer relationships and identifying new markets. In particular, Schwab developed futures-trading programs, simplified its mutual-fund offerings, and launched Internet-based products and services. Some of these probes, of course, went nowhere (Schwab aborted a line of credit cards and a foray into on-line mortgages). But those that did succeed enabled Schwab both to further differentiate itself from bare-bones discounters and to gain ground in markets dominated by full-service brokers.

Setting Pace and Rhythm Finally, as managers move from one horizon to another they must concern themselves with the speed and pace of change. You're already familiar with this aspect of strategy because you're familiar with the staging diamond of the five-elements strategy model. Many managers, however, fail to appreciate fully the role played by time and timing in formulating and executing strategy. Consider, for example, the various approaches to staging and pacing described in Exhibit 12.[30] Obviously, attention to pacing and staging can prompt a company to think more seriously about the need for constant experimentation and probing. The concluding example of 3M may partially explain why that firm is consistently able to generate new and innovative products.

Exhibit 12 Staging and Pacing in the Real World

British Airways	"Five years is the maximum that you can go without refreshing the brand. . . We did it [relaunched Club Europe Service] because we wanted to stay ahead so that we could continue to win customers."
Emerson Electric	"In each of the last three years we've introduced more than 100 major new products, which is about 70 percent above our pace of the early 1990s. We plan to maintain this rate and, overall, have targeted increasing new products to [equal] 35 percent of total sales."
Intel	The inventor of Moore's Law stated that the power of the computer chip would double every 18 months. IBM builds a new manufacturing facility every nine months. "We build factories two years in advance of needing them, before we have the products to run in them, and before we know the industry is going to grow."
Gillette	Forty percent of Gillette's sales every five years must come from entirely new products (prior to its acquisition by P&G). Gillette raises prices at a pace set to match price increases in a basket of market goods (which includes items such as a newspaper, a candy bar, and a can of soda). Gillette prices are never raised faster than the price of the market basket.
3M	Thirty percent of sales must come from products that are fewer than four years old.

The Role of Implementation Levers   In terms of strategy implementation, the previous discussion provides you with some perspective on the type of strategy that needs to be implemented. In applying any implementation framework, the elements of the model must be balanced—in this case, a dynamic strategy should be reflected in organizational structures, systems, and processes that accommodate the strategic needs of firms in turbulent and hypercompetitive environments. One element of strategy formulation—staging—can also serve to bridge formulation and implementation because the staging component can specify how certain levers will be employed along the way.

Finally, both the strategic leadership of senior management and the culture of the organization that they foster should reflect a commitment to reasoned risk taking, learning, and responding to change. Indeed, it's hard to promote core values that support the strategy implementation in dynamic contexts if top management doesn't practice and champion them.

Summary of Challenges

1. *Distinguish the ways in which firms' strategies are related to dynamic contexts.*   Dynamism can have dramatic effects on the quality of a firm's strategy and it can undermine competitive advantage—sometimes with blinding speed, but more typically over some extended period of time. Indeed, as noted in the opening vignette, although it may seem that the music industry has changed overnight, many of the seeds for that dramatic change were sown and nourished over an extended period of time. Technological discontinuities can alter the basis of competition and the requisite resources and capabilities for competitive advantage. The speed of change in an industry itself is a significant factor; it can either complement or compound the effects of industry evolution, technological discontinuities, and globalization.

2. *Identify, compare, and contrast the various routes to revolutionary strategies.*   Revolutionary strategies are ones that do not take the existing rules of competition in the industry for granted but rather attempt to create value by approaching competition by violating some of these taken-for-granted rules. Reconceiving products and services, either by creating a new value curve or by separate function and form, can result in new offerings with high value-added for customers. Firms can also reconfigure the value chain, either by developing a new value chain or by compressing the existing value chain. Value can be created by redefining the arenas, either through focusing on the total possible market, rather than current customers served, or by spearheading industry convergence. Opportunities to increase margins are also found in rescaling the industry, either by consolidating the industry in search of greater economies of scale, or by downscaling the industry in search of profitable niche markets. Finally, revolutionary strategies can be found in reconsidering the competitive mindset, both by focusing on complementors and by shifting the competitive focus away from head-to-head competition and searching for areas where the competition has not yet ventured.

3. *Evaluate the advantages and disadvantages of choosing a first-mover strategy.*   First movers are firms that initiate a strategic action before rivals, such as the introduction of a new product or service or a new process that provides a traditional product or service of dramatically higher quality or at a lower price, or both. Second movers are relatively early movers (because they are still not last-movers), but delayed enough to learn from first movers. Effective second movers are sometimes referred to as *fast followers*. They are distinguished from late movers, whose tardiness penalizes them when the market grows. First movers do not always have an advantage because there are significant risks associated with being the first to introduce new products, services, and business models.

4. *Recognize when an incumbent is caught off-guard by a revolutionary strategy and identify defensive tactics to reduce the effects of this competition.*   As hard as they try, incumbents are not always successful in being the firm to revolutionize an industry and are caught off-guard by other incumbents or new entrants. In such cases, firms can resort to defensive tactics such as containment, neutralization, shaping, absorption, or annulment. They can also attempt to avoid surprise by taking out options on new businesses and technologies early in their life cycle (such as through investments in startups) that will give them the opportunity to acquire the new business at a later time on favorable terms should it prove to be a revolutionary idea.

5. *Explain the difficulties and solutions to implementing revolutionary strategies.*   Vision is critical in that it serves as a set of simple rules that describe the business and how it creates value. Although all five elements of strategy are important and must be managed in concert, the arenas and staging diamonds are perhaps most important in dynamic markets. And, like the five elements of strategy, a balance among the implementation levers is critical.

These levers must accommodate environmental turbulence and hypercompetitive environments. The strategic flexibility demanded of these environments requires that organization structure and systems can be easily decoupled and recombined as circumstances change. Rigid bureaucracy is generally incompatible with turbulent environments. Strategic leadership must further support the firm's ability to identify the need for and undertake strategic change.

Review Questions

1. What are four sets of challenges to sustained competitive advantage outlined in this chapter?

2. What is the relationship between first and second movers?

3. What is industry commoditization? What are two strategies a firm may undertake to combat industry commoditization?

4. What is a new-market-creation strategy?

5. What is a low-end disruption strategy?

6. What are the three levels of activity that underlie strategies for turbulent and hypercompetitive markets?

7. What is the role of timing and pacing in revolutionary strategies?

8. What five defensive strategies might industry incumbents pursue in dynamic markets?

9. How might you apply real-options analysis, financially and conceptually, in the context of revolutionary strategies for turbulent and hypercompetitive markets?

10. What are the implications of dynamic strategies for strategy formulation and implementation?

Experiential Activities

Group Exercises

1. If you were the CEO of Napster (which started out as Roxio in the opening vignette), what material from this chapter would be most relevant to you? How would this material help you to formulate a strategy? What might key components of that strategy be? Now put yourself in Microsoft's shoes; would you see either Sonic Solutions or Napster as a threat? If so, what strategy would you formulate in response?

2. Review the list of first- and second-mover firms in Exhibit 9. What specific resources and capabilities do you think successful first movers must possess? What specific resources and capabilities do you think successful second movers and fast followers must possess? Do you think that a firm could be both a first mover and fast follower if it wanted to be?

Ethical Debates

1. Some firms manage disruptive strategy threats by investing in the firms that bring them to market, so that if the threat turns out to be wildly successful it can still benefit from it financially. Is this a purely business decision or are there ethical concerns as well?

2. You learned how incumbents can be blindsided by disruptive strategies. Litigation appears to be a prominent tool that incumbents can use to at least slow new entrants' growth. What might be some of your ethical concerns when using litigation to manage competition? Do you think that a firm's size will affect its ability to use this tactic? Does this matter?

How Would YOU DO THAT?

1. Pick an industry and use the box entitled "How Would *You* Do That? 1" as a template to map its value curve. What are the key success factors that define industry participation? Does there appear to be more than one strategic group in this industry operating with different value curves? Can you come up with a new value curve that would change the industry?

2. Identify a firm that you believe is pursuing a revolutionary strategy. How do its actions map onto the four-actions framework?

Go on to see How Would You Do That at www.prenhall.com/carpenter&sanders

Endnotes

1. N. Wingfield and E. Smith, "With the Web Shaking Up Music, a Free-for-All in Online Songs," *Wall Street Journal,* November 19, 2003, A1; N. Wingfield and E. Smith, "Microsoft Plans to Sell Music over the Web," *Wall Street Journal,* November 17, 2003, A1; www.roxio.com (accessed June 28, 2005). "Napster Lives Again as Legal Distributor of Music on the Web," *The Wall Street Journal,* 25 February 2003, A10; N. Wingfield, "Roxio Agrees to Acquire Napster Assets," *The Wall Street Journal,* November 18, 2002, B4.

"Napster Achieves Number One Market Share in On Demand Music Subscriptions With Over 830,000 Subscribers and Will Exceed Fourth Quarter Guidance," *PR Newswire,* April 3, 2007; "Napster Subscriptions in Decline," *PC Magazine Online,* August 3, 2006; Emmanuel Legrand, "Napster: the Final Shutdown," *Music & Media,* September 14, 2002 p1(2); Gavin O'Malley, "Subscription Survivor?" *Advertising Age,* September 4, 2006 p6; "Market Commentary on Napster Inc." *M2 Presswire,* April 3, 2007.

2. Adapted from K. G. Smith, W. J. Ferrier, and C. M. Grimm, "King of the Hill: Dethroning the Industry Leader," *Academy of Management Executive* 15:2 (2001), 59–70.

3. D. C. Hambrick and J. W. Fredrickson, "Are You Sure You Have a Strategy?" *Academy of Management Executive* 15:4 (2001), 48–59.

4. M. Chen, "Competitor Analysis and Interfirm Rivalry: Toward a Theoretical Integration," *Academy of Management Review* 21 (1996), 100–134; M. Chen and D. C. Hambrick, "Speed, Stealth, and Selective Attack: How Small Firms Differ from Large Firms in Competitive Behavior," *Academy of Management Journal* 38 (1995), 453–482.

5. A. M. Brandenburger and B. J. Nalebuff, *Co-Opetition* (New York: Currency Doubleday, 1996).

6. K. G. Smith, W. J. Ferrier, and C. M. Grimm, "King of the Hill: Dethroning the Industry Leader," *Academy of Management Executive* 15:2 (2001), 59–70.

7. K. Rangan and G. Bowman, "Beating the Commodity Magnet," *Industrial Marketing Management* 21 (1992), 215–224; P. Kotler, "Managing Products through Their Product Life Cycle," in *Marketing Management: Planning, Implementation, and Control,* 7th ed. (Upper Saddle River, NJ: Prentice Hall, 1991); P. Kotler, "Product Life-Cycle Marketing Strategies," in *Marketing Management,* 11th ed. (Upper Saddle River, NJ: Prentice Hall, 2003), 328–339.

8. P. Anderson and M. L. Tushman, "Technological Discontinuities and Dominant Designs: A Cyclical Model of Technological Change," *Administrative Science Quarterly* 35 (1990), 604–633.

9. G. A. Moore, "Darwin and the Demon: Innovating within Established Enterprises" *Harvard Business Review* 82:7/8 (2004), 86–92.

10. S. Brown and K. Eisenhardt, *Competing on the Edge* (Boston: Harvard Business School Press, 1998).

11. These examples are drawn from an extensive and detailed list provided by C. Christensen and M. Raynor, *The Innovator's Solution* (Boston: Harvard Business School Press, 2003).

12. Adapted from W. C. Kim and R. Mauborgne, "Blue Ocean Strategy," *California Management Review* 47:3 (2005), 105–121.

13. W. C. Kim and R. Mauborgne, "Value Innovation: The Strategic Logic of High Growth," *Harvard Business Review* 75:1 (1997), 102–113; Kim and Mauborgne, "Charting Your Company's Future," *Harvard Business Review* 80:6 (2002), 76–82.

14. W. C. Kim and R. Mauborgne, "Blue Ocean Strategy," *California Management Review* 47:3 (2005), 105–121; Wine Institute, "Strong Sales Growth in 2004 for California Wine as Shipments Reached New High," April 5, 2005 (accessed July 12, 2005), www.wineinstitute.org; www.elitewine.com/site/index.php?lang=en&cat=news&art=159 (accessed July 12, 2005).

15. Adapted from W. C. Kim and R. Mauborgne, "Blue Ocean Strategy," *California Management Review* 47:3 (2005), 105–121.

16. The concept of the value net is common among game theorists, but was popularized by A. Brandenburger & B. Nalebuff in *Coopetition: A revolutionary mindset that combines competition and cooperation* (New York: Currency Doubleday, 1997).

17. M. E. Porter, *Competitive Strategy* (New York: Free Press, 1979), 232–233.

18. For a particularly rich discussion of these differences, see S. Schnaars, *Managing Imitation Strategies* (New York: Free Press, 1994), 12–14.

19. G. Tellis, S. Stremersch, and E. Yin, "The International Takeoff of New Products: Economics, Culture, and Country Innovativeness," *Marketing Science* 22:2 (2003), 161–187.

20. A. Goolsbee and J. Chevalier, "Price Competition Online: Amazon versus Barnes and Noble," *Quantitative Marketing and Economics* 1:2 (June, 2003), 203–222.

21. Adapted from S. Schnaars, *Managing Imitation Strategies* (New York Free Press, 1994), 37–43.

22. Schnaars, *Managing Imitation Strategies,* 37–43; J. Covin, D. Slevin, and M. Heeley, "Pioneers and Followers: Competitive Tactics, Environment, and Growth," *Journal of Business Venturing* 15:2 (1999), 175–210.

23. This framework is adapted from A. Afuah, *Innovation Management: Strategies, Implementation, and Profits,* 2nd ed. (New York: Oxford University Press, 2003). An earlier version appears in Schnaars, *Managing Imitation Strategies,* 12–14.

24. www.riaa.org (accessed July 28, 2005).

25. www.kodak.com (accessed July 15, 2005).

26. R. D'Aveni, "The Empire Strikes Back: Counterrevolutionary Strategies for Industry Leaders," *Harvard Business Review* 80:11 (November 2002), 5–12.

27. M. Amram and N. Kulatilaka, *Real Options: Managing Strategic Investment in an Uncertain World* (New York: Oxford University Press, 1998); E. Teach, "Will Real Options Take Root? Why Companies Have Been Slow to Adopt the Valuation Technique," *CFO Magazine,* July 1, 2003, 73.

28. See, for example, S. Kauffman, *At Home in the Universe: The Search for the Laws of Self-Organization and Complexity* (New York: Oxford University Press, 1995); M. Gell-Mann, *The Quark and the Jaguar* (New York: W. H. Freeman, 1994); J. Casti, *Complexification: Explaining a Paradoxical World through the Science of Surprise* (New York: HarperCollins, 1994); R. Lewin, *Complexity: Life at the Edge of Chaos* (New York: Macmillan, 1992).

29. Examples drawn from S. Brown and K. Eisenhardt, *Competing on the Edge: Strategy as Structured Chaos* (Boston: Harvard Business School Press, 1998).

30. Brown and Eisenhardt, *Competing on the Edge.*

Developing Corporate Strategy

Developing Corporate Strategy

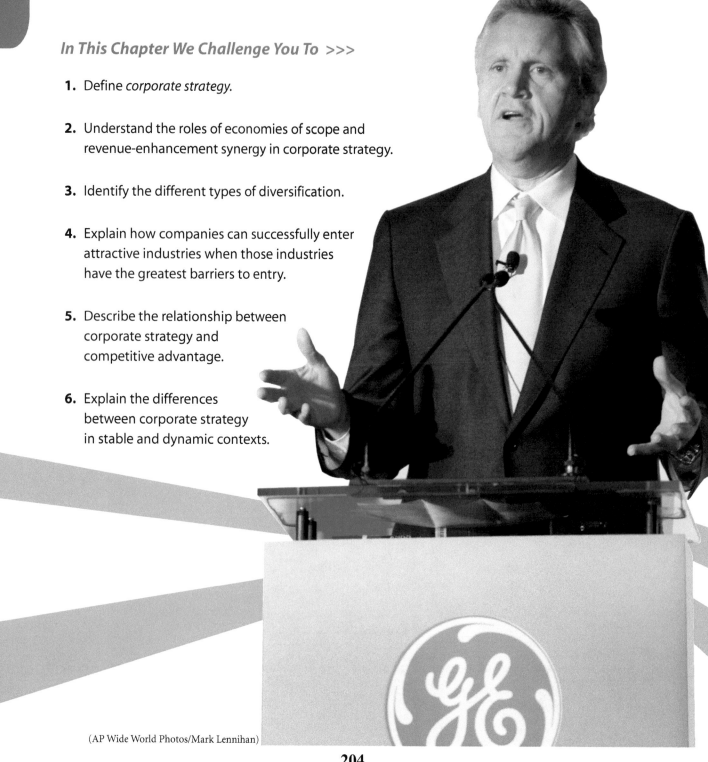

In This Chapter We Challenge You To >>>

1. Define *corporate strategy*.

2. Understand the roles of economies of scope and revenue-enhancement synergy in corporate strategy.

3. Identify the different types of diversification.

4. Explain how companies can successfully enter attractive industries when those industries have the greatest barriers to entry.

5. Describe the relationship between corporate strategy and competitive advantage.

6. Explain the differences between corporate strategy in stable and dynamic contexts.

(AP Wide World Photos/Mark Lennihan)

Diversification
at GE, 3M, *and*
MITY Enterprises

(Diane Austin/Prentice Hall)

*G*eneral Electric   General Electric (GE) was established in 1892 as a merger between two manufacturers of electrical equipment, Thomson-Houston Electric Co. and Edison General Electric Co. (of which Thomas Edison was one of the directors).[1] GE's early products included such Edison inventions as lightbulbs, elevators, motors, and toasters. In 1896, GE was among the 12 original companies to be included in the newly created Dow Jones Industrial Average, and it's the only one that's still on the list.

By 1980, GE was earning $25 billion in revenues from such diverse businesses as plastics, consumer electronics, nuclear reactors, and jet engines. By 2007, its revenues were an astounding $163 billion and its businesses spanned consumer and commercial finance, health care, industrial, infrastructure, and news and entertainment. GE CEO Jeffrey Immelt described the range of GE: "We're not a monolithic company," Immelt said. "We have a $17 billion healthcare business that competes in a $4 trillion industry that's growing 8 percent a year. I can grow that business 8 percent. I've got a consumer-finance business in a $40 trillion global market growing 10 percent a year." How did GE evolve from an electronics company to an enormous conglomeration of many businesses? Over the years, GE developed some of the businesses through its own research and development (R&D) efforts. However, many of its current operations are the result of acquisitions. Indeed, GE is one of the most frequent acquirers of other businesses in the world. Between January 2000 and December 2004, GE acquired more than 250 different companies and spent more than $78 billion to do so. Despite its diversity of operations, GE stays competitive by following a vision that its CEO John F. (Jack) Welch formulated in 1981. Welch announced that GE would participate only in high-performing businesses in which it could be the number-one or number-two competitor. This gave GE a vision for growth as well as disciplined criteria for adding or divesting business lines. GE divested itself of many of its businesses, including air conditioning, housewares, and semiconductors, but it remains one of the most diversified companies in the U.S., if not the world. Today, the company's products and services include aircraft engines, locomotives and other transportation equipment, appliances (kitchen and laundry equipment), lighting, electric distribution and electric control equipment, generators and turbines, nuclear reactors, medical imaging equipment, commercial insurance, consumer finance, and network television (NBC).

Describing his strategy for the future, Immelt said in 2007, "We continue to execute on our strategy to invest in leadership businesses. Our focus remains on building faster growth, higher margin businesses. Since the beginning of the year, we have announced $15 billion of acquisitions in fast growth platforms in oil and gas, healthcare, and aviation. We continue to exit slower growth and more volatile businesses, and we are currently reviewing the potential disposition of our plastics business." The company's success has earned it the respect of the business community. In 2007, GE was named the top company on *Fortune* magazine's "America's Most Admired Companies" list, making 2007 the seventh year of the last ten in which GE was voted number one.

3M Minnesota Mining and Manufacturing (3M)—perhaps best known for its Post-it Notes and Scotch tape products—was originally founded in 1902 to sell corundum (an extremely hard mineral that is used as an abrasive) to grinding-wheel manufacturers. Within a couple of years, the fledgling company was specializing in sandpaper, but it wasn't until the 1920s, when it began focusing on technological innovation, that 3M hit its stride. Two products—Scotch-brand masking tape (introduced in 1925) and Scotch-brand cellophane tape (1930)—became so successful that they virtually guaranteed the company a long and prosperous future. Today, 3M has six operating units—industrial and transportation; display and graphics; health care; safety, security, and protection; electro and communications products; and consumer and office products. With nearly $23 billion in annual revenues, the company makes thousands of products, ranging from asthma inhalers to Scotchgard™ fabric coatings.

Coupled with enormous R&D spending (over $1 billion per year), 3M's policy of allowing scientists to dedicate 10 percent of their working time to experimentation has yielded a number of highly profitable innovations. Of course, not all divisions and innovations have been equally successful, and the company has spun off some divisions, including low-profit imaging and data storage ventures. 3M closed its audiotape and videotape businesses and got out of billboard advertising.

3M has entered most of its businesses through internal innovation, but it recently increased its pace of acquisitions. Between January 2000 and December 2004, 3M completed only 10 acquisitions and spent only a little more than $500 million on these deals in total. But in 2006 alone, the company completed 19 acquisitions and spent $900 million on them. The acquisitions ranged from a German firm that makes personalized passports to a Brazilian company that provides earplugs, eyewear, and hand cream. Despite the recent acquisitions, CEO George Buckley sees growth through external acquisitions as secondary to growth through internal invention. "We'll build first where 3M is strong, defend and expand market presence, and build size and scale," Buckley said. "We will also grow through continuous invention and reinvention in our core businesses—the marketplace manifestations of 3M imagination and 3M innovation." Beyond growing the core business, Buckley will look for acquisitions that expand 3M into adjacent markets. "Acquisitions will help us enter adjacent markets and build business in new spaces more quickly," Buckley said. 3M's healthy mix of businesses cushions the company from disruptions in any single market. "The unique nature of 3M's business model lends power unseen elsewhere," Buckley said. "At 3M, we have some real magic."

MITY Enterprises In contrast to corporate giants GE and 3M, MITY Enterprises is a small $55 million company founded just 20 years ago. MITY's first product was a lightweight, durable folding-leg table. Since then, the company has diversified into other product lines, including chairs and other low-cost furniture. The company looks for acquisitions, but for a company MITY's size, acquisition targets are not easy to find. Instead, MITY focuses on internal growth through innovation. "We believe that new product development will continue to propel our growth," said MITY CEO Bradley Nielson. "With that in mind, we are working on new chair lines, staging, dance floors, new healthcare chairs, and additional fencing and accessories."

Not all new product introductions work out. As Nielson said in 2006, "When we entered the year, we were just coming off a failed next-generation table experiment that was diluting our earnings base. However, rather than spending time licking our wounds, we quickly shifted gears and began executing a new plan." The new plan included taking the failed technology from the failed table experiment and applying it to a new area: fences. Like MITY's furniture, the fence panels are durable. "The panels are impact resistant, won't bow or sag in the sun, need no sanding, painting, or other kinds of maintenance, [and] are faster and easier to install than concrete or stone," Nielson said. The new product line is doing well, and MITY will continue developing innovative products. "Our growth is not dependent on making an acquisition," Nielson said. "We can do just fine going without."

As can be seen from these brief descriptions, many firms operate in more than one business. Some firms, like GE, participate in an incredible number of seemingly unrelated business operations. Others, like 3M, have grown into many businesses. Still others, like MITY Enterprises, are smaller companies, but they, too, seem to grow to a point where they venture out of their original businesses to experiment in other product lines. In this chapter, we will introduce you to the basic concepts necessary to understand and manage corporate strategy, including the diversification of firms. <<<

Corporate Strategy

Why would a firm that makes lightbulbs also make elevators? If you're in the table business, does it make sense to be in the chair business, too? If your core business activities result in innovative new products, should you retain ownership of these products and the units responsible for them, or does it make more sense to sell them? Questions such as these are fundamental to corporate strategy.

Corporate strategy must address issues related to decisions about entering or exiting an industry. Specifically, effective corporate strategies must answer three interrelated questions:

- In which business *arenas* should our company compete?

- How can we, as a corporate parent, add value to our various lines of business?

- How will diversification or our entry into a new industry help us compete in our other businesses?

At the same time, however, corporate strategy also deals with issues affecting the overall management of a multibusiness enterprise, such as top-level efforts to orchestrate synergies across business units. **Synergy** occurs when the combined benefits of a firm's activities in two or more arenas are more than the simple sum of those benefits alone. After all, corporate-level strategy must maintain strategic coherence across business units and facilitate cooperation (or competition) among units in order to create value for shareholders. Thus, although fundamentally related to each other through the common goal of achieving competitive advantage, business strategy and corporate strategy have different objectives.

Most large and publicly traded firms are amalgamations of business units operating in multiple product, service, and geographic markets (often globally); they are rarely single-business operations. Obviously, companies approach corporate strategy in different ways, and as you can see from Exhibit 1, corporate portfolios can be built in a number of different ways. Although MITY Enterprises has diversified into new products, they're all related to the institutional furniture market niche. At the other end of the spectrum, GE not only makes everything from lightbulbs to locomotives, but offers financial services for virtually any business or consumer need. In between is 3M. This company's business units, though highly diversified, reflect common core competencies—the unique resources and knowledge that a company's management must consider when developing strategy—in innovation and adhesive technology.[2]

Recall that we introduced the important fact that most firms are multiproduct organizations in our earlier discussions of industry analysis, value chains, and market segmentation. That's why we're now going to discuss in some detail the ways in which managers can create (and squander) value through **diversification**. In this chapter, we'll focus on six key aspects of corporate strategy as it affects diversification decisions:

1. We'll review our understanding of corporate strategy and define *diversification*, and show how both concepts have changed over time.

2. We'll identify the potential sources of economic gain that make diversification attractive.

3. We'll describe alternative forms of diversification.

4. We'll present a rationale, or logic, for guiding corporate decisions about adding businesses.

5. We'll revisit the relationship between corporate strategy and competitive advantage.

6. We'll amplify our discussion of the roles of corporate strategy in dynamic contexts.

We will build our discussion around many of the elements of the strategy diamond. This framework is useful because it allows you to choose those elements of strategy formulation and implementation that are essential to developing a firm's corporate strategy under specific conditions. ◆ As was made apparent in the chapter's opening vignette, a firm's corporate strategy usually evolves over time. All three of our firms in the vignette have entered and/or exited business arenas. They have used the various major vehicles of strategy to facilitate these changes. The economic logic of diversification often incorporates such levers to achieve synergy and transfer

synergy Condition under which the combined benefits of activities in two or more arenas are greater than the simple sum of those benefits.

diversification Degree to which a firm conducts business in more than one arena.

 Economic Logic

Exhibit 1 Diversification Profiles

GE Product Scope

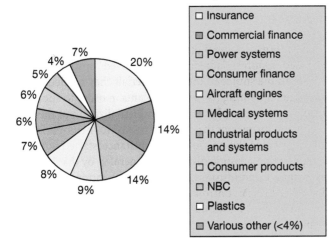

- 20%
- 14%
- 14%
- 9%
- 8%
- 7%
- 6%
- 6%
- 5%
- 4%
- 7%

□ Insurance
■ Commercial finance
□ Power systems
□ Consumer finance
□ Aircraft engines
■ Medical systems
□ Industrial products and systems
□ Consumer products
□ NBC
□ Plastics
□ Various other (<4%)

GE Geographic Scope

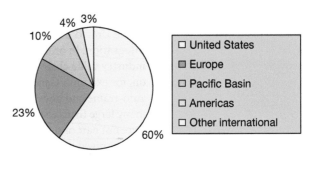

- 60%
- 23%
- 10%
- 4%
- 3%

□ United States
■ Europe
□ Pacific Basin
□ Americas
□ Other international

3M Product Scope

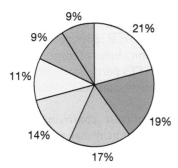

- 21%
- 19%
- 17%
- 14%
- 11%
- 9%
- 9%

□ Health care
■ Industrial
□ Display and graphics
□ Consumer and office
□ Safety and protection
□ Electrical and communications
□ Transportation

3M Geographic Scope

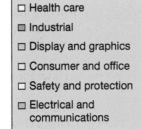

- 40%
- 26%
- 25%
- 9%

□ United States
■ Asia/Pacific
□ Europe and Middle East
□ Latin America, Africa, and Canada

MITY Enterprises Product Scope

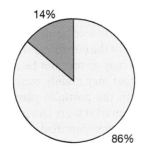

- 14%
- 86%

□ Multipurpose room furniture
■ Healthcare seating

MITY Enterprises Geographic Scope

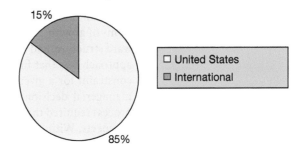

- 15%
- 85%

□ United States
■ International

knowledge between business units. The timing and pacing of such moves must be orchestrated in ways that do not negate the possible benefits of diversification.

THE EVOLUTION OF DIVERSIFICATION IN THE UNITED STATES

vertical integration
Diversification into upstream and/or downstream industries.

In the United States, the first form of organizational diversification was probably **vertical integration**. In order to secure needed resources, large firms often moved "upstream" in the industry value chain—that is, closer to the source of the raw materials they needed.[3] Early on, for example, General Motors began operating its own steel plants in order to supply its auto-frame and body factories. During the early phases of the industrialization of the U.S., many large firms also began investing in businesses that, though related to their operations, were not part of their original industry value chains. DuPont, for instance, started out making gunpowder and eventually applied the scientific discoveries generated by that business to enter new businesses, such as dynamite and nitroglycerin (1880), guncotton (1892), and smokeless powder (1894). Ultimately, DuPont controlled most of the U.S. explosives market. The company then diversified into paints, plastics, and dyes until antitrust action forced it to divest some of its explosive powder business.

In the late nineteenth century, the booming U.S. economy fostered a period of rapid consolidation. The Sherman Act of 1890 introduced federal antitrust law and led to the eventual breakup of many large monopolistic companies. In 1891, for instance, the courts ordered Rockefeller's Standard Oil to split into six separate companies. Similar rulings broke up other companies deemed to be anticompetitive.

By the 1960s, many large firms began expanding into areas unrelated to their core businesses, because this type of growth was generally exempt from antitrust restrictions. Unrelated diversification became a corporate strategy of choice, and soon a breed of corporations emerged that was characterized by curious mixes of operations. ITT's portfolio managed to accommodate telephones, donuts, hotels, and insurance. For a brief history of the diversification of ITT over time, see Exhibit 2.

conglomerate Corporation consisting of many companies in different businesses or industries.

Although it addressed certain problems entailed by antitrust constraints, the **conglomerate** model raised new issues of its own. How could a company manage a portfolio of far-flung enterprises? The need to address such questions fostered experiments in new management tools and models. One of the most popular of these tools was **portfolio planning**. Without knowing it, you are probably already familiar with the conglomerate version of portfolio planning (see Exhibit 3).

portfolio planning Practice of mapping diversified businesses or products based on their relative strengths and market attractiveness.

Portfolio planning was initially intended to help managers evaluate the diversified firm and achieve a balanced portfolio of large, stable businesses and high growth ones, such that resources could be channeled to fuel growth. Its basic purpose was to guide resource allocation among businesses, help make choices that achieve a balanced portfolio (in terms of growth, cash generation, cash needs, and so on), set performance hurdles and reward structure, and set business unit strategy. A key assumption of the portfolio planning approach was that firms were capital constrained—while this may or may not be a real constraint for a given firm, it is a pretty strong assumption that may unduly constrain managerial decision making. Regardless, the starting point in the portfolio planning process required the firm to analyze businesses in terms of their market share and growth prospects. With one variation of this tool, for instance, a company identified all of its businesses that were "dogs"—those businesses in which it didn't have a strong competitive position, typically based on low relative market share, and that were located in bad industries (i.e., mature or low-growth industries). Such businesses were then earmarked to be sold. Businesses that had very strong competitive positions but were in slow-growth industries were referred to as "cash cows." Portfolio planning dictated that cash cows should be maintained because the cash flow could be channeled into promising high-growth businesses ("stars").

Exhibit 2 A Brief History and Genealogy of a Conglomerate

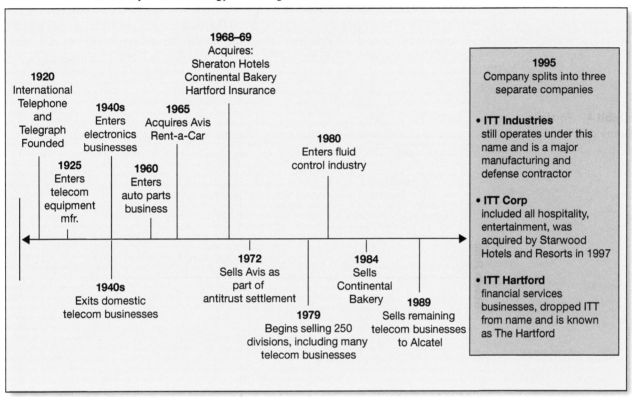

1920
International
Telephone
and
Telegraph
Founded

1925
Enters
telecom
equipment
mfr.

1940s
Enters
electronics
businesses

1960
Enters
auto parts
business

1965
Acquires Avis
Rent-a-Car

1968–69
Acquires:
Sheraton Hotels
Continental Bakery
Hartford Insurance

1980
Enters fluid
control industry

1940s
Exits domestic
telecom businesses

1972
Sells Avis as
part of
antitrust settlement

1979
Begins selling 250
divisions, including many
telecom businesses

1984
Sells
Continental
Bakery

1989
Sells remaining
telecom businesses
to Alcatel

1995
Company splits into three
separate companies

• **ITT Industries**
still operates under this
name and is a major
manufacturing and
defense contractor

• **ITT Corp**
included all hospitality,
entertainment, was
acquired by Starwood
Hotels and Resorts in 1997

• **ITT Hartford**
financial services
businesses, dropped ITT
from name and is known
as The Hartford

Business Unit Competitve Position or Market Share

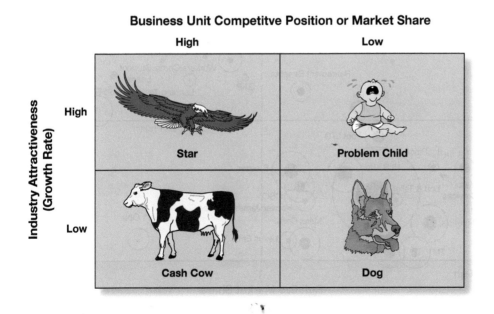

Exhibit 3 A Portfolio
Planning Lens on
Diversification

Exhibit 4 shows the portfolio models for MITY, along with one for a highly diversified financial services company in 2007. In simple matrices, like that for MITY, you can use the size of the circle to represent the market share of that business in a particular industry. More elaborate versions of the matrix involve plotting out the size and profitability of each business. For instance, with the diversified financial services firm in Exhibit 4, the size of the in-

Exhibit 4 Portfolio Planning at Two Firms

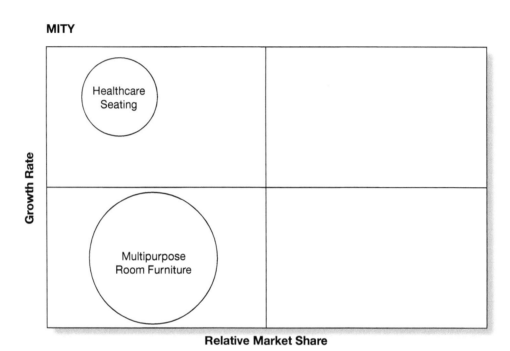

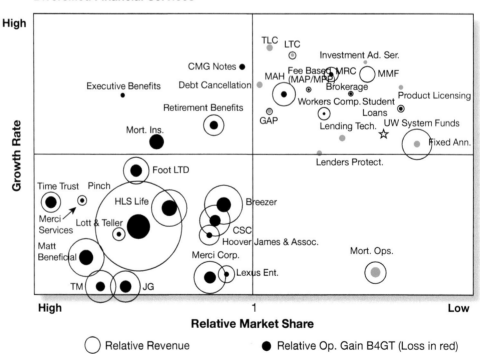

ner circle tells you the relative amount of revenue that business generates for the firm, while the color inside indicates whether or not it is profitable.

Several aspects of the more simplistic aspects of the portfolio planning approach have been debunked. The most basic reason is that it provides no fundamental competitive logic for which businesses should be entered and which should be maintained. Moreover, the sources of synergies among businesses—beyond the generation and usage of cash—are not recognized. Nor is there any accounting for the VRINE-based resources and capabilities that allow a firm to be successful in one business, but perhaps not another. Overly simplistic tools like this lead to questionable diversification moves such as a telecommunication company entering the hotel industry simply because the growth opportunities are attractive. Sears, for instance, used the model early in its history to diversify into growth industries like credit cards (Discovery), stock brokerage (Dean Witter), real estate brokerage (Coldwell-Banker), and insurance (Allstate). While Sears looked at these moves as logical, and aimed to develop a one-stop shopping strategy around what it perceived to be a mature retail business (Sears Department stores), these moves also led it to stop investing in the core retail business. Unfortunately for Sears, upstart Wal-Mart viewed retailing as a growth industry, and changed the rules of competition so dramatically in retailing that it almost put Sears out of business, and did lead to the demise of many retailers such as Kmart and others. Ironically, Wal-Mart is pursuing a similar one-stop shopping strategy (it has added groceries and is trying to enter the consumer banking industry), but Wal-Mart is still aggressively investing in its core retail business and making sure that it builds strong synergies among its portfolio of owned and partner businesses.

Despite the problems with the portfolio planning model, as demonstrated by Sears application of it, modified versions of the portfolio planning tool have been developed to help managers analyze the performance of single-industry and diversified companies as well as help them isolate performance problems. For instance, by plotting out businesses, managers can visually critique why and where there are or should be synergies between different business units, and identify those that might no longer fit the larger economic logic of the firm's corporate strategy. Similarly, managers can integrate what they know about product or industry life cycles with the portfolio visualization tool. As you can see in Exhibit 5, again using the example from the same diversified financial services firm portrayed in Exhibit 4,

Exhibit 5 A Portfolio Model that Accounts for the Life Cycle of Products

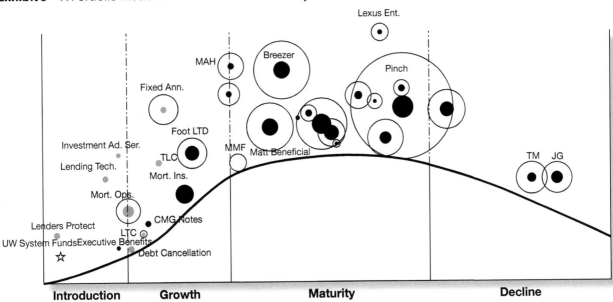

213

most of the firm's business activity is in relatively mature markets. This visual accounting of the businesses helped to motivate managers to invest more heavily in new product and service development. Beyond this modification, the portfolio management tool still helps managers communicate and align business unit managers' incentives and growth objectives. At a very basic level, particularly in firms with many business units, it provides a useful way to communicate and evaluate business unit strategies, and then relate them to corporate goals and objectives in changing environments. Since strategy is ultimately about making tradeoffs—what will the firm do and what won't it do—the portfolio approach clearly and visibly shows managers what the firm is doing, and what tradeoffs they are and are not making. We will introduce you to other portfolio models—ones that plot out industry characteristics or look at the intersection of industry characteristics and VRINE characteristics—that further incorporate aspects of dynamic strategy later in the chapter. You will have the opportunity to work with these portfolio-based tools in How Would *You* Do That? 1 and 2.

Shareholder dissatisfaction, especially on the part of institutional investors, coupled with the threat of hostile takeover opportunities, put pressure on conglomerates to reorganize in more manageable forms. Unwieldy portfolios of unrelated business units began to give way to more focused portfolios of related operations.[4] This move toward a more focused corporation can be seen in the more recent years of ITT, as illustrated in Exhibit 2.

Business history is littered with stories of failed growth and diversification strategies. The lesson taught by such cases is pretty clear: In and of itself, diversification not only doesn't necessarily create shareholder value but may in fact dissipate it. However, as we'll see later in the chapter, the logic behind *certain types* of diversification remains compelling. Indeed, substantial empirical evidence indicates that some forms of diversification can create significant shareholder wealth. Which types or forms of diversification are these? In the next part of the chapter, we'll identify and discuss the conditions necessary for value creation and the tools that can be used to increase its likelihood.

Economic Logic of Diversification: Synergy

Expanding the firm's scope—whether the addition of new vertical, horizontal, complementary, or geographic arenas—doesn't necessarily create value for shareholders. Strategists need to understand the sources of potential value creation from diversification, and they need to know how to determine whether a firm can leverage those sources. That's why we're going to turn to two concepts that are critical in evaluating opportunities for diversification and value creation: *economies of scope* and *revenue-enhancement*. Collectively, these are often referred to as *synergy*. However, they are two different economic logics for the possible profits from diversification. ◆

Economic Logic

ECONOMY-OF-SCOPE SYNERGIES

economy of scope Condition under which lower total average costs result from sharing resources to produce more than one product or service.

Economies of scope are one of the two key factors in determining whether a corporate strategy is adding value through the diversification of its business portfolio.

Recall that economies of scope are reductions in average costs that result from producing two or more products jointly instead of producing them separately. The concept of economies of scope can be represented by the following formula:

$$\text{Average costs } (X, Y) < \text{Average costs } (X) + \text{Average costs } (Y)$$

Economies of scope are possible when the company can leverage a resource or value chain activity across more than one product, service, or geographic arena. Although we focus on productive resources for the sake of presentation, you should recognize that economies of scope are possible in all value-chain activities, not simply production. For instance, comarketing of two products within one company may be less costly than marketing them separately in two companies (it may also help increase revenue-enhancement synergies, but we'll discuss that point later). For instance, it may have been less costly to market and distribute Sobe drinks within PepsiCo than it was to market it as a stand-alone product before PepsiCo purchased Sobe.

Sources of Economy-of-Scope Synergies   What tactics result in economies of scope? Economy-of-scope savings generally result when a firm uses common resources across business units. Or to put it another way: Whenever a common resource can be used across more than one business unit, the company has the *potential* to generate economies of scope. If, for instance, the cost of material that's common to two or more products is lower when purchased in greater quantity, then jointly producing two products may increase purchase volume and, therefore, cut costs. The ability to join the procurement function in this case and buy materials jointly creates an economy of scope.

Likewise, a manufacturing facility that achieves minimum efficient scale for one product may have excess capacity that it can put to use in producing other products. In this case, the total cost for both products will be lower because the cost of the common facility can be spread across two businesses. Sometimes the common resource is located farther down the firm's value chain. For instance, if a firm distributes products through a system with access to a large customer base, it may be able to add products to that system more cheaply than competitors launching similar new products that may need to create dedicated distribution networks from scratch. Coke and Pepsi enjoy such economies of scope in the markets for soft drinks, noncarbonated beverages, and bottled water.

REVENUE-ENHANCEMENT SYNERGIES

Another manifestation of synergy is revenue enhancement. **Revenue-enhancement synergy** exists when total sales are greater if two products are sold and distributed within one company than when they are owned by separate companies. Put another way, while economies of scope relate to cutting costs, revenue-enhancement synergies relate to growing revenues. In short, it's the difference between synergies that allow you to make more money by saving on expenses and those that allow you to grow the business! This can be represented by the following formula:

$$\text{Total revenues } (X, Y) > \text{Total revenues } (X) + \text{Total revenues } (Y)$$

Simply put, if two business units X and Y are able to generate more revenue because they're collectively owned by a single corporate parent than if they are in separate companies, the strategy of common ownership is synergistic.

Sources of Revenue-Enhancement Synergies   Revenue-enhancement synergy may result from a variety of tactics, such as bundling products that were previously sold separately, sharing complementary knowledge in the interest of new-product innovation, or increasing shared distribution opportunities.

Consider how Disney leverages its various resources to create revenue-enhancement synergies. The result of its web of collaborative activities is a consistent stream of new revenue sources that demonstrate a direct line between creativity in product design and financial acumen.[5] At the same time, Disney's collaborative context doesn't specify the forms that synergies must take; it merely reflects the principle that they should be profitable for all of the units involved. Two movies, for example, *The Little Mermaid* and *The Lion King,* became television shows. Another, *Toy Story,* was rolled out as a video game. Both *The Lion King* and another movie, *Beauty and the Beast,* became smash-hit Broadway musicals. The managers

revenue-enhancement synergy   When total sales are greater if two products are sold and distributed within one company than when they are owned by separate companies.

of Disney Tokyo share best practices with managers at Disney World in Orlando and Euro Disney outside Paris. Big Red Boat, a cruise line that specializes in Caribbean vacations, and Disney World, which offers vacation packages in Orlando on Florida's east coast, collaborate to build traffic in both venues. Characters from one animated series make cameos in others, and all shows are circulated through Disney's lineup of cable- and network-television channels, which include all or part of ABC, ESPN, A&E, E! Entertainment, and The History Channel. The voices of both live-action and animated characters circulate through Radio Disney.

Revenue-enhancement synergies generally arise from bundling and joint-selling opportunities. In recent years, for example, firms in the financial services industry have been actively acquiring or merging with firms in adjacent sectors in order to bundle products for current customers in different sectors.

A more specific example is found in the opening vignette. Founded in Orem, Utah, in 1987, MITY Enterprises originally made folding tables targeted at such institutional users as schools and churches. A decade later, when the company found itself with excess capacity in its Orem plant, managers began thinking about growth options. Because MITY's technology could be used to manufacture chairs and other types of furniture as well as tables, the company decided to expand into complementary products. MITY thus achieved synergy in two ways:

- Because expansion didn't require a new plant, the cost of the existing facility was spread across the various operations needed for different products.

- Because its manufacturing and distribution operations were geared toward multiple products, MITY's customers were more likely to buy more than one of its products, thus generating incremental sales that the firm could not otherwise have gained.

Similarly, firms in various sectors of the financial services industry have been actively acquiring and merging with firms in adjacent sectors in order to be able to bundle related products and cross-sell to existing customers.

ECONOMIC BENEFITS OF DIVERSIFICATION

Because mutual gains may be derived from either cost savings or revenue-enhancement synergies, a corporation that maintains ownership over multiple business units may have an advantage over competing businesses that are owned and managed separately. A company achieves this so-called "parenting advantage" when the joint cash flows of two or more collectively owned business units exceed the sum of the cash flows that they would generate independently.

When their collective market value exceeds the independent market values of a portfolio of business units, the financial markets will typically recognize the existence of a parenting advantage. Of course, the market doesn't compare business units by assigning both collective and independent value. Investors, however, can make reasonable estimates of a business unit's potential independent value. How? By using the market multiples (e.g., price earnings ratios or other similar multiples) of independent competitors in the industry within which its business units compete to compare the parent corporation's market value with the combined hypothetical values of its business units.

How and When to Seek Synergy
Two processes can generate synergy: sharing resources and transferring capabilities. We've discussed resource sharing extensively in our discussion of economies of scope. Transferring capabilities is actually a special case of resource sharing that can create both cost savings and revenue enhancement. Yum! Brands, for instance, can transfer knowledge about site location, franchise development, and internationalization from one restaurant brand to another. Black & Decker can share knowledge about small electric motors across its power tool and kitchen appliance units. Honda transfers knowledge gained about high-performance engines from its Formula 1 racing activities

216

not only to its automobile division, but also to units that produce motorcycles and lawncare and recreational equipment.

LIMITS OF DIVERSIFICATION BENEFITS

Remember, however, that neither economies of scope nor revenue enhancement materialize simply because firms expand into new lines of business. In other words, it's not *necessarily* cheaper to produce two products jointly in a single firm than separately in distinct firms. Indeed, in many cases, diversification creates **diseconomies of scope**—average cost increases resulting from the joint output of two or more products within a single firm.

diseconomies of scope
Condition under which the joint output of two or more products within a single firm results in increased average costs.

The critical question is *when economies of scope are likely to materialize.* Often, firms that can't demonstrate that diversification has generated economies of scope or revenue-enhancement synergies are forced to divest themselves of some units. During the 1990s, AT&T attempted to reap synergies across such businesses as long-distance telephone services, wireless cell phone service, and cable TV. However, it was never able to generate the cross-selling and synergistic outcomes it projected. Thus, in 2002 the company made the decision to split the company apart; some divisions were split off as separate companies, others were sold to competitors. The restructuring at AT&T reflects a failed diversification strategy; the sale of the surviving long-distance company to SBC Communications further testifies that AT&T's forays into new industries did not create the value and shareholder enthusiasm its leaders had hoped for. Ironically, SBC Communications changed their name to AT&T after acquiring the company. But, names can be deceiving; it is the shareholders and managers of SBC Communications that now own and manage the assets of the original AT&T long distance company. Of course, such divestitures are not always the result of failed diversification. Sometimes, a firm is quite successful but because of a change in strategy decides to divest itself of some successful businesses.

As the AT&T example illustrates, it often turns out that the collective value of a firm's portfolio is less than the total hypothetical value of the same businesses operated independently. In this case, the strategy of common ownership dissipates potential shareholder value. When investors—and corporate raiders, in particular—suspect the prospect of a significant diversification discount (i.e., the profits to be gained from buying the parent firm and selling off its portfolio piecemeal), a firm becomes a prime candidate for takeover and forced restructuring. Many investors have made huge profits by gaining control of an overly diversified company and selling various parts to firms in related areas—firms that are often willing to pay premium prices for operations related to their own.

Two things increase a firm's level of diversification: the number of separate businesses it operates and the degree of relatedness of those businesses. Relatedness is typically assessed by how similar the underlying industries are. The most diversified firms are those that own lots of businesses in very disparate industries; this is known as **unrelated diversification**. Firms that own many businesses clustered in a few industries are pursuing what is known as **related diversification**. Both forms of diversification can create management problems.

unrelated diversification
Form of diversification in which the business units that a firm operates are highly dissimilar.

related diversification Form of diversification in which the business units operated by a firm are highly related.

The harmful side effects of too much diversification include increased transaction and bureaucratic costs and burgeoning complexity. As firms become larger and multidivisional, corporate office functions tend to grow rapidly. If not held in check, these bureaucratic costs may exceed the benefits of diversification. Likewise, diverse firms may fall victim to doing too much internally and underutilize outside suppliers. Often the transaction costs of sourcing externally are sufficiently lower than the costs of organizing this activity internally. Finally, diversification increases firm complexity. For instance, the organization of a firm with ten businesses that span five industries is inherently more complex than a firm of the same size that operates only in one or a few industries. Complex firms are more difficult to manage than simple, focused firms. Research shows, for example, that diversified firms pay significantly higher compensation to attract and retain top management personnel than more focused firms of similar size.[6] Why? Because there are fewer top executives who are capable of managing complex firms. Bureaucratic costs, transaction costs, and complexity can all impede management's designs to create synergies.

If diversified firms are more difficult to manage—that is, if it's demonstrably harder to realize the benefits of diversification—then it stands to reason that there are real limits to those benefits. Indeed, research indicates that there's a point at which both the benefits of diversification and firm performance begin to decline. Exhibit 6 illustrates the relationship between diversification and two measures of firm performance—*return on assets* (ROA) and *total shareholder returns* (TSR).

In analyzing the data for the S&P 500 and S&P midcap firms over an eight-year period, we find that the relationship between diversification and performance takes the form of an inverted U (∩). At the median level of diversification, performance is much higher than at low levels of diversification (25th percentile) or high levels of diversification (75th percentile). These findings tell us that, on average, although diversification seems to benefit shareholders up to a point, it begins to dissipate value at high levels of diversification. Moderate values are typically achieved by firms which, like 3M, are active in several businesses that are somewhat related to each other.

When examining the relationship between diversification and performance reviewed in Exhibit 6, it is important to understand that there are exceptions to these averages. Some highly diversified firms perform quite well. For instance, GE is very diversified and over the long-term has performed very well, much better than most firms diversified at that level (and even single business firms). High levels of diversification, such as the conglomerate firm, can be very effective strategies in countries with developing capital markets. When capital markets are not as efficient as they are in developed countries, diversified firms can internally generate lower costs of capital than they can obtain in capital markets. Consequently, it can be efficient for firms to diversify and own more businesses than would be efficient in countries such as the United States, the United Kingdom, or Germany.

RESOURCE RELATEDNESS AND STRATEGIC SIMILARITY

To create economies of scope and revenue-enhancement synergies, a firm's resources should match its business activities. For this reason, whether they're thinking about en-

Exhibit 6

Diversification and Performance in S&P 500 and S&P Midcap Firms

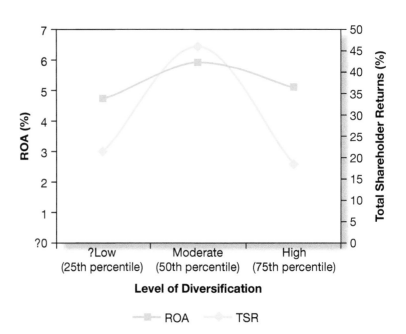

tering a new business arena or evaluating the suitability of a firm's portfolio for a proposed diversification move, strategists must assess the extent to which a firm's resources and capabilities match the needs of potential subsidiaries. One way to assess this match is in terms of how related the businesses are. When unrelated diversification is taken to the extreme—when there are many businesses and they are largely unrelated—firms are referred to as *conglomerates*. When there's a good match between the resource needs of parent and subsidiary—when diversification is related—it's more likely to create value. It's not critical, however, that both parent and subsidiary possess the *same* set of resources and capabilities. Indeed, in seeking to diversify, many firms are trying to acquire and bundle complementary resources and capabilities. The key issue is whether the match or fit between resources will help the parties compete more effectively.

Strategic Similarity   Parent firms and their subsidiaries need to assess their fit on more than just the resources it takes to compete. In determining fit, we want to know if the strategies required to compete in the various businesses of the firm are similar. A firm's strategy affects the way in which managers view the firm's competitive activities and make critical resource allocation decisions. In general, it is easier to manage a firm that does not require dissimilar strategies across business units. For instance, the jobs of the top executives at 3M and GE are significantly more complex than at MITY Enterprises—and this would be the case even if MITY were as large as these other firms.

If the strategies of its businesses are similar, a firm's managers can respond more quickly and effectively to strategic issues. Conversely, when strategies differ significantly, managers will generally be slower and less decisive. Decision-making delays can be hazardous, especially in high-speed industries such as cell phones and computer peripherals; perhaps more important, dissimilarity in dominant logic increases the likelihood that when managers finally do make decisions they'll make bad ones.

Not surprisingly, the strategic characteristics of businesses in a diversified portfolio may vary widely. Two businesses, for instance, may depend on very different technologies, industry competitive structures, and customer-buying routines. Strategic dissimilarity, therefore, can make it much more difficult to manage the portfolio. The more similar the contexts across which its businesses compete, the easier it is to manage a firm's portfolio and to create value through economies of scope and revenue-enhancement synergy.

The maximum opportunities to exploit potential economies of scope and revenue enhancement synergies lie at the intersection of two dimensions: (1) the fit among parent–subsidiary resources and (2) the fit of parent–subsidiary strategies. Conversely, the least promising opportunity for creating synergies occurs when there's a misfit on both of these same dimensions. When there's a misfit, managers need to make organizational adjustments. Later in this chapter, we'll present two models that can help determine these adjustments.

ULTERIOR MOTIVES FOR DIVERSIFICATION

In addition to reducing costs and increasing revenue-enhancement opportunities, managers may have self-serving motives for diversification—motives that aren't necessarily in shareholders' best interests. Among these, we'll mention three: *risk reduction, empire building*, and *compensation.*

At first glance, risk reduction would seem to be a natural reason for diversifying. In fact, it's probably the reason cited most often by students who haven't yet been formally introduced to the pros and cons of corporate diversification. Why isn't the strategy of reducing risk by diversifying generally in shareholders' best interests? Because it's much cheaper for the shareholders themselves to diversify in other ways. They can, for example, diversify equity risk by building a diversified stock portfolio—a strategy that, compared to the cost of diversifying a corporate portfolio, is fairly inexpensive.

When executives embark on growth and diversification because they desire to manage a larger company, they are said to be engaging in empire building. Rarely will empire building result in shareholder value or higher margins. However, empire building almost always results in greater notoriety and prestige for top executives. Although some executives may pursue empire building simply because of hubris, there are opportunistic reasons why they would do so as well. This simple reason is that executives of larger companies are paid more than executives of smaller companies. The main determinant of how much CEOs are paid is company size. Therefore, growing and diversifying the company generally results in executives being paid more.

Types of Diversification

A firm that wants to expand the scope of its operations has several options. In this section, we'll show how a company can expand its arenas, the three dimensions of *vertical*, *horizontal*, and *geographic*.

VERTICAL SCOPE

vertical scope The extent to which a firm is vertically integrated.

Sometimes a firm expands its **vertical scope** out of economic necessity. Perhaps it must protect its supply of a critical input, or perhaps firms in the industry that supply certain inputs are reluctant to invest sufficiently to satisfy the unique or heavy needs of a single buyer. Beyond such reasons as these—which are defensive—firms expand vertically to take advantage of growth opportunities. Vertical expansion in scope is often a logical growth option because a company is familiar with the arena that it's entering.

In some cases, a firm can create value by moving into suppliers' or buyers' value chains if it can bundle complementary products. If, for instance, you were to buy a new home, you'd go through a series of steps in making your purchase decision. Now, most homebuilders concentrate on a fairly narrow aspect of the homebuilding value chain. Some, however, have found it profitable to expand vertically into the home financing business by

Homebuilders like Pulte and D. R. Horton have found a way to create value by moving down the home-buyer's value chain. Both companies now offer mortgage services, a complementor to the home building industry, making it easier for customers to buy their homes. Pulte and D. R. Horton benefit as well because they earn the revenues associated with mortgage financing.
(Corbis Digital Stock/Royalty-Free/Corbis)

220

offering mortgage brokerage services. Pulte Homes Inc., one of the largest homebuilders in the country, set up a wholly-owned subsidiary, Pulte Mortgage LLC, to help buyers get financing for new homes. This service not only simplifies the home buying process for many of Pulte's customers, but it also allows Pulte to reap profits in the home financing industry. Automakers and dealers have expanded into financing for similar reasons.

The Pitfalls of Increased Vertical Scope   Although a firm's business segments lie adjacent along an industry's value chain, the structural features of the industries of these business segments (e.g., the industry five forces and complementors) may be fundamentally different. Thus, even though an adjacent segment is profitable, it doesn't follow that it's a good area for a firm to enter. Perhaps, for example, the firm doesn't have the resources needed to compete against established firms. Similarly, incumbents may enjoy significant cost advantages in performing the activities of their segment. Finally, the unwritten rules of competition in a segment, as well as the nature of strategic interactions, may be fundamentally different from those in a firm's base industry. A company should conduct thorough internal, industry, and competitor analyses before moving vertically into an adjacent segment of its industry value chain.

HORIZONTAL SCOPE

A firm increases its **horizontal scope** in one of two ways:

- By moving from an industry market segment into another, related segment; or

- By moving from one industry into another (unlike vertical-scope expansion, the movement here is into other industries not in the firm's existing value chain of activities).

horizontal scope   Extent to which firm participates in related market segments or industries outside its existing value-chain activities.

The degree to which horizontal expansion is desirable depends on the degree to which the new industry is related to a firm's home industry. Industries can be related in a number of different ways. They may, for example, rely on similar types of human capital, engage in similar value-chain activities, or share customers with similar needs. Obviously, the more such factors that are present, the greater the degree of relatedness. When, for example, Coke and Pepsi expanded into the bottled water business, they were able to take advantage of the skill sets that they'd already developed in bottling and distribution. Moreover, because bottled water and soft drinks are substitutes for one another, both appeal to customers with similar demands.

However, when Pepsi expanded into snack foods, it was clearly moving into a business with a lesser degree of relatedness. Although the distribution channels for both businesses are similar (both sell products through grocery stores, convenience stores, delis, and so forth), the technology for producing their products are fundamentally different. In addition, although the two industries sell complementary products—they're often sold at the same time to the same customers—they aren't substitutes.

Cost Savings and Revenue Enhancement Opportunities   Why is increased horizontal scope attractive? Primarily because it offers opportunities in two areas:

- The firm can reduce costs by exploiting possible economies of scope.

- The firm can increase revenues through synergies.

Because segments in closely related industries often use similar assets and resources, a firm can frequently achieve cost savings by sharing them among businesses in different segments. The fast food industry, for instance, has many segments—burgers, fried chicken, tacos, pizza, and so on. YUM! Brands Inc., which operates KFC, Pizza Hut, Taco Bell, A&W Restaurants, and Long John Silvers, has embarked on what the company calls a "multibrand" store strategy. Rather than house all of its fast food restaurants in separate outlets, YUM! achieves economies of scope across its portfolio by bundling two outlets in a single facility. The strategy works, in part, because customer purchase decisions in horizontally related industries are often made simultaneously: In other words, two people walking into a bundled fast food outlet may desire different things to eat, but both want fast food, and both are going to eat at the same time. In addition, some of these combinations allow two food services that cater to purchases with different peak hours to share physical resources that would otherwise be largely unused during off-peak hours.

Profit Pools One tool managers can use to evaluate adjacent market opportunities (whether vertical, horizontal, or complementary) is the **profit pool**. Beginning with a modified version of the firm and industry value chain, the profit pool can help you incorporate key complementary businesses near the point at which a firm is directly involved in customer transactions. The profit pool helps identify the size of value-chain segments (according to total sales) and the attractiveness of each segment (according to segment-by-segment profitability). Exhibit 7 illustrates the application of this tool to the auto industry in Europe and the global music industry.[7] Specifically, notice that sales volume for a segment is indicated visually by its width, while its profitability is shown by its height. As a map of the industry value chain, it reveals the breadth and depth of its alternative profit pools—each of the points along an industry's value chain at which total profits can be calculated.[8] The Western European profit pool is estimated to be approximately $62 billion, based on $885 billion in total revenues. In contrast, Exhibit 7 shows the United States' music industry profit pool to be about $10 billion, based on total industry revenues of $46 billion.

Some profit pools, of course, will be deeper (i.e., more profitable) than others. Moreover, depth may vary within a given value-chain segment. In the manufacturing segment of the PC industry, for instance, Dell enjoys much higher profit margins than Gateway. Segment profitability may also vary widely by product and customer group. Note that profit pools aren't stagnant; like industries in general, they change over time. Finally, and perhaps most importantly, the profit pool reminds us that *profit* concentration in an industry rarely occurs in the same place as *revenue* concentration.

Thinking in terms of profit pools also highlights a basic managerial mistake that's often made when developing corporate strategy. Firms often pursue strategies that focus on growth and market share on the assumption that profits automatically follow growth and size. *Profitable* growth, however, requires a clear understanding of an industry's profit pool. A profit-pool map, for example, will reveal the segments in which money is actually being made in an industry. More importantly, it may show where profits *could* be made. Consider, for instance, the consumer truck-rental business, in which U-Haul, Ryder, Hertz-Penske, and Budget are fierce competitors.[9] U-Haul, though the first entrant and largest player, faced significant disadvantages in the 1990s. Because its fleet was older, its maintenance expenses were considerably higher than those of competitors with newer fleets. U-Haul also charged lower prices than competitors. Lower revenues, coupled with higher expenses, generally result in lower margins. Indeed, U-Haul was barely breaking even on truck rentals. At the same time, however, U-Haul actually outperformed all of its competitors. Why? U-Haul beat its competitors because it went beyond its core business of truck rentals. It seized opportunities in complementary businesses that were relatively untapped, such as moving and storage accessories. By selling boxes, trailers, temporary storage space, tape, and other packing materials that truck renters needed, U-Haul squeezed out 10-percent operating margins in an industry in which the average was less than 3 percent. In How Would *You* Do That? 1, we walk you through the steps necessary to calculate the profit pool for a given industry.

profit pool Analytical tool that enables managers to calculate profits at various points along an industry value chain.

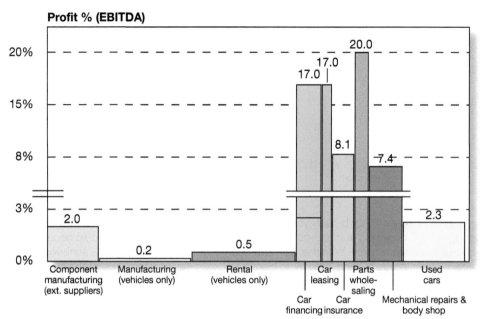

Exhibit 7a The European Auto Industry's Profit Pool

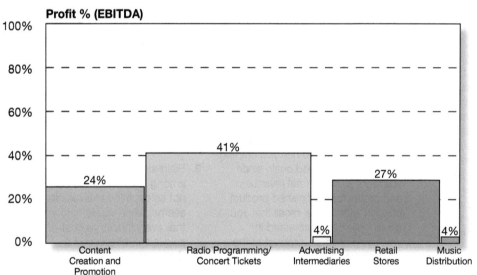

Exhibit 7b Global Music Industry's Profit Pool

GEOGRAPHIC SCOPE

A firm typically increases **geographic scope** by moving into new geographic arenas without altering its business model. In its early growth period, for instance, a company may simply move into new locations in the same country. More often, however, increased geographic scope has come to mean *internationalization*—entering new markets in other parts of the world.

For a domestic firm whose operations are confined to its home country, the whole globe consists of potential arenas for expansion. Remember, however, that just as different industries can exhibit different degrees of relatedness, so, too, can different geographic markets, even those within the same industry. We can assess relatedness among different national

geographic scope Breadth and diversity of geographic arenas in which a firm operates.

Six Steps to a Profit Pool

The profit pool tool is an easy tool to understand. It also gives you a ready means for thinking about the boundaries of your focal industry where profits come from in a particular industry (or arena, in strategy diamond terms). Your profit pool analysis essentially follows six steps:

1. Define the profit pool in terms of its boundaries and the value-chain activities that are relevant to profit creation now and in the future. Think about the coffee industry, for example. For coffee, what are the key value chain inputs? You could go back as far as the farmers who grow the coffee beans, and even to specific coffee growing geographic arenas or arenas related to the variety or quality of coffee bean. Assuming that coffee growers are one end of the spectrum in this first step, you then want to identify the other end of the spectrum. So for coffee, does your interest in the industry stop at the coffee wholesalers (who sell bulk coffee to institutional and retail buyers), or do you move to institutional and retail buyers like Sysco Foods or Procter & Gamble, respectively, or all the way to consumer coffee purveyors like Starbucks or Dunkin Donuts, which sell ready-to-drink coffee products? Since you are already getting a good sense of what we mean by value chain activities in a given pool, you can see how those activities might vary by how narrowly or broadly you define the beginning and end-points of the value chain. With this start and end-points in hand, now try to identify some of the intermediate value chain activities. Sticking with coffee, coffee-bean selection and roasting are important value chain activities in the larger coffee profit pool value chain since they determine the ultimate character of the final product.

2. Estimate the size of the profit pool. The size of the profit pool is the cumulative profits of all profit-pool activities for a given arena. One easy starting pointing in this step is to get figures on the total revenues and profits for all players in a given arena—this analysis has you starting at the top of the food chain since you want to know total revenues and profits for the finished product (though with coffee, recall that you could have been interested in wholesale product, product at the institutional or retail level, or the ultimate business to consumer level like a Starbucks coffee shop). In general, it is a good idea to think more broadly than narrowly about the scope of an industries value chain because, as in the case of coffee, if you stopped at wholesaling you would be missing pretty big pieces like institutional and retail sales, and ultimately the arena occupied by players like Starbucks (wouldn't you like to have been the person who imagined that the coffee profit pool could become what Starbucks has achieved? 0). Taking Starbucks, or the business-to-consumer coffee arena as your profit pool, then in this step you would want to estimate the total sales and profitability of all players in this pool. While these data are hard to come by, market research companies like Mintel (often available through your library) can help you estimate market size and profitability, though typically on a country or regional basis. Investment bank reports, SEC documents, and data bases like Compustat will provide profitability and other data at a business unit level.

3. Estimate how profits are distributed among value chain activities. This is not as daunting of a task as it seems, when you remind yourself that every industry's cost-of-goods sold is the reflection of a downstream industry's total revenues and a determinant of that downstream industry's profitability. So where Step 2 has you aggregate revenues and profits for your focal profit pool, Step 3 has you disaggregate revenues and profits among the key value chain activities supporting the target profit pool. Keep in mind that this analysis is at an industry level so, in the case of the ready-to-drink coffee-consumer business, you would still want to

include coffee wholesalers, retailers, and roasters in your analysis (i.e., estimating their industry sales and profitability) even though you know that Starbucks has gone around them, roasts its own coffee, and works directly with coffee growers. Just like a good five-forces + complements industry analysis, your objective in profit pool analysis is to understand profit opportunities in an industry, now and in the future.

4. This is your reality-check step. Stand back and look at the value chain sales and profits across each of the activities and see how they reconcile with those of the focal profit pool. Try to reconcile inconsistencies by collecting additional data or doing further probing of the existing qualitative or quantitative data. Step 5 may give you some insights into why you are having difficulty reconciling the data in each value chain activity with the total revenue and profitability data you have compiled for the profit pool of interest.

5. Graph the profit pool. This fifth step is one reason why profit pool analysis is so powerful—because of the visual imagery it creates for you to explain industry profitability and the distribution and tradeoffs between sales and profitability across segments. The vertical axis on your profit pool grid, just as you see in the examples in Exhibit 7, should be industry profitability and the horizontal axis should be total industry revenues. You can play around with these, using percentages instead of absolute values, though the visual impression should be pretty similar across the two variants. The examples in Exhibit 7 show percentages on the vertical access and actual dollars on the horizontal access. Just like a food chain, work from left to right where the first segment you plot on the left hand side is the first segment in the industry profit pool. So with

coffee, this would be the coffee bean growing industry (or different geographic, quality, or other (like organic, free-trade, etc.) segments of the coffee bean growing industry if they are relevant to your objectives. The height of each segment will reflect the segment's profitability, while the width will represent its sales. In the coffee profit pool, given that grocery stores are high volume but low profit businesses, you could imagine that segment of the profit pool to be very low (low profitability relative to other segments in the profit pool) but very wide in terms of sales volume.

6. You have probably learned a lot about the determinants of industry and firm profitability through the first five steps of your profit pool analysis. The sixth and final step is the most interesting and creative. In this step you have the opportunity to do at least two things. First, you can step back and look at the value chain that comprises the profit pool and imagine the business potential were you to integrate some of these activities within a firm, or eliminate them altogether. We've already given you the example of Starbucks, and how it bypassed the retail and wholesale channel, integrated roasting to provide distinctive coffee (ironically, they instruct their roasters to burn the beans more than other roasters!). IKEA would be an example of a firm that eliminated the value chain activity of furniture assembly, and actually outsourced it to you and me as consumers. Most recently, the T-shirt design house, ThreadFree, has eliminated fashion designers from its value chain cost structure. Through its web-site, thousands of customers submit T-shirt designs, its web-community picks one as the winner, and as a result 100% of the new T-shirt design is sold out as quickly as it is produced (the design winner receives a $2000 design award).

Second, in this final step you can strive to identify *complements* and adjacent value chain arenas (sometimes called *adjacencies*) where additional value could be tapped or increased demand created. A traditional example of this is where General Motors has its own financial services arm (which is very profitable), and many car and recreational vehicle companies have found that they can sell more products when they also can provide on-the-spot financing. This is an example of a complementary business that has been integrated into the General Motor's corporate strategy. The European auto industry profit pool, shown in Exhibit 7a, shows this incorporation of financial services like insurance and financing into the industry profit pool. Complements like the iPod and SNOCAP (musician to consumer direct sales), are examples of complements that could be added to the music industry example in Exhibit 7b.

An adjacent business is somewhat different. The example of U-Haul presented earlier in the chapter is a great example of how U-Haul has exploited adjacencies. It makes much more profit on packaging material than it does on the rental of trucks. The use of adjacencies is not a new phenomenon. For instance, not long after Xerox introduced the photocopier (and actually created that industry), it found that it had a captive audience for copier paper sales, and had greater sales volume and profits on the sale of copy paper than on copiers! You have surely heard the saying that razor companies give away the handles to make money on the replacement razor blades.

markets by examining a number of factors, including laws, customs, cultures, consumer preferences, distances from home markets, common borders, language, socioeconomic development, and many others.

Economies of Scale and Scope

Geographic expansion can be motivated by economies of scale or economies of scope. R&D, for example, represents a significant, relatively fixed cost for firms in many industries, and when they move into new regions of a country or global arenas, they often find that they can spread their R&D costs over a larger market. For instance, the marginal cost for a pharmaceutical firm to enter a new geographic market is lower compared to the R&D and clinical trial costs involved in bringing a new drug into the U.S. market. Once the costs of development and entry are covered, entering new geographic markets not only brings in new revenues, but because fixed costs have been spread over the new, larger market, the average cost for all the firm's customers goes down. It should come as no surprise, then, that industries with relatively high R&D expenditures, such as pharmaceuticals and high-tech products, are among the most globalized.

Strategy and the Local Environment

Sometimes, firms expanding into new geographic markets find that they must adapt certain components of their strategies to accommodate local environments. In this country, for instance, Dell is famous for the business model that allows it to skip middlemen and go directly to suppliers and customers. In its early years, Dell experimented with a retail distribution strategy but quickly retrenched. As it has expanded into some international markets such as India and China, however, Dell has found that it must, even temporarily, delay the implementation of its direct model, at least for the consumer and small business markets, although it worked well for government and large business buyers. Why? Basically because it needs local intermediaries to help develop both a base of business and acceptable levels of awareness among those particular buyers. Once the market has been penetrated to a sufficient degree, the direct model is implemented and used to reach consumers and small businesses.

Although Dell provides a nice example of adaptation, most global firms tend to approach the subject of corporate strategy from the perspective of their domestic market—such an ap-

In the United States, Dell has traditionally sold its computers straight to consumers without going through intervening middlemen or retail stores. In Asia, however, this strategy works only with institutional buyers, such as governments, schools, and businesses. As a result, Dell had to change its distribution strategy there. (CORBIS–NY/© Yang Liu/CORBIS. All rights reserved.)

proach can be problematic. Microsoft is a case in point here. The respective regulatory authorities of the U.S. and the countries of the E.U. employ very different traditions and models of competition, which in turn means that strategies must vary across these important markets. Had you not been aware of these differences, you might think that Microsoft implemented an ideal resource-based corporate strategy in its diversification into Europe. It bundled its Windows operating system with the Explorer browser and other software to increase customers' perceptions of value and, therefore, willingness to pay. It also used its extensive experience with PC software and operating systems and applications to better penetrate the market for software and operating systems in the server market, where customers are primarily businesses. Finally, Microsoft also tried to lock out competitors by including its Media Player as a standard feature in both its server and home PC operating systems.

The E.U. took exception to this strategy.[10] The European Commission recently signaled it would keep up the pressure on Microsoft, saying the company's "illegal behavior is still ongoing." It also warned that it remains concerned about Microsoft's "general business model," saying that it "deters innovation and reduces consumer choice in any technologies which Microsoft could conceivably take an interest in and tie with Windows in the future." In addition to a fine of over $600 million, the E.U. gave Microsoft 90 days to release versions of its Windows operating systems for home PCs and servers without the Windows Media Player and begin providing rivals access to the details of the code underlying its proprietary server systems. This is not the first time such differences in regulatory environments have been ignored or underestimated by global firms. Just a few years earlier, the European Commission's ruling dealt a fatal blow to the all-but-done merger between Honeywell and GE.[11]

Strategies for Entering Attractive New Businesses

So, what new businesses should a firm enter if it is contemplating diversification? We've already mentioned that the business should require the same or related resources and that it should have strategic similarity. But, there are literally thousands of possible businesses that a firm might enter, how else might managers narrow down the search? Certainly, some businesses will be more attractive than others. Among other things, attractive industries tend to benefit from higher levels of profitability. So, a manager might target a high-profit business that requires related resources and that is strategically similar to the firm's core business. However, there are reasons that industries have higher average profits; one critical reason is that it likely has strong entry barriers. Consequently, the most attractive markets are generally the hardest to enter. There are three ways to solve this paradox. First, entry barriers can be circumvented by acquiring a company already in the industry. Second, a firm can enter in a manner that incumbents don't initially take notice of your entry. Third, entry should exploit something that the new entrant can do with a cost advantage over incumbents and other new entrants. We outline three methods for accomplishing this that are based on concepts you have already learned earlier.[12] These methods are not mutually exclusive strategies; they are often used in combination to formulate robust entry moves into attractive industries.

FOCUS ON A NICHE

Recall the concept of generic strategic positions. These are low cost leadership, differentiation, focus cost leadership, and focus differentiation. Entering an attractive industry is difficult to do if making a direct assault on incumbents' strongholds. One way to enter and not attract lots of attention and retaliatory behavior is to focus the entry on a niche in the market. One type of niche to look for is a segment of the market whose needs are currently underserved. Consider the soft drink market. Coca-Cola and PepsiCo enjoy gross margins of more than 60 percent and return on assets of over 17 percent.[13] Many firms have attempted to enter the industry, but few have succeeded in establishing competitive positions. A successful niche entry to consider is the case of Red Bull. Rather than enter into the heart of the market, Red Bull entered the niche market of energy drinks.

Red Bull markets its nonalcoholic and functional energy drink in more than 100 countries. The nonalcoholic drink contains the amino acid taurine, B-complex vitamins, caffeine, and carbohydrates. Austrian Dietrich Mateschitz discovered the drink while doing business in Thailand. He formed a joint venture with the Thai businessman and adapted the drink for Austrian tastes.

Red Bull entered the United States in 1997 with little fanfare but city by city introduced the product and targeted the young adult market. The drink's popularity grew quickly and eventually captured more than 70 percent of the U.S. market for energy drinks, and rapid growth industry in and of itself. Of course, even though this was a niche market, that kind of growth captured the attention of Coca-Cola and PepsiCo, and many other firms and entrepreneurs. Red Bull's market share has slipped into the 40s, but the market has grown significantly as well, so Red Bull's sales continue to climb.

USING A REVOLUTIONARY STRATEGY

Entering an attractive industry is risky because it will get the attention of incumbents. In our first example, we suggested that entering by targeting a niche would provide some protection because incumbents often ignore niche markets. Likewise, entering with a revolutionary strategy will afford some protection because such a strategy breaks with the convention of the incumbents. Because it is so different from the status quo, incumbents generally are predisposed to think such a strategy is inferior, unwise, or risky. It is only after such a strategy proves successful that incumbents will rally to try to protect their ground. By then, it is often too late.

There are several ways a strategy can be revolutionary. For illustrative purposes, we use reconfiguring the value chain as an example, but successful new-business entry could be accomplished with any revolutionary strategy. One of those strategies was to reconfigure the value chain. Recall the example of Skype. How did Skype enter the telecom services industry with established and well-financed incumbents? It used a completely new value chain. Rather than rely on the existing telecom infrastructure, Skype used Voice-over-Internet-Protocol (VOIP) that allowed their customers to utilize their PCs to place calls, thereby bypassing the entire value chain of incumbents and giving them a totally different (and lower) cost structure. The service was targeted to price sensitive customers, so initially it was able to avoid direct retaliation from incumbents.

Pixar, part of the Walt Disney Company since its acquisition in 2006, provides another example of diversification. You will see value-chain reconfiguration here, but facets of other revolutionary strategies as well. In 1986, Steve Jobs purchased the computer graphics division of Lucasfilm, Ltd. for $10 million and established an independent company named Pixar. With the new animation technologies that it developed and controlled, Pixar began to experiment with film shorts and commercials. The technology allowed Pixar to cast lifelike characters without the cost of their care and feeding. While you may not be familiar with Pixar as a technology company, you probably have heard about Toy Story—the breakthrough film launched as a joint Disney/Pixar production in 1995. At that time, Toy Story provided the most dramatic glimpse of the promise of this new animation technology for global media market. Pixar is an example of a technology company diversifying into commercial (i.e., advertising) and then consumer animation (i.e., short and long animated feature films). As a result of this value-chain configuration, the core technology of many animated films was drastically changed, to the point that Disney abandoned its traditional animation approach in 2005.

LEVERAGE EXISTING RESOURCES

Successful new entrants use resources they already control, and possibly supplement these with a partner's resources, to leapfrog entry barriers. Consider Wal-Mart's entry into the soft drink business in the early 1990s. What resources Wal-Mart could bring to the table were shelf space and a top-flight distribution network. However, it did not have any capability in formulating soft drinks or bottling them. So, it partnered with Cott Corporation from Canada to develop Sam's Choice. By leveraging its resources with those of Cott, Wal-Mart has been able to capture approximately 5 percent of the soft drink market since its entry into softdrinks.

Recall the opening vignette from Chapter 1 about Under Armour. Under Armour initially entered the performance apparel market and established a loyal customer base. Its reputation for manufacturing high-quality performance apparel, combined with its brand image, were combined to help it enter the football cleat market. Under Armour leveraged these resources and product design to such an extent that they were able to capture 20 percent of the football cleat market share overall, and an amazing 40 percent of the market for cleats priced over $70! But Under Armour didn't enter the football cleat market as an end-game strategy. They view it as a stepping stone to allow entry into the broader athletic footwear market in future years. They used the resources they had to develop an entry strategy for cleats, but they plan to accumulate the resources (e.g., experience, expertise, distribution channels) in this niche area of footware to allow easier entry into the broader market later.

COMBINATION STRATEGIES

You have probably noticed in the examples of the three entry strategies reviewed above that several of the examples actually have elements of two or more of the strategies. For instance, Skype combined its reconfigured value chain with a niche strategy; they specifically targeted price-sensitive customers who would tolerate inferior quality. Wal-Mart's entry into soft drinks was a combination of leveraging their existing resources (e.g., shelf space and distribution network) with a reconfigured value chain; they did not distribute through typical retailers, they make no attempt to secure fountain drink contracts, and they do not stock vending machines except at their own properties.

The key to entering an attractive business is to do so in an indirect way; an entry strategy that does not directly assault the incumbents and immediately threaten their profitability. Pursuing niche markets initially is often ignored by incumbents because they represent customers that the incumbents were previously serving. Reconfiguring the value chain and leveraging existing resources help protect firms entering attractive markets. A reconfigured value chain gives the entrant a cost advantage and leveraging existing resources gives the entrant something to build off of that incumbents and other possible new entrants are likely to lack.

Competitive Advantage and Corporate Strategy

At the business level, competitive advantage reflects the relative position of a firm compared to positions of industry rivals. At the corporate level, it reflects management's success in creating more value from the firm's business units than those units could create as standalone enterprises or subsidiaries. Our goal is to identify the conditions under which the strategy of owning a corporate portfolio of businesses creates value for shareholders.

You are already familiar with the element of arenas in business strategy. Sometimes a firm chooses a corporate strategy of competing in only one arena. However, the corporate strategy of many firms involves operating in more than one arena. Corporate strategy becomes more complicated if the competitive or operational characteristics of those arenas differ in some way, whether subtly or substantially. Ultimately, it is the combination of arenas, resources (i.e., VRINE), and implementation that determines whether the corporate strategy leads to competitive advantage.

ARENAS

 Arenas

Theoretically, a firm can compete in any combination of discrete business arenas. In practice, of course, firms rarely enter arenas randomly but rather select those that are logically connected to the arenas in which they already participate. ◆ The key to logical connection is *relatedness*. Businesses can be related along several different dimensions, including similarity in markets, use of identical resources, and reliance on comparable dominant logic.

Resources provide the basis for corporate competitive advantage. The nature of corporate resources varies along a continuum, and whether the resources are specialized or general dictates the limits of a firm's scope, the manner of organizational control and coordination, and the effectiveness of corporate headquarters. Although most firms maintain some degree of relatedness among the various businesses in which they participate, some combinations require greater relatedness than others. Finally, it's not always easy to determine the dimensions along which corporate businesses are related.

Some conglomerates are actually portfolios of strategic business units within which several related businesses are combined for management purposes. GE, for instance, participates in such far-flung enterprises as jet engines, elevators, light bulbs, appliances, and financial services. Each of these businesses, however, is located in a business unit with conceptually similar units.

RESOURCES

As we saw in Chapter 3, resources and capabilities are tangible or intangible, and their usefulness in creating a competitive advantage depends on five factors: (1) how valuable they are, (2) whether they're rare in the industry, (3) whether they're costly to imitate, (4) the availability of substitutes, and (5) whether the firm has complementary capabilities to exploit them. At this point, we need to remember that these factors apply to the usefulness of resources in creating competitive advantage at the *business* level. At the corporate level in the VRINE framework (e.g., valuable, rare, inimitable, nonsubstitutable, exploitable), they must be supplemented by an additional factor: namely, how *specialized* or *general* a firm's resources are.

specialized resources
Resource with a narrow range of applicability.

Specialized Resources
Specialized resources have a narrow range of applicability. Knowledge about fiber-optics, for example, is fairly specialized, whereas managerial know-how and skill are more general in nature. Granted, fiber-optics has many uses in multiple contexts (such as telecommunications, electronics, routing and switching equipment), but its utility is more limited than that of a general resource such as general managerial skill.

general resources Resource that can be exploited across a wide range of activities.

General Resources
General resources can be exploited across a wide range of activities. For instance, expertise in efficient manufacturing and mass-marketing techniques can be exploited in any number of contexts. In fact, many companies have created significant shareholder value by leveraging these general resources across different businesses engaged in a variety of industries. General resources aren't confined to narrow applications, and the extent of resource specialization affects both a firm's scope and its organizational structure.

IMPLEMENTATION

Implementation levers include organizational structure, systems and processes, and people and rewards. Strategic leaders use these levers to implement strategies. The success with which diversified firms are managed in accord with key organizational features has a significant effect on the level of value that can be created through their portfolios. Implementation levers that are critical for corporate strategy vary from firm to firm, but some of the more important levers to achieve successful diversification include knowledge-transfer mechanisms, coordination mechanisms, rewards, and corporate oversight.

Knowledge transfer enables a diversified firm to apply superior performance results observed in one organizational business unit to other units that are not performing as well. In practice, knowledge transfer is difficult because it may not be entirely clear what is causing the superior performance in the high-performing unit. Three mechanisms facilitate knowledge transfer. First, just the knowledge that superior results are being achieved in another business unit can be used to reset performance expectations for future performance in other units. In this case, no real knowledge of actual practices is transferred, but the superior performance is used to create stretch goals that motivate learning in other units. Second, underperforming units can study the operational practices of high-performing business units to determine the source of superior performance. Finally, knowledge transfer is perhaps best facilitated when members of lower-performing business units simply seek advice from the higher-performing units. It is often the case that high-performing business units have explicit routines and practices that can be detailed by key employees in those units.[14]

Coordination mechanisms are the management systems and processes that facilitate intrafirm activity. Coordination depends on a variety of structural mechanisms, including reporting relationships, informal meetings and exchanges, and detailed policies and procedures for such activities as intrafirm transfer pricing. Greater relatedness of businesses within a firm requires more intense coordination across business units. Why? Because resources in highly related diversified firms are often shared across business units. Illustratively, more cross-business coordination is needed at 3M than at GE. For instance, adhesive technology is used in multiple divisions in 3M, and this knowledge sharing requires coordination. Alternatively, knowledge transfer or resource sharing (other than cash) does not occur between GE's jet engine and consumer finance divisions. Consequently, 3M can generate more revenue-enhancement synergy between related units than GE can generate between unrelated businesses, but to reap these possible benefits requires that energy and resources be devoted to coordination efforts.

Successful diversification may require adjustments in how managers are compensated and rewarded. Generally speaking, a firm with a broad (highly diversified) portfolio should reward managers differently than a focused or related diversified firm.[15] Why? In a firm with a broad scope, division-level managers do not share resources and cooperate to implement their strategies. Consequently, it is more effective to reward managers for the performance of their divisions than to reward (and punish) them for the performance of divisions that they have no control of or influence over. Conversely, in a related diversified firm, managers of different divisions are generally required to share resources and cooperate to implement their strategies. As a result, it is more effective to reward managers for the firm's collective performance than to focus all rewards on division-level performance. For instance, when division-level profits drive bonuses, managers have little incentive to help other divisions.

When corporate-level management grows unwieldy, it can be a drag on corporate earnings. What factors should determine the size and organization of corporate-level management? Basically, two factors govern this decision: the firm's resources and the scope of its involvement in disparate arenas. When a firm's portfolio contains numerous unrelated units that aren't significantly interdependent, it doesn't need heavy corporate-level oversight; there's not much that corporate-level management can do to add value on a day-to-day basis (a good example is Warren Buffet's Berkshire Hathaway Inc.). By contrast, when a firm's portfolio consists of highly interdependent businesses, more corporate-level control is needed to facilitate the sharing of resources and to oversee interbusiness transactions (e.g., S. C. Johnson, whose businesses include insect control, home cleaning, and plastic products).

Now that we've identified the ingredients of a good corporate strategy, we need to remind ourselves that it's the alignment of these ingredients in support of a firm's mission and vision that makes it possible for its managers to implement the firm's corporate strategy and create competitive advantage at the corporate level. Indeed, the configuration of these elements will determine whether a firm achieves corporate-level competitive advantage.

Corporate Strategy in Stable and Dynamic Contexts

By this point, you probably have a strong suspicion that corporate strategy is developed according to the relative dynamism of the context in which an organization operates. You are, of course, correct, and in this section we'll see how corporate strategy is designed to take dynamic context into account. Moreover, because alliances and acquisitions are vehicles for both business and corporate strategy, we'll elaborate on this theme in subsequent chapters as well. We'll see, for example, that, depending on whether a firm's context is stable or dynamic, different strategy vehicles are likely to play different roles. In particular, alliances and acquisitions have different implications for the allocation of a firm's resources and capabilities. We'll show that because certain issues arise in both stable and dynamic contexts, differences are often matters of emphasis. At the same time, however, we'll stress the point that even if the *content* of strategy is similar in both stable and dynamic contexts, the dynamism of the context will still have an effect on its *implementation*.

CORPORATE STRATEGY IN STABLE CONTEXTS

Many of the traditional notions of the relationship between diversification and corporate strategy are based on analyses of companies operating in relatively stable contexts. As we've seen, historically a firm may have diversified into a high-growth industry because growth prospects in its current industry were unattractive. That's why Kansas City Southern (KCS), a railroad, got into financial services in the late 1960s and soon owned almost 90 percent of the Janus Group of mutual funds. But recall, too, our observation that this form of unrelated diversification often fails. Indeed, due to an obvious lack of synergy between the rail industry and mutual funds—plus an increasing level of management conflict between its railroad and mutual-fund divisions—KCS divested Janus in 1999 (a move widely approved by the market).[16]

Stable Arenas and Formal Structures As we've seen, creating synergies among its businesses is an important part of a corporation's strategy. Synergies can come from shared know-how, coordination of business-unit strategies, shared tangible resources, vertical integration, and pooled negotiating power.[17] In relatively stable environments, such synergies are typically conceived as functions of static business-unit arenas and the formal structural links among them. Corporate-strategy objectives focus primarily on synergies as means of achieving economies of scope and scale. In fact, corporate strategy explicitly defines the form and extent of the coordination and collaboration among business units. Thus, the managers of individual units are often compensated according to a combination of division- and corporate-level performance. Generally speaking, the overarching objective of corporate strategy in a stable environment is ensuring that the firm operates as a tightly interwoven whole.

The best example of such strategy in action is probably the related diversified firm. Masco Corporation, a multibillion-dollar manufacturer and distributor of plumbing fixtures and other home building and home repair supplies, is just such a firm. Starting with Delta Faucets in the early 1960s, Masco built a diversified portfolio of manufacturing businesses by acquiring well-run firms in a variety of industries. Today, Masco is one of the leading makers of home improvement and home building products and a powerhouse in the do-it-yourself industry dominated by such retail chains as Home Depot and Lowe's. We've summarized the breadth of Masco's holdings in Exhibit 8. Operating a tightly knit set of businesses is an effective corporate strategy for Masco. Why? Primarily because each business alone is unattractive, and by combining them under one corporate roof, Masco gives them greater selling and merchandising power in dealing with aggressive customers such as Home Depot. In addition, because its businesses are sufficiently related, Masco can leverage manufacturing, design, marketing, distribution, and merchandizing expertise across them.

CORPORATE STRATEGY IN DYNAMIC CONTEXTS

Masco's strategy would be problematic for firms competing in more dynamic contexts. Adaptec Inc., for instance, was once an integrated maker of both computer hardware and software. The strategy was logical because the firm could extract synergies from operations in such complementary businesses. Adaptec soon discovered, however, that rapid changes in technologies and advances by competitors were weakening its ability to maneuver well in both areas. In 1999, therefore, Adaptec spun off its software side as Roxio through an IPO.

Even a seemingly focused business like Palm, which makes PDAs, can find it difficult to perform well in both hardware (Palm Pilot PDAs) and software (the Palm operating system), accordingly, Palm actually split into two separate companies. Ironically, as late as 2000, 3Com, then a supplier of computer, communications, and compatibility (network-interfacing) products, spun off Palm as a separate business for similar reasons.[18] In turn, Palm used the proceeds from its own IPO to strengthen its position in the market for handheld devices and operating systems. 3Com now concentrates on its core networking business, along with research and development in emerging technologies.

Diversification in Dynamic Contexts   Despite the examples of Adaptec and 3Com, both of which have used divestitures to increase corporate focus, diversification can be a viable strategy in dynamic contexts. Bear in mind, however, that firms seeking to diversify in dynamic contexts usually need strong resources and capabilities in the areas of learning, knowledge transfer, and rapid responsiveness. If corporate ownership hinders nimbleness and response time in a dynamic environment, it's more likely to be an encumbrance than an advantage. It's hard enough to manage competitively in dynamic contexts without having to struggle under excess layers of corporate hierarchy.

Coevolution   The ebbs and flows of firms' corporate strategies in dynamic contexts are best described as a web of shifting linkages among evolving businesses—a process that some researchers call **coevolution**.[19] Borrowed from biology, the term *coevolution* describes successive changes among two or more ecologically interdependent species that adapt not only to their environment but also to each other. Business units coevolve when senior managers do not target specific synergies across business units but rather allow business-unit managers to determine which linkages do and don't work. As business-unit managers search for fresh opportunities for synergies and abandon deteriorating linkages, internal relationships tend to shift. As in the organic world, coevolution can result in competitive interdependence, with one unit eventually absorbing another or rendering it unnecessary. Coevolution means that cross-business synergies are usually temporary, and managers must learn to deal with the fundamental tension that results from the agility afforded by fewer linkages and the efficiency afforded by more. Finally, research suggests that in successful coevolving compa-

coevolution   Process by which diversification causes two or more interdependent businesses to adapt not only to their environment, but to each other.

Exhibit 8 Masco:
A Holding Company at
a Glance

Domestic	International
Cabinet and Related Products	
d-Scan Inc.	AlmaKüchen, Germany
Diversified Cabinet Distributors	Alvic, Spain
KraftMaid	Aran Group, Italy
Merillat	Berglen Group, UK
Mill's Pride	Grumal, Spain
Texwood Industries	Moores Group Ltd., UK
Zenith	Tvilum-Scanbirk, Denmark
	Xey, Spain
Plumbing Products	
Aqua Glass	A & J Gummers, UK
Brass Craft	Breuer, Germany
Brasstech	Bristan Ltd., UK
Delta Faucet	Damixa, Denmark
H&H Tube	Glass Indromassaggio SpA, Italy
Mirolin	Hansgrohe AG, Germany
Peerless Faucet	Heritage, UK
Plumb Shop	Hüppe, Germany
Watkins Manufacturing	NewTeam Limited, UK
	Rubinetterie Mariani, Italy
	S.T.S.R., Italy
Decorative Architectural Products	
Behr	Avocet, UK
Franklin Brass (Bath Unlimited)	SKS Group, Germany
GAMCO (Bath Unlimited)	
Ginger	
Liberty Hardware	
Masterchem	
Melard (Bath Unlimited)	
Vapor Technologies	
Specialty Products	
Arrow Fastener	Alfred Reinecke, Germany
Cobra	Brugman, Holland
Computerized Security Systems (CSS)	Cambrian Windows Ltd., UK
Faucet Queens	Duraflex Ltd., UK
Gamco/Morgantown Products	Gebhardt, Germany
MediaLab	Griffin Windows, UK
Milgard Manufacturing	Jung Pumpen, Germany
PowerShot Tool Company	Missel, Germany
	Premier Manufacturing Ltd., UK
	Superia Radiatoren, Belgium
	Vasco, Belgium

nies, managers, rather than trying to control, or even predict, cross-business-unit synergies, simply let them emerge in the "natural" course of corporate operations.[20]

Ironically, of course, coevolution means that units owned by the same corporation are potentially both collaborators and competitors. This paradoxical relationship is perhaps easiest to detect when a firm operates both traditional and e-business units. It's less obvious when it arises because new technologies have emerged to threaten established processes, but the costs of allowing a competitor—even one with which you share a corporate umbrella—to gain a technological advantage are often steep. In dynamic contexts, corporate strategy usually takes the form of temporary networks among businesses, and if strategic alliances are added into the mix, the network may include companies that the corporation doesn't own as well as those it does.

Divestitures and corporate spinoffs can be effective strategic vehicles for dealing with disruptive innovations, and they also figure frequently in stories of corporate coevolution.[21] Because disruptive technologies compete with established technologies, it may not be enough to simply reorganize them as new units under the same corporate umbrella. The resulting problems from retaining ownership of the disruptive part of the business range from the creation of messy internal politics to simply starving the new business of resources so that it eventually fails. We've summarized the key differences between corporate strategies in stable and dynamic contexts in Exhibit 9. The box entitled "How Would *You* Do That? 2," demonstrates how you might evaluate dynamic corporate strategy at Disney.

Vehicles

Stable Contexts	Dynamic Contexts
Top management team emphasizes collaboration among the businesses and theform of that collaboration.	Top management team emphasizes the creationof a collaborative context that is rich in termsof content and linkages.
Collaboration is solidified through stable structural arrangement among wholly-ownedbusinesses.	Collaboration is fluid, with networks beingcreated, changed, and disassembled betweencombinations of owned and alliancebusinesses.
Key objectives are the pursuit of economies ofscale and scope.	Key objectives are growth, maneuver-ability,and economies of scope.
The business units' roles are to execute theirgiven strategies.	The business units' roles are to execute theirstrategies and seek new collaborativeopportunities.
Business units' incentives combine businesswith corporate-level rewards to promotecooperation.	Business units' incentives emphasize business-level rewards to promote aggressive executionand collaborative-search objectives.
Balanced-scorecard objectives emphasizeperformance against budget and in comparisonto within-firm peer unit.	Balanced-scorecard objectives gauge performance relative to competitors in terms ofgrowth, market share, and profitability.

Exhibit 9 Comparison of Corporate Strategies in Stable and Dynamic Contexts

Evaluating Diversification at Disney

To evaluate Disney's corporate strategy, we can use an adapted portfolio analysis. You learned about the problems with the traditional use of portfolio analysis, but it is still widely used in the modified form we present in this example. Disney's vision is to be the industry leader in providing creative entertainment experiences. The arenas in which Disney participates are focused on family entertainment and include media networks (41 percent), theme parks and resorts (28 percent), studio entertainment (24 percent), and consumer products (7 percent). A few of the fundamental resources that Disney shares across these arenas are the Disney name and legacy, the library of films and Disney's cast of animated and real-life characters, capabilities in the creation and management of world-class entertainment, and service-management expertise (this is obviously an abbreviated list of resources and capabilities).

Implementation is the glue holding these arenas and resources together. Although the company appears to be diversified into related arenas, each business is treated as a profit center, and managers are compensated according to business-unit performance. To overcome the lack of cross-division cooperation that this might motivate, Disney has historically relied on special "synergy management" positions. Imagine the powerful scope economies that are created when Disney launches a hit character and then leverages the

fictional personality through every channel, from toy licensing to Disney Radio. Just as important, however, is the skill with which Disney pulls the right implementation levers to make this synergistic dynamo work.

We want to evaluate how well Disney is doing with its corporate strategy. To do so, we will use a portfolio analysis tool that incorporates VRINE and other key strategy concepts that you have already learned about. We want to map Disney's business units along four dimensions: the size of the divisions, the VRINE characteristics of the division, the industry's five forces score, and the profitability of the divisions relative to competitors in these businesses. This 4-D exercise will allow us to visualize how well Disney is performing, given the industry contexts of each business and the resources and capabilities possessed by the divisions.

In Exhibit 10, we have tabulated the data for Disney's divisions using the tools you have learned earlier. For the five forces analysis, we rank each industry in which Disney participates.

For the VRINE analysis, we gave each division a score of 1 to 5, depending on whether its resources satisfy the VRINE requirements (e.g., 1 point given if the resources are valuable; 2 points if they are valuable and rare; 3 points if they are valuable, rare, and difficult to imitate; 4 points if they are valuable, rare, difficult to imitate, and non-substitutable; and 5 points if they meet the first four

requirements and the firm is able to exploit the resources. We also report the size of each division, the business unit profit margin, the weighted average profit margin for other firms in those industries, and the industry adjusted performance for each of Disney's business units (e.g., business unit profit margin minus the weighted average industry profit margin).

We can use this data to create a bubble chart in an Excel worksheet, which will make the data easier to interpret and present to managers. Bubble charts can plot three values. We use the VRINE scores for the X axis (i.e., the horizontal axis), the five forces score for the Y axis (i.e., the vertical axis), and the business unit size for the size of the bubble. After the chart is plotted, we then add the profit margin for each division using the text box feature. Exhibit 11 illustrates what we have found.

What do we learn from this type of portfolio analysis? Quite simply, it allows us to see whether Disney is creating synergy across its business units. Recall that synergy either results in economies of scope (which should lead to lower costs than competitors) or revenue enhancement, which should give us greater revenue relative to costs compared to competitors. Thus, if we've truly created synergy we should perform better than average. Portfolio analysis also helps us analyze the performance of the portfolio as a whole. For instance, we can see how business units perform relative to each other,

Exhibit 10 Comparison Portfolio Data for Disney

	Business Unit VRINE Score	Strength of Five Force Score	Business Unit Size ($ millions)	Business Unit Profit Margin	Industry Weighted Average Profit Margin	Industry Adjusted Business Unit Profit Margin
Parks and Resorts	5	3	9023	13%	19%	–5.88%
Media Networks	2	2	13207	21%	10%	10.81%
Studio Entertainment	2	4	7587	?	10%	–7.28%
Consumer Products	3	2	2215	23%	30%	–6.75%

which helps managers determine where they need to focus their attention.

So, how is Disney doing? Not too well, actually. Only Media Networks is performing above industry averages. The industry was scored as rather favorable (i.e., a low score for the level of the five forces). However, this will help all firms perform well in the industry, not just Disney. Perhaps

Media Networks is best exploiting the synergies of all the divisions, allowing it to perform better than its competitors. The other divisions are all under-performing their competitors.

We need to emphasize that we are using industry-adjusted performance to evaluate the portfolio. Why? A firm (or business unit) might perform at what appears to be a healthy clip. For

instance, the consumer product division of Disney achieves 23 percent profit margins, which are among the highest in the company. However, Disney's competitors in consumer products average more than 30 percent. So, actually, it would be a mistake to conclude that Disney is doing well in that division.

Exhibit 11 Disney Portfolio

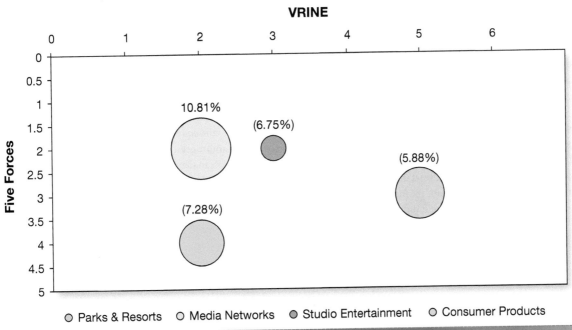

Summary of Challenges

1. *Define* **corporate strategy.** Corporate strategy encompasses issues related to decisions about entering and exiting businesses. A fundamental part of corporate strategy is the decision about what business *arenas* to enter and exit. However, corporate strategy also encompasses the overall management of the multibusiness enterprise, such as corporate headquarters' efforts to orchestrate the cross-business-unit synergies. Corporate strategy deals with the logic for owning more than one business within a firm.

2. *Understand the roles of economies of scope and revenue-enhancement synergy in corporate strategy.* Expanding the scope of the firm, whether vertically, horizontally, or geographically, does not necessarily create value. Value is created by either lowering costs or increasing revenues through diversification. This can take place when economies of scope result from diversification, such as when two businesses are able to share the same resources. Revenue-enhancement synergies can also create value. For synergies to be present because of joint ownership, the combined revenues of two distinct businesses must be greater when owned jointly than when operated independently. These economic gains are more likely when there is resource similarity between businesses and when the dominant logics necessary to manage the businesses are similar.

3. *Identify the different types of diversification.* Firms have several options when expanding the scope of their operations beyond the original business definition. In this chapter, we discussed the concept of diversification along three trajectories of new business arenas: vertical, horizontal, and geographic (global). Vertical scope is ownership of business activities along the firm's vertical value chain. Horizontal scope, typically called diversification, is increased by owning businesses in different industry segments or different industries entirely. Geographic scope entails moving into new geographic areas, typically new countries.

4. *Explain how companies can be successfully enter attractive industries when those industries have the greatest barriers to entry.* In the evolution of firms over time, most decide to expand into new businesses. The industries that attract the most attempts for new entry are industries that are more profitable on average than others. However, entry barriers make it difficult for firms to enter these industries, as evidenced by the fact that most new entrants to such industries earn profits far below the average of the industry, and even below what entrants to unattractive industries earn. To successfully enter an attractive industry a firm needs to orchestrate an indirect assault, not attack the incumbents in their strongholds, such as by entering in a niche segment of the industry. In addition, successful entrants leverage their existing resources and enter with a fundamentally different value chain than incumbents.

5. *Describe the relationship between corporate strategy and competitive advantage.* Competitive advantage at the corporate level is a function of the fit among arenas, resources, and organizational systems, structures, and processes. When these are connected in a coherent fashion, the corporation is more likely to achieve its long-term objectives. When resources are specialized, the firm will likely find greater value creation opportunities in a narrow scope of business arenas. Conversely, general resources can be applied across a greater spectrum of businesses. Firms with a broad scope of business activities have different demands for organization structure, systems, and processes than firms that are narrowly focused on a specific set of business arenas.

6. *Explain the differences between corporate strategy in stable and dynamic contexts.* In relatively stable environments, synergies are typically achieved through static definitions of the business-unit arenas and formal structural links among them. Corporate strategy objectives are aimed primarily at using synergies to achieve economies of scope and scale and, in fact, the strategy explicitly defines the form and extent of business units' coordination and collaboration. Firms in dynamic contexts must usually have strong resources and capabilities in the areas of learning, knowledge transfer, and rapid responsiveness for diversification to yield benefits. Otherwise, the nimbleness and responsiveness required of business units in dynamic contexts is dampened as a consequence of corporate ownerships being more of an encumbrance than an advantage. In dynamic environments, allowing managers of business units to pursue a pattern of synergistic relationships that mimics biological coevolution is generally more advantageous than corporate-forced synergistic relationships.

Review Questions

1. How does corporate strategy differ from business strategy?

2. How has the practice of corporate strategy evolved over time?

3. What is a conglomerate?

4. How can managers decide whether they should diversify into a new business?

5. What are the types of diversification and how is value created by each type?

6. What is the difference between economies of scope and synergies?

7. What is the relationship between diversification and firm performance?

8. What factors tend to limit the attractiveness of diversification?

9. How does a dynamic industry context affect the possible benefits of diversification?

Experiential Activities

Group Exercises

1. Choose two firms that are well-known to your group members—perhaps firms that you've done case analyses on in the past. For each of these firms, identify their vertical, horizontal, and geographic scope. Having done that, evaluate the resources that are necessary for each business arena for the firms. How similar are the resource requirements? Identify the dominant logic in each of their main lines of business (if you picked a very diversified firm, just choose the largest two or three business segments). How similar are they across the business divisions?

2. Try to apply the profit pool tool to another industry. Where would you turn for data to do this? How "friendly" is that data for the purposes of using this tool? If you are having trouble being precise, make informed estimates for what you are missing. You will likely find some profit pools that are deeper than others. Why are there big differences between segments? Which firms in the value chain are best able to enter these attractive segments?

Ethical Debates

1. Textbook publishers face growing competition on numerous fronts, including new models of textbook delivery. One such model provides students with online textbook content for "free," on the condition that students provide personal information about themselves to vendors like credit card, student loan, and cell phone companies. For any publisher that is considering diversification into this new media space, what might be some of the ethical issues?

2. You can imagine that firms in the alcohol, tobacco, or firearms businesses may feel a need to diversify into less scrutinized or regulated businesses. How might ethical issues related to these core businesses affect their ability to enter, or costs of entry, into new businesses? How might these ethical issues affect their ability to exit, or costs of exiting, their traditional businesses?

How Would YOU DO THAT?

1. The box entitled "How Would *You* Do That? 1" helps you see how a profit pool model is developed for a particular industry or geographic or product arena. You are given Starbucks and ready-to-drink coffee market as an example, but never shown a profit pool diagram for that industry. Using the resources you have available, try to map out the basic segment characteristics of this arena for the United States. Start with the narrow definition of the coffee business provided in the box. Finally, try to identify the complements or adjacencies that a company like Starbucks could exploit. Do you see new growth opportunities for Starbucks using all the steps of the profit pool tool?

2. "How Would *You* Do That? 2" applies a portfolio evaluation tool to Disney. Internally, Disney executives view one of their dynamic capabilities as that of being the best at creating world-class entertainment within financial constraints. What are your thoughts on this view? As you think about Disney and what you view as its resources and capabilities, and the insights you gain from evaluating Disney's portfolio of businesses, what arenas should it consider for future diversification or divestiture moves?

Go on to see How Would You Do That at www.prenhall.com/ carpenter&sanders

Endnotes

1. Corporate descriptions were compiled based on corporate histories on corporate Web sites (www.ge.com, www.3m.com, www.mityinc.com); business descriptions were compiled based on information available at www.hoovers.com (accessed July 15, 2005 and May 5, 2007); G. Colvin, "Q & A: On the Hot Seat," *Fortune*, November 27, 2006; "GE Reports Strong Fourth-Quarter and Full-Year Results for 2006," *Business Wire*, January 19, 2007; A. Fisher, "America's Most Admired Companies," *Fortune*, March 19, 2007, pp. 88–94; *MITY Enterprises Annual Report*, 2006; M. Moylan, "Whither 3M?" *Minnesota Public Radio*, February 28, 2007; "Economic Management," http://solutions.3m.com/wps/portal/3M/en_US/global/sustainability/s/governance-systems/management-systems/economic-management/ (accessed on May 4, 2007).

2. See especially C. K. Prahalad and G. Hamel, "The Core Competence of the Corporation," *Harvard Business Review* May–June (1990), 79–91; K. P. Coyne, S. Hall, J. D. Clifford, and P. Gorman, "Do You Really Have a Core Competency," *McKinsey Quarterly* 1 (1997), 40–54.

3. A. Chandler, *Strategy and Structure: Chapters in the History of the American Industrial Enterprise* (Boston: MIT Press, 1962).

4. G. F. Davis and S. K. Stout, "Organization Theory and the Market for Corporate Control: A Dynamic Analysis of Characteristics of Large Takeover Targets: 1980–1990," *Administrative Science Quarterly* 37 (1992), 605–633; G. F. Davis, K. A. Diekman, and C. H. Tinsley, "The Decline and Fall of the Conglomerate Firm in the 1980s: A Study in the Deinstitutionalization of an Organization Form," *American Sociological Review* 59 (1994), 547–570.

5. S. Wetlaufer, "Common Sense and Conflict: An Interview with Disney's Michael Eisner," *Harvard Business Review* 78:1 (2000), 44–48. See also K. Eisenhardt and C. Galunic, "Coevolving: At Last a Way to Make Synergies Work," *Harvard Business Review* (2000), 91–101.

6. A. D. Henderson and J. W. Fredrickson, "Information Processing Demands as a Determinant of CEO Compensation," *Academy of Management Journal* 39 (1996), 575–590; W. G. Sanders and M. A. Carpenter, "Internationalization and Firm Governance: The Roles of CEO Compensation,

Top-Team Composition, and Board Structure," *Academy of Management Journal* 41 (1998), 158–178.

7. The concept of profit pools has been around for decades but this particular tool is adapted from O. Gadiesh and J. L. Gilbert, "Profit Pools: A Fresh Look at Strategy." *Harvard Business Review* 76:3 (1998), 139–147.

8. O. Gadiesh and J. L. Gilbert, "Profit Pools: A Fresh Look at Strategy," *Harvard Business Review* 76:3 (1998), 139–148.

9. For more details on this example and other examples, see Gadiesh and Gilbert, "Profit Pools."

10. J. Kanter, D. Clark, and J. R. Wilke, "EU Imposes Sanctions on Microsoft—Fine, Disclosure Penalties Aim to Undercut Dominance; Continued Pressure Signaled," *Wall Street Journal*, March 25, 2004, A2; M. Wingfield, "DOJ Calls EC's Record Fine of Microsoft 'Unfortunate,'" *Dow Jones Newswires*, March 25, 2004; B. Mitchener and J. Kanter, "Monti's Initiatives on Commerce Leave an Enduring Mark," *Wall Street Journal*, March 25, 2004, A2.

11. Y. Akbar, "Grabbing Victory from the Jaws of Defeat: Can the GE-Honeywell Merger Force International Competition Policy Cooperation?" *World Competition* 25:4 (2002), 26–31.

12. The ideas in this section draw heavily from the work of Bryce and Dyer. D. J. Bryce and J. H. Dyer, 2007. Strategies to Crack Well-Guarded Markets. *Harvard Business Review* 85(5): 84–92.

13. Based on the companies' 10K filings for 2006. The averages over the past decade are consistent with these figures.

14. G. Szulanski, R. Cappetta, and R. J. Jensen, "When and How Trustworthiness Matters: Knowledge Transfer and the Moderating Effect of Causal Ambiguity," *Organization Science* 15 (2004), 600–613.

15. C. W. L. Hill, M. A. Hitt, and R. E. Hoskisson, "Cooperative versus Competitive Structures in Related and Unrelated Diversified Firms," *Organization Science* 3 (1992), 501–521.

16. A. Stone, "Can Kansas City Southern Keep Its Janus Spin-Off on Track?" *Business Week,* August 31, 1999, 27.

17. M. Goold and A. Campbell, "Desperately Seeking Synergy," *Harvard Business Review* 76:5 (1998), 131–143.

18. L. Bransten and S. Thurm, "For Palm Computers, an IPO and Flashy Rival," *Wall Street Journal,* September 14, 1999, B1.

19. Eisenhardt and Galunic, "Coevolving"; S. Brown and K. Eisenhardt, *Competing on the Edge* (Boston: Harvard Business School Press, 1998).

20. Eisenhardt and Galunic, "Coevolving"; Brown and Eisenhardt, *Competing on the Edge.*

21. C. Christensen, *The Innovator's Dilemma* (New York: Harper Collins, 1997).

Looking at International Strategies

Looking at International Strategies

In This Chapter We Challenge You To >>>

1. Define *international strategy* and identify its implications for the strategy diamond.

2. Understand why a firm would want to expand internationally and explain the relationship between international strategy and competitive advantage.

3. Use the CAGE framework to identify desirable international arenas.

4. Describe different vehicles for international expansion.

5. Apply different international strategy configurations.

6. Outline the international strategy implications of the static and dynamic perspectives.

(NewsCom/Justin Sullivan/Getty Images)

Dell *goes* *to* China

"Today there are one billion people on-line worldwide, and many of the world's second billion users are right here in China," said Michael Dell, chairman and chief executive of Dell Inc. "We intend to earn their confidence and their business." Mr. Dell was speaking in Shanghai in 2007. His company was the world's second-biggest PC maker and the third largest in China. The company had come a long way since 1999, when Mr. Dell first put plans for the company's expansion into China in motion.

In 1999, Dell had a negligible presence in many regions of the world, most notably China, where it ranked a distant seventh in PC sales. This lagging position bothered Dell executives because computer industry analysts were predicting that by 2002, China would become the second-largest PC market behind the

United States. Consequently, in 1999 Dell set the ambitious goal of achieving 10 percent of its global PC sales from China by 2002, which would amount to nearly 50 percent of PC sales for the entire Asian region.

"Faster sales growth in China could really give Dell a boost because of how big the market is and how much potential it has," said William Bao Bean, an analyst with Deutsche Securities in Hong Kong. According to Dell, only about seven in 100 people own PCs in China. About 25 million PCs were sold in China in 2006. What's more, China's economy grew 10.7 percent in 2006, the fastest rate in more than a decade. Increasing wealth is making electronic goods like computers more affordable to a larger section of the population. "Smaller cities and towns are really where the growth is in China because incomes are rising and people are shopping for their first computers," Bean added.

Dell's overall approach in China is to stay flexible. Its direct-selling model works well with commercial buyers. But to reach first-time computer consumers, the company is opening physical stores—called "experience stores"—in Nanjing, Chongqing, and Tianjin. The reason, as Bryan Ma, a research director at International Data Corp., explained, is that "Consumers are accustomed to buying things with cash, touching and feeling a product in a store and getting instant gratification, rather than calling into a call center or placing an order on-line and waiting a few days for the machine to arrive." Dell China says that its purpose for opening the stores is to have Chinese consumers able to get in touch with Dell's products and enjoy the unique advantages of these products. On August 4, 2006, Dell opened its first product experience store in China in Chongqing. Opening an experience store may be a surprising move for the king of direct-sell, but Michael Dell understands the importance of flexibility: "The thing I've been saying internally is the direct model is not a religion. It's a great strategy, [and it] works well; there are things we can do with it. But that's not the only thing we can do as a company."

Michael Dell is optimistic about Dell's future in China: "We have a lot of opportunity" in the consumer market, he says, "You'll see a lot more products" like the ones he unveiled in March 2007.

For many U.S. companies, China is attractive simply due to its size, but it is also a competitive environment fraught with many hazards—and it can turn potential profits into a cash-flow black hole. Sourcing components and products from China has proven successful for many global firms, although some companies such as Mattel have faced serious quality and safety problems. The Chinese consumer market appears to be an entirely different matter. By 1999, for example, Motorola and Kodak had already sunk many millions of dollars into China hoping for large domestic market share and commensurate profits but instead were reeling from enormous and continuing losses. Dell's management was not ignorant of these warning signals but viewed the situation as "if we're not in what will soon be the second-biggest PC market in the world, then how can Dell possibly be a global player?"

The Dell-in-China situation showcases all five elements of the strategy diamond. It also shows how a firm must engage these elements flexibly and entrepreneurially to do business in markets different from their home markets. That is, internationalizing firms face challenges as to how to be global yet local at the same time and to what extent they should be global or local. China is a relatively new geographic arena for Dell. Within this country arena, Dell is targeting certain market segments, or subarenas; it is also using different channels as part of its market segmentation strategy.

In terms of vehicles, and regardless of global location, Dell typically goes it alone in assembly and distribution, entering into alliances only for its inputs and raw materials. A key facet of Dell's competitive advantage is distribution via its Dell Direct model—an on-line PC assembly and sales-on-demand powerhouse. In China, however, Dell initially formed alliances with independent distributors for the consumer market, a channel it had learned to exploit in its earlier entry into India. This was a risky move for Dell but also one that showed that management recognized that it had to be flexible and act in a locally sensitive fashion in approaching new geographic markets. Dell initially planned to use Chinese distributors, as it had in India, and then migrate sales over a five-year period to the typical kiosk sales model it employs in other parts of the world, further allowing it to leverage its Dell Direct model. Dell was able to draw immediately on the model for the large multinational-firm market, with which it already had established customer relationships. It could also use the Dell Direct model for the government-users market. As in all of its other markets, Dell's intended strategy was based on a performance-for-value logic and its Dell Direct service model to maintain its solid relationships with corporate and government clients in China.

In terms of staging, Dell flipped its distribution model on its head. This is a third example of how the company flexibly adapted its historic strategic approach to enter into China. In the United States, Dell built its Dell Direct model through the direct-to-consumer market; it entered the corporate-customer market only after it had established a strong, profitable foothold with consumers. In China, however, the Dell Direct market was more commercially viable with corporate customers, who have both the cash and access to infrastructure to make the Dell Direct model work effectively. Although Dell initially worked through distributors in China for the consumer market, its staging plan was to migrate these consumers eventually to its Dell Direct model.

Finally, Dell's economic logic is one of both scale and scope economies. It can leverage its size to gain the best terms and prices for the best technologies for the products it sells. It can use this cost advantage to compete in China and at the same time further enhance the Dell Direct model's footprint on the global computer market. So far, it appears that Dell's global strategy, and its flexible approach to entering countries like China, is paying off. Michael Dell said the company's overall business in China was strong, growing, and profitable. Dell's revenue in China increased 26 percent in 2006. Dell's revenue share in China is about 20 percent, which is double its 10-percent share of product shipments, because the company also sells services and other products beyond PCs there.

Nonetheless, Dell is facing strong competition. On December 9, 2004, IBM announced the sale of its entire PC division to Lenovo, a Chinese multinational firm. This left Dell, Hewlett-Packard, and Lenovo as the world's top three PC makers. At the time, industry analysts were placing their bets on wildly efficient Dell to broaden its lead, both globally and in China, by the middle of 2007. Dell seemed invincible using the low-cost model. Now, however, other companies have figured out how to make and sell PCs as cheaply as Dell. Exhibit 1 shows the respective market positions of the top five desktop, notebook, and PC makers, with HP leading the pack.

To respond to the fierce competition in China, Dell will have to cut its costs. Just a few weeks after CEO Michael Dell's heralded trip to the Middle Kingdom, local Chinese media report that Dell China has formulated a plan to reduce staff at the end of April 2007. According to the plan, Dell China will reduce up to 13 percent of the staff in each of its departments. The reports say that it is urgent for Dell to reduce its staff because its operational expenditures increased remarkably over ten consecutive quarters, but its revenue per employee dropped to the lowest level in seven years. <<<

247

Exhibit 1 Global PC
Industry Market Share
Comparables

Exhibit 1 Global PC
Industry Market Share
Comparables

Company	Global Market Share	Annual Sales Growth
HP	17.4%	23.9%
Dell	13.9%	−8.7%
Lenovo	7.1%	9.3%
Acer	6.8%	33.1%
Toshiba	3.8%	24.5%
Rest of Market	51.0%	3.8%
Total Market	100.0%	7.4%

International Strategy

international strategy
Process by which a firm approaches
its cross-border activities and those
of competitors and plans to approach
them in the future.

What is *international strategy?* When should managers consider such a strategy? A firm's **international strategy** is how it approaches the cross-border business activities of its own firm and competitors and how it contemplates doing so in the future. In the narrowest sense, a firm's managers need only think about international strategy when they conduct some aspect of their business across national borders. Some international activities are designed to augment a firm's business strategy, such as sourcing key factors of production to cheaper labor markets (i.e., attempts to become more competitive within a core business). Other international activities represent key elements of the firm's corporate strategy (i.e., entering new businesses or new markets). Whether expanding internationally to reinforce a particular business's strategy or as part of a corporate strategy, international expansion is a form of diversification because the firm has chosen to operate in a different market.

Throughout this text, you have been exposed to many organizations, including those focused on one primary geographic region and others that are very global in their operating scope. For some organizations, a global mindset pervades managerial thinking and is explicit in the firm's vision, mission, goals, objectives, and strategy. With other firms, international strategy may be very new. Regardless of the case, a firm must carefully prepare for an international strategy through the analysis of all the dimensions of the strategy diamond.

The preventative cure for domestic-strategy myopia, and surefire pathway to a global mindset, is a broad awareness of the international landscape. Exhibit 2 highlights some of the top global trends that executives consider relevant to the competitive fortunes of their businesses.[1]

These trends suggest new market opportunities, such as the growth of consumer demand in emerging markets. They also suggest new concerns and constraints, particularly those related to natural resources and the environment. We encourage you to learn about these broader trends, different countries, and national cultures and internalize a cosmopolitan view of international strategy. In the broadest sense, a firm needs to consider its international strategy when any single or potential competitor is not domestic or otherwise conducts business across borders. Increasingly, it is this latter context that makes it imperative that almost all firms think about the international dimensions of their business, even if they have no international operations whatsoever. Thus, international strategy essentially reflects

Exhibit 2 Global Trends to Watch

Trend	Examples
Shifting of economic activity between countries and regions	Growth in demand for energy and basic materials (such as steel and copper) is moving from developed countries to developing ones, predominantly in Asia. Demand for oil in China and India, for example, will nearly double from 2003 to 2020, to 15.4 million barrels a day. Asia's oil consumption will approach that of the United States—the world's largest consumer—by the end of that period.
Shifting of economic activity within countries and regions	The story is not simply the march to Asia. Shifts within regions are as significant as those occurring across regions. For example, by 2015 the Hispanic population in the United States will have spending power equivalent to that of 60 percent of all Chinese consumers.
Growing number of consumers in emerging economies	Economic growth in the developing world will usher nearly a billion new consumers into the global marketplace over the next decade, as household incomes reach the level (around $5,000) associated with discretionary spending. Although these consumers will have less spending power than do their counterparts in the developed world, they will have similar demands as well as access to global brands. Many industries, therefore, face polarized markets where premium and no-frills offerings are squeezing middle-of-the-road offerings.
Increasing availability of knowledge and the ability to exploit it	Knowledge is increasingly available and, at the same time, increasingly specialized. The most obvious manifestation of this trend is the rise of search engines (such as Google) and online marketplaces (such as eBay and Amazon) that make an almost infinite amount of information available instantaneously.
Increasing global labor and talent markets	Ongoing shifts in labor and talent will be far more profound than the widely observed migration of jobs to low-wage countries. The shift to knowledge-intensive industries highlights the importance and scarcity of well-trained talent. The increasing integration of global labor markets, however, is opening up vast new talent sources. The 33 million university-educated young professionals in developing countries is more than double the number in developed ones. For many companies and governments, global labor and talent strategies will become as important as global sourcing and manufacturing strategies. For instance, in India there are about 245,000 Indians answering phones from all over the world about credit card and cell phone offers, along with bill collection. This type of skill shift is repeated across areas from data-input to programming to copyediting.
Resource and environmental strains	As economic growth accelerates—particulary in emerging markets—demand for natural resources is growing at unprecedented rates. Oil demand is projected to grow by 50 percent in the next two decades, and without large new discoveries or radical innovations supply is unlikely to keep up. Similar surges in demand across a broad range of commodities are being seen as well. In China, for example, demand for copper, steel, and aluminum has nearly tripled in the past decade. Evidence is emerging that one of our scarcest natural resources—the atmosphere—will require dramatic shifts in human behavior to keep it from being depleted further.

the choices a firm's executives make with respect to sourcing and selling its goods in foreign markets, and dealing with foreign competitors who enter their markets.

It probably comes as no surprise to you that all of the world's largest corporations are global as well. A simple review of the top-20 firms among *Fortune*'s Global 500 provides you with a snapshot of these global behemoths each year, in terms of who is largest and who has the best global reputation. As you can see in Exhibit 3, some of these large firms, seen at the beginning of 2007, had revenues greater than many countries' GDP!

And, with the exceptions of Wal-Mart and GE, the mix of top firms is clearly clustered among the oil and gas, automotive, banking, and insurance industries.[2] Even among this special group, you can see that firms vary significantly in terms of their international presence. What may be surprising, however, is the increasing presence of arguably tiny firms that are global very early in their lives, such as Logitech (which started in Switzerland and California and was global from inception) and Skype (which started in Sweden and went global in a year, and was recently acquired by EBay).

As you work through this chapter, you will see how international strategy must be reflected in all facets of the strategy diamond. Exhibit 4 summarizes some of the key strategic questions that firms must answer about the strategy diamond, such as Dell did in the opening vignette, as they expand into international markets.

Exhibit 3   Top 20 Global Companies Based on Revenue

Rank	Company	Country/HQ	Industry	Revenues ($ millions)	Profits ($ millions)	% Foreign Sales
1	Exxon Mobil	USA	Oil and Gas	339,938.0	36,130.0	69.14%
2	Wal-Mart Stores	USA	Retail	315,654.0	11,231.0	22.35%
3	Royal Dutch Shell	UK/Netherlands	Oil and Gas	306,731.0	25,311.0	57.25%*
4	BP	UK	Oil and Gas	267,600.0	22,341.0	70.17%
5	General Motors	USA	Automotive	192,604.0	–10,567.0	37.77%
6	Chevron	USA	Oil and Gas	189,481.0	14,099.0	55.19%
7	DaimlerChrysler	Germany	Automotive	186,106.3	3,536.3	14.64%
8	Toyota Motor	Japan	Automotive	185,805.0	12,119.6	63.23%
9	Ford Motor	USA	Automotive	177,210.0	2,024.0	49.32%
10	ConocoPhillips	USA	Oil and Gas	166,683.0	13,529.0	30.37%
11	General Electric	USA	Diversified	157,153.0	16,353.0	45.45%
12	Total	France	Oil and Gas	152,360.7	15,250.0	76.01%
13	ING Group	Netherlands	Banking	138,235.3	8,958.9	77.12%
14	Citigroup	USA	Banking	131,045.0	24,589.0	32.38%
15	AXA	France	Insurance	129,839.2	5,186.5	17.00%
16	Allianz	Germany	Insurance	121,406.0	5,442.4	70.72%
17	Volkswagen	Germany	Automotive	118,376.6	1,391.7	72.80%*
18	Fortis	Belgium	Banking	112,351.4	4,896.3	15.94%
19	Crédit Agricole	France	Banking	110,764.6	7,434.3	43.0%
20	American Intl. Group	USA	Insurance	108,905.0	10,477.0	48.77%

*Royal Dutch Shell and Volkswagen report domestic sales as sales in Europe.

250

Exhibit 4 The Five Elements in International Strategy

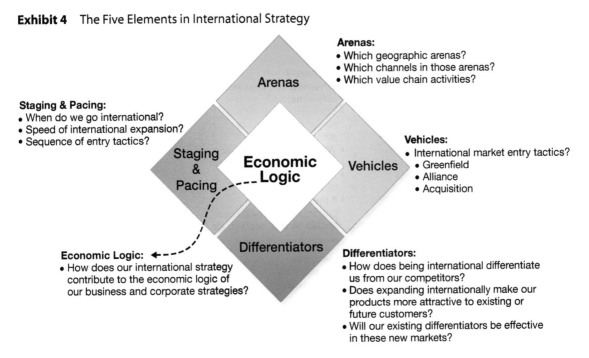

Arenas:
- Which geographic arenas?
- Which channels in those arenas?
- Which value chain activities?

Staging & Pacing:
- When do we go international?
- Speed of international expansion?
- Sequence of entry tactics?

Vehicles:
- International market entry tactics?
  - Greenfield
  - Alliance
  - Acquisition

Economic Logic:
- How does our international strategy contribute to the economic logic of our business and corporate strategies?

Differentiators:
- How does being international differentiate us from our competitors?
- Does expanding internationally make our products more attractive to existing or future customers?
- Will our existing differentiators be effective in these new markets?

International Strategy and Competitive Advantage

Why, where, and how? Using the strategy diamond and another simple framework we refer to as the 1-2-3 Model, these are the three basic questions that international strategy must answer. While there is obviously a lot of analysis that must go into answering them, these three basic questions—summarized in Exhibit 5—will put you in a good position to determine the scale and scope of your international strategy.

Too often, executives make international strategy choices based on what competitors are doing, instead of starting with answers to fundamental strategy diamond questions like: (1) *Why* should we expand into another geographic arena (is the economic logic compelling and do our differentiators apply)?; (2) If so, *where*—which new geographic arena?; and (3) If this arena, then *how*—what vehicles will we use, and how should entry be staged and paced? Notice, for instance, that Dell identified the need to be a global player based on its growth objectives, customer needs, and opportunities to garner new customers. These needs fit with the economic logic of Dell's strategy. They also leveraged Dell's differentiators—relationships with customers and Dell's quality image. Dell then identified China as an important stepping stone—or stage—in its global growth aspirations. Finally, it chose an entry strategy—starting with an alliance with Indian distributors—for staging its efforts to do well in the new China market.

Given the complexities and risks of managing business activities across borders, it is imperative to understand why any firm would take on the often significant costs of doing so in terms of time, dollars, and managerial attention. One reason is simply necessity. Increasingly, many experts in the field of strategic management view global expansion as necessary for just about every medium and large corporation. This opinion is based on a few basic observations: (1) that capital markets and employees favor fast-growing firms, and many domestic markets in developed countries are becoming saturated; (2) that efficiencies in all value-chain activities are linked across borders, and the linkages and pressures for efficiency continue to escalate; (3) new market opportunities are present in developing economies; (4) that knowledge is not uniformly distributed around the world, and new ideas increasingly

Exhibit 5 Your 1-2-3 Model of Internationalization

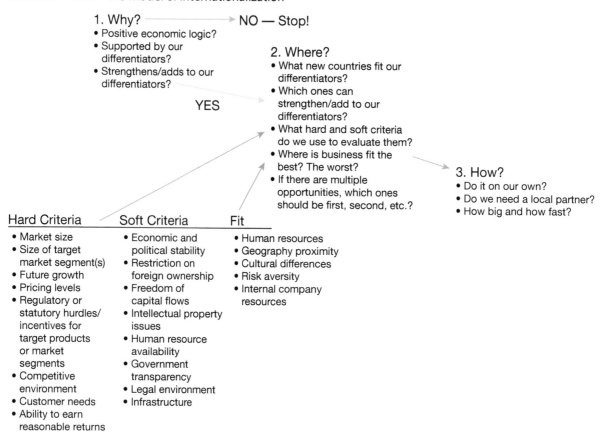

1. Why? ————————→ NO — Stop!
- Positive economic logic?
- Supported by our differentiators?
- Strengthens/adds to our differentiators?

YES

2. Where?
- What new countries fit our differentiators?
- Which ones can strengthen/add to our differentiators?
- What hard and soft criteria do we use to evaluate them?
- Where is business fit the best? The worst?
- If there are multiple opportunities, which ones should be first, second, etc.?

3. How?
- Do it on our own?
- Do we need a local partner?
- How big and how fast?

Hard Criteria
- Market size
- Size of target market segment(s)
- Future growth
- Pricing levels
- Regulatory or statutory hurdles/ incentives for target products or market segments
- Competitive environment
- Customer needs
- Ability to earn reasonable returns

Soft Criteria
- Economic and political stability
- Restriction on foreign ownership
- Freedom of capital flows
- Intellectual property issues
- Human resource availability
- Government transparency
- Legal environment
- Infrastructure

Fit
- Human resources
- Geography proximity
- Cultural differences
- Risk aversity
- Internal company resources

are coming from emerging economies; (5) that customers themselves are becoming global at both the organizational level in terms of the growth and proliferation of multinationals and at the individual level in terms of consumer preferences; and (6) that competitors are globalizing, even if your organization is not.[3]

THE PROS AND CONS OF INTERNATIONAL EXPANSION

International expansion is no panacea for corporate-growth needs, and it is inherently hazardous even when it promises revenue opportunities. For instance, at the beginning of the 1990s, PepsiCo established an ambitious goal to triple its international sales from $1.5 billion to $5 billion within just five years. PepsiCo aggressively pursued this growth, yet it failed to keep pace with the growth of international markets and actually lost ground to Coca-Cola. While Coke was reaping the benefits of the growth of soft drinks in international markets, Pepsi's international market share actually shrank.[4] Pepsi's experience demonstrates that simply participating in international markets does not equate to having a competitive advantage to exploit international opportunities. Indeed, if you consult *Fortune*'s list of the largest global firms, you will typically find Wal-Mart at the top of that list. Yet, Wal-Mart's non–U.S. operations do very poorly in comparison to its domestic business. Global expansion can just as easily contribute to profitability as it can detract from it. The key is to align international expansion with the firm's strategy in a way to exploit and further develop firm resources and capabilities.[5] Ultimately, the benefits must outweigh the costs, and more often than not, questions about a firm's nondomestic profitability take years to answer. The opening vignette on Dell demonstrates the ups and downs associated with international strategy and the necessary alignment of the elements of strategy and the firm's resources and capabilities. In addition to the possible benefits of international expansion, a firm incurs a number of costs when diversifying its business operations around the globe.[6] The costs of geographic diversification include the liabilities of newness and foreignness, and governance and coordination costs.

Liabilities of Newness and Foreignness *Liability of newness* can be thought of as a disadvantage (cost disadvantage or other disadvantages) associated with being a new player in the market. For instance, a firm suffering from a liability of newness does not initially gain benefits from the learning curve. Likewise, *liability of foreignness* is the disadvantage a firm faces by not being a local player. This disadvantage may be cultural, in that the firm's managers do not understand local market conditions. It may also be political, such as when the firm does not understand local laws or have relationships in place to manage the local regulatory environment.

Firm managers contend with many challenges when establishing operations in a new country, including the logistics of purchasing and installing facilities, staffing, and establishing internal management systems and external business networks. Costs associated with establishing a new business can put a new foreign division in a disadvantageous position relative to local or more established foreign competitors. These types of disadvantages tend to dissipate with time as the division gains local experience, which in turn diminish the negative influence of liability of newness and foreignness.

Costs Associated with Governance and Coordination Although the disadvantages of newness and foreignness typically decline over time, governance and coordination costs are disadvantages that tend to increase as international diversification increases. Some of the issues that increase governance and coordination costs include information distortion as it is transferred and translated across divisions and countries. Coordination difficulties and possible misalignment between headquarters and divisional managers in international firms increases as international diversification increases, much as in highly diversified domestic firms. Because every country has a relatively unique business environment, the more country environments a firm must deal with, the greater the difficulty and cost of coordinating operations across these diverse environments.

Offsetting Costs and Benefits As shown in Exhibit 6, the costs associated with internationalization can offset the possible benefits of operating in multiple markets.[7] A firm's level of internationalization, shown on the horizontal axis, refers to the degree to which it has tapped foreign markets, particularly for product or service sales. The potential economic benefits of internationalization are modest at first, and then become quite significant before the marginal benefits level off. These potential increases in revenue must of course be balanced with the costs of internationalization. Costs are significant in early efforts to internationalize. After a presence is established, economies of scale and scope kick in, and the incremental costs of further expansion are minimal. However, bureaucratic and management costs can spike at extreme levels of internationalization. This increase in costs is similar to the notion of diseconomies of scale and scope introduced in earlier chapters. Consequently, research suggests that performance gains from internationalization come not at the early stages but at moderate to high levels; however, at very high levels of internationalization, firms tend to suffer performance declines.[8] The key for managers is to find a way to exploit the possible advantages of economies of scale and scope, location, and learning without having them offset by the excessive costs of internationalization. The tradeoff between costs and benefits of internationalization results in an S-curve relationship between internationalization and firm performance.

Exhibit 6 Costs and Benefits of Internationalization

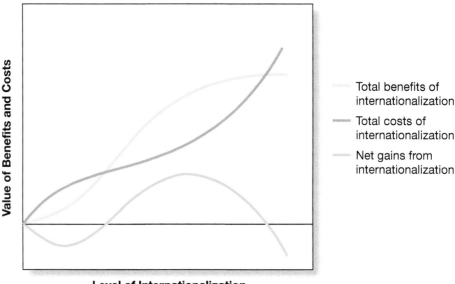

Level of Internationalization

- Total benefits of internationalization
- Total costs of internationalization
- Net gains from internationalization

KEY FACTORS IN INTERNATIONAL EXPANSION

International strategy, particularly in the form of international expansion, can contribute to a firm's competitive advantage in a number of interrelated ways. The four most important aspects are *economies of scale and scope, location, multipoint competition,* and *learning.* While most of these aspects are directly related to the economic logic of a firm's strategy, they also can contribute to the differentiators. Firms must understand the specific benefits in one or more of these areas if they are to proceed with international expansion plans.

Global Economies of Scale and Scope

Referring back to the strategy diamond, international strategy affects a firm's economic logic through its implications for economies of scale and scope. ◆ Larger firms are not necessarily more efficient or more profitable, but in some industries, such as pharmaceuticals and aircraft manufacturing, the enormous costs of new-product development require that the firm be able to generate commensurate sales, and this increasingly requires firms to have a global presence.

For instance, R&D costs are skyrocketing in many industries. This requires that firms in those industries seek a larger revenue base, typically outside of their home countries. This relationship is demonstrated by strategy research showing that the performance benefits from R&D increase with a firm's degree of internationalization: Firms generate more profits out of their R&D investments if they are also highly global.[9] One reason for this is that there is a minimum threshold of R&D investment necessary to launch a new product. When the firm can amortize those costs across many markets, it can in effect lower its average cost per sale. It is interesting to note that, when graphed, the relationship between performance, R&D investment, and internationalization further demonstrates the S-curve relationship between internationalization and firm performance discussed earlier in this chapter. Such economies of scale can also be realized for intangibles, such as a firm's brand, much as CitiGroup, McDonald's, and Coca-Cola leverage their brands in practically every country in the world.

Scale and Operating Efficiency The larger scale that accompanies global expansion only creates competitive advantage if the firm translates scale into operating efficiency. As you learned in Chapter 5, cost savings are not axiomatic with larger scale. Larger scale must be managed to avoid diseconomies of scale. As with economies of scale in general, the potential scale economies from global expansion include spreading fixed costs over a larger sales and asset base and increasing purchasing power.[10] Attempts to gain scale advantages must

254

be focused on resources and activities that are scale sensitive, and it means that these resources and activities must be concentrated in just a few locations.[11] However, if these resources and activities are concentrated in a few locations, they can become isolated from key markets, which may lead to delayed responses to market changes. For instance, until Dell established a regional office and manufacturing facility in Brazil (Eldorado do Sul), its sales and service record in Brazil suffered.

Economies of Global Scope A specialized form of scope economies is available to firms as they expand globally. Recall that scope economies were defined as the ability to lower average costs by sharing a resource across different products. Numerous scope economies are available to firms that expand globally. For example, CitiGroup, McDonald's, and Coca-Cola profit from scope economies to the extent that the different country markets share the benefits of brand equity that these firms have built up over time. The opening vignette on Dell, too, provides several examples of scope as well as scale economies across different geographic and customer markets, starting with its ability to take advantage of its brand; its capability to leverage its Dell Direct sales model and related Internet sales and support technologies; its experience and relationships with distributors in India and then China; and its different geographic units' ability to pool their purchasing power for key components, such as CPUs, from powerful suppliers like Intel.

Consider how a supplier to McDonald's could exploit economies of global scope, which in turn provide it with economies of scale in production and other related value-chain activities. McDonald's needs the same ketchup products in Europe and South America as it does in the United States. A vendor with sufficient global scope to satisfy McDonald's worldwide demand for ketchup would be an attractive sourcing alternative to McDonald's compared with sourcing this supply from numerous local suppliers.[12] In this case, global scope gives a supplier an opportunity to generate revenue that it would be unable to generate in the absence of global scope. Of course, McDonalds' global scope also gives it access to more suppliers from around the globe, including local suppliers in many markets. Local suppliers may also have some advantages over global players in terms of being able to provide more immediate service and greater knowledge of local business practices. Thus, firms like McDonald's are in the enviable position of being able to source the lowest cost inputs and use lower local prices and service levels to force global suppliers to keep prices down and service levels high.

Attempts to gain economies of scope also face numerous hazards as well. Although economies of scope are possible as resources are shared across markets, strategy must still be executed at the national level.[13] In cases such as China, the United States, and Europe, where the "nation" is actually composed of distinctly different subgeographic markets (cantons in Switzerland, countries in other parts of Europe, states in the United States, and provinces in China), successful execution at the local level is further complicated. This can easily lead to tension between the need to identify and satisfy the local client contact and the aim of lowering costs by sharing resources and having actions coordinated across markets.

Location National and regional geographic location has an impact on competitive advantage as well, because of its implications for input costs, competitors, demand conditions, and complements. A basic five-forces industry analysis can be used to determine the importance of a given location. The analysis of industry structure should include such features as barriers to entry, new entrants, substitutes, and existing competitors, both domestic and international. Related and supporting industries that are forward and backward in the value chain, as well as true complements, also need to be identified.

With such an analysis in hand, the value chain and five-forces analysis can be geographically segmented to consider how and why rivalry may play out differently in different geographic arenas. ◆   In terms of customers, for instance, an analysis of consumption trends among the top 25 countries in the global soft drink industry shows that India and China

Arenas

Huge international chains, such as McDonald's, are able to achieve economies of scope, thereby lowering the costs of inputs they purchase both globally and in local markets.
(AP Wide World Photos)

exhibit fairly steady growth. A firm's managers can thus assess the desirability of investing in one market versus another, the competitive consequences of such an investment, and the value-chain activities needed to locate in each region. For instance, India and China may be prime locations to launch new growth initiatives for large players like Coca-Cola and Pepsi. Such an analysis should show how the firm's strategy has connected the dots, so to speak, in terms of linking resources, capabilities, and locations—and in this case, the choice of a new geographic arena should be consistent with the other facets of the firm's strategy, as seen in the strategy diamond.

Arbitrage Opportunities Beyond the five-forces and value-chain assessment, location differences also present an opportunity for arbitrage. Arbitrage represents the age-old practice of buying something in one market and selling it another market where it garners a higher price. Historically, the value added in such arbitrage was simply tracking down a desirable commodity, such as spice, tea, or silk, from a faraway land, and transporting it to a market that would pay a premium for it. Companies can improve performance and potentially build competitive advantage by optimizing the location of their value-chain activities. Significant cost differences for different types of value-chain activities exist around the globe. A firm that can optimize the intercountry cost differences better than its rivals will have a cost advantage. The caveat here is that arbitrage opportunities may be fleeting in that once they are identified, competitors who lack entry barriers can quickly realize them as well. Therefore, a firm that relies on arbitrage as a core part of its competitive strategy must possess greater capabilities in continually identifying new arbitrage opportunities as well as in increasing entry barriers for competitors trying to follow it.

Multipoint Competition Firms can develop competitive advantages through multipoint competition. **Multipoint competition** refers to the situation when a firm competes against another firm in multiple product markets or multiple geographic markets (or both). For instance, Proctor and Gamble and Unilever not only compete head to head in personal care products around the globe, they also compete in the soaps and detergents markets. When the firm competes in multiple international markets, as a special kind of multipoint

multipoint competition
When a firm competes against another firm in multiple product markets or multiple geographic markets (or both).

tactic, the stronghold assault becomes available. *Stronghold assault* refers to the competitive actions a firm takes in another firm's key markets, particularly when the attacking firm has little presence in that market. In the case of international strategy, stronghold assault refers to attacks on the geographic markets that are most important to a competitor's profitability and cash flow. A classic example of international stronghold assault is provided by the actions of French tire manufacturer Michelin and the U.S. tire company Goodyear in the 1970s.[14] Early on, both firms had negligible market presence in each other's respective domestic markets (Europe and the United States). Michelin became aware of Goodyear's intent to expand its presence in Europe, so it started selling its tires in the United States at or below its actual cost. Although these sales were a miniscule part of Michelin's overall sales, Michelin's sales tactic forced Goodyear to drop its prices in the United States, and hence lower the profitability of its largest market.

Such multipoint competitive tactics often initially benefit customers at the expense of competitors until a new market equilibrium is reached. Moreover, Michelin's low-price ploy earned it a larger share of the U.S. market, such that the lost profits in the United States began to take a toll on Michelin's overall profitability. In addition, nothing prevented Goodyear from doing the same thing in Michelin's home markets, further eroding both firms' profitability. Eventually, both firms ended up in the international courts charging each other with "dumping"—selling goods below cost in a foreign country.

Even today, stronghold assault is a motivation for global investment, but as the Michelin case highlights, it must be used with care and is typically not sustainable. Therefore, firms that employ this tactic should also have strategies in the staging component that take into account when and how the firm will shift from price competition to more sustainable bases of competition. For this reason, stronghold assault is used not only to underprice a competitor's products in its home market but also to simply eliminate the competitor's home market monopoly. Just as with the cola wars, the Michelin–Goodyear war left the industry landscape forever changed, and both firms had to adjust their strategies to survive in the new industry structure that resulted.

Learning and Knowledge Sharing

Learning is very important to the success of a firm's international strategy for a variety of reasons. At the very least, a firm with operations that cross borders must learn how to cope with different institutional, legal, and cultural environments. For the most successful firms, international expansion is used as a vehicle for innovation, improving existing products in existing markets, or coming up with new ideas for new markets. It is one thing to use such tools as the five-forces, value-chain, and other frameworks to identify profit or arbitrage opportunities, for instance, but it is quite another thing to exploit them successfully and profitably. For instance, Michelin initially shipped products to the United States and didn't care whether it made money on them because it viewed any losses as insignificant. But eventually that tactic caused the U.S. market to grow in importance as part of the French tire maker's overall global sales, and it had to reckon with making this part of its business profitable or admit defeat and abandon the U.S. market—one of the auto industry's largest and most profitable markets.

Similarly, Dell first used Indian then Chinese distributors in serving the consumer segment in China, but this is a much less profitable vehicle and differentiator than its core distribution and sales engine—the Dell Direct model. Dell's goal was to migrate from its Chinese distributors and eventually learn enough about the Chinese marketplace to use its direct-sales vehicle, which can be accessed through kiosks placed in busy foot-traffic locations. Like the product-diversified firm, the geographic-diversified firm must somehow learn how to ensure that the benefits of being international outweigh the added costs of the infrastructure necessary to support its nondomestic operations.

Learning and local adaptation appear to be particularly difficult for U.S. firms, even when they are very big firms that already have an international presence. For instance, with nearly a half-billion dollars in annual sales, Lincoln Electric completed its largest acquisition ever in 1991—the $70-million purchase of Germany's Messer Gresheim, a manufacturer of welding equipment, which was Lincoln's core business.[15] Although Lincoln maintained the bulk of its business in the United States, it had over 40 years of marketing and manufacturing experience in Canada, Australia, and France. Moreover, the company was in the process of aggressively ramping up manufacturing and sales operations in Japan, Venezuela, Brazil, the Netherlands, Norway, and the United Kingdom. With the acquisition of Gresheim, as with the other newly established international operations, Lincoln's management simply assumed that it could transplant its manufacturing approach, aggressive compensation and incentive systems (Lincoln pays employees only for what they produce), and culture—the three key success factors in the U.S. business—to the newly obtained German and other foreign operations. Within a year, the European operations were in disarray; losses were mounting in Japan and Latin America; and Lincoln reported a quarterly consolidated loss of $12 million—the first quarterly consolidated loss in the company's 97-year history.

Although Lincoln eventually recovered from the brink of disaster and ruin, it only did so after top management recognized and took steps to remedy the harsh reality that it had insufficient international experience, a dearth of experience in and knowledge about running a globally dispersed organization, and no understanding of how to manage foreign operations and foreign cultures. Part of its salvation involved scaling back many of the foreign operations it had acquired, giving the firm breathing room to develop its international operating and managerial capabilities. As a consequence of its learning from its failures abroad, Lincoln is now a global success story, as summarized in excerpts from its 2006 annual report shown in Exhibit 7.

Learning, Knowledge, Transfer, and Innovation Beyond the rather obvious aspects of learning shown in the Lincoln Electric case, a firm that has operations in different coun-

Exhibit 7 Global Strategy at Lincoln Electric

To Our Shareholders: During 2006, the continued strong worldwide demand for our products, combined with the effective execution of our global strategy, contributed to another year of excellent performance for Lincoln Electric. By maintaining our focus on the five key components for excellence—people development, customer service, operational efficiency, global expansion, and innovative products—we have been able to take advantage of many opportunities in rapidly growing markets around the world.

We are expanding our footprint, strengthening our global leadership position in the welding industry and taking advantage of significant growth opportunities. Our performance has been strong everywhere we operate—in North America, Europe, Asia, the Middle East and Latin America—and we have gained market share in each of these regions.

From a global perspective, we are strengthening our position in emerging markets while continuing to serve existing markets. In Asia, specifically China, which stands to be the largest market for welding products for the foreseeable future, we are significantly increasing our manufacturing capacity for flux cored wire. We also are constructing a new facility in India to begin production of consumables in 2007, and we have recently expanded capacity at our Indonesia consumables plant.

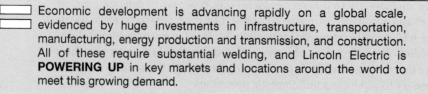

Economic development is advancing rapidly on a global scale, evidenced by huge investments in infrastructure, transportation, manufacturing, energy production and transmission, and construction. All of these require substantial welding, and Lincoln Electric is **POWERING UP** in key markets and locations around the world to meet this growing demand.

Source: Lincoln Electric Annual Report

tries has the opportunity to increase innovation and transfer knowledge from one geographic market to another. For example, SC Johnson's European operations learned about a product that involved the combination of household pesticides and a simple plug-in device. In Europe, this product was sold in stores to consumers who needed a cheap and efficient deterrent for mosquitoes and other annoying insects. SC Johnson demonstrated its ability to learn from its European operation by transferring the technology to its fragrance division in the United States, thus giving rise to a whole new category of air fresheners called Glade PlugIns.[16]

A second facet of this form of learning is to locate a firm or a particular aspect of its operations in a part of the world where competition is the fiercest. So, for example, a U.S. automaker might locate a product facility in Japan. Ironically, although one goal of such a move is actually to compete on Japan's own turf against incumbents Toyota and Honda, the learning objective is to try to emulate and learn from Japan's auto manufacturers' leading-edge production practices and transfer that advanced knowledge to the U.S. company's plants in other parts of the world, such as the United States, Canada, and Mexico. Similarly, because France and Italy are leaders in the high-fashion industry, companies such as DuPont and W. L. Gore & Associates, which aim to compete with leading-edge fabrics such as Lycra and Gore-Tex, place high value on those countries as production and marketing locations because of the learning opportunities about future customer preferences (e.g., touch, feel, color, etc.). In this view, the strategically most important markets will be those that feature not only intrinsic market attractiveness but an opportunity to learn and innovate in ways that can improve the organization's operations, products, and services around the globe.[17]

Sharing Knowledge Across Business Units Finally, large multinationals can exploit opportunities for inter-business-unit collaboration, which results in valuable knowledge sharing.[18] Sharing knowledge across business units has several tangible benefits. First, it enables firms to transfer best practices across national and business-unit boundaries. Because these best practices are proprietary—and probably tailored to the idiosyncrasies of the firm—they are more likely to result in competitive advantage than borrowing best practices from other firms. Why? Because all competitors have access to that information as well.

An example of this type of knowledge sharing is illustrated by a case study of British Petroleum (BP). A U.S. business unit that operates service stations was looking for novel ways to reduce costs in BP convenience stores. A manager borrowed ideas from colleagues in the Netherlands and the United Kingdom about how to reduce working-capital requirements. Copying these practices and implementing them in the United States resulted in a 20-percent reduction in working capital.

Sharing knowledge across business units can also uncover revenue-enhancement opportunities. The country manager of GlaxoSmithKline in the Philippines found a new drug therapy for tuberculosis in the company's R&D lab in India. Although this therapy was not widely known within the company because it represented a very small slice of the multinational firm's business, it represented a huge market opportunity in the Philippines and other developing countries, where tuberculosis is more widespread than it is in Europe and the United States.

Using CAGE to Choose Foreign Countries

Now that you have answered the *why* question of international strategy, you must move on to answer the *where* question. But the world is a big place, so where do you start? Some markets are growing so quickly that their sheer size merits consideration. Exhibit 8 presents the top ten countries in terms of population, in addition to information on GDP, and GDP growth.[19]

The European Union and the United States have the most global Fortune 500 firms, 172 and 114 respectively, as of the start of 2007. And, as you might expect, Brazil, Russia,

Exhibit 8 Comparative Country Information of the Top 10 Markets by Population

Country	Est. Population 2007	Labor Force	Internet Users	GDP (in $ millions)	Average GDP Real Growth Rate (%)
China	1,321,851,888	798,000,000	123,000,000	10,000,000	10.50
India	1,129,866,154	509,300,000	60,000,000	4,042,000	8.50
European Union	460,827,146	222,700,000	247,000,000	12,820,000	2.80
United States	301,139,947	151,400,000	205,327,000	12,980,000	3.40
Indonesia	234,693,997	108,200,000	16,000,000	935,000	5.40
Brazil	190,010,647	96,340,000	25,900,000	1,616,000	2.80
Pakistan	164,741,924	48,290,000	10,500,000	427,300	6.50
Bangladesh	150,448,339	68,000,000	300,000	330,800	6.10
Russia	141,377,752	73,880,000	23,700,000	1,723,000	6.60
Nigeria	135,031,164	48,990,000	5,000,000	188,500	5.30

India, and China (you will often see them referred to collectively as BRIC) figure greatly into the landscape of developing economies where there is great opportunity married with great risk. Moreover, these four particular markets are giving rise to a new breed of savvy global competitor. They are shaking up entire industries, from farm equipment and refrigerators to aircraft and telecom services, and changing the rules of global competition (see Exhibit 9 for one view of how they are shaking things up in strategy and competition).[20]

The CAGE Framework   Generally, the greater the distance covered and the greater the value differences between the disconnected markets, the greater the profit potential that arises from arbitrage. However, greater distance also tends to be accompanied by greater entry costs and risks.

Although most people tend to think of distance in geographic terms, in the area of international strategy distance can also be viewed in terms of culture, administrative heritage, and economics. As summarized in Exhibit 10, this broader **CAGE framework**—Culture, **A**dministrative, **G**eographic, and **E**conomic—provides you with another way of thinking about location and the opportunities and concomitant risks associated with global arbitrage.[21] CAGE-related risks would be most relevant in industries in which language or cultural identity are important factors, the government views the products as staples or as essential to national security, or income or input costs are key determinants of product demand or cost. CAGE asks you to look at countries and regions, try to assess the degree to which they are different or similar along many of the PESTEL dimensions, and then try to estimate the implications of such differences for a firm that wishes to move into a new geographic market.

Application of the CAGE framework requires managers to identify attractive locations based on raw material costs, access to markets or consumers, or other key decision criteria. For instance, a firm may be most interested in markets with high consumer buying power, so it uses per capita income as the first sorting cue. This would result in some type of ranking. For example, one researcher examined the fast food industry and found that based on per capita income, countries such as Germany and Japan would be the most attractive markets for the expansion of a North American-based fast food company. However, when the analysis was adjusted for distance using the CAGE framework, the revised results showed that Mexico ranked as the second-most-attractive market for international expansion, far ahead of Germany and Japan.[22]

CAGE framework Tool that considers the dimensions of culture, administration, geography, and economics to assess the distance created by global expansion.

Exhibit 9   The Emerging Market Boom

In the world of global strategy and competition, new contenders are hailing from seemingly unlikely places, developing nations such as Brazil, Russia, India, China, and even Egypt and South Africa. They are shaking up entire industries, from farm equipment and refrigerators to aircraft and telecom services, and changing the rules of global competition. These changes are consistent with those presaged by the trends you learned about in Exhibit 8.2.

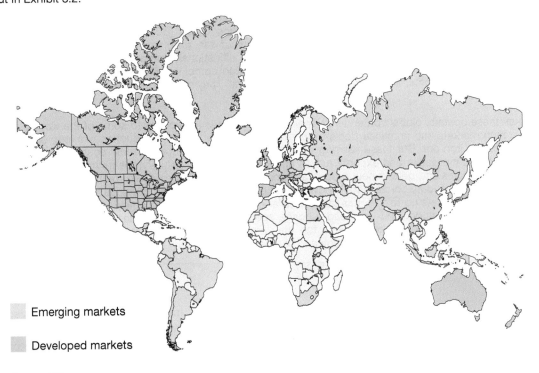

Emerging markets

Developed markets

Grey—Other

Unlike Japanese and Korean conglomerates, which benefited from protection and big profits at home before they took on the world, these emerging economy upstarts are mostly companies that have prevailed in brutally competitive domestic markets, where local companies have to duke it out with homegrown rivals and Western multinationals every day. As a result, these emerging champions must make profits at price levels unheard of in the United States or Europe. Indian generic drugmakers, for example, often charge customers in their home market as little as 1% to 2% of what people pay in the United States. Cellular outfits in North Africa, Brazil, and India offer phone service for pennies per minute. Yet these companies often thrive in such tough environments. Egyptian cellular operator Orascom boasts margins of 49%; Mahindra's pretax profit rose 81% in 2006.

Some already are marquee names. Lenovo Group, the Chinese computer maker, made waves in 2005 by buying IBM's $11 billion PC business. Indian software outfits Infosys, Tata Consultancy Services, and Wipro have revolutionized the $650 billion technology services industry. Johannesburg brewer SABMiller PLC is challenging Anheuser-Busch Cos.' leadership right in the United States.

These companies are just the first wave. The biggest international cellular provider? Soon it may be Mexico's América Móvil, which boasts more than 100 million Latin American subscribers and led BusinessWeeks's 2006 rankings of the world's top information technology companies. Never heard of Hong Kong's Techtronic Industries Ltd.? If you buy power tools at Home Depot Inc., where its products now fill the aisles, you probably know some of the brands it manufactures: Ryobi, Milwaukee, and RIDGID. Brazil's Embraer has surged past Canada's Bombardier as the world's No. 3 aircraft maker and is winning midsize-jet orders that otherwise

(continued)

Exhibit 9 Continued

would have gone to larger planes by Airbus and Boeing. Western telecom equipment leaders have long looked down on China's Huawei Technologies Co. as a mere copier of their designs. But in 2006, Huawei snared $8 billion in new orders, including contracts from British Telecommunications PLC for its $19 billion program to transform Britain's telecom network.

Many more companies are using their bases in the developing world as springboards to build global empires, such as Mexican cement giant Cemex, Indian drugmaker Ranbaxy, and Russia's Lukoil, which has hundreds of gas stations in New Jersey and Pennsylvania. Boston Consulting Group (BCG) recently published a report describing the amount of progress as "surprising," in view of the progress made by emerging-market companies in the last few years. BCG identified 100 emerging multinationals that appear positioned to radically transform industries and markets around the world. The 100 had combined $715 billion in revenue in 2005, $145 billion in operating profits, and a half-trillion dollars in assets. They have grown at a 24 percent annual clip in the past four years.

What makes these upstarts global contenders? Their key advantages are access to some of the world's most dynamic growth markets and immense pools of low-cost resources, be they production workers, engineers, land, petroleum, or iron ore. But these aspiring giants are about much more than low cost. The best of the pack are proving as innovative and expertly run as any in the business, astutely absorbing global consumer trends and technologies and getting new products to market faster than their rivals. Techtronic, for example, was the first to sell heavy-duty cordless tools powered by lightweight lithium ion batteries. Jetmaker Embraer's sleek EMB 190, which seats up to 118, has taken smaller commercial aircraft to a new level with the fuselage design that offers the legroom and overhead luggage space of much larger planes. Globalization and the Internet allow these emerging market firms to tap the same managerial talent, information, and capital as Western companies. In most industries, strategy and competition have clearly become a global game.

Any international expansion strategy would still need to be backed up by the specific resources and capabilities possessed by the firm, regardless of how rosy the CAGE analysis paints the picture. Think of international expansion as a movement along a continuum from known markets to less-known markets; a firm can move to more CAGE-proximate neighbors before venturing into markets that are portrayed as very different from a CAGE-framework perspective. Let's look at each dimension of CAGE.

Cultural Distance Culture happens to be the first facet of CAGE, in terms of the acronym, but it also can be the most practically perplexing facet for managers. Culture is sometimes referred to as the software of the mind, in that it has a sometimes invisible but indelible influence on people's values and behaviors. *Cultural distance,* then, has to do with the possible differences existing in relation to the way individuals from different countries observe certain values and behaviors.

A number of researchers have identified significant cultural differences among countries. Among these, for instance, Geert Hofstede drew together distinct cultural differences he observed around the following dimensions: power distance (the extent to which individuals accept the existence of inequalities between subordinates and superiors within a hierarchical structure); uncertainty avoidance (individuals' willingness to coexist with uncertainty about the future); individualism (how the individuals in a society value individualistic behaviors as opposed to collective ones); predominant values (regarding quantity or quality of life, that is, whether more importance is given to material aspects or a stronger emphasis is laid on interpersonal relationships); and long-term or short-term orientation (the focus on future rewards or the concern about the maintenance of the stability related to the past and the present).[23] A cross-section of these cultural dimensions for a sampling of developed and developing countries around the world are presented in Exhibit 11.

Exhibit 10 The CAGE Framework

Cultural Distance	Administrative Distance	Geographic Distance	Economic Distance
Attributes Creating Distance			
Different languages Different ethnicities: lack of connective ethnic or social networks Different religions Different social norms	Absence of colonial ties Absence of shared monetary or political association Political hostility Government policies Institutional weakness	Physical remoteness Lack of a common border Lack of sea or river access Size of country Weak transportation or communication links Differences in climates	Differences in consumer incomes Differences in costs and quality of: • natural resources • financial resources • human resources • infrastructure • intermediate inputs • information or knowledge
Industries or Products Affected by Distance			
Products have high linguistic content (TV) Products affect cultural or national identity of consumers (foods) Product features vary in terms of size (cars), standards (electrical appliances), or packaging Products carry country-specific quality associations (wines)	Government involvement is high in industries that are: • producers of staple goods (electricity) • producers of other "entitlements" (drugs) • large employers (farming) • large suppliers to government (mass transportation) • national champions (aerospace) • vital to national security (telecom) • exploiters of natural resources (oil, mining) • subject to high sunk costs (infrastructure)	Products have a low value-of-weight or bulk ratio (cement) Products are fragile or perishable (glass, fruit) Communications and connectivity are important (financial services) Local supervision and operational requirements are high (many services)	Nature of demand varies with income level (cars) Economies of standardization or scale are important (mobile phones) Labour and other factor cost differences are salient (garments) Distribution or business systems are different (insurance) Companies need to be responsive and agile (home appliances)

From Exhibit 11 you can see, for instance, that the United States has one of the lowest scores for uncertainty avoidance (i.e., a culture with a high tolerance for uncertainty), and one of the highest scores for individualism (i.e., a highly individualistic culture). These differences may influence the success of a strategic initiative due to the way a new product is perceived by consumers, or the effect they have on how a firm traditionally manages its operations. You have already been introduced to the global trials and successes of Lincoln Electric, for example. One of its key strategic weapons was the use of highly individualistic pay practices, which resonate well with its U.S. employee stakeholders. However, as you can see from Exhibit 11, the German culture is not as individualistic, and this offers a partial explanation for the initial failure of this management tool in Germany.

Administrative Distance *Administrative distance* reflects the historical and present political and legal associations between trading partners; for example, colonial ties between trading partners, or participation in common trading blocs. This facet of CAGE asks you to examine whether there are historical or current political factors that might favor or impede a business relationship between a company and a new country market. NAFTA, for instance, decreased the administrative distance between U.S. firms and Mexico and Canada.

Exhibit 11 Cultural Differences Among Countries

Country	Power Distance	Individualism	Masculinity	Uncertainty Avoidance	Long-term Orientation
Arab World	80	38	52	68	na
Brazil	69	38	49	76	65
China	80	20	66	30	118
Germany	35	67	66	65	31
India	77	48	56	40	61
Japan	54	46	95	92	80
Philippines	94	32	64	44	19
South Korea	60	18	39	85	75
Sweden	31	71	5	29	33
United Kingdom	35	89	66	35	25
United States	40	91	62	46	29

*Hofstede estimated these values for the region comprised of Egypt, Iraq, Kuwait, Lebanon, Libya, Saudi Arabia, and United Arab Emirates. Long-term orientation was not included in his estimates.

Similarly, historical political hostilities between the United States and Cuba make it virtually impossible (and illegal) for most U.S. firms to do business there.

As you can imagine, trade practices between countries can be significantly affected by laws and regulations enacted at the national or international level. Because they affect fundamental business practices, they often affect the competitive position of firms as well. Some of the key legal considerations for U.S. firms include the following:

■ **Free Trade Agreements.** Since presidential Trade Promotion Authority (TPA) was restored in 2002, the United States has embarked on an unprecedented effort to open foreign markets to U.S. exports by expanding its network of free trade agreements (FTAs). In 2003 and 2004, negotiations for FTAs with Chile, Singapore, Australia, and Morocco were concluded and subsequently approved by Congress. The latter two came into force in 2005; the FTAs with Chile and Singapore are already generating impressive results. U.S. exports to Chile, for example, increased by 28 percent in the first year of the agreement's implementation.

■ **Import Laws.** Under longstanding U.S. law, harm to U.S. companies caused by dumped products can be offset by antidumping duties if U.S. government investigating agencies—the Commerce Department and the International Trade Commission—are satisfied that certain criteria are met. Similarly, these two agencies can impose countervailing duties on subsidized imports to offset harm caused to U.S. industries by those imports. And numerous other laws are designed to restrict imports on grounds ranging from public health and safety to national security to protection of intellectual property. Such laws are still on the books, even though the recently established World Trade Organization has as a mandate continuing efforts to reduce such practices worldwide.

■ **Foreign Corrupt Practices Act (FCPA).** This U.S. federal law, amended to include OECD antibribery conventions, requires firms to have adequate accounting controls in place, but is most commonly known for its antibribery provisions. The antibribery provisions of the FCPA make it unlawful for a U.S. person, and certain foreign issuers of securities, to make a payment to a foreign official for the purpose of obtaining or retaining business for or with, or directing business to, any person. Since 1998, they also apply to foreign firms and persons who take any action in furtherance of such a corrupt payment while in the United States. The definition of foreign official is broad. For example, an owner of a bank who is also the brother of the minister of finance would qualify as a foreign official according to the U.S. government. There is no materiality to this act, which makes it illegal to offer even a penny as a bribe. The government focuses on the intent of the bribery more than the amount of it.

■ **Intellectual Property Protection.** Patents and trademarks are territorial and must be filed in each country where protection is sought. A U.S. patent or trademark does not afford protection in another country. However, the Patent Cooperation Treaty (PCT) streamlines the process of filing patents in multiple countries. By filing one patent application with the U.S. Patent and Trademark Office (USPTO), U.S. applicants can concurrently seek protection in up to 127 countries. Notable exceptions to this process include China. Indeed, if a firm enters the China market with a product but does not register its mark at China's Trademark Office, one of the firm's competitors, distributors, or partners may be able to register the trademark before them and bar them from manufacturing or selling the products with their mark in China. Despite international attention to the importance of intellectual property rights, their protection remains problematic in many developing countries. At the www.stopfakes.gov website, maintained by the U.S. Department of Commerce, there are intellectual property protection toolkits for Brazil, China, Korea, Malaysia, Mexico, Peru, Russia, and Taiwan—countries identified as among the most problematic.

Geographic Distance How far apart are trading partners in physical terms: the size of the country, differences in climates, and nature of transportation and information networks? You can think of *geographic distance* as absolute, in terms of the miles or kilometers that separate a firm from another market or supplier. Technology, however, has shrunk distance in terms of transportation time, and now with digital products and services, almost entirely eliminated geographic distance as a constraint of trade between some markets.

One of the most dramatic changes in trade was facilitated by the shipping container, which in many cases moves seamlessly between one country, shipping channels, and another country. The most recent example, of course, where distance has been reduced is with the case of the Internet. W.W. Grainger, for example, a leader in the U.S. maintenance, repair, and overhaul (MRO) industry, found that the Internet provided it a ready sales vehicle into European markets. Prior to the Internet it could not justify an investment in a far-flung European brick-and-mortar presence. With the Internet, its storefront in Europe became virtual.

Economic Distance Finally, *economic distance* captures fundamental differences relating to income, the distribution of wealth, and the relative purchasing power of segments of a geographic market. This has been one of the biggest barriers, for instance, in the way of U.S. firms success selling products in emerging markets. In global terms, this is the four billion people who live on less than $2 per day. The phrase "bottom of the pyramid" is used in particular by people developing new models of doing business that deliberately target that market, typically using new technology. An example of a product that is designed with the needs of the very poor in mind is that of a shampoo that works best with cold water. Such a product is marketed by Hindustan Lever (part of the Unilever family of firms).

How would you calculate economic difference? You should have ready access to information on per capita income and relative purchasing power across countries. In the following "How Would *You* Do That? 1," you can see a sample per country per capita income difference for a cross-section of countries. This data will give you a sense of the income that individuals or companies may have to spend on a new product or service. At the same time, you should gain an understanding of the pricing for comparable products or services. This is why economic distance also includes the economics of supply for comparable or

YOU DO THAT? 1

Putting CAGE to Work at Virgin Mobile

The starting point for your CAGE analysis is something called a country attractiveness portfolio (CAP). A CAP is created using data on a country or region's per capita income, along with data on some aspect of the market's desirability, such as market penetration or per capita spending on a focal product or service. With this information, you would have two reference points that you plot on a grid, for each country. For instance, if you were Virgin Mobile, a U.K.-based cell phone company with an interest in entering a new geographic arena outside of its home European Union market, you would want to collect information on the percentage of the population that uses cell phones in other countries, along with country per capita income. By looking at the CIA's 2006 World Factbook, which is summarized in Exhibit 12, you found

the following information (you also happened to collect information on each country's population, since that will give you an idea of the percentage of people who have cell phones, or the current market penetration for cell phones in each country).

Since you were smart enough to rank order the data by cell phones, you can see that China has the biggest actual market. In some markets you see that the number of cell phones in use actually exceeds the labor force, which means that kids and retired people must be using them as well. Your next step is to plot out some of this data on a grid, so you have a better visual image of the possible market arenas. This is where the population data come in. You simply plot each country's location on the grid using number of cell phones on the X axis, and per capita income on the

Y axis—then use the bubble size to give you a rough impression of the relative opportunity presented by each market, in terms of the actual population. We picked population because it maps well to the idea of the potential cell phone market, but you could use other aggregated indicators like gross domestic product, number of factories, and so on. The best dimension is one that can give you an idea of the country's market size for the particular product or service you are analyzing. Exhibit 13 shows you your CAP, using population as an indicator of market size.

Had you not been reading this chapter, you would have concluded that you were done with your analysis. Based solely on the information in Exhibit 13, what country would you have chosen for Virgin's expansion move? And sadly, this is why so many

Exhibit 12 Market Characteristics

Rank	Country	Cell Phones	Per Capita Income	Population
1	China	334,824,000	$7,600	1,321,851,888
2	European Union	314,644,700	$29,400	460,827,146
3	United States	194,479,364	$43,500	301,139,947
4	Japan	91,473,900	$33,100	127,433,494
5	Russia	74,420,000	$12,100	141,377,752
6	India	69,193,321	$3,700	1,129,866,154
7	Brazil	65,605,000	$8,600	190,010,647
8	Mexico	38,451,100	$10,600	108,700,891
9	South Korea	36,586,100	$24,200	49,044,790

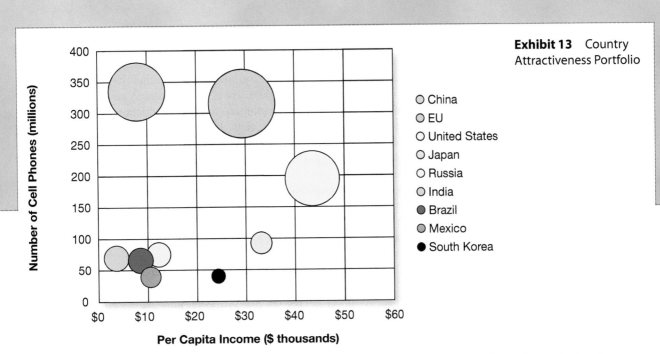

Exhibit 13 Country Attractiveness Portfolio

○ China
○ EU
○ United States
○ Japan
○ Russia
○ India
● Brazil
● Mexico
● South Korea

CAP's are fundamentally flawed. The information in Exhibit 13 does give you an idea of the relative attractiveness of each country market, and you can see their relative size related to per capita income, and so on. For a company like Virgin, they would probably like to enter a new country market where income is high, and the market is very big. They do fine in Europe, and as you can see from Exhibit 12 (and 13), that market is both big and relatively rich. However, these exhibits do not tell you how well Virgin is prepared to enter those markets—you only know that they are big, but will they be big (as in a homerun) for Virgin? The third and final step is to adjust the size of the bubbles upward or downward for CAGE-based differences along the dimensions of culture, administration, geography, and economics. This will tell you how attractive each country is, *after adjusting for the critical CAGE differences*. For instance, this would probably lead you to discount all the markets, other than the U.S. market, and you might adjust the U.S. market upward. A CAGE-adjusted CAP is shown in Exhibit 14.

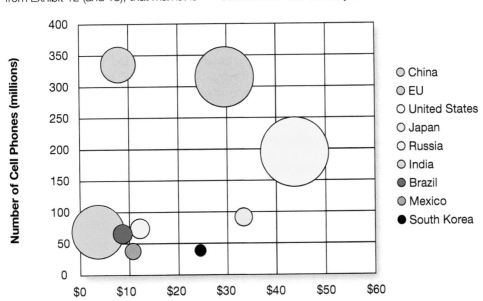

Exhibit 14 CAGE-Adjusted CAP for Virgin Mobile

○ China
○ EU
○ United States
○ Japan
○ Russia
○ India
● Brazil
● Mexico
● South Korea

substitute products in a market. For instance, processed cheese (like Velveeta) tends to cost less than fresh cheese in U.S. supermarkets, and low relative price is a key selling point for processed cheese. A recent U.S. entrant to the Brazilian cheese market assumed this same price relationship. After setting up their factory, however, they found that fresh cheese was very good *and* cheap in Brazilian supermarkets. The company wrongly assumed they would have a price advantage, when in fact the economics of cheese production in Brazil typically made processed cheese a higher-priced, and relatively less attractive, product.

Based on the CAGE-adjusted CAP you calculated for Virgin, for instance, you would probably recommend that Virgin Mobile should think about entering the U.S. market. Beyond this work, a full analysis could consider how a company's own characteristics operate to increase or reduce distance from foreign arenas. ◆ Companies with a large cadre of cosmopolitan managers, for instance, will be less affected by cultural differences than companies whose managers are all from the home country. Other company characteristics can help or hurt as well. In Virgin's case, consideration of company-specific features make the United States even more attractive. For instance, Virgin's parent company, Virgin Atlantic Airways, has a pretty sexy image in the United States, particularly in the demographic that would be the ideal target market for Virgin Mobile. Despite starting well behind companies like Orange or Vodafone in the United Kingdom, Virgin has become the fastest-growing cell phone provider in that country, with more than 700,000 customers added in its first 15 months of operation.

 Arenas

So what have we learned by using CAGE in the context of Dell and Virgin Mobile, and international expansion more generally? You should now see that the CAGE framework can be used to address the questions of where to expand internationally (which arena) and how to expand (by which vehicle). It can also help you map out the staging and pacing of your strategic international expansion moves so as to maximize the strategy's anchoring in the firm's VRINE-based resources and capabilities. You can see the CAGE-based logic at work in recent moves by Indian and Chinese competitors, for instance. Chinese technology-based companies like Lenovo are offering their products (laptops in Lenovo's case), but outsourcing the service side to English-speaking Indian firms. In contrast, a number of Indian companies have bought third- and fourth-tier U.S. or European manufacturers, and used their proximity to China to outsource production to China. Finally, a firm with an already large, but diverse, global presence can use CAGE to reevaluate which countries to stay in, and which ones to exit.

The opening vignette about Dell further demonstrates the usefulness of the CAGE framework. As you saw in the case of Dell, the vehicles it used to enter China were just as important in its China strategy as the choice of geographic arena it entered. For Dell's corporate clients in China, a CAGE framework would reveal relatively little distance on all four dimensions, even geographic, given the fact that many PC components are sourced from China. However, for the consumer segment, the distance is rather great, particularly on the dimensions of culture, administration, and economics. One outcome here could have been Dell's avoidance of the consumer market altogether. However, Dell opted to choose an alliance with distributors whose knowledge base and capabilities enabled it to better bridge the CAGE-framework distances until it was in a position to engage its Dell Direct model with consumers (staging and pacing).

Entry Vehicles into Foreign Countries

The strategy diamond says that a critical element of a firm's strategy is how it enters new markets. Now that you have answered questions about economic logic and desired geographic arena, your international strategy must answer the "how" question. How will you enter that new market? With international strategy, these new markets just happen to be in different countries, with different laws, infrastructure, cultures, and consumer preferences. The various entry mechanisms are referred to as *vehicles of strategy*. Consequently, a critical

Exhibit 15 Choice of Entry Vehicles

```
                        ┌─────────────────┐
                        │   Choice of     │
                        │ Entry Vehicle   │
                        └─────────────────┘
         ┌─────────────────────┴─────────────────────┐
┌──────────────────┐                        ┌──────────────────┐
│ Nonequity Vehicles│                        │  Equity (FDI)    │
└──────────────────┘                        │   Vehicles       │
                                            └──────────────────┘
```

Exports	Contractual Agreements	Alliances and Joint Ventures (JVs)	Wholly Owned Subsidiaries
Direct exports	Licensing/ franchising	Minority JVs	Greenfield investments
Indirect exports	Turnkey projects	50/50 JVs	Acquisition
Others	Contracted R&D	Majority JVs	Others
	Comarketing	Strategic alliances (within dotted areas)	

element of international expansion is determining which vehicles to use to enter new global markets. The first choice that managers must make is whether they will enter a foreign country with a vehicle that requires the firm to put some, or even considerable, capital at risk. As shown in Exhibit 15, firms can choose among a variety of nonequity and equity vehicles for entering a foreign country.[24] ◆ Exhibit 16 provides you with examples of the vehicles chosen by different firms around the world.[25]

 Vehicles

The second choice that managers must make is the type of the vehicle. Typically, each type of vehicle offers differing levels of ownership control and local presence. Although firms can expand internationally in a number of different ways, we present them to you under three overarching foreign-country entry vehicles: *exporting, contractual agreements* and *alliances,* and *foreign direct investment (FDI),* either through the acquisition of a company or simply starting one from scratch. At the end of this section, we will briefly discuss the use of importing as a foreign-country entry vehicle; it is somewhat of a stealth form of internationalization.

Foreign-country entry has been viewed historically as a staged process. Like the industry life cycle, the internationalization life cycle starts with a firm importing some of its raw materials or finished product for resale at home, followed perhaps by exporting products or raw materials abroad, and lastly ending in some type of partial or full ownership of plant, equipment, or other more extensive physical presence in a foreign country. These stages could be accomplished using vehicles ranging from simple contracts for purchases or sales on a transaction basis, through alliances, and perhaps even via mergers or wholesale acquisitions. Lincoln Electric, which was discussed in the previous section, offers an example of international growth through acquisition.

Over time, research has suggested that although some firms do follow such stages, they are better viewed as being more descriptive than predictive. Specifically, some firms follow the stages, starting with importing through foreign direct investment, whereas others jump right to the direct investment stage as their first internationalization effort.[26]

Exhibit 16 Vehicles for Entering Foreign Markets

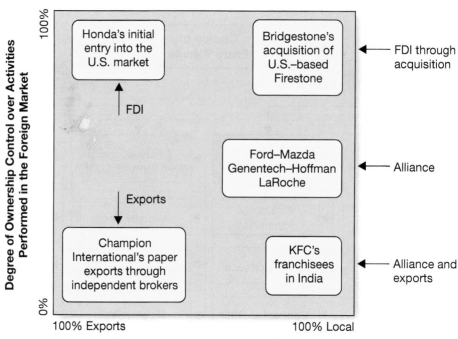

It is also helpful to note that the different entry vehicles have differing degrees of risk and control. For instance, a company that is only exporting its products abroad is typically risking its payment for the product, and perhaps its reputation if the product is not serviced well in the foreign locale. This also shows how little control the exporter has over the downstream activities once it has shipped the product. Although the exporter may have some legal or distribution agreement with local firms, this is very little control compared

South African Breweries, the maker of Castle Lager, successfully entered one of the largest beer markets in the world—the United States—by acquiring Miller Brewing Company in 2002. The combined corporation is known as SABMiller.

(SABMiller plc)

270

to ownership of local factories or distribution, or partial ownership through some form of alliance. In this section, we will walk you through these alternative entry vehicles.

EXPORTING

Exporting is exactly the opposite of importing; it can take the form of selling production or service inputs or actual products and services abroad. With the advent of the Internet and electronic banking, the physical entry barriers to becoming an exporter are lower than ever before. Although the importer is ultimately responsible for the issues relating to customs, packaging, and other trade requirements, the exporting firm will generally only be successful to the extent that it can deliver a product or service that meets customers' needs.

exporting Foreign-country entry vehicle in which a firm uses an intermediary to perform most foreign marketing functions.

Costs of Exporting
Exporting is a popular internationalization vehicle with small firms because the costs of entering new markets are relatively minimal with this vehicle. Exporters generally use local representatives or distributors to sell their products in new international markets. The main costs associated with exporting are transportation and meeting the packaging and ingredient requirements of the target country. Consequently, exporting is most common to international markets that are relatively close to the domestic market or to markets in which competitors and substitutes for the firm's products are not readily available. A large percentage of the born-global firms discussed later in the chapter used exporting as a vehicle to go global quickly.[27]

Contractual Agreements
Contractual agreements are an entry vehicle where a firm typically relies on another to manage their market presence. The contract itself can take a variety of forms, from a verbal agreement to an extensive legal document, but often relates to one of the following four types of agreements.

contractual agreement An exchange of promises or agreement between parties that is often enforceable by the law.

Licensing and Franchising
Exporting can take the form of shipping a product overseas and leaving marketing and distribution up to a foreign customer. It can also take the form of licensing or franchising, turnkey projects, R&D contracts, and comarketing. Due to some of the characteristics of these latter vehicles, as shown in Exhibit 15, such contractual arrangements are often considered a form of strategic alliance. Licensing and franchising provide a case in point. When a firm licenses its products or technologies in another country, it transfers the risk of actually implementing market entry to another firm, which pays the licensor a fee for the right to use its name in the local country. Franchising in a foreign country works similarly to franchising in a domestic market. A firm receives a sign-up fee and ongoing franchise royalties in exchange for teaching the franchisee how to open and operate the franchisor's business in the local market.

The risk, of course, to the licensor or franchisor is that the licensee or franchisee will violate the terms of the agreement, either to the detriment of the product or service itself, by refusing to pay agreed-upon fees or royalties or simply selling a copy of the product or service under another name (that is essentially stealing the intellectual property entirely). The primary risks to the franchisee or licensee are that the product or service will not perform as promised or that the licensor or franchisor will do something that diminishes the market attractiveness of the product or service.

Turnkey Projects, R&D Contracts, and Comarketing
The latter three forms—turnkey projects, R&D contracts, and comarketing—are specialized contractual agreements whereby a firm agrees to build a factory, conduct a specific R&D project, or comarket or cobrand a product such that the contracting firm has used it as a foreign-market entry vehicle. For example, the Norwegian firm Kvaerner A/S contracts to build paper mills and deep-sea oil rigs for Brazilian paper and petroleum companies; the German firm Bayer AG

contracts a large R&D project to the U.S. firm Millennium pharmaceuticals with the work undertaken in both firms' respective countries; McDonald's in Japan packages its kids meals with characters that are familiar to Japanese children based on characters like Pokémon or Hello Kitty that are popular at the time.

ALLIANCES

Alliances are another common foreign-market entry vehicle. Because we devote an entire chapter to alliances later in the text, here we simply explain why alliances are so commonly used for international expansion. Often, alliances are chosen because of government regulations. For example, only recently did the Chinese government allow non-Chinese ownership of companies in China. As a result, firms could only enter China through various partnerships. Alliances may also be used as an international-strategy vehicle due to management's lack of familiarity with the local culture or institutions or because the complexity of operating internationally requires the firm to focus on the activities it does best and to outsource the rest. Some combination of these three factors—regulations, market familiarity, or operational complexity—typically explain why alliances are so often used by firms competing internationally. For instance, Virgin Mobile partnered with Sprint when it initially entered the U.S. market in 2002.

FOREIGN DIRECT INVESTMENT

foreign direct investment (FDI) Foreign-country entry vehicle by which a firm commits to the direct ownership of a foreign subsidiary or division.

greenfield investment Form of FDI in which a firm starts a new foreign business from the ground up.

Foreign direct investment (FDI), as the term implies, is an international entry strategy whereby a firm makes a financial investment in a foreign market to facilitate the startup of a new venture. FDI tends to be the most expensive international entry tactic because it requires the greatest commitment of a firm's time and resources. FDI can be implemented in several ways, such as through acquisitions or through a so-called greenfield alliance—the startup of a foreign entity from scratch. This latter form of FDI is called **greenfield investment**. In the previous section, we reviewed how alliances can be a vehicle to foreign market entry. As you will learn in Chapter 9, alliances do not require any equity investment. However, many alliances do involve equity investment, and when they do in the context of foreign market entry, it is a special case of greenfield investment. For instance, DaimlerChrysler and BMW each invested $250 million to start a new engine factory in Curitiba, Brazil.

Acquisitions and Equity Alliances Because greenfield investment usually involves the greatest risk, expense, and time, many firms pursue FDI through acquisitions or alliances (you will learn more about these particular strategy vehicles in Chapters 9 and 10). Acquisitions provide the firm with rapid entry because the firm purchases existing businesses that are already staffed and successfully operating. For instance, when the battery maker Rayovac entered Brazil in 2005, it did so by purchasing Microlite, the dominant battery maker in Brazil. Similarly, South African Breweries purchased Miller Brewing in 2002 to gain an instant presence and production capacity in one of the largest beer markets in the world, the United States.

After its horrendous experiences with rapid international expansion, Lincoln Electric amended its corporate policy on FDI: It now engages only in FDI through alliances with local players in order to maximize the knowledge needed about local market conditions, both in terms of production and market demand. Sometimes alliances are dictated by the necessity to have a certain proportion of local content in a product, such as a car or motorcycle, in order to sell the product into a nonlocal market. Brazil and China are two examples of countries that have stringent local-content laws. Minimum efficient scale is another explanation for the use of alliances as an FDI foreign-entry tactic.

For example, the DaimlerChrysler and BMW alliance mentioned earlier was necessary because neither company could justify the volume of production needed by the new plant to justify it economically. Therefore, the two firms joined forces to form Tritec, a state-of-the-art automotive engine factory that supplies parts for BMW's Mini Cooper assembly plant in the United Kingdom and DaimlerChyrsler's PT Cruiser assembly plants in Mexico, the United States, and South Africa.[28]

IMPORTING AND INTERNATIONAL STRATEGY

In many ways, **importing** is a stealth form of internationalization because firms will often claim they have no international operations and yet directly or indirectly base their production or services on inputs obtained from outside their home country. Firms that engage in importing must be knowledgeable about customs requirements and informed about compliance with customs regulations, entry of goods, invoices, classification and value, determination and assessment of duty, special requirements, fraud, marketing, trade finance and insurance, and foreign trade zones. Importing can take many forms, from the sourcing of components, machinery, and raw materials to the purchase of finished goods for domestic resale to outsourcing production or services to nondomestic providers.

importing Internationalization strategy by which a firm brings a good, service, or capital into the home country from abroad.

Outsourcing and Offshoring
This latter activity, international outsourcing, has taken on the most visible role in business and corporate strategy in recent years. International outsourcing is not a new phenomenon. For instance, Nike has been designing shoes and other apparel for decades and manufacturing them abroad. Similarly, Pacific Cycle does not make a single Schwinn or Mongoose bicycle in the United States but instead imports them from Taiwanese and Chinese manufacturers. It just seems that international outsourcing is new because of the increasingly rapid pace with which businesses are sourcing services, components, and raw materials from developing countries such as China, Brazil, and India.

Information technologies (IT), such as telecommunications and the widespread diffusion of the Internet, have provided the impetus for the international outsourcing of services as well as factors of production. Such *business process outsourcing (BPO)* is the delegation of one or more IT-intensive business processes to an external nondomestic provider which, in turn, owns, administers, and manages the selected process based on defined and measurable performance criteria. Sometimes this is referred to as **offshoring** because the business processes (including production/manufacturing) are outsourced to a lower-cost location, usually overseas. Offshoring refers to taking advantage of lower-cost labor in another country. Although outsourced processes are handed off to third-party vendors, offshored processes may be handed off to third-party vendors or remain in-house. This definition of offshoring includes organizations that build dedicated captive centers of their own in remote, lower-cost locations. The many U.S. firms that have established *maquiladoras* (assembly plants) in Mexico are examples of offshoring without outsourcing.

offshoring Moving a value chain activity or set of activities to another country, typically where key costs are lower.

Firms in such service- and IT-intensive industries as insurance, banking, pharmaceuticals, telecommunications, automobiles, and airlines seem to be the early adopters of BPO. Of the industries just mentioned, insurance and banking are able to generate savings purely because of the large proportion of processes they can outsource, such as claim processing, loan processing, and client servicing through call centers. Among those countries housing BPO operations, India appears to be experiencing the most dramatic growth for services that require English-language skills and education. BPO operations have been growing 70 percent a year and are now a $1.6 billion industry, employing approximately 100,000 people. In India alone, BPO has to grow only 27 percent annually until 2008 to deliver $17 billion in revenues and employ a million people.[29]

More generally, foreign outsourcing and offshoring locations tend to be defined by how automated a production process or service can be made, the relative labor costs, and the transportation costs involved. When transportation costs and automation are both high, then the knowledge-worker component of the location calculation becomes less important. You

273

can see how you might employ the CAGE framework to evaluate potential outsourcing locations. However, in some cases firms invest in both plant and equipment and the training and development of the local workforce. Brazil is but one case in point, with examples from Ford, BMW, Daimler-Benz, and Cargill. Each of these multinational organizations is making significant investments in the educational infrastructure of this enormous emerging economy.[30]

International Strategy Configurations

How a firm becomes involved in international markets—which appears to be increasingly important, if not obligatory, for many if not all firms—differs from how it configures the interactions between headquarters and country operations. It is important to note that international-strategy configuration is as much about strategy formulation as it is about implementation, because management is making choices about which value-chain components to centralize, where to centralize those operations geographically, and the degree to which those decentralized and centralized value-chain activities will be managed and coordinated. Remember, too, that strategy helps a firm manage important tradeoffs that differentiate it and its products from competitors.

RESOLVING THE TENSION BETWEEN LOCAL PREFERENCES AND GLOBAL STANDARDS

In this section, we discuss the underlying tensions created between a firm's attempts to be responsive to the local needs of diverse sets of customers and yet remain globally efficient. Meeting the ideal tradeoff between customizing for local needs and achieving cost efficiencies requires further tradeoffs with respect to the firm's value chain regarding which activities will be standardized and which will be locally tailored. These are the central tradeoffs a firm must wrestle with in designing and managing its international strategy.

Globalizing firms must reconcile the natural tension that exists between local preferences and global standards. The domination of local preferences over the search for global efficiencies, left unchecked, often leads to what strategy researchers describe as *market fragmentation*.[31] In addition, local adaptation of products and services is significantly more expensive than relying on global standards. Consequently, attempting to achieve high levels of local responsiveness will almost always lead to higher cost structure.[32] A product that is uniform across markets is highly efficient to produce because the firm can simply design a factory of the most efficient size in a location that most efficiently balances the costs of inputs with the transportation costs of getting outputs to the desired markets. If this product has the same brand around the world, then marketing and promotion efforts are similarly focused on that single brand. However, even products like Coca-Cola, which appear to be ubiquitous, have different flavorings, packaging, and promotion constraints in each market. Some of these constraints are a function of local regulatory pressures; others reflect underlying differences in consumers' tastes. Just as important, other constraints are a function of the competitive norms that have prevailed in the industry, either globally or locally. The variations of international strategy configurations that we cover in this section—making tradeoffs between local responsiveness and global efficiency—are summarized in Exhibit 17.[33]

We will also speak briefly about born-global firms in this section because more and more organizations appear to have operations that span national borders early in their existence. As you will see, born-global firms employ an amalgam of exporting and FDI, but do so much more rapidly than firms have in the past. In the strategy diamond, exporting and FDI are considered vehicles, and the timing and sequencing of the usage are viewed in the context of staging. Each of these vehicles provides a firm and its management with experience and knowledge about cross-border business practices.

Exhibit 17 International Strategy Configurations and Local/Global Tradeoffs

	Relatively Few Opportunities to Gain Global Efficiencies	Many Opportunities to Gain Global Efficiencies
Relatively High Local Responsiveness	**Multinational Vision** Build flexibility to respond to national differences through strong, resourceful, entrepreneurial, and somewhat independent national or regional operations. Requires decentralized and relatively self-sufficient units. **Example:** MTV initially adopted an international configuration (using only American programming in foreign markets) but then changed its strategy to a multinational one. It now tailors its Western European programming to each market, offering eight channels, each in a different language.	**Transnational Vision** Develop global efficiency, flexibility, and worldwide learning. Requires dispersed, interdependent, and specialized capabilities simultaneously. **Example:** Nestlé has taken steps to move in this direction, starting first with what might be described as a multinational configuration. Today, Nestlé aims to evolve from a decentralized, profit-center configuration to one that operates as a single, global company. Firms like Nestlé have taken lessons from leading consulting firms such as McKinsey and Company, which are globally dispersed but have a hard-driving, one-firm culture at their core.
Relatively Low Local Responsiveness	**International Vision** Exploit parent-company knowledge and capabilities through worldwide diffusion, local marketing, and adaptation. The most valuable resources and capabilities are centralized; others, such as local marketing and distribution, are decentralized. **Example:** When Wal-Mart initially set up its operations in Brazil, it used its U.S. stores as a model for international expansion.	**Global Vision** Build cost advantages through centralized, global-scale operations. Requires centralized and globally scaled resources and capabilities. **Example:** Companies such as Merck and Hewlett-Packard give particular subsidiaries a worldwide mandate to leverage and disseminate their unique capabilities and specialized knowledge worldwide.

Emphasize Local Responsiveness Each of the configurations identified in Exhibit 17 presents tradeoffs between global efficiency and local responsiveness. Recognize that in reality, most firms' international strategy configurations vary slightly or significantly from those shown in Exhibit 17. By definition, strategy must be internally consistent and externally oriented. However, management must make judgments as to what an external orientation means in terms of how the strategy takes competitive pressures and consumer preferences into account. At the same time, management must also make judgments about the firm's internal resources and capabilities to support a particular international-strategy configuration. This explains why firms with seemingly very different international-strategy configurations can coexist in the same industry.

When Lincoln Electric first embarked on becoming a global firm, it had relatively independent operations in many markets around the world. It used its strongest national

cross-subsidizing Practice by which a firm uses profits from one aspect of a product, service, or region to support other aspects of competitive activity.

positions to **cross-subsidize** market-share battles or growth initiatives in other countries. Such an approach is essentially a portfolio of geographically removed business units that have devoted most of their resources and capabilities to maximizing local responsiveness and uniqueness. Firms which, like Lincoln Electric, employ this configuration have the objective to develop a global presence but may or may not use the same brand names in each market or consolidate their buying power or distribution capabilities.

Emphasize Global Efficiencies with Some Local Advantages

Another configuration centralizes some resources, such as global brand and distribution capabilities, in order to achieve costs savings; but decentralizes others, such as marketing, in order to achieve some level of localization. This strategy is common among firms that have created something in their home market that they wish to replicate in foreign markets, allowing them the economies of scale and scope necessary to create and exploit innovations on a worldwide basis. Heavy R&D companies such as Intel and Pfizer fit this mold: Even though the products that they produce are relatively standardized around the world, local marketing and distribution channels differ.

Emphasize Global Efficiencies

This configuration focuses only on global efficiency. A tradeoff is made between local responsiveness and the lower costs associated with global efficiency. With this configuration, production and sourcing decisions are designed to achieve the greatest economies of scale. Firms following this configuration potentially sacrifice the higher prices that follow customization, but they are counting on the likelihood that their products or services will meet enough needs to be demanded without finely tuned customization. Firms in commodity industries such as steel and copper, such as BHP-Billeton, fall into this category. Because end customers make purchase decisions based on price alone, the firm is organized to realize the lowest possible production costs.

Seek to Exploit Local Advantages and Global Efficiencies

The final international-strategy configuration that we discuss is one that attempts to capitalize on both local responsiveness and global efficiency. When successfully implemented, this approach enables firms to achieve global economies of scale, cross-subsidization across markets, and the ability to engage in retaliatory and responsive competition across markets. This configuration is available to companies with high degrees of internationalization. However, as with any other strategic tradeoff, it is extremely difficult to find the balance between cost efficiencies and the ability to customize to local tastes and standards. McDonald's is often used as an example of a firm that fits this configuration because it uses its purchasing power to get the best prices on the global commodities it uses for inputs, yet tries to tailor its menu offerings to fit local tastes and cultural preferences.

BORN-GLOBAL FIRMS

One reason that global strategy—and the four international strategy configurations—will become an increasingly important topic is the fact that more and more firms, even very small ones, have operations that bridge national borders very soon after their founding. Perhaps appropriate for the Internet age, this new breed of firms that emerged in the 1990s is being dubbed "born global" because their operations often span the globe early in their existence. A common characteristic of such firms is that their offerings complement the products or capabilities of other global players, take advantage of global IT infrastructure, or otherwise tap into a demand for a product or service that at its core is somewhat uniform across national geographic markets. Although many firms may fall into this category by virtue of their products, the operations and customers of born-global firms do actually span the globe. Born-global firms position themselves globally, exploiting a combination of exporting and FDI.

Logitech, the computer-mouse and peripherals company, is perhaps one of the best early examples of a successful born-global firm.[34] It was founded by two Italians and a Swiss, with operations and R&D initially split between California and Switzerland. Logitech's primary focus was on the PC mouse, and it rapidly expanded production to Ireland and Taiwan. With its stylish and ergonomic products, Logitech had captured 30 percent of the global mouse business by 1989, garnering the startup a healthy $140 million in revenues. Today, Logitech is an industry leader in the design and manufacture of computer-peripheral devices. It has manufacturing facilities in Asia and offices in major cities in North America, Europe, and Asia Pacific and employs more than 6,000 people worldwide.[35]

How to Succeed as a Global Startup   Successful global startups must complete two phases. In the first phase, managers ask, "Should my firm be a global startup?" If they can answer "yes" to all or most of the follow-up questions entailed by phase 1, then they need to be sure that they can quickly build the resources and capabilities identified in phase 2. Research has shown that those firms unable to connect the dots in phase 2 were forced to cease operations after short, albeit sometimes lively, adventures.[36]

During phase 1—*and before moving on to phase 2*—managers should consider questions that will help them determine whether the firm should be a global startup:

- Does the firm need human resources from other countries in order to succeed?

- Does the firm need financial capital from other countries in order to succeed?

- If the firm goes global, will target customers prefer its services over those of competitors?

- Can the firm put an international system in place more quickly than domestic competitors?

- Does the firm need global scale and scope to justify the financial and human capital investment in the venture?

- Will a purely domestic focus now make it harder for the firm to go global in the future?

If the answer to all or most of these questions is "yes," managers can commit to moving the firm into phase 2 and put together the tools they will need to move the firm into the global market:

- Strong management team with international experience

- Broad and deep international network among suppliers, customers, and complements

- Preemptive marketing or technology that will provide first-mover advantage with customers and lock out competitors from key suppliers and complements

- Strong intangible assets (Logitech has style, hipness, and mindshare via their brand)

- Ability to keep customers locked in by linking new products and services to the core business, while constantly innovating the core product or service

- Close worldwide coordination and communication among business units, suppliers, complements, and customers

So why do we introduce the concept of global startups at this point in the text? One reason is because of their increasing prevalence, which is driven, in part, by globalizing consumer preferences, mobile consumers, large global firms, and the pervasiveness of the Internet and its effects. The second reason, which should become clear after reading the next section, is that dynamic contexts typically give rise to the need for firms to strive for a global presence and to understand global markets early in their evolution.

International Strategy in Stable and Dynamic Contexts

A recent McKinsey study suggests that the creativity that some companies have found in emerging economies, and that have resulted in inexpensive but high-quality products, will now compel incumbents to go down the same road.[37] This assertion gets at the heart—the question of urgency and timing—of how international strategy is approached in relatively stable versus dynamic contexts. ◆ Moreover, it also suggests that industries that might have been considered relatively stable will increasingly take on dynamic characteristics as a result of global competition. In many ways, what you have learned so far about business and corporate strategies in dynamic contexts is equally applicable in purely domestic and already globalizing organizations. The key difference, however—a difference that we hope is apparent after reading this chapter—is that cross-border business adds another level of complexity to both strategy formulation and execution and, that unfortunately, such complexity may be unavoidable for firms in dynamic contexts.

 Staging & Pacing

GLOBAL CONTEXT AND INDUSTRY LIFE CYCLE

Recall from earlier chapters that we differentiated between external- and internal-based views of strategy. The internal view emphasizes resources, capabilities, and activities as the source of competitive advantage; whereas the external view draws attention to how firms need to adapt or modify their competitive positions and strategies to the external environment to position themselves in a manner conducive to superior returns. These views have implications for the dynamic nature of international strategic action, as well. Taking the external perspective, for instance, typically draws managerial attention to the dynamic nature of the industry life cycle and how that drives decisions to internationalize. Specifically, as an industry matures, the international implications of industry structure—and therefore strategic choices and firm behavior—should change in fundamental ways.[38]

First-Mover Advantage   In the introductory stage of an industry's life cycle, the external perspective would expect firms to engage in few exports, largely because the market for the industry's products is still highly uncertain and there are few accepted quality, service, or technological standards. As you will see, the length of this stage may vary significantly by country. Firms should begin to export during the growth stage of industry life cycle because new firms enter the market and compete for existing customers. Early movers in the domestic market then have an opportunity to be early movers in foreign markets as well and to continue growth even as domestic competition heats up. As the industry matures, exports gain even more steam in the face of domestic market saturation, and firms start producing products abroad to satisfy foreign demand and to search for global efficiencies. Industry shakeout and consolidation also tend to follow industry maturity, and consolidation through acquisitions leads to a few large global companies.

Staging and Geographic Markets   Similarly, when discussing international strategy from an external perspective, the fact that geographic markets differ in many legal, cultural, and institutional ways—differences which, in turn, are likely to have implications for product demand—must also be taken into account. Indeed, demand characteristics of geographic markets have been shown to evolve at different rates. For example, the time from new-product introduction to the growth stage (sometimes called market takeoff) in Portugal may occur after a longer period of time than the same transition in Denmark. Indeed, although the average period of time between a new-product or new-service introduction and market takeoff is 6 years, a new product takes only about 4 years to take off in Denmark, Norway, and Sweden, compared to 9 years in Greece and Portugal (the United States averages 5.3 years).[39]

Role of Arenas in Global Strategies   Identification of arenas ensures that the most critical national markets are identified and brought into the plan. Similarly, even with thoughtful treatment of staging and arenas, structures, systems, and processes must be in complete alignment with the firm's vision and global intent. A firm that strives to execute the most complex global strategy—the transnational strategy—must have enormous investments in its ability to coordinate and integrate activities around the globe, complemented by customer characteristics that enable such a global strategy to create true value.

Resources and Global Strategy   The resource-based perspective has important implications for international strategy in dynamic contexts as well. It is here, too, that the questions of staging and geographic arenas from the strategy diamond model are critically important to effective international strategies. From the resource-based perspective, staging is important because the firm's global resources and capabilities do not materialize overnight. Lincoln Electric's experience is a case in point here. Lincoln's pace of international expansion exceeded its organizational capabilities to integrate foreign acquisitions, let alone manage them once they were integrated. Lincoln also attempted to internationalize almost exclusively through acquisitions. However, research on foreign expansion reveals that the firms most successful at internationalizing combine greenfield investments with acquisitions and alliances.[40] Simply expanding through greenfield investment can lead to inertia and lack of learning. Acquisitions help broaden a firm's knowledge base. However, exclusive reliance on acquisitions is not only costly but makes knowledge transfer and learning more difficult. Firms that balance greenfield investments and acquisitions seem to transfer more knowledge and create more value than firms that rely on either process exclusively.

Capabilities and Global Strategy   One of the fundamental ideas of having a dynamic view of strategy is to continuously build and renew firm capabilities. Many born-global firms fall into this dynamic-context category nearly from inception. By continuously evolving its stock of resources and capabilities, a firm maximizes its chances of adapting to changing environmental conditions. Thus, when a firm decides to enter a particular new foreign market, it must also embark on developing the resources necessary to make that market-entry decision a success. At the same time, what it learns in those new geographic markets should be evaluated for application or adaptation to existing market positions.

In addition, as a firm internationalizes and becomes more dependent on a particular foreign location, the need for high-level capabilities to perform the local activities increases commensurately.[41] For instance, as Ikea expands around the globe, its ability to understand local furniture markets increases. However, these needs are greatest in markets where it faces the most exposure; Ikea's early missteps in the United States have been attributed to lack of market intelligence.[42] This leads us to our closing section on global strategy in dynamic contexts.

DEVELOPING A MINDSET FOR GLOBAL DYNAMIC COMPETITIVENESS

Given the emphasis on the importance of leadership skills throughout this text, it should come as no surprise that what may make or break the effectiveness of a firm's international strategy is the internationally related capabilities and global mindset of the firm's executives, particularly in dynamic markets. Moreover, such capabilities and mindset may enable one firm to change a once relatively stable competitive context into a dynamic and vibrant one.

Global Perspective   The global mindset has two distinct but related dimensions. The first dimension is something that strategy researchers simply refer to as global perspective.[43] Executives with a global perspective require a combination of specific knowledge and skills. In terms of knowledge, executives with a global mindset have an appreciation for the fact

279

that countries and their peoples differ culturally, socioeconomically, and sociopolitically; view those differences as potential opportunities as opposed to threats; and can link such differences to necessary adaptations in business operations. In addition, they also recognize that the management processes guiding those business operations must also be adapted to cultural, socioeconomic, and sociopolitical differences.

As opposed to conventional and routine cross-country transfers, companies are exposing managers to problem-solving situations in different business environments. An interesting example in this context is Dell Computer. Traditionally, Dell's practice has been to use local managers to run its outfits in different parts of the world. For important functions, Dell uses teams of specialists who move around the world providing expertise in specific areas. One such team which picked up design expertise while setting up Dell's manufacturing facilities in Texas, has been spending time in countries such as Ireland, Malaysia, China, and Brazil to set up plants there. In each of these countries, the team spends typically six months to one year.

Learning on a Worldwide Scale   In many ways, the second dimension of a global mindset requires the first dimension as a foundation. The second dimension is the capacity to learn from participation in one geographic market and transfer that knowledge to other operations elsewhere in the world. This means that the firm not only has globally savvy executives, but that these executives form an effective network of communication throughout the organization on a worldwide scale. You can tell that a firm and its managers possess this second dimension when the firm is routinely able to take knowledge gained in one market and apply it elsewhere, as was demonstrated in the case of SC Johnson's transfer of a plug-in household insect repellent product from Europe to the development of a new category of air-freshener products in the United States—Glade PlugIns.

Ironically, many global firms, and even more so with less global ones, are not very effective at retaining their managers once they return from an international assignment. These managers are either *expatriates*—someone from the home country who has moved abroad temporarily—or, increasingly, *inpatriates*—a manager recruited from the "local" market for their local business savvy. This apparent disconnect between a need for globally-seasoned executives and their retention by the firms that need them most can be explained by two factors. First, when the managers accept an international work assignment they often lose contact with the elements of the organization where strategy is formulated, such as corporate headquarters. In the case of inpatriates, they may never have had an opportunity to establish a strong network and power base at headquarters. Second, the expatriates' or inpatriates' firms do not have a repatriation plan in place to take advantage of their expertise. Because they have-been-out-of-sight-and-out-of-mind, there is no ready way to plug them into the top management team.

Obviously, the development of a global mindset is more easily said than done. Our hope is that, given the fact that there are very few industries or markets untouched by global competition (just look around your classroom, for instance, and you will likely see at least one person from another country), you will take it upon yourself to start investing in your own global mindset.

Summary of Challenges

1. *Define* international strategy *and identify its implications for the strategy diamond.* A firm's international strategy is how it approaches the cross-border business activities of its own firm and competitors and how it contemplates doing so in the future. International strategy essentially reflects the choices a firm's executives make with respect to sourcing and selling its goods in foreign markets. A firm's international activities affect both its business strategy and its corporate strategy. Each component of the strategy diamond may be affected by international activities.

2. *Understand why a firm would want to expand internationally and explain the relationship between international strategy and*

competitive advantage. Firms often expand internationally to fuel growth; however, international expansion does not guarantee profitable growth and should be pursued to help a firm build or exploit a competitive advantage. International expansion can exploit four principle drivers of competitive advantage: economies of scale and scope, location, multipoint competition, and learning. However, these benefits can be offset by the costs of international expansion, such as the liabilities of newness and foreignness, and governance and coordination costs.

3. *Use the CAGE framework to identify international arenas.* CAGE stands for *c*ultural distance, *a*dministrative distance, *g*eographic distance, and *e*conomic distance and is a tool to help you better understand the firm-specific implication of a country attractiveness portfolio (CAP). You learned how to identify a portfolio of geographic markets and rank them on their relative attractiveness. The first step involved gathering data on personal income and market performance for a particular segment or industry. The second step involved creating a CAP by plotting the data on a grid to observe relative differences in attractiveness across countries. The third step asked you to make judgments about relevant CAGE dimensions and apply them to your CAP.

4. *Describe different vehicles for international expansion.* Foreign-country entry vehicles include exporting, alliances, and foreign direct investment (FDI). Exporters generally use local representatives or distributors to sell their products in new international markets. Two specialized forms of exporting are licensing and franchising. Alliances involve partnering with another firm to enter a foreign market or undertake an aspect of the value chain in that market. FDI can facilitate entry into a new foreign market and can be accomplished by greenfield investment or acquisition.

Although importing is not technically a form of international expansion, it does provide firms with knowledge, experience, and relationships on which future international expansion choices and activities can be based.

5. *Apply different international strategy configurations.* The different forms that international strategies may take are driven by tradeoffs in attempts to customize for local needs and to pursue global cost efficiencies. The first configuration seeks to achieve high levels of local responsiveness while downplaying the search for global efficiencies. The second configuration seeks relatively few global efficiencies and markets relatively standard products across different markets. The third configuration seeks to exploit global economies and efficiencies and accepts less local customer responsiveness (i.e., more standardized products). The fourth configuration attempts to simultaneously achieve global efficiencies and a high degree of local product specialization.

6. *Outline the international strategy implications of the stable and dynamic perspectives.* Cross-border business adds another level of complexity to both strategy formulation and execution, and unfortunately such complexity may be unavoidable for firms in dynamic contexts. As products mature, firms' international strategies evolve, often moving from little global involvement during the introductory phase to high degrees of internationalization in mature markets. Resources need to be renewed more rapidly in dynamic markets. Thus, when a firm enters a new foreign market, it must also embark on developing the resources necessary to make that market-entry decision a success. In addition, what is learned in new markets can be leveraged for application in existing markets. Obviously, these objectives can be best achieved when managers with an international mindset are in place.

Review Questions

1. What is meant by *international strategy?*

2. Which aspects of the strategy diamond are related to international strategy?

3. What are the four most important ways a firm's international strategy can be related to its competitive advantage?

4. What three foreign-country entry vehicles are emphasized in this chapter?

5. What is typically the most cost- and time-intensive entry vehicle?

6. What are characteristics of firms that fit the four international strategy configurations discussed in this chapter?

7. On what two dimensions do the four international strategy configurations differ?

8. What does the external perspective tell you about international strategy in dynamic contexts?

9. What does the resource-and-capabilities-based perspective tell you about international strategy in dynamic contexts?

10. What role do managers play in effective international strategies, particularly in dynamic contexts?

Experiential Activities

Group Exercises

1. Why have firms typically followed an international strategy path that started with importing or exporting, followed by alliances, and then FDI? What risks do born-global firms face in trying to do all of these at once? What resources and capabilities must they possess to do all of these effectively?

2. Are all Internet firms global by definition? What opportunities and barriers does the Internet present to firm internationalization?

Ethical Debates

1. You have successfully grown your local pasta company and while traveling in other countries you found that you might be able to produce and sell your product profitably there as well. In exploring these opportunities further, you were surprised to find that one of these countries has much stricter ingredients labeling and contents laws, while the other country much looser ones (in comparison to those of your home country, which you considered to be pretty strict to begin with). All three opportunities look to be profitable, regardless of the differences in regulations. Which regulations do you abide by in each country? The strictest ones, or the respective country standards, even if they are different?

2. As you learned in the section exploring CAGE, the Foreign Corrupt Practices Act is a U.S. federal law that makes it illegal for a citizen or corporation of the United States or a person or corporation acting within the United States to influence, bribe, or seek an advantage from a public official of another country. You, as an employee of a U.S. firm, are bidding for a contract in a foreign country where you understand that bribery is a common practice. Does the U.S. law put your firm at a competitive disadvantage? What should you do?

How Would YOU DO THAT?

1. Refer to the box entitled "How Would *You* Do That? 1." Pick another industry that is of interest to you. What did you identify as your indicator of potential market size? What market performance indicator did you use (for instance, in the example we used current cell phone usage)? How different were your CAP and CAGE-adjusted CAPs?

Go on to see How Would You Do That at www.prenhall.com/ carpenter&sanders

Endnotes

1. "Acting on Global Trends: A McKinsey Global Survey," *The McKinsey Quarterly*, 7, May 2007, www.McKinsey.com.

2. Information provided on companies' respective websites. General information on the global Fortune 500 can be found at www.Fortune.com.

3. The imperatives are summarized in A. Gupta and V. Govindarajan, "Managing Global Expansion: A Conceptual Framework," *Business Horizons* 43:2 (2000), 45–54.

4. R. Tomkins, "Battered PepsiCo Licks Its Wounds," *The Financial Times*, May 30, 1997, 26.

5. A. K. Gupta and V. Govindarajan, "Converting Global Presence into Global Competitive Advantage," *Academy of Management Executive* 15 (2001), 45–56.

6. J. W. Lu and P. W. Beamish, "International Diversification and Firm Performance: The S-Curve Hypothesis," *Academy of Management Journal* 47 (2004), 598–609.

7. J. W. Lu and P. W. Beamish, "International Diversification and Firm Performance: The S-Curve Hypothesis," *Academy of Management Journal* 47 (2004), 598–609.

8. Lu and Beamish, "International Diversification and Firm Performance."

9. Lu and Beamish, "International Diversification and Firm Performance."

10. A. D. Chandler, *Scale and Scope: The Dynamics of Industrial Capitalism* (Cambridge, MA: Harvard University Press, 1990).

11. Gupta and Govindarajan, "Converting Global Presence into Global Competitive Advantage."

12. Gupta and Govindarajan, "Converting Global Presence into Global Competitive Advantage."

13. Gupta and Govindarajan, "Converting Global Presence into Global Competitive Advantage."

14. K. Ito and E. L. Rose, "Foreign Direct Investment Location Strategies in the Tire Industry," *Journal of International Business Studies* 33:3 (2002), 593–602.

15. This anecdote is based on an interview with Lincoln Electric's chairman emeritus in D. Hastings, "Lincoln Electric's Harsh Lessons from International Expansion," *Harvard Business Review* 77:3 (1999), 163–174.

16. Based on information from a personal interview with Sam Johnson.

17. Adapted from A. Gupta and V. Govindarajan, "Managing Global Expansion: A Conceptual Framework," *Business Horizons* 43:2 (2000), 45–54.

18. The points in this paragraph draw heavily on the work of M. T. Hansen and N. Nohria, "See How to Build a Collaborative Advantage," *Sloan Management Review* Fall (2004), 22–30.

19. CIA World Factbook, www.cia.gov.

20. Based on surveys reported in *Business Week* and Grant Thornton LLP. See *2007 Grant Thornton International Business Report* at www.gti.org, and "Emerging Giants Multinationals from China, India, Brazil, Russia, and even Egypt are coming on strong. They're hungry—and want your customers. They're changing the global game," *Business Week*, July 31, 2006, Cover Story.

21. P. Ghemawat, "The Forgotten Strategy," *Harvard Business Review* 81:11 (2003), 76–84. Recreated from www.business-standard.com/general/pdf/113004_01.pdf.

22. P. Ghemawat, "Distance Still Matters," *Harvard Business Review* 79:8 (2001), 1–11.

23. G. Hofstede, *Culture's Consequences. International Differences in Work-Related Values* (Newbury Park, CA: Sage Publications, 1980); G. Hofstede, *Culture's and Organizations. Software of the Mind* (London: McGraw-Hill, 1991).

24. Adapted from Y. Pan and D. Tse, "The Hierarchical Model of Market Entry Modes," *Journal of International Business Studies* 31 (2000), 535–554.

25. Examples drawn from A. Gupta and V. Govindarajan, "Managing Global Expansion: A Conceptual Framework," *Business Horizons*, March/April 2002, 45–54.

26. J. Johanson and J. Vahlne, "The Internationalization Process of the Firm," *Journal of International Business Studies* 8 (1977), 23–32; F. Weidershiem-Paul, H. Olson, and L. Welch, "Pre-Export Activity: The First Step in Internationalization," *Journal of International Business Studies* 9 (1978), 47–58; A. Millington and B. Bayliss, "The Process of Internationalization: UK Companies in the EC," *Management International Review* 30 (1990), 151–161; B. Oviatt and P. McDougall, "Toward a Theory of International New Ventures," *Journal of International Business Studies* 25 (1994), 45–64.

27. O. Moen, "The Born Globals: A New Generation of Small European Exporters," *International Marketing Review* 19 (2002), 156–175.

28. www.tritecmotors.com.br

29. Gupta and Govindarajan, "Managing Global Expansion."

30. www.fordfound.org, www.tritecmotors.com.br, and www.cargill.com.br.

31. G. Hamel and C. K. Prahalad, "Do You Really Have a Global Strategy?" *Harvard Business Review* 63:4 (1985), 139–148.

32. Gupta and Govindarajan, "Converting Global Presence into Global Competitive Advantage."

33. Adapted from C. Bartlett, S. Ghoshal, and J. Birkenshaw, *Transnational Management* (New York: Irwin, 2004). Note that Bartlett and Ghoshal distinguish among international, multinational, global, and transnational strategies. We have found these distinctions are difficult for students to apply and have chosen to use the underlying dimensions of local responsiveness and global efficiency as the tradeoffs that international strategy emphasizes.

34. B. Oviatt and P. McDougall, "Global Start-Ups: Entrepreneurs on a Worldwide Stage," *Academy of Management Executive* 9:2 (1995), 30–44.

35. www.logitech.com.

36. Summarized from Oviatt and McDougall, "Global Start-Ups."

37. J. S. Brown and J. Hagel, "Innovation Blowback: Disruptive Management Practices from Asia," *McKinsey Quarterly* January (2005).

38. M. Porter, *Competitive Advantage* (New York: Free Press, 1998).

39. G. Tellis, S. Stremersch, and E. Yin. "The International Takeoff of New Products: Economics, Culture and Country Innovativeness," *Marketing Science* 22:2 (2003), 161–187.

40. F. Vermeulen and H. Barkema, "Learning Through Acquisitions," *Academy of Management Journal* 44 (2001), 457–476; M. A. Hitt, M. T. Dacin, E. Levitas, and J. Arregle, "Partner Selection in Emerging and Developed Market Contexts: Resource-Based and Organizational Learning Perspectives," *Academy of Management Journal* 43 (2000), 449–467.

41. Gupta and Govindarajan, "Converting Global Presence into Global Competitive Advantage."

42. "Furnishing the World," *The Economist*, November 19, 1994, 79–80.

43. B. Kedia and A. Mukherji, "Global Managers: Developing a Mindset for Global Competitiveness," *Journal of World Business* 34:3 (1999), 230–251.

Understanding Alliances and Cooperative Strategies

Understanding Alliances and Cooperative Strategies

In This Chapter We Challenge You To >>>

1. Explain why strategic alliances are important strategy vehicles.

2. Identify the motivations behind alliances and show how they've changed over time.

3. Compare and contrast the various forms and structures of strategic alliances.

4. Explain alliances as both business- and corporate-level strategy vehicles.

5. Understand the characteristics of alliances in stable and dynamic competitive contexts.

6. Summarize the criteria for successful alliances.

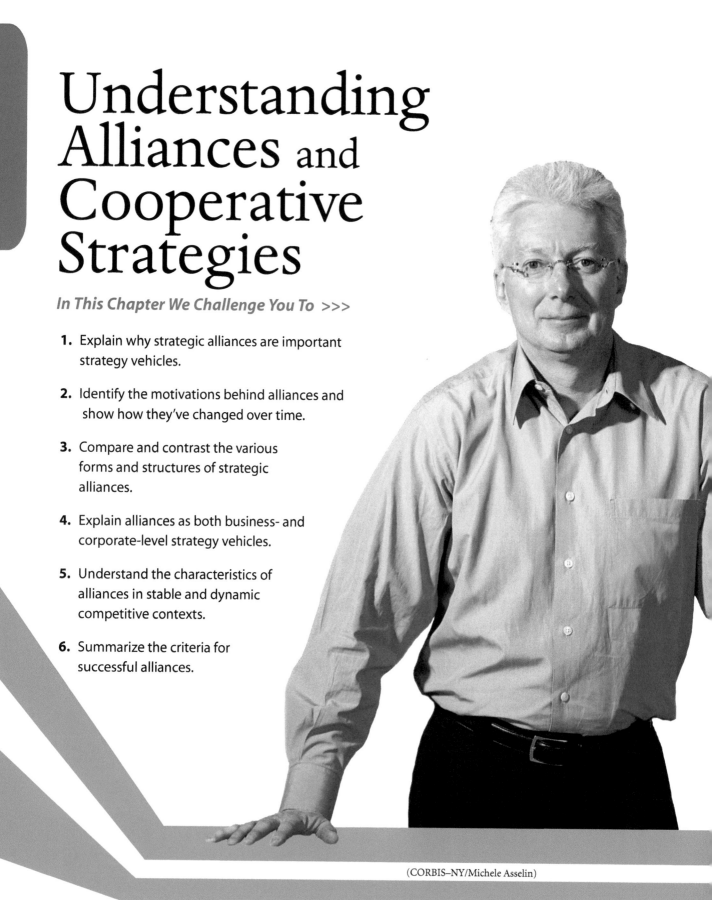

(CORBIS–NY/Michele Asselin)

An Alliance *that* Fits Like *a* Glove[1]

(Diane Austin)

Procter & Gamble's Mr. Clean brand, launched in 1958 with a muscle-man sailor as the mascot, had become a 98-pound weakling in the liquid cleaner segment by the 1990s. Jeffrey Weedman, P&G Vice President of External Business Development, saw the problem. "Mr. Clean is a singleproduct line and we aren't focusing enough on it," he told Nancy Bailey of Nancy Bailey & Associates. "Nancy, why don't you take the Mr. Clean brand and see what you can do with it." Bailey & Associates specializes in brand extension licensing, and Bailey went right to work finding an alliance partner who could help revitalize the Mr. Clean brand. Bailey found Jordan Glatt, President of Magla, a $30 million unbranded manufacturer of household gloves. Magla excelled at making high-quality products, but gloves are a commodity product, which, if undifferentiated and unbranded, can't command a premium price. Mr. Clean, on the other hand, was a well-known brand looking to expand beyond its core liquid-cleaner line. An alliance between the two companies could help both. In just 60 days, P&G and Magla signed an agreement to market a line of Magla household gloves under the Mr. Clean name. Glatt was "excited about the prospects of producing upscale household gloves under the Mr. Clean brand name and developing creative packaging and promotions to further distinguish our products," he said. Magla would use the Mr. Clean trademark and pay P&G royalties, but Magla would remain separate from P&G and would sell directly to the big retailers. The deal brought a strategic line extension for Mr. Clean while expanding the customer base and distribution channels for Magla. Describing the agreement, Glatt said, "A partnership with P&G provides Magla with a great niche-marketing opportunity. Mr. Clean has widespread name recognition." Similarly, Scott Lazarczyk, Brand Manager of Mr. Clean, explained the benefit to P&G: "This licensing agreement is a great example of how we're leveraging the Mr. Clean brand across product categories that add to our current offerings."

In an age of speed, alliances make sense. If done right, they can help a company grow faster, introduce new products faster, or expand into new areas less expensively. As Glatt said, "An added benefit from working with P&G is that we could hook in to their national FSCIs [free-standing coupon inserts] that appear in newspapers, which make the P&G and Magla products look like a seamless Mr. Clean product line. A company our size could never afford this type of investment." What's more, the alliance helped Magla expand overseas. Mr. Clean is known overseas as Mr. Proper in mainland Europe, Don Limpio in Spain (*limpiar* is the Spanish verb for "to clean") and Mastro Lindo ("Master Clean") in Italy. Glatt said, "The Mr. Clean brand provides us with a wonderful opportunity to enter the European market with a leading brand with high awareness and an exceptional reputation."

Pursuing an alliance is an important strategic consideration for growth. Indeed, Glatt initially came up with the idea of using alliances long before the Mr. Clean opportunity presented itself. In the 1990s, Glatt was debating with his top managers about whether to launch a line of work gloves. Magla already made gloves for household chores, so adding a line of work gloves made strategic sense. But Glatt and his team realized that pursuing such an expansion strategy would be risky because Glatt knew that Magla had neither the brand name nor the retail connections to enter the home improvement market. Glatt worried that a big player like Stanley Works (a company known for its hardware and tools) could easily get into the market. Glatt decided to circumvent the potential problems of expansion and potential competition through an alliance with Stanley. He signed a licensing deal for Magla to make and sell work gloves under the Stanley name. In 2005, Glatt continued with his alliance strategy, this time entering into an agreement with the American Red Cross to market a complete line of branded medical gloves. The partnership was the first of its kind for the American Red Cross, with a portion of the proceeds from the sale of each retail package going directly to benefit the organization's relief efforts. The alliance strategy has paid off for Glatt—by 2006, his company's revenues had more than tripled to $100 million. Said Glatt: "Partnerships have turned us into a new company."

For its part, giant P&G is likewise benefiting from its alliances. P&G expanded the Mr. Clean brand even further through alliances with other companies. Its alliance with automotive and chemical supplier Old World Industries yielded a Mr. Clean Premium Windshield Wash. Even better, P&G's strategic alliance with Old World covers other P&G brands beyond Mr. Clean. For example, Old World is producing a specialty automotive version of P&G's Febreze air fresheners and Swiffer dusters that bring these two brands out of the home and into the car. For the Febreze auto line, Old World tailored Febreze into a lightly scented formula made specifically to eliminate odors in car interiors.

Successful alliances have led P&G's Jeff Weedman to coin "Weedman's Corollary": The second deal takes one-half of the time of the first deal. The third deal takes one-third of the time, and so on. And that law appears to have worked well for P&G, Magla, and Stanley. The subsequent deals are not only faster, but they also tend to be more profitable. Weedman's corollary means that P&G looks for ways to extend its alliances with good partners. P&G benefits from sustained collaborations and discovers new value creation opportunities that it previously did not know about. Small businesses can bring the giant company ideas it needs. As Jeff Weedman says, "This isn't a revolutionary idea. It's just smart business." <<<

Strategic Alliances

Why do firms enter alliances? Are most alliances successful? Was the agreement between P&G and Magla typical? How long do typical alliances last? Are alliances really a form of courting prior to the acquisition of one party by another? Or, does one party use the alliance to gain knowledge at the expense of the other party? By the end of this chapter, you should be able to answer these and many other questions about the formation, implementation, and termination of strategic alliances. Like most relationships, alliances have a beginning and an end. As you work through the chapter, you'll see that the opening vignette on P&G and Magla features many of the characteristics of strategic alliances. Alliances often enable participants to share in investments and rewards while reducing the risk and uncertainty that each firm would otherwise face on its own. In addition, shared activities enable each organization to focus its resources on what it does best. Finally, alliances foster economies of scale and scope—both within the partner firms and between partners and the alliance vehicle—that companies wouldn't otherwise be able to achieve, at least not in the same cost-effective manner.

Studies have shown that companies that participate most actively in alliances outperform the least-active firms by 5 to 7 percent.[2] And most alliances average seven years in duration before they are dissolved, or one of the parties to the alliance buys out the other. Some might argue that this 5 to 7 percent performance premium results from the fact that better-run firms are also simply better at initiating and managing alliances. In the early 1990s, for instance, BMW and DaimlerChrysler determined jointly that the minimum efficient economic scale of a small automobile engine facility would be a plant capable of producing 400,000 engines annually. Separately, however, each firm had internal demand for only 200,000 engines per year. The solution? An alliance through which they shared the cost of building a new plant large enough to turn out 400,000 engines. BMW uses the motors in its line of Mini Coopers, and DaimlerChrysler uses them in both its Neon and PT Cruiser lines.

Remember, however, that alliances are not strategies in and of themselves. Rather, as you will recall from the strategy diamond, which represents the five elements of the strategy diamond, an alliance is simply one *vehicle* for realizing a strategy. ◆ In addition, an effective alliance must be consistent with the economic logic of the strategy. The firm must also have the managerial capabilities to create economic value through cooperative arrangements, not simply the actions that are internal to the firm. In this chapter, we'll review the critical features that firms must master if they're going to use alliances effectively and in a manner that's consistent with the economic logic underpinning their overall strategies.

 Vehicles

Exhibit 1 The Value Chain

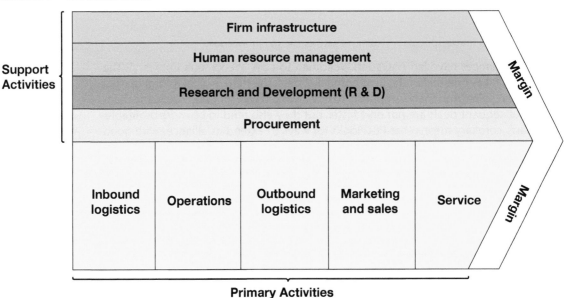

A **strategic alliance** is a partnership in which two or more firms combine resources and capabilities with the goal of creating mutual competitive advantage. An alliance may involve sharing resources related to only one key activity in the partners' value chain, such as R&D. See Exhibit 1 for a generic reproduction of the value chain model.

As shown in Exhibit 2, however, an alliance may involve coordination across many value chain activities. For example, the partners may work together to develop new products via shared R&D and also cooperate on the production and marketing of the new products. Indeed, the number and combinations of linkages is practically endless.

Note, too, that an alliance may be strategic to one firm and only tactical or operational to the other. This distinction is typically a function of the relative size of the alliance partners, and the truly unique character of the alliance function. Wal-Mart, for example, has long sought to reduce the number of its suppliers through a variety of so-called *sole-sourcing* and *just-in-time supply agreements*. Both types of agreements mean that a buyer has chosen only one or a few suppliers for its raw materials, and with the just-in-time arrangement, it expects that the supplier will provide the buyer with those materials at the exact point in time that they are needed in the production or sales cycle. In terms of investment in distribution infrastructure, sales volume, and concentration of sales to one buyer, such agreements may be strategic for the supplier but not necessarily to Wal-Mart, which is rarely dependent on any one supplier. In 1994, for instance, when Rubbermaid sought to raise its prices to Wal-Mart, its single largest customer, the giant retailer responded by dropping Rubbermaid products from every one of its stores.[3] Only after Rubbermaid was acquired by Newell in 1999 was it restored to Wal-Mart's good graces.

GROWTH OF ALLIANCES

Given its attractive features—as well as increasing competitive intensity in most industries—it shouldn't be surprising that the use of alliances as a strategy vehicle has grown dramatically in the last few decades. As a percentage of revenues, alliances ballooned from 2 to nearly 16 percent between 1980 through 1995. In particular, as of 2007, it is believed that large multinational corporations will have over 20 percent of their total assets tied up in al-

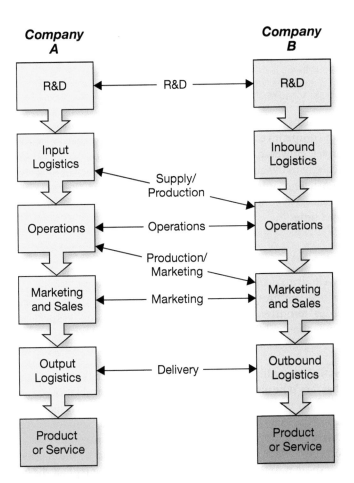

Exhibit 2 Possible Points of Value Chain Coordination in an Alliance

liances.[4] If outsourcing arrangements were factored into this calculation, then the percentage of assets related to alliances would surely be much higher. For U.S. firms, alliance partners are largely, and not surprisingly, concentrated in Asia and Europe.

FAILURE RATES

Note, however, that despite their apparent popular use, the failure rate for alliances is about 50 percent (and nearly 70 percent in some cases). An alliance can be deemed a failure when one or more of the partners did not achieve its objectives and, in more dismal cases, when one partner benefited but the other partner was left worse off competitively. Clearly, alliances can be high-risk as well as high-return vehicles for realizing a firm's strategy.[5]

Interestingly, however, such a high failure rate doesn't surprise economists and many other experts. Why? Most economic theories assume that, left to their own devices, individual entities will behave in their own *self-interest*. The success of an alliance, of course, depends on the willingness of partners to subordinate their own interests to those of the alliance, but even when partners start out by suspending self-interest, circumstances can change dramatically over time, compromising even the best of intentions.

In the remaining sections of this chapter, we'll examine the various forms that alliances can take, and we'll show how the objectives underlying them have evolved over time. We'll discuss alliances as strategy vehicles and explain the risks to which they're prone. We'll also focus on the ways in which both the objectives and structures of alliances vary in stable versus dynamic contexts. Finally, because so many alliance failures are due to faulty implementation, we'll conclude by discussing four specific ways to improve the probability of alliance success.

Why Alliances?

Not surprisingly, firms participating in effective alliances can improve their competitive position and gain competitive advantage. Remember that one alternative to an alliance is a purchase contract. However, there are significant limits as to what can and cannot be contracted, particularly in dynamic contexts. Put bluntly, contracts alone are not always sufficient to coordinate and control partners' behaviors. In this section, we review how the use of alliances is related to competitive advantage and how the motivation for using alliances has evolved over time.

ALLIANCES AND COMPETITIVE ADVANTAGE

Alliances can help firms achieve their objectives in several ways. Alliances not only spread the risk of business ventures by sharing that risk with other firms; they also give firms access to knowledge, resources, and capabilities that the firm might otherwise lack. Alliances achieve these potential building blocks of competitive advantage in four ways: *joint investment, knowledge sharing, complementary resources,* and *effective management.*[6]

Joint Investment Alliances can help to increase returns by motivating firms to make investments that they'd be unwilling to make outside a formal alliance relationship. This advantage is particularly important in light of the fact that productivity gains are possible when activities linked in the value chain are supported with transaction-specific investments.

In many situations, a supplier won't make an investment pertaining specifically to an exchange with one buyer. Why? Because the investment would tie the supplier too closely to one buyer and expose it to too much risk, the greatest risk being that the buyer reneges on its commitment to buy the supplier's products or services or grinds the supplier down on price due to its dependence on the single buyer.[7] For instance, if you invested $10 million in a piece of equipment that made products that could be sold only by Wal-Mart, you would be very dependent on Wal-Mart because of the asset specificity of such an investment. A buyer, therefore, often integrates backward vertically in the value chain, making the necessary investment to internalize the supply. The supplier's hesitancy, however, can be overcome if the buyer is willing to enter a formal arrangement that reduces the supplier's risk. Both supplier and buyer can benefit not only from gains in efficiency but also from savings in the bureaucratic costs entailed by vertical integration.

Knowledge Sharing One common reason of entering into alliances is to learn from partners. Learning, however, requires partners to cooperate in transferring knowledge. Although partners may not be equally capable of absorbing knowledge, two factors can help to facilitate the transfer of knowledge: (1) mutual trust and familiarity between partners; and (2) consistent information-sharing routines, such as that obtained through higher-level executive contact, integrated information systems, and employee swapping and cross-company career paths. As an example of the latter, John Deere regularly exchanges key employees with alliance partner Hitachi in certain product segments.

Complementary Resources A firm's resources and capabilities are the primary sources of competitive advantage. When partners combine resources and capabilities, they may be able to create a stock of resources that's unavailable to other competitors in the industry. If that stock combines complementary resources and capabilities, then the alliance may be able to generate a shared advantage. Finally, if the combination of resources and ca-

292

pabilities is valuable and rare, the alliance may be able to generate greater profits than the sum of the partners' individual profits. Thus, when Nestlé and Coke combined resources to offer canned tea and coffee products, the alliance offered a vehicle that was more attractive than going it alone due to complementarities between the parties.[8]

Effective Management   One way to judge the appropriateness and effectiveness of an alliance is through comparing its costs with the alternatives of an arm's-length transaction or formal internal integration (providing the activity internally or buying a company that can provide the activity). The second way to judge whether an alliance is effective is if it helps build a competitive advantage. This evaluation process is referred to as a *buy or make* decision, with alliances lying somewhere in between the two extremes—this is sometimes called make, buy, or ally.

Look at the principle from the following perspective: A potential problem in any alliance is that one partner may take advantage of another. To minimize this risk, many alliances call for formal protection mechanisms, such as equity investments (which should align incentives) or formal contracts (which should outline expected behavior and remedies for violations). Although such mechanisms are costly, they may still be cheaper than formal integration of activities within one firm. However, some experts argue that the true cost savings of alliances comes to those firms that can rely on less formal managerial control over their partners' behavior and instead depend on self-enforcement and informal agreements. Informal arrangements, of course, require a great deal of trust, which is likely to develop only after multiple dealings between partners.[9] We'll address the subjects of learning and trust more fully in the concluding section of this chapter.

Recall from the VRINE framework that resources and capabilities are the basis of competitive advantage only when they satisfy certain criteria: They must be valuable, rare, difficult to imitate, and supported by organizational arrangements. If an alliance (or network of alliances) is a vehicle that helps the firm's strategy satisfy these criteria, it has probably developed a collaborative advantage that helps one or more of the member firms achieve a competitive advantage over rivals outside the alliance.

ALLIANCE MOTIVATION OVER TIME

Although the overarching motivation behind alliances—the pursuit of competitive advantage—hasn't changed, the ways in which alliances contribute to such advantage have. This is one reason why it is so critical for you to understand strategic management from a dynamic perspective. In the late 1980s, in an effort to better understand why alliances were becoming increasingly common, the consulting firm Booz-Allen began studying the alliance practices of 1,000 U.S. firms. Among other things, the study revealed dramatic changes in the motivations that impelled firms to enter alliances over the course of several decades.[10] Note, these drivers represent *cumulative* needs.

As shown in Exhibit 3, alliances formed during the 1970s emphasized product and service performance.[11] The alliance strategy of Corning Glass Works (now called Corning) exemplifies this focus. Its alliance with Dow (Dow-Corning) allowed Corning to leverage its advanced glass-making capabilities in new products and new markets, and creating scale and scope economies, both at home and abroad. In the 1980s, firms tended to stress the building and reinforcing of market position. Microsoft and Intel, for example, joined to informally establish the Wintel alliance. Microsoft's Windows family of operating systems functioned best on PCs with Intel's chips, and as long as Microsoft kept increasing processing-speed requirements, Intel could count on consistent product demand. In some ways, P&G's alliance with Magla is a position alliance, since P&G can leverage Magla's strengths in gloves with its own brands to enter new markets or reinforce existing market positions.

Exhibit 3 Cumulative Motivation of Alliances Over Time

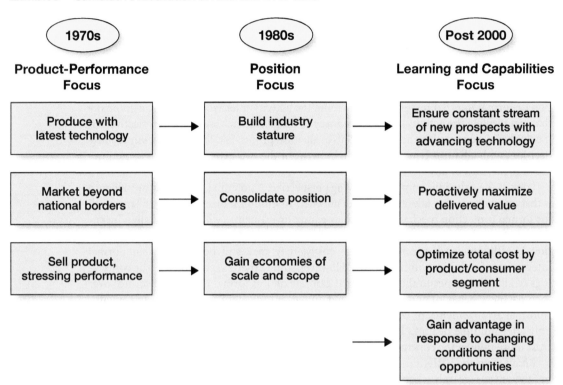

More recently, corporations have begun to emphasize more complex benefits, such as organizational learning and the development and accumulation of valuable resources and capabilities. In this vein, we can look at the case of the bicycle distributor Pacific Cycle. Recall that Pacific is sort of the Nike of bikes—it designs and distributes its bikes, but outsources production entirely to overseas factories in China. While Pacific does have its own design team in the United States, it relies heavily on its suppliers for new product ideas. In fact, these suppliers have the capability of rapidly building prototypes of new bikes that Pacific can then quickly test market in its major venues. As a reward for such innovativeness, Pacific will often grant the production contract for the new bike to the factory that invented it. Thus, Pacific and its suppliers have a shared gain in any successful products that are brought to market.

Form and Structure of Alliances

Note that we've been using the term *strategic alliances* as a catchall term. In reality, cooperative arrangements can take a number of forms. Exhibit 4 summarizes the vast continuum of forms that cooperative arrangements, including strategic alliances, may take. As you can see, the two primary dimensions on which alliances can be categorized are the nature of the *time commitment* (e.g., timeframe and resources) and respective *investment commitment* of the alliance and inputs into the alliance (ranging from cash to people to technology).

Whether or not a particular alliance is deemed as strategic will depend on the degree to which one or both parties' survival or competitive advantage depends on the alliance. For instance, a contract to supply coffee to a company's offices might be important, but there is no shared equity involved (no cross investment), and the relationship can probably be easily replaced by another provider. However, a contractual relationship between an enterprise software provider like SAP and its client, while perhaps not strategic for SAP, is mission critical for SAP's customer because such software is likely to be the lifeblood of their operations.

Exhibit 4 Degrees of Alliance Intensity

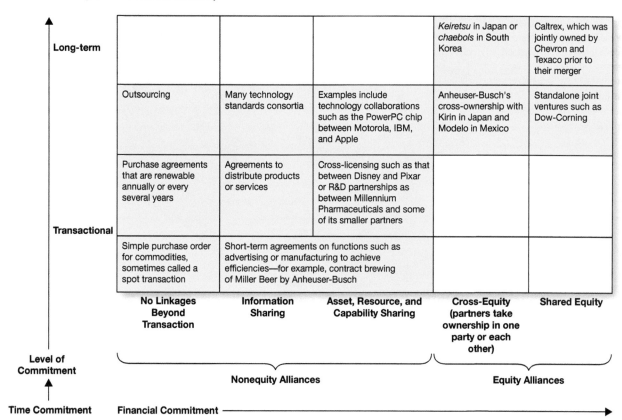

JOINT VENTURES AND OTHER EQUITY ALLIANCES

The form of an alliance depends on such factors as legal structure and the number and objectives of participants. In a **joint venture**, for instance, two companies make equity investments in the creation of a third, which exists as an independent legal entity. This is the case with Dow-Corning, which, as the name suggests, is a joint venture between Dow and Corning; if mapped to Exhibit 3, it would fall under the shared-equity category. Many joint ventures are 50/50 splits in ownership and control, but they need not be equal partnerships. As you can probably imagine, each partner typically wants 51% ownership, so that they have technical control over the alliance. In reality, partners usually identify the specific aspects of the alliance that they are most interested in, so the respective ownership question becomes less of a stumbling block.

It isn't necessary, however, for an alliance to create a separate legal entity or share equal ownership. In many cases, **equity alliances** involve unequal partners. This may be the case when one partner owns a greater percentage of the alliance's equity than another partner; when a separate legal entity is not established, and one partner instead takes partial ownership of the other partner; or when contracts are used to govern the sharing and respective rights regarding contributed assets, resources, or capabilities. Millennium Pharmaceuticals, for example, prefers arrangements in which larger partners take a percentage ownership not only in Millennium itself, but also a minority-percentage interest in any alliance with a separate legal structure. (It also manages several strategic alliances with traditional 50/50 splits.[12])

joint venture Alliance in which two firms make equity investments in a third legal entity.

equity alliance Alliance in which one or more partners assumes a greater ownership interest in either the alliance or another partner.

Dow Corning Corporation, the Michigan-based silicon-products maker, is a joint venture between Dow and Corning, as its name suggests. In joint ventures, partners often invest on an equal basis and split corporate ownership and control down the middle.
(Photo courtesy of The Dow Corning Corporation)

NONEQUITY ALLIANCES

The most common form of strategic alliance involves neither equity interest nor separate organizations. Arrangements such as *sole-sourcing, just-in-time supply agreements, licensing, cobranding,* and *franchising* often fall under the heading of *nonequity alliances.* The coffee company example provided earlier fits this category.

nonequity alliance Alliance that involves neither the assumption of equity interest nor the creation of separate organizations.

Nonequity alliances are typically contracts that call for one firm to supply, produce, market, or distribute another's goods or services over an extended period of time, but without substantial ownership investments in the alliance. Starbucks, for instance, has extended the presence of its brand into a number of customer-contact locations through alliances with such companies as Barnes & Noble (bookstore cafés), United Airlines (in-flight coffee service), Dreyer's (coffee ice cream), Pepsi (Frappuccino ready-to-drink coffee), and Kraft (ground and whole coffee beans distributed through grocery stores). The various strategic roles that these nonequity alliances play for Starbucks are shown in Exhibit 5.[13]

MULTIPARTY ALLIANCES

consortia Association of several companies and/or governments for some definite strategic purpose.

Thus far, we've described alliances involving two partners. Other types of alliances, such as **consortia**, usually involve many participants, perhaps even governments. The primary contribution to these cooperative arrangements is information, though there may be some cost sharing as well. Perhaps the most complex multifirm alliances are those in the technology arena. SEMATECH, for example, is a consortium of semiconductor manufacturers established in the mid-1980s to prop up the U.S. semiconductor industry, which at the time was considered to be of strategic importance to national defense. To some extent, SEMATECH's cooperative structure was modeled after joint projects by which Japanese semiconductor producers were responsible for advancing their collective technological competencies in the late 1970s.[14] The consortium has since evolved to include both U.S. and non–U.S. firms, and a related venture called SEMI/SEMATECH (or SEMI) is an alliance of suppliers to the semiconductor industry.[15]

Exhibit 5 Starbuck's Universe of Alliances

Alliances as Strategy Vehicles

You probably are beginning to realize this, but almost any organization is a potential alliance partner, and deciding with whom to partner is a matter of a firm's business and corporate strategies. The challenge is to, first, determine if you are going to use alliances as a strategy vehicle and then, second, begin to identify potential partners.

ALLIANCES AND BUSINESS STRATEGY

Let's start by considering factors related to business strategy—strategy that determines how a firm competes in a chosen industry. A quick review of the five-forces model and related complementors of industry structure reinforces the number and variety of a firm's potential partners. Who might these allies be?

- **Rivals.** Are there opportunities to partner with rivals? Although there are certainly legal prohibitions against cooperative arrangements among competitors that harm consumers, rivals will often engage in strategic alliances. The various airline alliances, such as One World and Star, are a case in point. Sometimes a company may partner with a competitor to manage surplus production demand or to help it manage excess capacity. Beer companies collaborate in production and distribution for instance—if a truck can deliver two breweries' products to the same market then both companies benefit from the cost sharing. Similarly, breweries often contract with competitors to brew their beer when their demand outstrips capacity. This has been one of the secrets of success for Sam Adams. Sam Adams creates the beer recipes but then has the beer produced by Anheuser-Busch, Miller Beer, and others.

- **New entrants.** Industry incumbents can ally with new entrants to diversify or to co-opt a future potential rival. Wal-Mart's alliance with the Mexican retailer Cifra is a good example of this. If you know a new competitor has an interest in your market, one firm can take the initiative to work together with the other, usually with the end-game strategy of merging the two entities.

297

- **Suppliers.** Increasingly, firms are developing alliances with key suppliers. These can take on the form of sole-sourcing and just-in-time arrangements or include more complex forms, such as Tritec, in which the supplier is formed by two rivals. This alliance approach can take several forms. For instance, SC Johnson sells many of its products in Wal-Mart. However, since SC Johnson is so good at merchandising its products, Wal-Mart has designated SC Johnson as the category manager for several lines of products. What this means is that SC Johnson is responsible for stocking its own goods on Wal-Mart's shelves, but also for coordinating and merchandising all the other producers' products in, say, the category of household cleansers. As a result, SC Johnson is in a much stronger position, and can improve its merchandising skills, and Wal-Mart benefits by having the best in the business managing this part of its in-store merchandising.

- **Customers.** The customer-incumbent relationship is the flip side of the incumbent-supplier relationship. This is most often seen in business-to-business relationships. For instance, when Copeland Corporation developed a new line of air conditioning units, it partnered with its customers to provide that part, while the end-user like Trane or Rheem manufactured the rest of the air conditioning unit. This situation is very analogous to the Intel inside story. Intel makes the chips, but its alliances with Apple and Dell and others ensures that they are the leading edge processor in those machines.

- **Substitutes.** These products and services pose a threat to the incumbent. Through an alliance, this threat can actually be exploited. For instance, soy milk is a clear substitute for dairy milk. Instead of actively competing against the growing market for soy milk, Dean Foods established a joint venture with, and then acquired, industry leader Silk. You can see how you can employ this same logic with any substitute. If there is an opportunity to collaborate, and offer consumers broader choices, then perhaps both parties will gain through the alliance.

- **Complementors.** Recall that complements are those products or services that, when bundled together, create greater value than when acquired separately. An alliance between an industry incumbent and a complement can lock out competitors. As a case in point, most major fast-food chains provide Coke or Pepsi products, not both. We elaborate further on this aspect of managing alliance strategy below.

The Value Net Model and Co-opetition

One way to think about all of the players identified in the industry structure model in a manner that highlight possible alliance possibilities is to rearrange the players into the **value net model**. See Exhibit 6.[16] Notice that in this model we place the firm of interest in the center and link it to all possible exchange partners. In allowing them to identify opportunities for cooperative relationships among all possible exchange partners and even competitors, the value net model helps managers find alternatives to conventional win-lose business scenarios.

value net model Map of a firm's existing and potential exchange relationships.

How might a firm establish a cooperative relationship with a competitor? Consider a firm like Motorola, which may in some business situations be a competitor to Intel, such as in the sale of microprocessors. In other situations, it may be in a partnership with Intel, such as in the development of a new technology. Still in other situations, Motorola might be a customer of Intel, sourcing key components for a particular product.

Co-opetition The term **co-opetition** refers to a situation in which firms are both competitors and cooperative partners. The purpose of co-opetition is to find ways of increasing the total value created by parties in the value net, not just determining how to compete for

co-opetition Situation in which firms are simultaneously competitors in one market and collaborators in another.

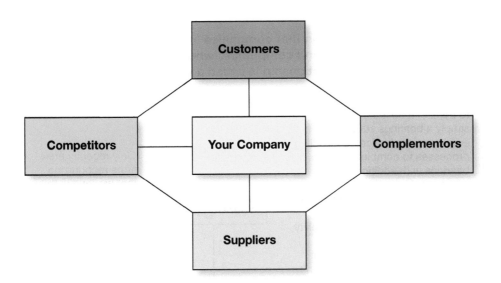

industry profits. The value net helps managers find potential partners; in other words, it helps them to identify those parties that are possible complementors rather than just competitors. In the following two sections we illustrate how the value net can be applied to various types of alliances.

Alliances can figure into most aspects of business strategy, but they generally provide a means of managing competitive pressures, uncertainty, or both. Business-strategy alliances tend to fall into two major categories: *vertical alliances* or *horizontal alliances*.

Vertical Alliances

A **vertical alliance** is formed when a firm partners with one or more of its suppliers or customers (typically, the latter only occurs in business-to-business relationships). This is exactly the type of alliance we referred to in the section about supplier and customer alliances earlier. The purpose of a vertical alliance is to leverage partners' resources and capabilities in order to meet two goals: (1) to create more value for the end customer and (2) to lower total production costs along the value chain. In a sense, the vertical alliance is an alternative for vertical integration, the *corporate* strategy whereby a firm takes ownership of downstream supply or upstream distribution or other marketing functions.

Jeffrey H. Dyer, a prominent strategy professor who specializes in the study of strategic alliances, has found that vertical alliances can create lean value chains by reducing total supply-chain costs in four areas: transaction, quality, product-development, and logistics costs:[17]

- *Transaction costs* are often lower among alliance partners than among firms in third-party arm's-length transactions.

- Because quality is often improved, *quality-related costs*—those associated with defects, returns, and warranty work—go down.

- When partners share knowledge and human capital and focus their efforts on improving product design and quality, vertical alliances can control *product-development costs.*

- Reduced warehousing and transportation costs not only reduce inbound *logistics costs* but result in lower inventory costs as well.

vertical alliance Alliance involving a focal firm and a supplier or customer.

Exhibit 7 An Example of Co-opetition

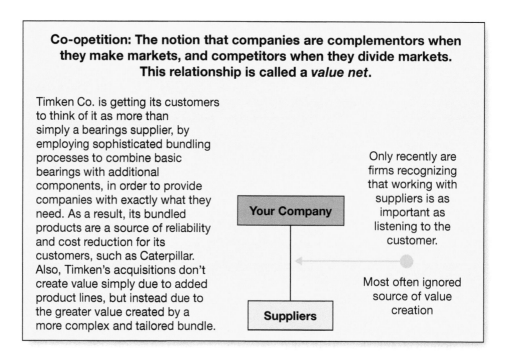

Co-opetition: The notion that companies are complementors when they make markets, and competitors when they divide markets. This relationship is called a *value net*.

Timken Co. is getting its customers to think of it as more than simply a bearings supplier, by employing sophisticated bundling processes to combine basic bearings with additional components, in order to provide companies with exactly what they need. As a result, its bundled products are a source of reliability and cost reduction for its customers, such as Caterpillar. Also, Timken's acquisitions don't create value simply due to added product lines, but instead due to the greater value created by a more complex and tailored bundle.

Only recently are firms recognizing that working with suppliers is as important as listening to the customer.

Most often ignored source of value creation

Your Company

Suppliers

Vertical alliances also improve value to the customer by making it possible for alliance partners to increase speed to market, improve quality, introduce newer technologies and features, and respond more quickly to market changes. Exhibit 7 shows how Timken applies the net value to vertical integration alliances by bundling its product offerings.

Horizontal Alliances **Horizontal alliances** are partnerships between firms in the same industry. These types of alliances enable competitors, or potential competitors, to gain a presence in multiple segments of an industry. As a component of a firm's value net, a horizontal alliance, which gives a company access to multiple segments of an industry, can create value in a number of ways. First, it can reduce risk. For instance, when two oil exploration firms enter into a joint venture, they spread the risk entailed by the costs of drilling. Likewise, Kraft's alliance with Starbucks gives it a super-premium coffee brand that it can distribute through the grocery channel to complement not only its Maxwell House and Yuban brands in the same channel but also its Gevalia brand in the direct-marketing and business-to-business channels. Mondavi's various alliances with top wine producers in Chile, Italy, Argentina, and France give it access to a broader range of high-quality wines than it could support if it had to rely solely on its own resources.

Horizontal alliances can also help partners achieve greater efficiency. Thus, when McDonald's and Disney cooperate in promotions, each leverages its advertising expenditures. In addition, although Disney benefits from McDonald's promotion of Disney characters and programming, McDonald's benefits from the popular appeal of Disney characters, which appear as toys in products aimed at kids.

Finally, horizontal alliances foster learning in the development and innovation of new products. SEMATECH and the Automotive and Composites Consortium (launched by GM, Ford, and Chrysler) are good examples of learning alliances. In the case of SEMATECH, for instance, all U.S.–based semiconductor manufacturers pooled their

horizontal alliance Alliance involving a focal firm and another firm in the same industry.

knowledge to improve the production process and were collectively able to turn the competitive tide against the rising dominance of Japanese firms. The Apple–Sony partnership that developed the PowerBook is a good example of firms using horizontal alliances to access complementary skills. Finally, horizontal alliances can help firms overcome political obstacles. In China, for example, the Otis Elevator–Tianjin joint venture enabled Otis to enter an attractive and growing market that at the time was inaccessible without a local partner.

Let's return for a moment to the concept of co-opetition, which is based on the principle that firms must often cooperate and compete simultaneously. Because horizontal alliances make allies of competitors, it's crucial that all parties understand the conditions that favor success in such ventures. First, they're potentially beneficial when partners' strategic goals converge and competitive goals diverge. When, for instance, Philips and DuPont collaborated to make compact discs (CDs), neither firm was invading the other's markets for other products. In addition, horizontal alliances are more likely to succeed when the partners are chasing industry leaders, as when Asian semiconductor-chip makers collaborated in making memory chips in an effort to cut into Intel's market share. Finally, in successful horizontal alliances, all partners acknowledge the fact that, though each must be willing to share knowledge, each can and must protect proprietary skills. For example, the Fuji Photo–Xerox alliance, established in 1962, allows the two makers of copiers and printers to collaborate in the Japanese and Pacific Rim markets. In return for access to these markets, Fuji is entitled to a 75-percent share in the joint profits. Fuji agreed to the arrangement because it believed that it could protect its film business in these markets; Xerox, meanwhile, believed that the venture would not endanger its copier business elsewhere in the world.

CORPORATE AND INTERNATIONAL STRATEGIC ALLIANCES

Although alliances are typical business strategy vehicles, they can also be vehicles for corporate and international strategy. In the first case, the alliance facilitates product or service diversification within an existing market, while in the second case the alliance facilitates entry and competition in another geographic market. ◆ Arenas

Alliances and Corporate Strategy   Corporate strategy is largely concerned with two activities:

- Determining the right mix of businesses in the corporate portfolio

- Ensuring that this mix creates shareholder value

Let's consider each of these activities in terms of decisions about alliances. As for portfolio mix, alliances are vehicles for exploring and implementing diversification options. Through its office-copier business, for instance, a company like Xerox may have developed a set of technologies that may provide access into the intensely competitive desktop-copier and computer-printer businesses. In an alliance with a strong partner like Fuji Photo of Japan, it can share the risk and development costs related to an uncertain diversification move. Similarly, through its alliance with Magla, P&G diversified into household gloves and Magla diversified into branded consumer products.

Corporations can also use alliances to create value across a portfolio of individual businesses. At first glance, for example, you might think of venture capitalists (VCs) and their various investments as independent entities. They do, however, represent strategic alliances. How so? Whereas the VC provides capital and managerial expertise, the entrepreneurial firm provides an opportunity for new products. From a corporate-strategy

301

perspective, the VC firm can create more value for its investments by identifying key individuals in one firm who could help create value for its other units. The VC firm Softbank, for example, leverages its investments in broadband-application and broadband-provider companies by circulating its best and brightest managers and technologists among its wholly owned companies as well as those in which it has investments.[18] Likewise, a diversified firm can also broker relationships among its portfolio businesses.

Alliances and International Strategy Finally, as shown in the example of the international partnership between Dell Computer and its Asian distributor, a firm's international strategy should issue from its business- and corporate-strategy objectives. Many of the alliances that we've described in this chapter are international in nature: either they involve partners from different countries or the alliance itself is headquartered in a country different from those of the partners. Cross-border alliances differ from domestic alliances in that governments, public policies, and national cultures often play significant roles. Also important, of course, are differences in workplace regulations and socioeconomic conditions.

In some cases, a firm can only do business in another country through an alliance. For instance, a U.S. firm that wishes to do business in Saudi Arabia can only do so if it has a partner with a local firm. In fact, the partner has to be a member of the Saudi Royal family. Alliances are not just a vehicle used by U.S. firms. Many Chinese companies are buying U.S. and European high-technology firms, and then partnering with Indian companies for the customer service component. Similarly, Indian firms are buying large manufacturing firms in Latin America, the United States, and Europe, and then through alliances outsourcing production to more efficient facilities in China.

Not surprisingly, in international contexts, decisions about internal and external vehicles through which to execute a firm's strategy are much more complex than in domestic contexts. Multinational corporations, for instance, may be better than alliances in facilitating the flow of knowledge across borders. Analysis of patent citations by semiconductor companies suggests that multinationals are better than both alliances and market forces in fostering cross-border knowledge transfer, primarily because they can use multiple mechanisms for transferring knowledge and are more flexible in moving, integrating, and developing technical knowledge.[19]

ALLIANCE NETWORKS

Related to the study of the strategic functions of alliances is the concept that alliances are taking on characteristics of networks. Network theory has two implications for organizational practice. First, as alliances become a larger component of a firm's strategy, the strategy discussion will shift from particular alliances as a vehicle to networks of alliances as a vehicle. In this sense, the firm is operating as a hub, or node, in a complex array of owned, partially owned, and nonowned businesses. Looking back at the value net portrayed in Exhibit 6, you can imagine how multiple alliances among complementors, competitors, suppliers, and customers might easily come to resemble a web of complex network relationships.

Second, as networks themselves take on the characteristics of organizations, competition among networks should arise both within and across industries. Exhibit 8 lists several alliance networks formed in the past, some of which have been dissolved or restructured as the nature of the partners' relationships or the competitive environment has evolved. The clearest current example of network competition can probably be found in the airline industry, where three alliances—Star, One World, and Sky Team—are battling for air passengers. [20]

Perhaps more dramatic still are the alliance networks that are battling over emerging technological standards. As you can see in Exhibit 9, Sun, HP, IBM, and MIPS, are all plac-

Business or Industry	Selective Rival Constellations
Hardware and Software for Interactive TV	▸ Motorola, Scientific Atlanta, Kaleida ▸ Time Warner, Silicon Graphics ▸ Intel, Microsoft, General Instruments ▸ H.P., TV Answer
Video CDs	▸ Sony and Philips ▸ Toshiba, Time Warner, Matsushita, others
Global Telecommunications	▸ AT&T Worldpartners (includes 12 partners) ▸ British Telecom and MCI ▸ Sprint, Deutsche Telekom, France Telecom
Automobiles and Trucks	▸ G.M., Toyota, Isuzu, Suzuki, Volvo ▸ Ford, Mazda, Kia, Nissan, Fiat, VW ▸ Chrysler, Mitsubishi, Daimler-Benz
Biotechnology Research	▸ Genentech network ▸ Centocor network
Pharmaceutical Marketing (United States)	▸ Merck and Medco (merger) ▸ SmithKline and DPS (merger) ▸ Eli Lilly and PCS (merger) ▸ Pfizer and Value Health ▸ Pfizer, Rhône-Poulenc, Caremark, others
Global Airline Services	▸ Delta, Swissair, Singapore Airlines, SAS ▸ KLM and Northwest ▸ British Airways and USAir
Global Comercial Real Estate Services	▸ Colliers International (44 companies) ▸ International Commercial (23 companies) ▸ Oncore International (36 companies) ▸ New America Network (150 companies) ▸ Cushman & Wakefield (52 alliances) ▸ CB Commercial (70 affiliates) ▸ Grubb & Ellis (six affiliates)

Exhibit 8 Different Alliance Networks

ing bets on certain technological standards, and they have a vast array of partners helping them to battle their respective parts of the fray.[21]

Importantly, the fortunes of the many small firms in the network are dependent upon the success of the larger group. Just as beta and VHS battled it out, with VHS being the eventual winner, so too will this battle have its winners and losers. What is clear, however, is that the loser is typically not a single firm, but instead many of the smaller players aligned with the network core. If one of these battles is lost, it means less to SUN, HP, IBM, or MIPS, but it can make or break the fortunes of a much smaller firm.

Finally, there is another variation of alliance networks where a focal firm sets itself out as the hub of an enormous wheel of alliance relationships. The most dramatic example of the new organization form is P&G, and it has dubbed this aspect of its strategy as "Connect +

Exhibit 9 Alliance Networks of Sun, HP, IBM, and MIPS

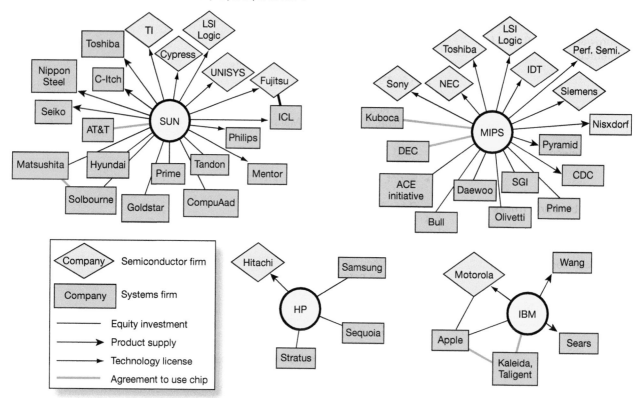

Develop," instead of the traditional notion of research and development. Exhibit 10 summarizes P&G's view, and in particular, how it comes from the CEO himself.

P&G even maintains a Connect + Develop (C+D) website that invites new potential partners. While P&G is no slacker when it comes to investment in new products—2006 R&D spending amounted to about $2 billion across 150 science areas—by the company's own calculations, its C&D activities with just its top 15 suppliers provides it access to more than 10,000 new products, and an estimated combined R&D staff of 50,000! P&G's goal is to have over 50 percent of its new products originated through the C&D process by 2010.

RISKS ARISING FROM ALLIANCES

As we mentioned in the introduction to this chapter, one of the potential benefits of an alliance is the reduction of risk or uncertainty borne by any one party. With that said, however, we must point out that cooperative ventures can be risky. There are six potential alliance risks:

- **Poor Contract Development** This problem is relatively self-explanatory. Typically, the hardest part of drawing up good alliance contracts is negotiating rights, particularly those pertaining to termination prior to the intended maturity date.

- **Misrepresentation of Resources and Capabilities** This issue arises when a partner *misrepresents*, intentionally or unintentionally, the quality or quantity of a resource or capability—say, a crucial technology or the availability of staff with particular skill sets— that its partners deem critical to the success of the venture.

Exhibit 10   Welcome to P&G's Connect + Develop Website

Connecting with the world's most inspired minds. Developing products that improve consumers' lives.

We've collaborated with outside partners for generations—but the importance of these alliances to P&G has never been greater.

Our vision is simple. We want P&G to be known as the company that collaborates—inside and out—better than any other company in the world.

I want us to be the absolute best at spotting, developing and leveraging relationships with best-in-class partners in every part of our business. In fact, I want P&G to be a magnet for the best-in-class. The company you most want to work with because you know a partnership with P&G will be more rewarding than any other option available to you.

A. G. Lafley

Chairman of the Board,

President and Chief Executive

The Procter & Gamble Company

Source: The Procter & Gamble Company http://pg.t2h.yet2.com/t2h/page/homepage

- **Misappropriation of Resources and Capabilities** *Misappropriation* occurs when one partner takes something of value, whether to the partner itself, to the alliance, or to both. Sometimes misappropriation is so endemic that would-be partners garner reputations for misappropriation. China, for example, has a notoriously poor reputation when it comes to protecting intellectual and trademark property rights.

- **Failure to Make Complementary Resources Available** Related to the risk of misappropriation is the risk that a partner may fail to make available a promised complementary resource, such as a valuable technology or the people with the skills needed to implement or design new products or processes.

- **Being Held Hostage Through Specific Investments** Sometimes, even when such resources are made available, the firm that needs them may become so dependent on the alliance that it's virtually held hostage. Resources can range from a proprietary technology that the partnership controls or simply a production capability controlled by one of the partners. Trek Bicycles, for example, outsources much of its production to an Asian manufacturer called Giant. The alliance allows Trek to focus on the design, marketing, and distribution of high-quality bikes. In turn, Giant enjoys economies of scale in production. Giant, however, is also a competitor of Trek and, given Trek's dependence on Giant's production capabilities, Giant could conceivably raise its prices to Trek in order to gain price advantage over Trek in the latter's primary markets. Or consider the arrangement by which Rayovac (Spectrum) licenses its core battery technology from Matsushita, on whom it was dependent for a key technology.

- **Misunderstanding a Partner's Strategic Intent** The Trek and Rayovac examples provide a jumping off point for exploring another alliance risk. Both Trek and Rayovac are not only dependent on their partners for a critical resource, but they're much smaller than their partners and much weaker financially. It would be relatively easy for Giant to exploit and weaken Trek—perhaps eventually buy it out for relatively little investment. Likewise, Matsushita could raise licensing fees for its battery technology or even suspend Rayovac's access to it altogether. In addition, although Matsushita sells consumer electronics products (under the Panasonic label), its share of the U.S. battery market is quite small. Conceivably, one way of increasing it would be to weaken Rayovac, undermining its U.S. competitor to the point at which it would become an easy acquisition target. In each case, then, it's crucial for the vulnerable partner to have a strong sense of whether its larger partner is interested in a co-opetition strategy or a winner-take-all strategy.

Alliances in Stable and Dynamic Contexts

Another factor in determining whether an alliance is a suitable strategic vehicle is the level of stability or dynamism of a firm's competitive context. Relative dynamism of an industry context may affect an alliance decision in two ways:

- From a practical standpoint, relatively stable environments are much more forgiving of mistakes, such as poor choices in partners or alliance structures.

- Because they make maintenance and management easier, stable environments allow firms to participate in more alliances. Likewise, although wasted time, effort, and resources are undesirable in any situation, relatively stable contexts provide firms with the luxury of learning from their mistakes and regrouping.

Consider, for example, an alliance between Nestlé and Mars that allows Nestlé to put Mars-brand M&Ms in its ice creams. The success or failure of this alliance is not going to make or break either company. As we'll soon see, however, in dynamic contexts, competitive stakes are typically much higher, and any distraction of a firm's resources or managerial time and attention can have serious consequences. Particularly when dynamism is coupled with technological intensity. If, for instance, Millennium Pharmaceuticals chooses an unsuitable partner, it will lose time and money, and it also risks the possibility that while it's busy trying to manage the alliance, a competitor will make some advance in product or technology that gives it a significant advantage. Such risks place tremendous pressure on firms not only to choose the

Nestlé and Mars share an alliance whereby Nestlé is allowed to put Mars' M&Ms in its ice creams. Because the companies compete in a relatively stable competitive environment, however, the success or failure of the alliance isn't likely to make or break either firm.

(Frank LaBua, Inc.)

right partners (and the right number of partners), but to structure alliances so that they contribute to the development and enhanced value of its resources and capabilities.

RELATIVE STABILITY AND ALLIANCE MOTIVATION

Relative environmental stability of a firm's external context also affects the objectives that partners set for an alliance. In many ways, relative stability has played a role in the evolution of alliance motivation that we discussed previously. In relatively stable environments, for example, partners are typically seeking access to production technologies or markets. Their objective is essentially to consolidate market positions and generate economies of scope and scale.[22] These objectives also motivate firms in dynamic contexts, but under such conditions, firms are also motivated to use alliances as means of identifying new market threats and opportunities and of providing dynamic capabilities with which to respond to changes (and perhaps even to drive changes) in the competitive landscape.

RELATIVE STABILITY AND THE COEVOLUTION MODEL OF CORPORATE STRATEGY

Focusing on relative stability will also help us to better understand the coevolution model of corporate strategy. Recall that *coevolution* means orchestrating a web of shifting linkages among evolving businesses. In making alliances, a firm opts to develop vertical, horizontal, or complementary linkages with other firms instead of seeking them solely among wholly owned businesses. The use of alliances in such a web enables a firm to develop its specific dynamic capabilities in concert with the best resources and capabilities available. Just as important, alliances sustain a specific focused strategy. Periodically, for instance, certain alliances can be abandoned and others added. Thus, if a firm is pursuing, say, a growth strategy, the coevolution approach suggests that it drop alliances developed around commoditized products and add those with partners who are active on the technology frontier or in other forward-looking strategies for enhancing competitive advantage.[23]

What Makes an Alliance Successful?

Given the prevalence of alliances as a critical and valuable strategy vehicle, it is imperative for managers to understand the ingredients that make them successful, as well as the factors that can derail them. Professor Ben Gomes-Casseres, one of the world's leading experts in alliances, identifies ten features that separate successful alliances from unsuccessful ones. These are summarized in Exhibit 11.[24]

But how do you put these features into place? Strategy research has considered the ten features identified in Exhibit 11, and distilled out of them five particular areas where organizations can increase the probability of alliance success. As you will see in the final section of this chapter, some of these areas are related to relationships between the partners, while others relate to the experience and supporting structures put into place in a focal firm. These five areas are:

- Understanding the determinants of trust

- Being able to manage knowledge and learning

- Understanding alliance evolution

- Knowing how to measure alliance performance

- Creating a dedicated alliance function

The first four apply readily to firms of all sizes, both domestic and international. The last usually pertains to larger firms and those that otherwise use alliances as a key vehicle for strategy execution. Understanding what's involved in all five areas puts managers in a better position to design alliances that will contribute to a firm's competitive advantage.

Exhibit 11 Features of Successful Alliances

1. The alliance has a clear strategic purpose—alliances are never an end in or of themselves, they provide tools to achieve a business strategy

2. Good partner fit—a partner with compatible goals and complementary capabilities

3. Specialized partner roles—allocate tasks and responsibilities in the alliances in a way that enables each party to do what they do best

4. Create incentives for cooperation—working together never happens automatically, particularly when partners were former rivals

5. Minimize conflicts between partners—the scope of alliance and of partners' roles should avoid pitting one against the other in the market

6. Share information—continual communication develops trust and keeps joint projects on target

7. Exchange personnel—regardless of the form of the alliance, personal contact and site visits are essential for maintaining communication and trust

8. Operate with long time-horizons—mutual forbearance in solving short-run conflicts is enhanced by the expectation of long-term gains

9. Develop multiple joint projects—successful cooperation on one project can help partners weather the storm in less successful joint projects

10. Be flexible—alliances are open-ended and dynamic relationships that need to evolve in pace with their environment and in pursuit of new opportunities

UNDERSTANDING THE DETERMINANTS OF TRUST

It may be stating the obvious to say that alliances perform better when partners trust each other. Research suggests that a network of trustworthy partners can itself be a competitive advantage, as can be a reputation for trustworthiness.[25] Unfortunately, because not all partners are equally trustworthy, parties in alliances often must rely on a variety of mechanisms to safeguard their interests. Formal mechanisms, such as long-term contracts, stock ownership, and collateral bonds, can signal credible long-term commitments to alliance partners. They do not, however, ensure information sharing, which is critical to alliance success. Partners foster interorganizational trust by using understandable and predictable processes. Informal mechanisms, such as firm reputation and personal trust among managers and officers, are also keys to creating long-term value.

Mutual trust generates several benefits. It results in conditions that increase the value of the alliance and, therefore, the probability that it will contribute to competitive advantage.[26] As you might expect, trust leads to a greater willingness to make investments in assets customized to the alliance. When such partnership-specific investments raise the potential for hold-up, they're also more likely to yield the economies of scope and scale that make such partnerships pay off economically. The investment in Tritec by BMW and DaimlerChrysler is a good example, because both firms invested considerable time and dollars in the plant and it is delivering some of the most dependable and efficiently produced four-cylinder car engines in the industry.

Besides increasing learning by encouraging investment in mechanisms that promote greater information sharing, trust reduces the costs of monitoring and maintaining an alliance. Savings can result from such simple gestures as foregoing new legal agreements for small changes in the arrangement or from such critical decisions as an agreement to rely on a simple management structure rather than a more complicated structure requiring a board of directors.

Relational Quality

Because trust is so important to alliance performance, firms need to focus on the areas that affect it most. One approach to identifying these areas is called **relational quality**, which identifies four key elements in establishing and maintaining interorganizational trust.[27] You'll probably find one or more of these elements to be intuitively obvious, but research suggests that organizations don't do a good or consistent job of paying attention to them.

relational quality Principle identifying four key elements (initial conditions, negotiation process, reciprocal experiences, outside behavior) in establishing and maintaining interorganizational trust.

Initial Conditions The first element refers to the mutual attitudes of the parties before negotiations begin. Attitudes may be based on prior experiences or on reputation. Sometimes they reflect a larger set of political and economic circumstances. As we noted earlier, for example, China's reputation for condoning property-rights abuses would probably make a prospective partner wary of allying with a Chinese firm.

The Negotiation Process Prior experience with the process can influence the attitudes that any party brings to the negotiating table. Initial conditions provide a foundation for the development and upgrading of resources and capabilities, but the social interactions that characterize the negotiations process will determine whether any promise in the negotiations is eventually realized. Your own relationships provide a relevant example here. When you meet someone, for instance, you may feel positive about that person due to his or her behaviors or prior reputation. However, your interaction with that person after the initial meeting will determine whether a friendship and otherwise productive relationship develops.

Reciprocal Experiences Once some level of interorganizational trust is established, stock and flow reflect the partners' reciprocal experiences. Do they, for instance, share information openly, disclose potential problems, or behave in other ways that add to the stock of existing interorganizational trust?

Outside Behavior Trust is also a function of the reputation the organization develops as a consequence of its interactions with other organizations outside of the alliance. When Wal-Mart dropped Rubbermaid as a supplier, other suppliers undoubtedly became concerned about the degree to which the retailer could be trusted as a partner.

MANAGING KNOWLEDGE AND LEARNING

For many firms, learning from alliance partners is one of the primary objectives of entering an alliance. In addition to reflecting trust, the ability of a partner to learn increases the collective benefits derived by every partner in the alliance. However, wanting to learn, though obviously important, isn't enough to make learning take place.[28] Learning is enhanced if a firm develops specific processes for managing knowledge exchange. Some explicit activities enable firms to learn from alliances.

Learning and Supplier Support at Toyota
Toyota is one of the most successful firms at managing learning through alliance networks and provides a helpful example of knowledge management best practices. Research by Jeffrey H. Dyer highlights Toyota's success in managing its alliances so that knowledge and productivity gains accrue to all alliance members.[29] In studying Toyota's U.S. alliance networks, Dyer found that Toyota's U.S. suppliers were able to achieve efficiency gains in manufacturing that suppliers for GM and Ford couldn't match. In fact, Toyota's suppliers outperformed the other automakers' suppliers despite the disadvantage of being newer and at an earlier stage of the learning curve. Performance *improvements* far outpaced those of other suppliers, and *absolute* performance rapidly surpassed that of suppliers to American firms. Dyer suggests that these efficiency gains resulted from concentrated efforts to ensure that learning flowed both ways and that suppliers learned from each other, not just from Toyota. The strategy depends on the carmaker's Toyota Supplier Support Center (TSSC), which has twenty consultants working with U.S. suppliers.

Let's look at the process a little more closely. Toyota divides its suppliers into groups of six to twelve, with direct competitors assigned to separate groups. To keep interactions fresh, group composition changes every three years. Each group meets with Toyota consultants to decide on a theme for the year, such as styling, demographic fit, supplier relations, and so on. Representatives from each group visit each supplier's plant over a four-month period, examining operations and offering suggestions for improvement. Finally, Toyota hosts an annual meeting at which each group reports on the results of the year's learning activities.

The results have been impressive—an average improvement of 124 percent in labor productivity and inventory reductions of 75 percent. The lesson is quite clear: Alliances result in significant productivity gains when learning is facilitated by coordinated efforts to exchange knowledge and disseminate best practices within the network. Note, too, that such a high level of learning is made possible by an overarching commitment to mutual trust.

UNDERSTANDING ALLIANCE EVOLUTION

At the outset of this chapter, we asked whether you thought the outcome of Magla's alliance with P&G was a common one. You may not be surprised to learn that what starts out as an alliance may eventually become an acquisition.[30] In fact, one study found that nearly 80 percent of equity joint ventures end in the sale of one partner to another.[31] The researchers suggested that managers who don't look out for this twist in the road may run head-on into an unplanned divestiture or acquisition. Although some alliances are actually structured to terminate in the eventual transfer of ownership, most are not, and unplanned sales may erode shareholder value.

Of course, a sale that's well managed and planned in advance can be to a firm's advantage. The same study indicated that alliances can advance a firm's long-term strategy by providing companies with a low-cost, low-risk means of previewing possible acquisitions.

At the same time, it should come as no surprise that relationships between partners may change over time. Indeed, if one partner is aggressively pursuing a coevolution strategy that involves alliances, these changes should be monitored closely and included in the ongoing strategy of both the alliance and its partners. The box entitled Exhibit 12 provides a good example of well-managed coevolution through the Fuji-Xerox alliance.[32]

MEASURING ALLIANCE PERFORMANCE

Ironically, one reason for the high failure rate of alliances is the fact that few firms have effective systems for monitoring alliance performance.[33] In the short term, a lack of monitoring systems means that managers who are responsible for the alliance must rely more on intuition than on good information. The long-term consequences are even more serious: When problems do surface, it's much more expensive to fix them. Moreover, performance may have declined so drastically that one or more of the partners starts looking for ways to exit the alliance—an event that often starts a downward spiral toward more performance problems and eventual termination.

Although it may, therefore, seem eminently logical for firms to put monitoring systems in place, there are at least three barriers to getting it done:

- Partner firms often have different information and reporting systems. DaimlerChrysler and BMW, for instance, have quite different quality, production, and financial reporting systems. The systems at their alliance firm, Tritec, differ from those of both partners. The two carmakers have recently decided that, despite the expense in time and money, Tritec will "translate" its performance data into information that can be accessed through both DaimlerChrysler's and BMW's systems.

- Even when firms go to great lengths to gauge performance, the inputs that the alliance receives from its corporate parents can be difficult to track and account for. For example, say a manager from DaimlerChrysler joins a Tritec team and that team develops a novel new manufacturing approach. Very often it is difficult to determine whether it was the specific team member or the larger team that came up with the new idea.

- Similarly, it's also difficult to put a precise value on alliance outputs. What price or value, for example, would you attach to the alliance-based knowledge that a partner uses to improve operations in other parts of the organization?

DEDICATED ALLIANCE FUNCTION

Recent research indicates that cooperative strategies are more likely to succeed when a firm has a dedicated alliance function.[34] A dedicated alliance function may simply be one manager who is responsible for setting up, tracking, and dissolving the firm's alliances; however, typically this function is managed by a group of individuals working together as a team. In many ways, such a function is a structural solution to the need to manage trust, learning, evolution, and performance in a systematic fashion. Although some firms can't afford this added management function, the benefits make it worth looking for a way to fill this role. A

Exhibit 12

Coevolution in the
Fuji-Xerox Alliance

Some of the best examples of coevolution reinforce the important roles played by time and investments. Take the case of Fuji-Xerox, which provides some insight into the resources and capabilities acquired through alliances. This alliance between Fuji Photo and Xerox also provided fertile ground for the successful turnaround of Xerox itself by Anne Mulcahy.

The Fuji-Xerox alliance had been in place for several years, but it was not until early 1970 that it began to bear fruit as a source of competitive capabilities and knowledge for both the alliance and the partners. Xerox was in dire financial straits at the time, having positioned its products against then high-powered rivals such as Eastman Kodak and IBM but being undermined at the same time by low-cost Japanese manufacturers. The first transition was the transfer of Fuji Photo's manufacturing plants in 1970 to the Fuji-Xerox alliance and the resulting development of low-cost manufacturing capabilities by the venture. Following the development of these capabilities, from 1976 to 1978, Xerox initiated R&D and technology-reimbursement agreements between itself and Fuji-Xerox. This transfer agreement fostered the design and fabrication of copy machines for distribution in Europe and the United States.

Over the next decade, Fuji-Xerox continued to upgrade its resources and capabilities in low-end copiers and printers, and Xerox aggressively absorbed these advantages as they grew in importance in the global marketplace. For instance, following an agreement to allow Fuji-Xerox control over its own R&D, Fuji-Xerox began to internalize Japanese total-quality-control manufacturing processes. Xerox, in turn, adopted these processes, and at the same time used the Fuji-Xerox alliance as a platform to expand its own products' presence in Japan.

Ironically, the success and rapid growth for the Fuji-Xerox alliance was a function of the autonomy granted to it by its parents. By 1991, those parents established a new alliance, Xerox International Partners, to market the Fuji-Xerox printer mechanism outside of Japan to companies such as Hewlett-Packard, which were largely captive to the industry leader, Canon. At the same time, this same mechanism satisfied the majority of Xerox and Rank Xerox (another alliance) low-end copier sales. Although the alliances were largely autonomous, top executives at Xerox and Fuji-Xerox were careful to hold top-executive "summits" twice a year, exchange key personnel, and fund joint research programs to avoid redundant and wasteful R&D efforts.

It was on this platform of global success that Anne Mulcahy made a case for the acquisition of the color-printer division of Tektronix by Xerox in 2000. These color-printer capabilities were shared, not surprisingly, with Fuji-Xerox, which flourishes to this day, with Xerox owning 25 percent and Fuji Photo owning 75 percent.

firm might, for example, assign a chief alliance officer, whose responsibilities are outlined in Exhibit 13.[35]

The first two roles in the components of a dedicated-alliance-function process are often the most critical. Regardless of the levels of trust, learning, and capabilities that an alliance boasts, it won't be productive under either of the two following situations:

■ When there isn't a strong business case for the alliance as a vehicle

■ When assessment fails and there simply isn't a good fit between partners

Exhibit 13   A Dedicated Alliance Function

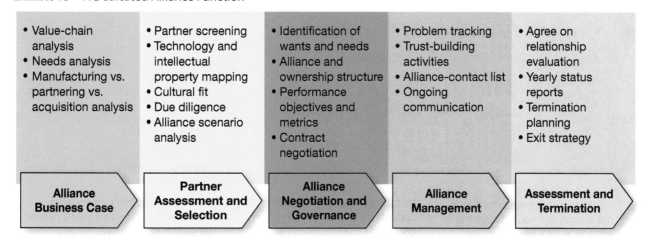

Good intentions alone do not make alliances work. Nothing can replace a good strategy that spells out the role of alliances in a firm's strategy and partner fit.

WHEN DO PARTNERS FIT?

The issue of fit isn't easy to resolve, and to do so, firms must be able to answer yes to the following questions:

- *Strategic fit:* Are the partners' objectives compatible? For how long?

- *Resource and financial fit:* Are the partners willing and able to contribute the resources and competencies?

- *Cultural fit:* Can the partners understand each other? Do they share the same business logic and commitment?

- *Structure, systems, and processes fit:* Can the decision-making and control mechanisms be aligned?

- *Additional fit criteria:* What other key questions should be on the table, such as timing, other alliances, alliance alternatives, environmental context, and competitive pressures?

Because we're interested in alliances as a strategy vehicle, the first question pertains to *strategic fit.* Researchers at the consulting firm of McKinsey and Company have identified lack of strategic fit as a common starting point for those alliances that eventually failed.[36] In many ways, the opening vignette on Magla provides an example of an alliance where strategic fit was good because Magla needed better access to the mass-market channels and capital than it could attain on its own. Sometimes, alliances between weaker and stronger firms even lead the weaker firm to a position of strength, in which case the alliance is usually dissolved, or in other cases in which the stronger partner acquires the weaker one. Partnerships among complementary equals tend to be the strongest and longest lasting. In some cases, competitive tensions and industry conditions may lead one partner to acquire the other, usually after about seven years. In other cases, the partners remain strong and independent. Some alliances, such as Fuji-Xerox, exemplify true co-evolution and are most likely to survive for much longer than seven years. In the case of Fuji-Xerox, the alliance has lasted several decades and has spawned additional complementary alliances.

YOU DO THAT? 1

Assessing Alliance Fit at Millennium Pharmaceuticals

Evaluating alliance opportunities is not simple, but you do have the advantage of a framework that helps you start the process. The first step is to develop a grid, shown in Exhibit 14 that lays out how well the potential partner fits with your firm.

Note that you should always include alternative potential partners, since you may be more likely to enter a bad deal when you have nothing to compare it to. This may sound silly, but many CEOs say that some of the most important alliance or acquisition decisions they have made, are the decisions not to do them! In this example, Millennium Pharmaceuticals was faced with a huge alliance opportunity with German firm Lundberg—it involved lots of cash and a savvy global partner with a great deal of experience. Why, then, would Millennium turn such a deal down? Using the following alliance-fit framework, and setting up Abbott Labs as the comparison alliance, Millennium decided that it was best to pass on the Lundberg alliance (though it turns out that the Abbott alliance was in the works):

- *Strategic fit?* In general, the strategic fit was good. However, Millennium had recently put together a very similar large alliance with Monsanto, and it was not clear how another deal would move Millennium's strategy forward.

- *Resource fit?* Other than money, the Lundberg did not bring much to the table in terms of new resources and capabilities. In fact, Millennium would be putting most of its unique capabilities to work, which in turn could stretch its technical and research staff with no benefit other than additional cash in the bank. At the time, Millennium was strong financially.

- *Cultural fit?* The potential partner was a large, private agribusiness firm, whereas Millennium was a relatively small, public biotech firm. In initial meetings, there was some indication with the potential partner that top management was keen on an alliance but that lower-level managers were out of the loop. Cultural misfit often arises when line managers are not involved in the alliance-building process from the very start.

- *Structural fit?* This, too, was a big question mark. Millennium's management had the impression that the partner would not grant it the autonomy or flexibility that it desired in its alliances. Thus, the structure appeared too rigid from Millennium's perspective.

- *Other questions?* Because Millennium was still contemplating other options and partnerships, it was not as if this was the only opportunity in the market. Finally, the top-management team determined that it was not excited about the alliance beyond the fact that the partner had a great reputation and brought lots of cash to the relationship.

So, you are probably asking what happened to Millennium after it passed up such a lucrative deal. Shortly thereafter, Millennium and Abbott formed a five-year alliance primarily for collaborative research and development in the area of metabolic diseases. The companies agreed to share equally the cost of developing, manufacturing, and marketing products on a worldwide basis. The arrangement with Abbott also includes an equity investment by Abbott in Millennium, amounting in total to $250 million over several years, and a technology exchange and development agreement. Moreover, Millennium and Aventis expanded their existing joint development pipeline to include an aggregate of eleven additional discovery projects that were previously pursued outside the joint collaboration by Millennium or Aventis. These new assets included chemokine receptors, kinases, and integrins, which are important as potential drug-development target classes in inflammatory disease research. As a result of this expansion, that alliance yielded approximately fifty jointly funded discovery projects. Soon, Millennium had created more than twenty alliances with leading pharmaceutical and biotechnology companies—close to $2 billion of committed funding. You can learn more about why Millennium sees such a network of alliances as a central vehicle in its strategy—to eventually become a full-fledged pharmaceutical firm—through its R&D page at www.millennium.com.

Exhibit 14 Comparing Alliance Opportunities

	Partner A—Lundberg	Partner B—Abbott Labs
Strategic Fit?	Good, but no new learning opportunities	Good and ample learning and growth opportunities
Resource Fit?	Cash resources, but cash is generic	Cash and technology resources, and technology is unique
Cultural Fit?	Likely to be poor	Good
Structural Fit?	Unknown	Good
Other Key Questions? • Capital market demands—who drives strategy here? • Timing—are capital markets hot or cold? • Timing—do we need another deal like this? • Timing—how plentiful and attractive are other alliance options? • Does "no" here mean no more options? • Again, other criteria? • What other key questions should be on the table?	Management was not excited about the deal	Management was excited about the deal—high level of motivation

The second question concerns *resource and financial fit.* This question deals with either the availability of a resource or the willingness and ability of a partner to make that resource available. Questions of *cultural fit* typically relate to the cultural characteristics of the organizations themselves. In the early years of SEMATECH, for instance, Intel's participation was problematic because Intel's highly competitive culture clashed with the cooperative culture being fostered by the consortium.[37] Though *structural fit* can be a simple matter of making financial reporting systems compatible, conflicts may arise over arrangements of authority and decision making.

Finally, in determining fit, a company should take situation-specific factors into consideration. Is the firm, for example, already involved in too many alliances? Is the timing right? Do competitive conditions currently favor alliances as a strategy vehicle? The box entitled "How Would *You* Do That? 1" shows what happened when Millennium Pharmaceuticals applied a checklist for assessing partner fit in determining whether to enter into an alliance with a potential partner. The answer, as you can see, was no.

Dyer's research shows that it's difficult to develop the rich alliance capabilities that will satisfy a checklist like Millennium's. At the same time, however, Dyer notes that firms that succeed in developing the requisite capabilities may be better competitors as a result. Not only may such capabilities contribute to near-term performance and competitive position, but they may also enhance the reputation of a company as a preferred partner. Wal-Mart, for example, though known as a very aggressive competitor, has established a solid reputation in Latin America as a dependable partner. As noted earlier, Wal-Mart is now leveraging these alliance skills and the reputation built through local partnerships to fuel its growth in China and Japan.

Summary of Challenges

1. *Explain why strategic alliances are important strategy vehicles.*
Alliances enable participants to share in investments and rewards, while reducing the risk and uncertainty that each firm must bear on its own. Such sharing also enables firms to focus their efforts on what they do best, while benefiting from the similarly focused efforts of their partner firms. In economic terms, alliances may lead to higher firm performance by enabling firms to realize economies of scope and scale that would otherwise not be realized if they had to operate on their own.

2. *Describe the motivations behind alliances and show how they've changed over time.* Although firms seek economies of scope and scale from alliances, their ultimate objective is that the alliance contributes to their competitive advantage. The VRINE framework can be applied to alliances. If the alliance creates something of value, has benefits that are both rare and difficult to imitate (including less costly imitation by a simple market purchase agreement or wholly owned business), and the partners are able to extract value from the alliance (i.e., the resources and capabilities in the alliance are supported by features of the organization), then a firm can reap competitive advantages. Over time, the basis for alliance advantage has shifted from simple efficiencies and economies of scope and scale to a vehicle for organizational learning and innovation.

3. *Identify the various forms and structures of strategic alliances.*
Alliances can take many forms. A joint venture is the most complex form because it results in the establishment of a third, independent entity. Joint ventures, in which partners contribute cash and other resources to the partnership, fall into the broader category of equity alliances. Nonequity alliances are the most common form of alliance. These typically take the form of contracts to supply, produce, market, or distribute a firm's goods or services. Sole-sourcing, just-in-time supply agreements, licensing, and cobranding are examples of nonequity alliances. Equity and nonequity alliances may involve many participants. Such alliances are sometimes called *industry associations, cooperatives,* or *consortia.*

4. *Compare and contrast alliances as business- and corporate-level strategy vehicles.* The five-forces model and value net are good tools for both identifying potential partners and reaffirming that just about any firm related to the business can be considered a potential partner. Business strategy alliances fall into two categories: vertical and horizontal. Vertical alliances link a focal firm to downstream raw materials and other critical inputs; upstream they link that same firm to marketing, arenas, and other channels of distribution. Horizontal alliances enable firms in one segment of the industry to partner with firms in other segments. Strategic alliances are also a useful vehicle for a firm's corporate and international strategies. Cross-border alliances differ from domestic-only alliances in that government, public policies, and national culture often play a more visible role. Alliances can also take on the characteristic of a network when clusters of companies compete against each other for customers or new technology standards. Finally, cutting across all these alliances are six risks that contribute to their failure or lackluster performance. These risks range from poor contract development to the misinterpretation of a partner's strategic intent.

5. *Understand the characteristics of alliances in stable and dynamic competitive contexts.* Just as strategies may vary according to context, so, too, should the expectations and design features of alliances as a strategy vehicle. Stable contexts afford firms the luxury of managing many alliances. Although the choice of alliance partners is always important, any one alliance failure is unlikely to break the company. However, in dynamic contexts the stakes are much higher. Such heightened stakes can take the simple form of greater dollar investments in new technological platforms but typically are manifest in a rapidly evolving environment where being in the wrong partnership today could mean the ultimate demise of the firm later. The use and design of alliances in dynamic contexts fits well with the coevolution model. That is, alliances are included in the firm's orchestration of a web of shifting linkages among evolving businesses.

6. *Summarize the criteria for successful alliances.* Five interrelated criteria for effective alliance implementation were emphasized in this chapter. First, firms must understand the determinants and benefits of trust. Alliances that are based on trust benefit from lower transaction costs, greater economies of scope and scale, and greater learning and knowledge management. Second, firms must be good at managing knowledge and knowledge flows. This means that they should establish learning objectives for each alliance and mechanisms for realizing them. The third criterion is the need to understand alliance evolution. Alliances may follow different pathways depending on their initial conditions and partner relations, and an understanding of both the role of initial conditions and the potential pathways will inform the establishment of an alliance and its management once it is in place. Linking the alliance to a performance management system is the fourth criterion. Such tracking will help to ensure both near-term benefits and the avoidance of problems that may fester for lack of attention. Finally, firms should consider the establishment of some systematic and coherent structural response to the unique and complex management challenges that alliances give rise to. This structure can take the form of an individual with the title of chief alliance officer or, where appropriate and financially feasible, the establishment of a dedicated alliance function.

Review Questions

1. What is a strategic alliance?

2. Do most strategic alliances succeed?

3. What forms can strategic alliances take?

4. What is the difference between an equity and a nonequity strategic alliance?

5. Provide an example of a nonequity strategic alliance.

6. Why do firms enter into alliances?

7. What are the three forms of strategic alliance that support business strategy?

8. What do the value net and industry structure models tell you about potential alliance partners?

9. How do alliances serve as a vehicle for corporate strategy?

10. What risks do alliances pose to partner firms?

11. How do alliances differ in stable and dynamic contexts?

12. What are the five critical criteria for successful alliances (hint: don't confuse these with the ten observations made about alliances in Exhibit 11)?

317

Experiential Activities

Group Exercises

1. Increasingly, firms such as P&G, Corning (www.corning.com) and Millennium Pharmaceuticals (www.millennium.com) claim to have a core competency and competitive advantage based on their ability to manage alliances. Develop statements that both defend and critique this proposition. Identify risks that firms run when their strategy is essentially a network of alliances.

2. Identify a firm and document its alliance activity over the past five to ten years (visit the Web site of a public firm, particularly the "history" page). Examine the list of officers at the company (these are always detailed in the annual report and often on the firm's Web site). Do they appear to have a dedicated alliance function? What kinds of changes would they have to make if they were to follow the recommendations on implementation levers necessary to achieve an effective dedicated alliance function? What would be the costs and benefits of such a change?

Ethical Debates

1. One of the biggest barriers for firms entering into alliances with foreign partners, and even domestic ones, are issues of trust. Does a well-crafted legal agreement prevent breaches of ethics by either party to the agreement?

2. You have seen many reports in the press about Adidas or Nike and how the working conditions of the foreign partners and suppliers are sometimes abysmal. Is this just a cost of doing business through foreign alliances or can firms do something to manage these situations?

How Would
YOU DO THAT?

1. The box entitled "How Would *You* Do That? 1" shows how Millennium Pharmaceuticals evaluated a potential alliance partner. Apply the Millennium fit framework to the alliances of another firm you are familiar with. Do these appear to be good alliances? Do any of the alliances suggest that your focal firm is on a pathway to acquire its partner or be acquired by it?

Go on to see How Would You Do That at www.prenhall.com/carpenter&sanders

Endnotes

1. "Growth: Hand In Glove," *Business Week*, Fall 2006, (accessed August 15, 2007), at http://www.businessweek.com/magazine/content/06_38/b4001838.htm; D. G. Thomson, *Blueprint to a Billion: 7 Essentials to Achieve Exponential Growth* (New York: Wiley, 2005); "Mr. Clean Expands Licensing Program Internationally," *PR Newswire*, January 10, 2002; "Magla Plans to Sell Household Gloves Under Procter & Gamble Mr. Clean Brand Name," *Business Wire*, January 16, 2000; *Magla Company Story* (accessed on April 25, 2007) at http://www.magla.com/geninfo/Type.cfm?Type=About&Level=General&Width=1878; "Magla Signs Licensing Agreement to Sell Disposable Exam Gloves Under the American Red Cross Brand Name," Press Release, February 23, 2006, accessed June 21, 2007; "Inspirational Consumers," *Brand Strategy*, July 12, 2005, p. 24; "Driving with Mr. Clean." *Grocery Headquarters*, January 2006, p. 96; "P&G Keeps Expanding Its Far-flung Empire," *Household & Personal Products Industry*, January 2007, p. 100; H. Chesbrough and K. Schwartz, "Innovating Business Models with Co-Development Partnerships," *Research-Technology Management*, January–February 2007, p. 55(5).

2. J. Harbison and P. Pekar, *Smart Alliances: A Practical Guide to Repeatable Success* (San Francisco: Jossey-Bass, 1998).

3. C. Wolf, "Rubbermaid Struggles to Put Lid on Problems: Company's Earnings Tumble after Price Increase Backfires," *Cincinnati Enquirer*, April 8, 1996, D1.

4. J. Cook, T. Halevy, and B. Hastie, "Alliances in Consumer Packaged Goods," *McKinsey on Finance*, Autumn 2003, 16–20.

5. J. Bleeke and D. Ernst, *Collaborating to Compete* (New York: John Wiley & Sons, 1993); D. Ernst and T. Halevy, "When to Think Alliance," *McKinsey Quarterly* 4 (2000), 46–55.

6. J. H. Dyer and H. Singh, "The Relational View: Cooperative Strategies and Sources of Interorganizational Competitive Advantage," *Academy of Management Review* 23 (1998), 660–679.

7. O. E. Williamson, *The Economic Institutions of Capitalism* (New York: Free Press, 1985).

8. G. Hamel and C. K. Prahalad, *Competing for the Future* (Boston: Harvard Business School Press, 1994).

9. J. B. Barney and M. H. Hansen, "Trustworthiness as a Source of Competitive Advantage," *Strategic Management Journal* 15 (1995), 175–190; Dyer and Singh, "The Relational View."

10. Harbison and Pekar, *Smart Alliances.*

11. Adapted from J. Harbison and P. Pekar, *Smart Alliances: A Practical Guide to Repeatable Success* (San Francisco: Jossey-Bass, 1998).

12. www.mlnm.com/media/strategy/index.asp (accessed July 15, 2005).

13. Adapted from J. D. Bamford, B. Gomes-Casseres, and M. S. Robinson, *Mastering Alliance Strategy: A Comprehensive Guide to Design, Management, and Organization* (San Francisco: John Wiley & Sons, 2003), p. 22.

14. For detailed discussions of the Japanese projects, see K. Flamm, *Mismanaged Trade? Strategic Policy and the Semiconductor Industry* (Washington, D.C.: Brookings Institution, 1996), 39–126; J. Sigurdson, *Industry and State Partnership in Japan: The Very Large Scale Integrated Circuits (VLSI) Project* (Lund, Sweden: Research Policy Institute, 1986). For a dissenting assessment, see M. Fransman, *The Market and Beyond: Cooperation and Competition in Information Technology Development in the Japanese System* (Cambridge: Cambridge University Press, 1992).

15. Semiconductor Equipment and Materials International, About Us (accessed June 6, 2005), at http://wps2a.semi.org/wps/portal/_pagr/103/_pa.103/259.

16. Adapted from A. Brandendburger and B. Nalebuff, *Co-Opetition* (New York: Doubleday, 1996).

17. J. H. Dyer, *Collaborative Advantage: Winning through Extended Enterprise Supplier Networks* (New York: Oxford University Press, 2000).

18. www.softbank.co.jp (accessed August 12, 2005).

19. P. Almeida, J. Song, and R. M. Grant, "Are Firms Superior to Alliances and Markets? An Empirical Test of Cross-Border Knowledge Building," *Organization Science* 14 (2002), 157–171.

20. Adapted from B. Gomes-Casseres, "Competing in Constellations: The Case of Fuji-Xerox," *Strategy and Business* First Quarter (1997), 4–16; www.fujixerox.co.jp/eng/company/history (accessed July 15, 2005) and the Xerox Fact Book (2005–2006), at www.xerox.com (accessed November 8, 2005).

21. Adapted from B. Gomes-Casseres, "Alliance Strategies of Small Firms," *Small Business Economics* 9 (1997), 33–44.

22. Harbison and Pekar, *Smart Alliances;* E. Bailey and W. Shan, "Sustainable Competitive Advantage Through Alliances," in E. Bowman and B. Kogut, eds., *Redesigning the Firm* (New York: Oxford University Press, 1995).

23. S. Brown and K. Eisenhardt, *Competing on the Edge* (Boston: Harvard Business School Press, 1997).

24. Adapted from B. Gomes-Casseres, "Critical Eye," www.criticaleye.net, June–August, 2004. See http://www.alliancestrategy.com/, for more alliance resources.

25. Barney and Hansen, "Trustworthiness as a Source of Competitive Advantage."

26. Dyer, *Collaborative Advantage.*

27. A. Arino, J. de la Torre, P. S. Ring, "Relational Quality: Managing Trust in Corporate Alliances," *California Management Review* 44:1 (2001), 109–134.

28. G. Probst, "Practical Knowledge Management: A Model That Works," *Prism* (Arthur D. Little Consultants), Second Quarter (1998), 17–29.

29. Information in this section is drawn from J. H. Dyer, *Collaborative Advantage.*

30. J. Bleeke and D. Ernst, *Collaborating to Compete* (New York: Wiley, 1993).

31. Bleeke and Ernst, *Collaborating to Compete.*

32. Adapted from B. Gomes-Casseres, "Competing in Constellations: The Case of Fuji-Xerox," *Strategy and Business* First Quarter (1997), 4–16; www.fujixerox.co.jp/eng/company/history (accessed July 15, 2005) and the Xerox Fact Book (2005– 2006), at www.xerox.com (accessed November 8, 2005).

33. J. H. Dyer, P. Kale, and H. Singh, "How to Make Strategic Alliances Work," *Sloan Management Review* 42 (2001), 121–136. According to the authors, 51 percent of the alliances surveyed had no performance monitoring systems, and only 11 percent believed that they had good systems in place.

34. Dyer, Kale, and Singh, "How to Make Strategic Alliances Work."

35. Adapted from J. H. Dyer, P. Kale, and H. Singh, "How to Make Strategic Alliances Work," *Sloan Management Review* 42:4 (2001), 121–136.

36. J. Bleeke and D. Ernst, "Is Your Strategic Alliance Really a Sale?" *Harvard Business Review* 73:1 (1995), 97–102.

37. L. D. Browning, J. M. Beyer, and J. C. Shetler, "Building Cooperation in a Competitive Industry: SEMATECH," *Academy of Management Journal* 38:1 (1995), 113–151.

Studying Mergers and Acquisitions

Studying Mergers and Acquisitions

In This Chapter We Challenge You To >>>

1. Explain the motivations behind acquisitions and show how they've changed over time.

2. Explain why mergers and acquisitions are important to strategy.

3. Identify the various types of acquisitions.

4. Understand how the pricing of acquisitions affects the realization of synergies.

5. Outline the alternative ways to integrate acquisitions and explain the implementation process.

6. Discuss the characteristics of acquisitions in different industry contexts.

(CORBIS–NY/Kim Kulish)

eBay + Paypal +Skype
How to Acquire Customers

(SNOCAP)

*S*trategy is important at every firm, but Meg Whitman, CEO of eBay, says that on the Internet "the landscape changes quarterly," which elevates strategy to a mission-critical task.[1] eBay, as most people know, is an Internet-based auction and marketplace site on which some 233 million registered customers buy and sell tens of thousands of products ranging from Beanie Babies to used cars. The company generates revenues through advertising and by charging listing and selling fees. For the 2007 year, eBay expected revenues between $7.2 billion and $7.45 billion.

eBay has grown fast, and acquisitions are part of Whitman's toolkit. Some acquisitions, like the purchase of Butterfields (a 140-year-old auctioneer of high-end merchandise) didn't work well and Butterfields was sold off three years later. Others, like eBay's purchase of PayPal in 2002, were greeted skeptically but have paid off. Whitman said she thought the PayPal acquisition was "one of the all-time great acquisitions, even though at the time people about had a heart attack that we paid $1.5 billion for PayPal. I mean, I got creamed in the press.'The woman is crazy. I cannot believe she paid $1.5 billion dollars for this, you know, stupid little company.'"

Indeed, PayPal didn't come cheap. The sale entailed a 100-percent stock transaction, and the price—about $1.5 billion—represented a 20-percent premium over PayPal's stock value prior to the announced acquisition. Thus, eBay paid a premium of about $250 million, and on the day that the sale was announced the market discounted eBay's stock price by 7 percent. After successfully negotiating and closing this transaction, Whitman was left with the reality of trying to make it work. She either had to identify significant cost savings or find new revenue-enhancement opportunities (i.e., synergies) in order to recoup the capital that was necessary to snag PayPal. Whitman's approach was to look for synergies. "The magic is, what opportunities do various combinations of our two assets open up?" As Whitman sees it, "eBay and PayPal was one of the most remarkable combinations because they made each business stronger on their own, and then created a whole new opportunity called merchant services." Most payment companies faced the problem that they couldn't get enough buyers to use the payment system and therefore couldn't get merchants to accept the payment form. But eBay provided PayPal with ready-made droves of customers. "PayPal became the *de facto* payment standard on the biggest locus of small business in the world, and as a result was able to extend off that market place," Whitman said. At the end of March 2007, PayPal had 143 million total accounts. Those accounts helped drive record TPV (total payment volume) of $11.36 billion the first three months of 2007 alone.

Let's take a closer look at the synergies between PayPal and eBay: PayPal's network builds on the existing financial infrastructure of bank accounts and credit cards to create a global payment system. Its revenue comes from the float in the personal accounts and fees charged for Premier and Business Accounts. Float can mean many things in finance, but in this case it refers to the fact that eBay has buyers' money, via PayPal, for a period of time and can invest those monies for profit between the time it receives the money and the time it pays it out to sellers. eBay management viewed PayPal's strategy as complementary to its own. Both business models, shown in Exhibit 1, for example, relied on transaction-based revenue sources. Neither required inventory or warehousing of merchandise, and neither maintained any sales force to speak of. Finally, both strategies called for high operating leverage and low capital requirements.

Just because there are synergies between two companies, however, doesn't mean that executing the acquisition plan is easy. For example, when eBay first bought PayPal, eBay executives debated whether to rename the company something like "eBay Payments" rather than PayPal. "In fact," Whitman admitted, "for a while on the website, it was called 'eBay Payments.' We were a little confused." Ultimately, however, the team decided that if PayPal was to grow as a system used by merchants beyond the eBay space, it had to retain its own brand identity. "We decided that eBay stands for e-commerce, it stands for connecting buyers and sellers. PayPal stands for payments," Whitman said. Had eBay called it eBay Payments, Whitman continued, "I don't think we'd have a merchant services business, because I'm not sure Dell.com would necessarily want eBay Payments as a payment module."

One of Whitman's latest acquisitions was of the Internet phone service startup Skype, which eBay bought in 2005 for as much as $4.1 billion (depending on how Skype performs). Whitman made the acquisition for several reasons: "We loved the Skype viral effect of how it had grown its user base—it looked a lot like eBay. You know, in the earliest

eBay Business Model

eBay's revenue comes from auction—posting fees paid by sellers.

Posts auction, pays fee

Wins auction

Contract and payment occur between buyer and seller

Seller

Buyer

PayPal Business Model

PayPal's revenue comes from float in the personal accounts and fees for premier and business accounts.

Sends money

Receives money (pays fee)

Payer

Payee

Exhibit 1 eBay and PayPal Business Models

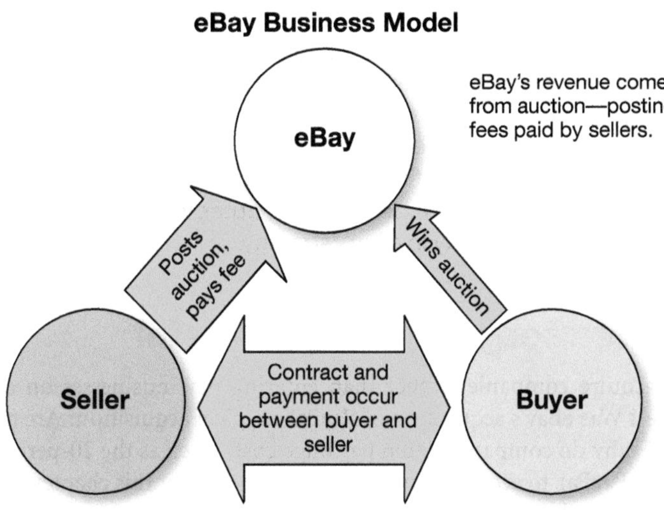

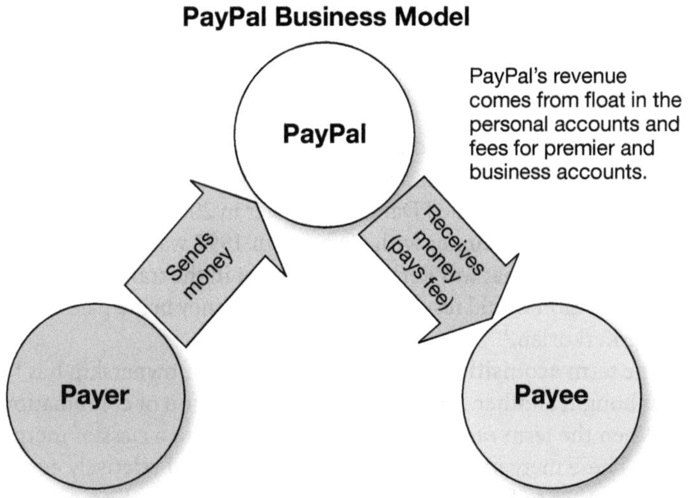

days, [it had] even more rapid adoption. So it was very clear to me that something quite unique was going on at Skype—it was pioneering a whole new technology, but building a thriving ecosystem of users, developers, hardware manufacturers, and chipset manufacturers."

Most of all, however, Skype added to synergies with Paypal and eBay. "In the case of eBay, [there is] communication synergy. And with PayPal, this whole notion of PayPal being the wallet on Skype, and every new Skype user getting a PayPal account and vice versa," Whitman said. "That's why we were so excited when we saw Skype—there's something here that will unlock the Skype business, and will enable each business to grow on its own," Whitman said. Skype had grown to 196 million registered users at the end of March 2007, representing a 107 percent increase from the 95 million users at the end of March 2006.

In short, Whitman's strategy boils down to three critical synergies among eBay's properties: that eBay buyers and sellers will talk using Skype (generating ad revenue for eBay);

that Skype callers will use PayPal to pay for their calls (the ones that aren't free, that is); and that Skype will encourage PayPal's expanding cross-border remittance business. This economic logic of eBay's strategy is summarized by Whitman: "We want to build the synergies between these businesses," Whitman said at a shareholder conference in 2006, "so that one plus one plus one equals a lot more than three." The jury is still out on the actual synergies and other benefits to be gained by eBay through the high-profile Skype acquisition, but as you will see later in the chapter, it appears that the PayPal leg of the trio is paying off handsomely in eBay's strategy. <<<

Motives for Mergers and Acquisitions

Why do firms acquire companies rather than entering new businesses on their own or through alliances? Was eBay's acquisition of PayPal a typical acquisition? Are most acquisitions successful? Why do companies often pay huge costs, such as the 20-percent premium that eBay paid for PayPal, to acquire another firm? By the end of this chapter, you should be able to answer these and other questions about mergers and acquisitions (M&As). Indeed, as you work through the chapter, you'll see that our opening vignette on eBay and PayPal introduces many of the features common to acquisitions.

DIFFERENCES BETWEEN ACQUISITIONS AND MERGERS

Although it is regular practice to use the terms *mergers* and *acquisitions* together, and sometimes interchangeably, they aren't the same thing. The differences can be subtle, and depending on who's using the terms and in what country, each term tends to have different meanings. Disputes over differences in legal definitions can end up in court. For instance, Chrysler investor Kirk Kerkorian sued DaimlerChrysler in 2001 for billions based on the argument that the marriage of Daimler with Chrysler in 1997 was actually an acquisition by Daimler and not a merger. What was Kerkorian's interest in the transaction being labeled an acquisition? An acquisition would result in much more money being paid to Chrysler shareholders, including Kerkorian.[2]

acquisition Strategy by which one firm acquires another through stock purchase or exchange.

Technically, the term **acquisition** means that a transfer of ownership has taken place—that one firm has bought another. A **merger** is the consolidation or combination of one firm with another.[3] When the term *merger* is used, it often refers to a class of mergers known as *mergers of equals*. These mergers are typically between firms of relatively equal size and influence that fuse together to form one new larger firm. Although there are many technical, legal, and detailed differences between mergers and acquisitions, for our purposes in understanding how they serve as vehicles of strategy, they are more similar than dissimilar. Consequently, we will focus on how firms use M&As to pursue their objectives.

merger Consolidation or combination of two or more firms.

We will emphasize the motives for M&As and the strategic implications of those motives. The motives behind M&As fall into three basic categories: *managerial self-interest*, *hubris*, and *synergy*. In this section, we'll review these three types of motives and assess the effects of M&As undertaken in pursuit of each of them. Because the first two motives usually don't reflect shareholders' best interests, the rest of the chapter will focus on M&As undertaken in pursuit of synergy.

MANAGERIAL SELF-INTEREST

managerialism Tendency of managers to make decisions based on personal self-interest rather than the best interests of shareholders.

Sometimes senior managers make decisions based on personal self-interest rather than the best interests of shareholders. We call this behavior **managerialism**. Conceivably, managers can make acquisitions—and even willingly overpay in M&As—in order to maximize their own interests at the expense of shareholder wealth. Executive compensation, for instance, tends to be linked to firm size. Managers might, therefore, enhance their paychecks by making acquisitions that accomplish nothing more than enlarging the firm.[4] As you have learned, getting bigger, in and of itself, does not create shareholder wealth.

Likewise, because year-end bonuses (and job security) are often tied to the firm's earnings, some managers might pursue diversification through M&A in order to stabilize annual earnings. Managers could, therefore, make acquisitions in order to boost earnings by diversifying the firm's revenue stream.[5] Certainly, organic growth could achieve the same goal but not as quickly. In any case, diversification of a firm's revenue stream creates little value for shareholders. Why? Because, as we've seen, they can diversify their personal securities portfolios much more cheaply.

HUBRIS

In the mid-1980s, economist Richard Roll proposed what he called the *hubris hypothesis* to explain, at least in part, why acquisition premiums are so large and yet acquisitions remain so common.[6]

As we've already pointed out, when a publicly traded firm is acquired by another firm, the purchase price almost always exceeds the target firm's market value. The average premium—the amount received by the target firm's shareholders in excess of the value of their stock—was between 30 and 45 percent during the 15-year period between 1989 and 2004. Why would anyone pay such a generous premium? After all, the target firm's market value prior to the acquisition bid was the market's best estimate of the present value of target firm's future cash flows.

According to Roll, managers not only make mistaken valuations but often have unwarranted confidence both in their valuations and in their ability to create value. This attitude, says Roll, reflects **hubris**—a Greek term denoting excessive pride, overconfidence, or arrogance. Hubristic managers may overestimate their own abilities to implement potential synergies.

A final word: Although we're going to focus on synergy as a motivation for acquisitions, you shouldn't ignore the other two motivations—managerialism and managerial hubris—when you're evaluating M&As. When managerialism and hubris are kept in check, acquiring firms are more likely to realize synergies and positive performance benefits.

hubris Exaggerated self-confidence that can result in managers' overestimating the value of a potential acquisition, having unrealistic assumptions about the ability to create synergies, and a willingness to pay too much for a transaction.

SYNERGY

When M&As are undertaken in pursuit of synergy, managers are guided by the belief that the value of two firms combined can be greater than the sum value of the two firms independently. This category includes all forms of M&As that are motivated by value creation. Synergy may derive from a number of sources, including reduced threats from suppliers, increased market power, potential cost savings, superior financial strength, economies of scope and scale, and the sharing and leveraging of capabilities.

Reducing Threats As was noted in Chapter 7, sometimes a supplier cannot or will not make an investment that's specific to an exchange with one buyer. Why might this situation arise? Perhaps the investment would tie the company too closely to one buyer, expose it to too much risk, or overtax its financial means. In such cases firms may need to integrate vertically, backward into the supply chain.[7] The quickest way to do this is through an acquisition. Some of Cisco Systems' acquisitions of network switch technology companies are examples of this type of backward integration.

Increasing Market Power and Access If a company improves its competitive position by means of a merger or acquisition, it may be possible to derive potential market power from the deal. Firms have market power when they can influence prices, and price competition is reduced significantly when rivalry is reduced. In the banking industry, for example, some mergers—especially those involving two moderate-sized banks—seem to have been motivated by a desire to improve market power. Thus, when First Union purchased Wachovia, the combined company vaulted into the number-four slot among U.S. banks. When Daimler merged with Chrysler in an effort to exploit potential synergies, its share in the global automotive market increased significantly. And the merger was designed to improve market access for both companies in geographic arenas where they were weak but their merger partner was strong. Another example of improved access is provided by PepsiCo. In 1992, for example, when PepsiCo still owned Pizza Hut, Taco Bell, and Kentucky Fried Chicken, it purchased Carts of Colorado (CC), a small food cart (e.g., kiosk) manufacturer, for $7 million, seeing it as the ideal means of installing new restaurants quickly and cheaply. Not only did the purchase give PepsiCo access to new cart technology, but it also provided it with an inexpensive means for quickly establishing fast food outlets in high-traffic locations. One of PepsiCo's first successful cart locations was in the Moscow metro system.

Realizing Cost Savings   Cost savings are the most common synergy and the easiest to estimate. Financial markets tend to understand and accept cost savings as a rationale and are more likely to reward savings-motivated M&As with higher stock prices than other forms of synergy. Revenue-enhancement opportunities, such as increasing total sales through cross-selling and enhanced distribution, also represent a significant upside in many M&As. It's more difficult, however, to calculate and implement revenue enhancement synergies (sometimes called *soft synergies*) than cost-saving synergies.

Increasing Financial Strength   Other synergies can be created by various forms of financial engineering. An acquisition, for instance, can lower the financing costs of the target firm when the two firms' respective credit ratings are markedly different and significant debt is involved. Such would be the case if a company with AAA-rated debt were to buy a B-rated company. Various tax benefits also provide unique financial synergies. If, for example, the target company has operating loss carry-forwards (i.e., financial losses that the IRS allows firms to apply to future years' earnings) that can't be fully utilized, the acquiring company can use them to reduce the tax bill of the combined firm.

Sharing and Leveraging Capabilities   Transferring best practices and core competencies can create value. This form of synergy is important in the resource-based view of competitive advantage. According to this view, one reason for acquiring another firm would be to absorb and assimilate the target's resource, knowledge, and capabilities—all of which may be primary sources of competitive advantage. When firms combine resources and capabilities through M&As, they may be able to create a bundle of resources that is unavailable to competitors. If the combined resources and capabilities are complementary, the competitive advantage may be long-term. If the combination is valuable and rare, the acquiring firm may be able to generate profits greater than the sum of the two firms' individual profits. Bear in mind, however, that transferring resources, knowledge, or capabilities can create long-term competitive advantage only if the cost of the acquisition doesn't exceed the cost to other firms of accumulating comparable resource stocks.

Mergers, Acquisitions, and Strategy

Three points need to be kept in mind when considering acquisitions as a part of a firm's corporate strategy. First, as with other elements of strategy, managers need to be clear about the economic logic: How does the acquisition help the firm earn profits? Second, managers need to consider alternatives to the acquisition, such as developing the new business internally rather than buying it. Third, acquisitions are fraught with hazards that can end up ruining the projected returns, and managers need to know what these hazards are and how to navigate around them.

THE VEHICLE AND ITS ECONOMIC LOGIC

Acquisitions enable firms to enter new businesses quickly, reduce the time and risks entailed by the process of starting new businesses internally, and rapidly reach minimum efficient scale. Research shows, however, that M&As come with significant risks and uncertainties of their own. Although some acquisitions succeed, such as eBay's acquisition of PayPal, others fail to produce anticipated synergies, resulting in small losses, and some fail miserably, resulting in huge losses. eBay, for instance, was forced to sell Butterfields at a significant loss in terms of both dollars and managerial time and attention. In this chapter, we'll discuss some of the keys to making acquisitions serve as an effective vehicle for growth and, at the same time, avoiding common potential pitfalls.

Mergers and acquisitions are not strategies in and of themselves; rather, as we're reminded in the strategy diamond shown in Exhibit 2, M&As simply represent one element of a strategy. Specifically, they are *vehicles* for realizing a strategy—that is, for entering or exiting a business.[8]

However, acquisitions have significant implications for other elements of strategy. Acquisitions take firms into new arenas. Acquisitions that result in diversification are used in the staging of corporate strategies. And finally, acquisitions have implications for the financial success of strategies—for the realization of the anticipated economic logic of the strategy.

Perhaps because they enable companies to accelerate their strategies, acquisitions are quite popular. The number of acquisitions over the past few decades suggests that they constitute a fundamental element of many firms' strategies. Exhibit 3 shows that M&A is not a new strategy vehicle, but its usage has grown dramatically in recent years.[9] The graph of aggregate M&A activity clearly displays a wave-like behavior with several notable peaks. The most intense quarter of M&A activity in Exhibit 3 is 1899:1, while the least intense quarter occurred during the Great Depression (1932:1). However, current M&A activity, as you will see in later exhibits, dwarfs these early peaks in both dollar volume and number of deals.

Research suggests that firms average about one acquisition per year, but of course, there's tremendous variance in firms' propensity for using acquisitions as a growth vehicle.[10] Not

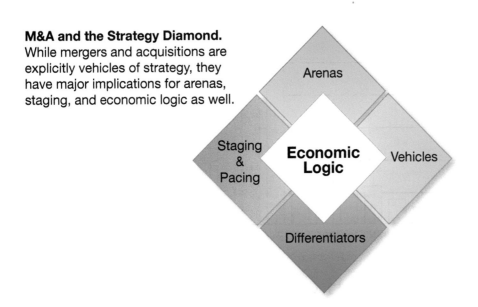

M&A and the Strategy Diamond.
While mergers and acquisitions are explicitly vehicles of strategy, they have major implications for arenas, staging, and economic logic as well.

Exhibit 2 The Place of Acquisitions in the Strategy Diamond

Exhibit 3 Long-term View of M&A Activity (Relative Frequency of Deals)

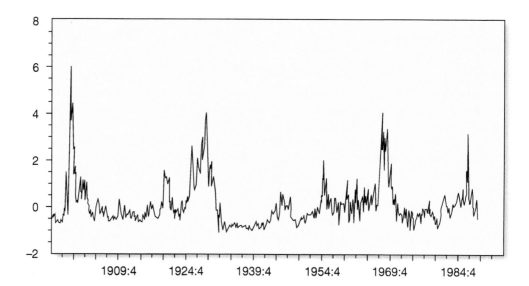

surprisingly, the financial success of any given acquisition depends on a number of factors and has a significant effect on the overall economic logic of a firm's strategy. As you can see in Exhibit 4, which summarizes acquisition activity involving U.S. firms between 1995 and 2006, the value of acquisitions involving U.S. firms demonstrates that acquisitions represent a major economic activity.[11]

Also, as shown in Exhibit 5, the frequency of cross-border M&A is on the rise.[12] Across all deals, over 40 percent of transactions were valued in excess of $1 billion; about 30 percent were in the $100 million to $500 billion range.

As you can also see from Exhibit 5, recent acquisition activity peaked near the turn of the century. That wave coincided with the tremendous bull market when firms used their inflated stock prices as currency to purchase other firms.

Exhibit 4 Recent M&A Activity

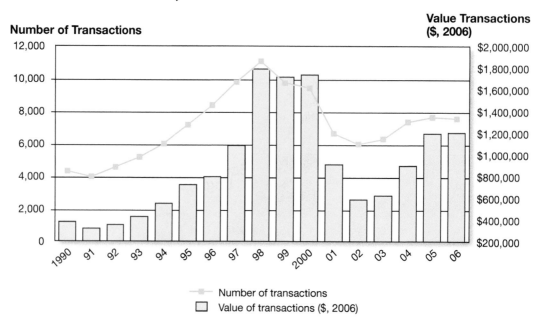

Exhibit 5 Global M&A Activity

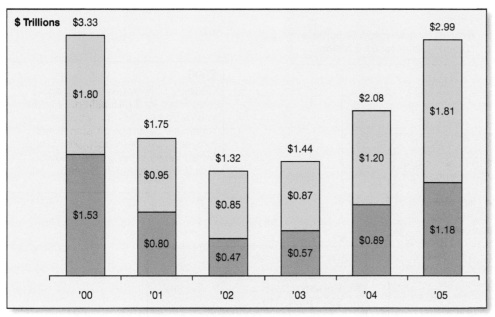

$ Trillions

Year	United States	All other	Total
'00	$1.53	$1.80	$3.33
'01	$0.80	$0.95	$1.75
'02	$0.47	$0.85	$1.32
'03	$0.57	$0.87	$1.44
'04	$0.89	$1.20	$2.08
'05	$1.18	$1.81	$2.99

☐ United States   ☐ All other

Despite—and because of—their economic consequences, M&As get a lot of bad press and receive criticism from scholars and consultants as well. We can attribute this criticism—at least in part—to the high visibility of many spectacular acquisition mistakes. Notable acquisition "mistakes" include AT&T's acquisition of NCR, Quaker's acquisition of Snapple, and AOL's acquisition of Time Warner. As is the case of so many acquisitions, the managers who made these deals seemed to be unable to make them work.

Quaker, for instance, purchased Snapple thinking that it could create profitable synergies between Snapple and its own Gatorade.[13] Apparently, however, Quaker failed to do its preacquisition homework, particularly when it came to the differences in the distribution networks of the two products. There were troublesome delays in implementing key aspects of the acquisition, and Snapple's market position in relation to newer brands was seriously eroded. The pressure from analysts and shareholders grew so intense that just two years after acquiring Snapple, Quaker pulled the plug on the acquisition and sold it for $300 million—a hefty $1.5 billion less than it paid for it. After just three years of repositioning Snapple, the new owner, Triarc, sold the brand for $1.45 billion to Cadbury Schweppes PLC, where it's now successfully positioned in a portfolio of brands run by a company with the capabilities necessary to build the Snapple brand. Snapple's financial-market roller coaster ride, which is illustrated in Exhibit 6, provides a good lesson in the combination of risks and opportunities that often accompany acquisitions as a strategy vehicle.

And while you might think that firms would learn from others' M&A mistakes, Daimler's recent sale of Chrysler for $7.4 billion, after having paid $36 billion for it in 1998, is striking evidence that hubris is alive and well in the world of M&A.

From what we've seen so far, it's clear that **divestiture**—the selling off of a business and the flip side of acquisition—is also a key strategic vehicle. eBay, AT&T, and Quaker all exited businesses by selling business units to competitors. In this chapter, we focus primarily on acquisitions as vehicles for entering or expanding businesses, but remember that closely related types of transactions enable firms to exit businesses as well.

When deciding to enter a new business, companies have alternative vehicles from which to choose, including *internal development*, *alliances*, and *acquisition*. Here, we'll explain why the

divestiture Strategy whereby a company sells off a business or division.

Exhibit 6 Ups and Downs at Snapple

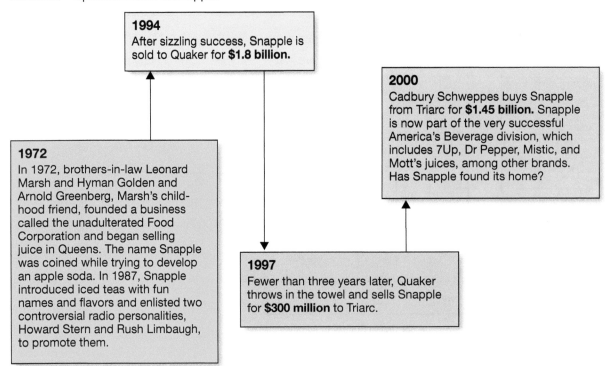

tradeoffs between internal development and acquisition—make or buy decisions—are important considerations when deciding whether to enter a new business through acquisition.

BENEFITS OF ACQUISITION OVER INTERNAL DEVELOPMENT

One of the primary advantages of acquisition over internal development is *speed*. Although an acquisition quickly establishes a foothold in a new business, internal development can take years. A corollary benefit is critical mass. An acquisition ensures that a firm enters a new business with sufficient size and viable competitive strength. The acquiring firm, for example, can be assured of entering at minimum efficient scale for cost purposes. As another advantage, acquisitions can provide access to complementary assets and resources. In developing a new business, a firm invests its existing stock of resources and capabilities, and although it may develop new resources and capabilities in the process, there's always the chance that it may simply expend existing resources. With an acquisition, new resources and capabilities can be integrated with those of the buyer, who may actually improve its competitive position in other businesses as well. Finally, entry by acquisition may foster a less competitive environment. By acquiring an existing firm in a new business, the buyer eliminates a competitor that would otherwise remain in the market.

DRAWBACKS OF ACQUISITION OVER INTERNAL DEVELOPMENT

Conversely, firms may find it preferable for several reasons to enter new businesses by means of internal development. First, acquisitions can be more expensive than internal development. Buyers often pay steep premiums for existing companies. In many cases, these premiums outweigh any potential benefits of the acquisition, and in some cases, they make it economically more viable either to enter through internal development or to avoid entry altogether. In short, firms may decide against entering new businesses because they aren't likely to generate sufficient return on capital to justify the premium cost. In addition, the acquiring firm will often inherit several unnecessary adjunct businesses. As an acquirer, you must either be willing to run these unwanted businesses or go through the administrative hassle of spinning them off.

Second, although acquisitions represent a major one-time commitment of resources, internal development entails incremental investment over time. The internal development process, therefore, allows for many points at which the project can be assessed and reevaluated before further investment is made. If, for example, economic circumstances change, a firm can pull the plug. Acquisitions, on the other hand, are typically all-or-nothing propositions.

Finally, organizational conflict may emerge as a potential problem; the eruption of *cultural clashes* can impede the integration of two firms. The process of integration requires significant effort, and firms may encounter setbacks or even failure. Because integration is such a major factor in making M&As work, we'll discuss it in greater detail later in the chapter.

As you can see, many potential roadblocks can make it difficult for firms to realize economic gains from acquisitions. And the greater the cost in capital and time required for integration, the more synergies managers will have to squeeze out of the deal.

Types of Mergers and Acquisitions

There are many types of M&As, and each has a particular purpose—a specific rationale for creating synergies. In this section, we'll survey the different forms of M&As and link the economic logic of each form to firm strategy.[14] Because the logic behind each form varies, so, too, do the criteria for their success.

TYPES OF ACQUISITIONS

Acquisitions can figure into most aspects of business strategy, but they're generally regarded as a means of managing competitive pressures, uncertainty, or both. Thus, business-strategy acquisitions, like business-strategy alliances, tend to be fundamentally related to the firm's core business through *vertical*, *horizontal*, or *complementary relationships*.

A vertical acquisition has three purposes:

- To secure a reliable supply

- To leverage the resources and capabilities of upstream activities in order to create more value for the end customer

- To reduce total production costs across the value chain

Coca-Cola and Pepsi each have engaged in several vertical acquisitions over the years as they have purchased independent bottling operations. These acquisitions are downstream vertical acquisitions. Recall from the opening vignette in Chapter 4 that Coke and Pepsi sell most of their core product (concentrate) to bottlers who then mix the concentrate with other ingredients, bottle the product, and distribute it to retail outlets. Coke and Pepsi were able to reduce some threats that were beginning to emerge from large bottlers, as well as infuse more efficiency into these downstream activities, by consolidating bottling operations into more efficient regional operations.

In contrast, horizontal acquisitions help expand the company's product offerings. The Cadbury Schweppes purchase of Snapple was a horizontal acquisition that helped expand the buyer's beverage portfolio, particularly in the growing juice and tea segment.

Best Buy's 2002 acquisition of the Geek Squad, a Twin Cities computer-support service, was a product-market extension.

A complementary acquisition involves a complementary business—one that increases the sale of another product. Best Buy's recent acquisition of the Geek Squad, a computer-support service, is a complementary acquisition: When computer-service capability is bundled with retail computer sales, each business potentially increases sales of the other's product.

A Complete Classification Because this simple breakdown of acquisitions into vertical, horizontal, and complementary relationships is a little oversimplified, let's take a look at the typology proposed by Harvard professor Joseph Bower, illustrated in Exhibit 7. It will give us a better understanding of the strategic logic behind five more commonly employed forms of acquisition.[15]

Though developed through a study of extremely large acquisitions (over $500 million), this schema provides a useful way of thinking generally about M&As.

Product and Market Extension In a *product-extension acquisition*, the acquiring company expands its product line by purchasing another company. Basically, the buyer has decided that it can reap higher rewards by buying a company with an existing product than by developing a competitive product internally. In a *market-extension acquisition*, one company buys another that offers essentially the same products as the buyer but has a platform in a geographic market in which the buyer has no presence.

The journey of Snapple that we described earlier in this chapter is an interesting example of two different companies using the same acquired firm for the purpose of product extension. Conceivably, Quaker Oats could have developed its own line of fruit juices, lemonades, and teas. At the time, however, Quaker management believed that an internally developed line would lag too far behind those of incumbent firms in the market segment. Likewise, Cadbury Schweppes certainly has the capability to develop new drinks internally but chose to cultivate expertise in extending product offerings through the acquisition of established brands.

geographic roll-up Strategy whereby a firm acquires many other firms in the same industry segment but in different geographic arenas in an attempt to create significant scale and scope advantages.

Geographic Roll-Ups A **geographic roll-up** occurs when a firm acquires several firms that are in the same *industry* segment but in many different *geographic* arenas. It's not the same strategy as market extension. With a roll-up, the acquiring company is trying to change the nature of industry competition in a fundamental way; it seeks to become a large

Exhibit 7   Bower's Classification of Acquisitions

	Product/Market Extension	Roll-up M&A	M&A as R&D	Overcapacity M&A	Industry Convergence
Example	Pepsi's acquisition of Gatorade	Service Corporation International's more than 100 acquisitions of funeral homes	Intel's dozens of acquisitions of small high-tech companies	DaimlerChrysler merger	AOL's acquisition of TimeWarner
Objectives	Synergy of similar but expanded product lines or geographic markets	Efficiency of larger operations (e.g., economies of scale, superior management)	Short cut innovation by buying it from small companies	Eliminating capacity, gaining market share, and increasing efficiency	Anticipation of new industry emerging; culling resources from firms in multiple industries whose boundaries are eroding
Percent of All M&A Deals	36%	9%	1%	37%	4%

regional, national, or international player in what's probably been a fragmented industry. The purpose of a roll-up is to achieve economies of scale and scope. Prior to its merger with First Chicago, for example, Banc One had grown from a small regional bank in Ohio to a large national bank by buying smaller local and regional banks around the country. (The merged company is called Bank One.) In a roll-up, the acquiring company usually retains the resources and management of acquired companies but imposes its processes on them.

Entrepreneur Bradley Jacobs made a fortune deploying the roll-up strategy to build two extremely successful companies in two different industries. In the waste-management business, Jacobs used United Waste Systems as a roll-up company to buy small trash-hauling firms in a fragmented industry. He later sold the company to USA Waste Services (now Waste Management) and used the proceeds to launch another startup—one that would use the same roll-up strategy to consolidate the equipment rental industry. He launched United Rentals by purchasing six heavy-equipment leasing firms and then proceeded to buy equipment rental companies all across the country. Through a series of more than sixty acquisitions in seven years, it has become the largest equipment rental company in the United States.

What's the rationale behind a roll-up strategy? Basically it's that a large regional or national player can achieve economies of scale that smaller local firms can't. Centralized management, for example, may improve overall operational effectiveness through large volume supply discounts. In addition, a national firm may have the resources to win customer accounts that smaller local firms don't have. United Rentals, for instance, may be able to win equipment rental contracts with large customers who want a single national provider for all of their heavy equipment needs.

M&As as R&D   Some firms use acquisitions in lieu of or in addition to internal R&D. Usually, the acquiring firm buys another company in order to gain ownership of its technology. The strategy is common in industries in which technology advances rapidly and in which no single company can do all the innovating that it needs to continue competing effectively.

Exhibit 8 M&A as R&D

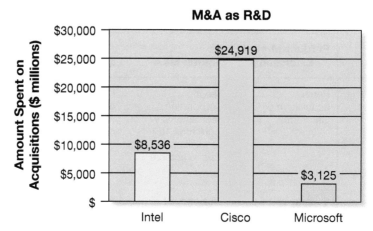

In the telecommunications equipment and computer industries, this strategy has been used to good effect by such firms as Cisco, Microsoft, and Intel. Exhibit 8 indicates how important acquisitions are to these companies as R&D vehicles.

First of all, bear in mind that the average U.S. company engages in approximately one acquisition per year. In the five-year period between 1999 and 2003, each of these three companies averaged more than ten acquisitions per year. All three companies allocate money for internal R&D, but each also spends considerable sums to acquire new technologies by buying startups that have made promising innovations. The strategy, of course, represents a tradeoff.

To get a better idea of what this tradeoff entails, consider the acquisition expenses of Intel and AMD. Both firms devote significant capital to traditional internal R&D projects. However, Intel made dozens of acquisitions during the past several years, whereas AMD made only three. This suggests that these two firms in the same industry have very different approaches to R&D. Intel apparently uses acquisitions as an opportunity to acquire potential future innovations from small startup companies with promising technologies.

Overcapacity M&As The purpose of an *overcapacity acquisition* is to reduce the number of competitors in a mature industry in which capacity exceeds decreasing demand. In essence, parties to an overcapacity acquisition are trying to consolidate the industry. Such is the case, for instance, when two companies in the same industry merge (or one acquires another) in order to rationalize the industry and reduce overcapacity. Overcapacity mergers are often explained as attempts to create economies of scale, but in many cases both companies are already large enough to be operating at a minimum efficient scale. Improved efficiencies come from reducing redundant operations and trimming the size of combined units. This was the rationale behind Daimler's acquisition of Chrysler (Daimler's recent sale of Chrysler for a significant loss is evidence of the difficulty implementing large acquisitions). The banking industry, in which firms are jockeying for market position and trying to create greater economies of scale, has experienced extensive overcapacity-M&A volume in the past decade.

Industry Convergence M&As When two industries start to overlap and become highly complementary, they begin to *converge*. When this happens, we see an increase in the level of M&As involving firms in the converging industries. In the media and entertainment industries, for example, Time Inc. had an extensive print media business and some cable operations (as well as HBO). Warner Brothers Inc. had a bigger presence in cable operations and a huge library of movies. In 1990, the two companies combined through Time's acquisition of Warner to form Time Warner (which acquired Turner Broadcasting in 1996 and which was later acquired by AOL in 2001) in order to consolidate media content and distribution. In response to the AOL–Time Warner combination, Viacom, whose core business was cable TV production and distribution, bought Paramount, a movie and TV producer (1993); Blockbuster, a chain of video outlets (1994); and the TV network CBS (2000). In

1996, Disney, already a media conglomerate, bought ABC, including cable broadcaster ESPN (1996). The entertainment industry's landscape continues to shift as firms try to find the right mix of businesses to compete effectively in converging industries.

The logic behind M&As in converging industries holds that such calculated investments will put firms in a better competitive position if and when industry boundaries erode. One can also view acquisitions in this environment as attempts by companies to acquire resources that, although less valuable in the present competitive environment, will be critical in projected new industry contexts.

Investor/Holding Company M&As Although we won't discuss this category in much detail, investor holding company M&A represents a significant portion of total acquisition activity. In investor/holding company transactions, independent investors or holding companies purchase existing firms. Such might be the case when an investment fund engages in a leveraged buyout of a company. Rather than merge the purchased company with other firms in its portfolio, the buyer tries to bring some management, operating, and financial discipline to the company, intending to sell it later at a profit. In other cases, investors (such as Warren Buffett's Berkshire Hathaway) purchase companies for long-term ownership and management.

International Acquisitions

Bower's classification doesn't provide a specific category for international M&As, but in Exhibit 5 you learned that they are fairly prevalent. Our analysis of data compiled by Thompson Financial Services reveals that since 1990, cross-border M&As have accounted for an increasing percentage of all M&A activity. However, the issues confronting firms during international acquisitions are significant and you may need to examine the issues of differing cultures, laws, and competitors very closely before executing an international acquisition. An international acquisition can be of any of the types reviewed (e.g., R&D, product/market extension, roll-up, convergence, overcapacity, holding company). Obviously, the use of acquisitions as a strategy vehicle by any firm wanting to enter a new international arena should flow from its business- and corporate-strategy objectives, but firms must be aware that the international context introduces significant complexity into M&A transactions.

Pricing and Premiums

In this section, we'll review some of the basic financial issues relating to potential M&A success. These issues include pricing, premiums, and the benefits of establishing a walk-away price.

PRICING

What is the right price to pay for an acquisition? You might imagine such an assignment from a future boss (or a finance professor on an exam!); however, in the real world there really is no single correct price for an acquisition or merger. Why? Simply because the value of a target depends on how well it fits with the acquiring company. A potential acquisition will have a different value for different buyers. The ultimate purchase price will depend on a number of specific factors, including the target's current market value, its intrinsic value, and the value to be gained from any potential synergies between the target and buyer. Intrinsic value and the value of potential synergies cannot be known with certainty; these values are estimated by managers of the acquiring firm, investment bankers, and outside analysts. The firm contemplating an acquisition can consider a number of factors when determining its offer price for another firm.

Market and Intrinsic Value

Of course, one of the first (and easiest) things to consider when evaluating a possible acquisition is the target's current market value. As the term suggests, **market value** is the current market capitalization of a firm, which is typically

market value Current market capitalization of a firm.

calculated by multiplying the number of shares outstanding by the firm's stock price. This value is theoretically the market's estimates of the current value of the firm's future cash flows. A firm's **intrinsic value**, however, is the present value of a company's future cash flows from existing assets and businesses for a particular owner or buyer. It can be higher or lower than a company's market value, with the difference reflecting a number of factors. Markets make important adjustments in the valuation of a firm, evaluating future growth opportunities that will result in products and generate additional cash flows, assessing discounts for bad management or excessive diversification, or awarding premiums to firms that are likely to become the targets of bidding wars themselves.

The **purchase price** is the value actually paid to the target firm's shareholders. Like market price, it may be either higher or lower than intrinsic value, but it's almost always greater than current market value. The only exception to this rule involves target firms that are in dire financial condition (e.g., Daimler recently had to pay a buyer to take Chrysler off its hands).

Why would a potential acquirer offer to pay more than a firm's market price in an acquisition? Recall that synergy is the economic value created by being able to reduce costs or increase revenues by operating in two or more businesses instead of a single business. Synergy is essentially another way of saying that two or more combined entities create economies of scope and scale. If a buyer perceives that an acquisition will offer synergy potential, it may rationally pay more than the current market value for another firm. When synergies exist, they have the effect of increasing the intrinsic value of a target firm for that buyer.

Because synergy is a function of the *strategic fit* of the acquiring and the target firms, each bidding firm may value the target differently. In addition, the market may react differently in evaluating different bidding firms. When, for instance, Vodafone and Bell Atlantic both made bids for AirTouch, Bell Atlantic's stock price dropped while Vodafone's price went up—even though Vodafone entered the bidding with a higher offer. Why? The market believed that Vodafone and AirTouch could achieve greater synergies than Bell Atlantic and AirTouch.

PREMIUMS

The difference between current market value and the final purchase price is called the **acquisition premium**. A premium is what induces shareholders of the target to sell their shares to new owners. Our analysis of the acquisitions tracked by Thompson Financial Services finds that in the United States, average acquisition premiums have ranged between 30 and 45 percent during each of the past fifteen years. For instance, a firm with a market value of $100 million would normally sell for a purchase price of between $130 and $145 million.

Paying premiums for acquisitions, however, presents a basic problem for managers of would-be acquirers. When the managers of an acquiring firm agree to pay a premium for a target firm, they must expect that they will be able to generate better returns by combining the firms than the firms would achieve independently. In other words, to justify paying a premium of 30 to 45 percent, managers will need to generate more net income from the combined companies than the market assumed would be realized before the announcement of the acquisition. Where is this increase in return supposed to come from? Apparently it is from the synergies achieved by the combined firms. Synergies, however, are not guaranteed and there are several managerial traps that can make synergies difficult to achieve. Some of the managerial problems will be discussed in more detail later in the chapter. First, let's consider the practical implication of premiums.

The Synergy Trap In a study of acquisition premiums, Mark Sirower of the Boston Consulting Group (BCG) discussed what he called the "synergy trap."[16] He argued that premiums present two problems for managers:

---

intrinsic value Present value of a company's future cash flows from existing assets and businesses.

purchase price Final price actually paid to the target firm's shareholders of an acquired company.

acquisition premium Difference between current market value of a target firm and purchase price paid to induce its shareholders to turn its control over to new owners.

1. Premiums increase the level of returns that must be extracted from the combined businesses.

2. Because of the time value of money, the longer it takes to implement performance improvements, the lower the likelihood that the acquisition will be successful. Consequently, any delays in implementing and extracting synergies increase the ante on required performance improvements.

Not surprisingly, paying too much for an acquisition can not only jeopardize the success of an acquisition, but it can also cause irreparable damage to the acquiring firm. Regularly in his letters to shareholders, Warren Buffett has reminded shareholders of Berkshire Hathaway that paying too much for a company can lead to disastrous effects. The box entitled "How Would *You* Do That? 1" goes into more depth on the issue of premiums and their effects on acquisition success and helps you gain confidence in calculating the required performance improvements associated with a particular acquisition premium. **Required performance improvements** are the annual increases in cash flow that are necessary to justify the level of premium paid. Calculating required performance improvements utilizes simple principles from discounted cash flow analysis that you've learned in your finance classes. The tools we provide you with in "How Would *You* Do That? 1" make the calculations even easier.

> **required performance improvements** The increases in combined cash flow of the acquiror and target that are necessary to justify the acquisition premium.

Reaching a Walk-away Price

Given what you now know about the synergy trap (and perhaps about Warren Buffett's shrewdness as a strategic investor), it shouldn't surprise you to learn that in 2000, when Coke CEO Douglas Daft tried to buy Quaker Oats in order to add Gatorade to the company's product line, board member Buffett opposed the idea. Buffett argued that the bidding by Coke and Pepsi had driven the premium too high and Coke should walk away from the negotiations. (The board sided with Buffett and withdrew from the bidding.) Similarly, in 2004, cable operator Comcast made a tender offer for Disney of 0.78 share of Comcast Class A stock for each Disney share. The stock market wasn't overly thrilled with the proposed deal and Comcast's share price dropped while Disney's increased. Comcast was forced to withdraw the offer, however, because the value of its stock subsequently dropped too far: There came a point at which Comcast would have to pay out too many shares to reach the offered value. In effect, that point was Comcast's "walk-away price."

Escalation of Commitment and the Winner's Curse

Establishing a walk-away price is relatively easy; sticking to it is not. One reason for this is that executives escalate the commitment to their initiative as they proceed through a transaction. This—coupled with excessive fear of failure—means that bidders are sometimes seduced into making questionable decisions. Bidders who allow their prices to get carried away (or allow themselves to get carried away with their bidding) often suffer from the so-called **winner's curse**. Although the bidders win the "prize," they're saddled with the consequences of having paid too much.

> **winner's curse** Situation in which a winning M&A bidder must live with the consequences of paying too much for the target.

The Acquisition Process

So far we've focused mostly on the technical side of M&As: what they are and how they're used as strategy vehicles, along with the roles of pricing and premiums. The success of M&As as a strategy vehicle, however, depends on much more than the choice of a good target and paying the right price. The process by which M&As are completed and targeted firms are integrated into acquiring firms can have a significant bearing on success or failure. Indeed, some experts say that the acquisition process is the single largest factor.[17]

The Impact of Premiums on Required Synergies

Assume that you worked for eBay prior to its acquisition of PayPal. You have learned from your division manager that PayPal will be folded into your division after the acquisition. Your boss, in a moment of pause from the hysteria surrounding the deal, has suddenly realized that she will be held responsible for integrating the acquisition and generating the synergies that Meg Whitman has been touting in discussions with Wall Street analysts. She turns to you and asks you to calculate just how much synergy she will have to deliver to make the deal a success. How would you translate the premium paid in this acquisition into actionable division budgets for the coming years?

This is not an entirely hypothetical question. Every time an acquisition is completed, it affects how division managers operate. Indeed, it often affects the targets that the CEO imposes upon them in terms of revenue targets and expense containment. To illustrate how this happens, let's go back to eBay's acquisition of PayPal. The opening vignette noted that eBay paid a premium of $250 million (a 20-percent premium over PayPal's market value prior to the acquisition).

Let's start with our objective: We need to know the synergy required to make the deal a success. Let's call this *required performance improvement*, or RPI for short. Understanding how to

calculate RPI is a useful managerial tool here. The RPI to justify a premium paid can be calculated with various degrees of sophistication, including the use of discounted uneven cash flows and probability statistics. But that level of sophistication isn't necessary to get in the ballpark.

We have simplified the various formulas and created a simple table of factors in Exhibit 9 that will help you understand the concept. The three factors that you'll need to know are (1) the premium expected to be paid, (2) the number of years before you expect synergies to be implemented (on the vertical axis) and (3) the cost of capital of the firm (on the vertical axis). Together, these are the factors that can be used to determine the annual synergies required to make the acquisition a success. The synergy trap calculation also assumes synergies are captured over a 10-year period, so if synergies start in year 1, that amount would need to be captured in each of the remaining 9 years as well. If they start in year 9, then they would need to be captured in 9 and 10, and so on.

Locate the intersection of the years assumed to make the synergies materialize and the cost of capital. Then multiply that factor by the premium paid to determine just how much synergy must be generated *each year* over the 10-year synergy period, depending upon when the synergies start, through the

combination of annual cost savings and new revenue improvements. If we assume that synergies will materialize immediately after the acquisition, then the amount of synergy that must be achieved is determined by simply multiplying the cost of capital by the premium. However, as you can see, as the years increase before synergies are implemented, or as the cost of capital increases, the amount of synergy that must be generated increases very quickly (the amount of synergy required is reflected in the yellow area of the exhibit).

In the case of eBay's acquisition of PayPal, the premium was approximately $250,000,000. So if the company thought that it would take two years to implement the synergies and it knew that their cost of capital was 15 percent, then the operational synergies required could be estimated by multiplying the premium by the factor as follows: $250,000,000 × 0.198 = $49,500,000. What does this number represent? It is the amount of additional net income that is needed *each* of the eight remaining years in a 10-year period. The acquisition of PayPal over and above the existing net income of both companies combined. eBay would have to find almost an additional $50 million in synergies just to pay for the premium.

Recall that synergies can take the form of increased revenues or reduced

Years Until Synergies Are Implemented	Cost of Capital		
	10%	15%	20%
0	0.100	0.150	0.200
1	0.110	0.173	0.240
2	0.121	0.198	0.288
3	0.133	0.228	0.346
4	0.146	0.262	0.415
5	0.161	0.302	0.498

Exhibit 9 Synergies Required to Justify a $10 Million Premium

costs for the combined firm, or both an increase in revenues and reduction of costs. Synergies can also be found in specific parts of the business such that one unit can grow faster or have a better cost position than it had previously. Ultimately, if it is considered a successful acquisition, the acquisition must leave the acquired and the acquiror better off than had the acquisition not been consummated.

While it is too early to tell how the Skype acquisition will turn out, and it is less obvious where the synergies from that deal might come from, we can at least provide a post-mortem on the PayPal deal. Here are the facts:

- eBay launches BillPoint in 1999 for online payments (though took a year to launch, and when finally up and running, PayPal had registered its millionth user)

- By mid-2001, eBay is losing $10–15 million yearly on BillPoint

- eBay buys PayPal in July 2002 for $1.5 billion, and eBay's cost of capital at the time was 15 percent

- eBay integrated PayPal in *one year*, with 74 percent of all eBay transactions by 2004, and 9 percent of U.S. e-commerce (5 percent globally)

- Experts point to the availability of PayPal as partial explanation for the exponential growth of eBay's total revenues, beyond those garnered by PayPal. While it is hard to point to the PayPal acquisition as the single source of eBay's growth, all indicators suggest that PayPal is a great example of a complement obtained through acquisition!

In summary, the synergy trap tool will help you evaluate what must be done with an acquisition if it takes place and considering some basic financial assumptions. Ironically, CEOs will comment that the best acquisitions are sometimes the ones they did not make, and the synergy trap tool lets the managers who must eventually integrate and make good on the purchase wrestle with whether or not the numbers made sense. Recall from our opening vignette that the business press considered the PayPal acquisition to be more hubristic than synergistic, but that in the end the deal proved a home run for eBay. You can bet though, as is the case in most acquisitions, that had the strategy not worked, many a critic would have said "I told you so!"

STAGES OF THE ACQUISITION PROCESS

Exhibit 10 summarizes the four major stages in an acquisition: *idea generation, justification* (including due diligence and negotiation), *integration,* and *results.* As the exhibit suggests, the M&A process really begins with the strategy because management has identified and prepared for M&A as a strategy vehicle, understands what strategic differentiators the firm will gain, bolster, or develop as a result of M&A, and has accounted for all the acquisition process stages in the staging and pacing facet of its strategy.

Problems at any of the first three stages can sow the seeds of failure.[18] This model identifies two types of problems: *decision-making problems* and *implementation* or *integration problems.* Decision-making problems can arise during the idea-generation, justification, and integration stages, whereas implementation problems occur during the integration stage. However, these integration problems could have their roots in an earlier stage of the process.

Idea   Integration starts with the strategy itself, since the strategy will have foreseen M&A as a critical vehicle for success. But once M&A is part of the strategy, then the *idea* is the impetus for the acquisition. Some firms have well-articulated strategies that state the conditions under which acquisitions will be the vehicle of choice for implementing strategic plans. Recall, for instance, the case of United Rentals' roll-up strategy: Acquisitions were a key vehicle in the firm's strategy. Conversely, Quaker Oats' purchase of Snapple was an opportunistic (and ill-considered) move. Whereas some firms have well-defined strategies, in terms of the role of M&A as strategy vehicles, others don't. Firms that do have clear concepts about the role of M&A in their strategy, and have the requisite M&A capabilities, can be more opportunistic in the use of acquisitions.[19]

Justification, Due Diligence, and Negotiation   The major analytical stage of an acquisition includes the processes that a firm goes through to develop the internal and external logic for the acquisition. Researchers Philippe Haspeslagh and David Jemison contend that several critical decisions must be made at this stage: strategic assessment, devel-

Exhibit 10
Acquisition Process
Stages

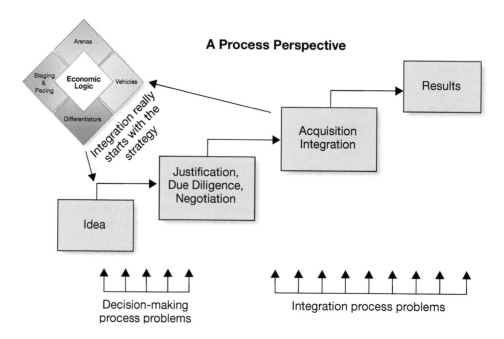

oping a widely shared view, a degree of specificity, organizational conditions, implementation timing, and a walk-away price.

■ *Strategic assessment* is the process of determining how an acquisition will contribute to overall strategy and competitive position. It should do more than analyze the target: It should address the issue of how the acquisition will affect the acquiring firm's pursuit of its core objectives. Managers should also make sure that their assessment isn't too static: It should consider the firm's future needs as its industry evolves.

■ Because many people will be involved in implementing an acquisition and integrating the target firm into the parent, it's important that the purpose and strategic logic of the acquisition be widely understood by members of the organization. The following is a list of eight questions that managers should ask at this stage of an acquisition:[20]

1. What is the strategic logic behind this acquisition? Does it correspond with the firm's strategy? Why this company?

2. Is the target industry attractive? What are the key segments? What is the prognosis about industry evolution?

3. If this is an international acquisition, what are the key differences between this country and our experience? Do these differences have performance implications?

4. Does an analysis of the target company (products and services, market position, customers, suppliers, distribution channels, costs, etc.) suggest that it is healthy and viable in the long term?

5. How well does this company fit with ours? What are the expected benefits, and what might impinge on the realization of those benefits?

6. How will the acquisition be integrated? Who will lead this process? How will we be organized?

7. Have alternative *scenarios* been considered? What is the outcome given reasonable, optimistic, baseline, and pessimistic assumptions?

8. Is the valuation reasonable? Is this acquisition priced at a premium or distress—priced? What do alternative valuation methods conclude (accounting-based, market-based, NPV, option)?

■ Managers should be as specific as possible in identifying the possible benefits and problems of an acquisition throughout the organization. This step is important for two reasons:

1. If operational managers aren't aware of the potential sources of synergies identified by upper management and the acquisition team, they'll have a hard time determining what's expected of them. Moreover, if they understand that synergies are needed but have little idea about how to gain them, the task is just as daunting. Let's go back to Quaker Oats' purchase of Snapple. Perhaps some acquisition managers understood Snapple's operations but no one seemed to understand fully the differences between the two industries' distribution systems. Operating-level managers were thus left to discover and deal with them through trial and error. A good deal of time and effort was wasted in trying to implement the acquisition in ways that simply were not in sync with Quaker Oats' business model.

2. Although identifying possible problems is also important, some acquisition teams tend to understate them, usually because they're afraid of causing key decision makers to shy away from the deal.[21] All in all, it's much better for all parties to know what

the potential roadblocks are; they can be dealt with more effectively if the acquisition team provides some suggested solutions.

Understand the Conditions Required for Creating Synergies Managers must understand the organizational factors on which key synergies hinge and the organizational conditions necessary to implement desired synergies. Synergies in a cross-border acquisition, for example, may depend on the transfer of a functional skill from one company to another. If so, executives at the acquiring firm must identify the managers and key employees who are critical to the transfer. Even when the numbers look good, more and more firms are scuttling acquisitions because of a lack of organizational fit—which can undermine possible synergies. Cisco Systems is one of the most successful high-technology acquirers; their screening criteria and means of achieving these criteria are summarized in Exhibit 11. Cisco regularly uses acquisitions to supplement internal R&D. However, Cisco discovered that the ability to realize synergies was to manage the entire process actively, from screening possible acquisitions to diligently managing the integration process.

Control the Timing of Implementation and Integration Timing is critical in most acquisitions. It's important because of the time value of money. In addition, stock markets can be volatile, which is important when a firm is paying for an acquisition with its own stock. Moreover, timing is critical because acquisitions cause major disruptions in both the target and acquiring firms. Many organizational problems arise from disruption in the lives of affected employees who may be impacted by the acquisition; such problems can be lessened if implementation and integration are achieved quickly. As you learned from the synergy trap tool, the more quickly that synergies can be realized through implementation and integration measures, the greater the premium a firm can afford to pay for the acquisition.

Establish a Walk-away Price Finally, managers should settle on the maximum price that they're willing to pay for the target firm. As we've already seen, it's wise to set a walk-away price early in the process, before rival bidders succumb to *escalation of commitment* and overestimate the value that they believe will be derived from the acquisition. Potential synergies are often uncertain and ambiguous, and they'll vary from one prospective buyer to

Exhibit 11
Organizational-Fit
Acquisitions Screening
by Cisco Systems

Screening Criteria	Means of Achieving Criteria
Offer both short- and long-term win-wins for Cisco and acquired company	• Have complementary technology that fills a need in Cisco's core product space • Have a technology that can be delivered through Cisco's existing distribution channels • Have a technology and products that can be supported by Cisco's support organization • Is able to leverage Cisco's existing infrastructure and resource base to increase its overall value
Share a common vision and chemistry with Cisco	• Have a similar understanding and vision of the market • Have a similar culture • Have a similar risk-taking style
Be located (preferably) in Silicon Valley or near one of Cisco's remote sites	• Have a company headquarters and most manufacturing facilities close to one of Cisco's main sites

the next. Problems arise when managers mistake a rival's higher bid as a signal that they've overlooked some attractive feature of the deal; in responding with a more competitive offer, they're often overpaying.

Integration Many acquisitions fail during the integration stage. The best means of integrating an acquisition varies from case to case, and failure to identify it can cancel any potential synergies that may have been derived from the deal. Determining the best process for implementing and integrating an acquisition means understanding potential interactions between the target and the acquiring firm. Because this stage is so important, we'll devote the next section to presenting a model for dealing with integration problems.

Integrating and Implementing an Acquisition

When one company acquires another it has several options for how the acquired company will be integrated into the firm. At one extreme, the acquired company may be granted near-complete autonomy. Warren Buffett's Berkshire Hathaway often treats its acquired companies this way. Alternatively, the acquiring company may attempt to fully integrate the acquired firm into its operations so that the two firms are melded into one.

How should managers decide whether an acquisition should be treated in a rather hands-off approach or be tightly integrated? Two concepts should be considered in making this decision—the strategic interdependence of the businesses and the need for organizational autonomy of the acquired business.

STRATEGIC INTERDEPENDENCE

Let's go back to one of the basic principles identified in this chapter: The primary purpose of M&As is to create synergies—value that can be created by combining two firms that isn't available to them as standalone firms. To what extent should the target firm and acquiring firm remain strategically interdependent? It depends on the types of resource sharing and skill transfers anticipated by the two firms. When the logic of the acquisition requires that they share tangible and intangible resources, the success of the deal usually requires a relatively high level of interdependence. Likewise, when the logic of the deal calls for transferring people with different functional skills in order to share knowledge, it entails more interdependence between the two organizational units than if it called simply for a transfer of general management skills. Alternatively, when the resources being transferred are primarily financial (say, borrowing power or excess cash), very little interdependence is required. Thus the first factor that determines how integration should be handled is the level of strategic interdependence between the acquiring firm and the acquired firm.

NEED FOR AUTONOMY

The second factor that should be considered is the target's need for autonomy. The value of some acquisitions lies largely in the retention of key people and transfers of capabilities. Key people, however, often leave once their firm has been acquired—especially when the acquisition disrupts their operating procedures and their autonomy in conducting them. Just how much autonomy should be granted an acquired firm? There's no single answer, of course, but the following is a good rule of thumb: The appropriate amount of autonomy depends on whether it is necessary to create value. Granted, even this response is a little too simple. Perhaps, for example, autonomy is necessary only in certain facets of the acquired firm's operations, whereas others can be easily assimilated.

When Swiss giant Nestlé set out to purchase British candy maker Rowntree York (makers of such candies as Kit Kat and Rolo) in order to extend its reach in chocolates and

345

confectionary markets, it found that it could not, in accord with its usual policy, fully integrate its latest acquisition. Rather, to get the deal approved by Rowntree, Nestlé had to allow Rowntree executives to remain in the United Kingdom and run the strategic office in charge of all confectionary businesses. Thus, in this case, autonomy was needed simply to get the managers of the target firm to support the acquisition and agree to the buyout. Cisco, the network company, has used acquisitions extensively as part of its strategy. Generally, they try to integrate the target as soon after the closing as possible. For instance, they attempt to have the target's products in its sales peoples' catalogues the moment the acquisition closes. In order to achieve this, they need the target firms to adopt all of Cisco's systems and be fully integrated. However, periodically, Cisco acquires a target that resists some aspect of Cisco integration. They claim that to be innovative, they need some organizational autonomy, and that their engineers want to work for a small and dynamic company, not a big, "bureaucratic" Cisco. Consequently, in a few cases, Cisco has deviated from their normal integration policy in order to complete a transaction that they deem is of strategic imperative.

THE IMPLEMENTATION PROCESS

No matter what approach managers take—fostering interdependence, autonomy, or some combination of these—they will be well served by reminding themselves that acquisition integration is a *process* and not an *event*. By analogy, think of acquisition integration as a comma in a sentence, not a period. To this end we can learn some lessons from so-called **serial acquirers**—companies that engage in frequent acquisitions—that will be useful in understanding how the process can be handled smoothly and effectively.

serial acquirers Company that engages in frequent acquisitions.

It's a Continual Process, Not an Event The best serial acquirers start the integration process during initial screening interviews and negotiations, well before closing the deal. M&A is already designed into the arenas, differentiators, vehicles, staging and pacing, and economic facets of their strategy (notice these comprise *all* five facets of the strategy diamond). During this process, called **due diligence**, executives and lower-level managers at both companies begin to plan for the postdeal structure of the combined firm. Although some pretransaction discussions can be awkward, they're essential in identifying both potential obstacles and additional opportunities. Once the deal is closed, specific decisions must be executed and prearranged organizational structures implemented. The lesson, in short, is that it's better to make tough decisions early rather than delaying them. Firms such as GE Capital and Cisco, which have successfully integrated many acquisitions (and some not so successfully), have found that initiating and pursuing a comprehensive integration and communications process is the lynchpin for success.

due diligence Initial pre-closing screening, analysis, and negotiations for an acquisition.

Integration Management Is a Full-time Job Many firms make the mistake of assuming that people at all levels in both organizations will work together to make the acquisition as seamless as possible. Unfortunately, so many organizational issues are involved in integrating an acquired company that line managers often can't oversee operations *and* manage the integration process. Many successful acquirers, therefore, appoint an *integration manager.* Ideally, this person will be someone from the due-diligence team who understands both companies. Having met many line managers in both organizations, the integration manager spearheads integration efforts, guiding newly acquired managers through the maze of the new organizational hierarchy.

At GE Capital, for instance, integration managers introduce both executives and employees of the acquired firm to the business requirements and organizational standards of the new parent company. They also deal with a number of seemingly mundane issues that have been found to hamper integration efforts, such as communicating information about benefits and human resources policies. They educate new employees about such idiosyncratic features of the firm as culture, business customs, and even acronyms. Finally, in order to prevent unnecessary overload and redundant activities, they channel information requests from the parent company to both new managers and those who are veterans of the original organization.

GE Capital has found that individuals with strong personal and technical skills make the best integration managers and typically draws candidates from one of two pools. First, the company recruits "high-potential individuals"—people with strong functional-area management credentials and leadership potential. These people function best as integration managers when the integration is highly structured and relatively uncomplicated. For more complex integrations, GE Capital relies on seasoned veterans who know the company well. Experience has shown that these individuals can be drawn from every functional area.

Key Decisions Should Be Made Swiftly

As we've already seen, speed is of the essence in the acquisition process simply because of the cost and the time value of money. Certain organizational factors also dictate swift integration. For one, employees—both those of the target firm and those of the acquiring firm—are naturally concerned about the impact of the acquisition on their jobs. As much as executives and managers would like everyone to feel like a team player with a secure place in the organizational lineup, when they're worried about their jobs, people succumb to distractions. Successful acquirers have found that it's best not to prolong the suspense: Decisions about management structure, key roles, reporting relationships, layoffs, restructuring, cost-cutting, and other career-affecting aspects of the acquisition should be announced as soon as possible—even within days of the acquisition announcement. Telling employees that everything will be "business as usual" is almost never being honest and will probably hamper the integration process. In addition, swift implementation of the integration process allows the firm to get on with its primary task—creating value. Because sluggish integration makes it more difficult to focus on this task, it weakens the value-creation process.

Integration Should Address Technical and Cultural Issues

When integrating acquisitions, most managers tend to focus on technical issues. At Cisco, for example, a key technical issue is the rapid integration of the target's products into the Cisco system so that sales representatives can begin selling the new product line. Successful integration means identifying and addressing such issues as early as possible.

Issues related to corporate culture should also be addressed immediately. Some of these issues are as simple as meeting and greeting new employees. The cultures of any two firms are bound to be different, and the faster managers and employees can meld the two organizations, the more smoothly the integration will proceed. Even when two organizations seem to have a lot in common, profound cultural differences may exist that could threaten successful integration. When, for instance, Franklin Quest merged with Covey, many observers expected cultural integration to be smooth. After all, the two businesses were highly complementary, and because both firms were located in Utah, they had similar employee bases. In addition, the two CEOs were well acquainted with one another. Surprisingly, however, the two cultures were highly dissimilar. For instance, Franklin Quest was built on a culture of efficiency, whereas Covey eschewed efficiency for effectiveness. Everything from products to company vision statements were tied to these critical underlying philosophies. During the acquisition process, executives dismissed these differences as semantics, but discovered during the integration phase that these were rather incongruent philosophies. In addition, more functional things, such as incompatible accounting systems, also impeded quick integration. Successful acquirers identify cultural clashes early; in fact, they may walk away from deals when the potential clashes are too severe.

Acquisitions in Different Industry Contexts

Not surprisingly, M&A activity varies across industries. It is determined largely by the development phase in which a given industry finds itself and by the extent of industry dynamism. In addition, competitive conditions will determine whether acquisition is a suitable strategy vehicle for a firm in a given industry and what the most viable type of acquisition may be. In this section, we'll discuss the role of M&As and industry context in terms of the industry life cycle and the level of industry-wide turbulence.

M&AS AND INDUSTRY LIFE CYCLE

Recall the model of industry life cycle and industry dynamics that we presented in Chapter 4. In this section, we'll use this model to illustrate how different types of acquisitions play different roles in each stage.

Introduction   During the introduction stage, acquisitions tend to involve the purchase of startup firms by well-established firms in related but more mature industry segments. Many partial acquisitions may occur, with established companies making equity investments in startups but not acquiring them outright. Thus, at this stage M&As tend to be R&D and product- and market-extension acquisitions.

Growth   During this phase, we see several types of acquisitions. Established companies from one industry segment may start entering other segments with greater frequency, looking mostly for proven and growing targets. Although some M&A activity may be for R&D, most of it is likely to be for the purpose of acquiring products that are proven and gaining customer acceptance. The geographic roll-up also becomes more common, especially at the end of the growth stage and through the maturity stage. In high-velocity industries, industry-convergence acquisitions appear and continue into the maturity stage.

Maturity   At this point, we begin to see overcapacity acquisitions. Why? During the growth stage, the industry witnessed the entry of new firms and aggressive expansion, with numerous competitors jockeying for competitive position. Capacity built during this period often exceeds the long-term needs of the segment, and as demand starts to flatten, companies see consolidation as a way to rationalize the industry. Overcapacity M&A activity continues throughout the decline stage of the cycle.

M&AS IN DYNAMIC CONTEXTS

Dynamic contexts are often home to firms that engage in acquisitions at a frantic pace. What is it about dynamic contexts that makes acquisitions such popular strategy vehicles? In Chapter 4, we discussed factors that can alter an industry landscape, particularly discontinuities and globalization. These factors tend to accelerate acquisitions. Note that within these two broad categories, many factors can affect the attractiveness of acquisitions as strategy vehicles. We'll focus on *technological change, demographic change, geopolitical change, trade liberalization,* and *deregulation.*[22]

Technological Change   In high-velocity industries, technological change and innovation can transpire at lightning speed, and some firms respond with aggressive acquisition campaigns. Both Cisco and Microsoft, for example, use acquisitions to ensure that innovation and technological change among competitors don't contribute to the erosion of their strong competitive positions.

Demographic Change   Demographic changes, such as the aging of the population and mass emigration, may alter customer profiles significantly. Spanish-language speakers, for instance, are an increasingly important market segment for U.S. media companies. Thus, when the Tribune Company merged with Times-Mirror in 2000, it acquired *Hoy*, the leading Spanish-language daily in New York and one of the fastest-growing publications of its kind. The Tribune Company has recently launched editions in Chicago and Los Angeles.

Geopolitical Change   Such events as the fall of the Iron Curtain, the emergence of the European Union, the opening of China, and conflict in the Middle East all have significant effects on the operations of global companies. In some cases, changes enhance opportunities for acquiring established companies in new locations. In others, they foster divestiture. For example, IBM was able to divest its personal computer division to the Chinese firm Lenova in 2005 largely because of the rapid growth and commercialization of the domestic Chinese marketplace, which was fostered by the loosening of some government interventions.

Trade Liberalization   Trade liberalization also opens new opportunities for doing business. In the wake of the European Union and the North American Free Trade Agreement (NAFTA), for example, cross-border acquisition activity increased in industries conducting business in those regions. Wal-Mart's acquisition of the successful Mexican retailing giant, Cifra, is a case in point. Geographic proximity and NAFTA make it cost-effective for Wal-Mart to stock its shelves in the United States with goods assembled in Mexico as well as provide otherwise more expensive U.S.–made goods to Mexican consumers through Cifra's outlets. Wal-Mart gained improved economies of scope and scale as a result of NAFTA.

Deregulation   Finally, deregulation has had a major impact on the volume of M&A activity in a number of industries. Prior to deregulation, for instance, the wave of M&As that swept the banking industry would not have been possible. Regulation and deregulation have also affected acquisitions and divestitures in the telecommunications industry. AT&T, for example, was allowed to exist as a virtual monopoly until 1984, when antitrust action forced its breakup. The seven so-called Baby Bells divided up local service, leaving the parent company, AT&T, with long-distance and telecom equipment businesses. Following subsequent deregulation, M&A activity has put the industry in a state of almost constant change.

M&AS AND COEVOLUTION

As with alliances, the use of acquisitions in dynamic contexts fits into the coevolution model of corporate strategy. Recall our definition of coevolution as the orchestration of a web of shifting linkages among evolving businesses. In the case of acquisitions, acquisitions can enable a firm to absorb the capabilities of their targets in order to develop specific dynamic capabilities in concert with the best resources and capabilities available on the market. Just as important, acquisitions (at least well-conceived ones) support a specific, focused strategy. Consequently, in keeping with this strategy, certain businesses are periodically pared off through divestitures and others added through acquisitions. If, for instance, the firm is pursuing a growth strategy, the coevolution perspective would suggest that it divest slow-growth businesses and products and acquire firms that are operating on the technology frontier or that offer some other basis for future competitive advantage.[23]

Summary of Challenges

1. *Explain the motivations behind acquisitions and show how they've changed over time.* The three basic motivations for acquisitions are synergy, manager self-interest, and hubris. Synergy is the primary motivation for acquisitions, and it can be generated in many different ways. Synergies can come from cost savings, revenue enhancements, improved competitive position, financial engineering, and the transfer of resources, best practices, and core competencies between targets and acquiring firms. Manager self-interest can motivate some acquisitions because many managers find it attractive to lead larger organizations, size and diversification can help smooth earnings, and compensation is higher for managers of large firms. This motive is known as *managerialism.* Hubris is exaggerated self-confidence, and it can result in managers overestimating the value of a potential acquisition, having unrealistic assumptions about the ability of an acquisition to create synergies, and being too willing to pay too much for a transaction. Thus, hubris results in more acquisitions than would be the case if it were kept in check.

2. *Explain why mergers and acquisitions are important to strategy.* Acquisitions enable firms to enter new businesses quickly. One of the key benefits of an acquisition over internal development of a new business is that the time and risks associated with business startup are reduced significantly. For instance, if the acquisition is of a firm of sufficient size, minimum efficient scale is achieved immediately. In addition, proven products are already in distribution. Acquisitions can also put firms in a position to achieve significant synergies—they can create value when the two firms combined are more valuable than when owned separately.

3. *Identify the various types of acquisitions.* Several types of acquisitions are possible, and each has a specific purpose. A product- or market-extension acquisition has the aim of expanding the products offered or markets served. A geographic roll-up is a series of acquisitions of firms in the same industry segment but in different geographic segments. A R&D acquisition is the purchase of another company for the purpose of acquiring its technology. An overcapacity, or consolidation, acquisition is the combination of two large firms in a mature industry that has excess capacity for slowing demand. An industry-convergence acquisition occurs when the boundaries between two industries start to fade and firms need to participate increasingly in both industries to be competitive; firms often use acquisitions to enter the converging industry. Finally, a significant portion of acquisitions are transactions by investors or holding companies (not an existing operating company) that are purchasing a company as an investment.

4. *Understand how the pricing of acquisitions affects the realization of synergies.* The pricing of an acquisition is critical to its success. The price of an acquisition normally exceeds its current market value by a significant premium. And although there is no one correct price for an acquisition target, managers of each potential acquiring firm can estimate the potential synergies between their company and the target. The price a firm is willing to pay for a target should be based on these synergies. Using Sirower's formula for acquisition premiums, managers can calculate the maximum premium they should be willing to pay. Likewise, if the price that is needed to make the acquisition is known first (such as in bidding situations), managers can easily estimate the required performance improvements that would be necessary. The greater the premium paid, the more synergies that must be extracted from the deal to make it economical. Likewise, the greater the premium, the more important it is to realize the synergies quickly.

5. *Outline the alternative ways to integrate an acquisition and explain the implementation process.* How an acquisition is integrated should be a function of the target firm's need for autonomy and the strategic interdependence between the target and the acquired company. Successful implementation requires recognition that acquisition integration is a continual process, that dedicated managers are required to oversee the process, that the process is enhanced by swift decisions, and that it focuses on both technical and cultural issues.

6. *Discuss the characteristics of acquisitions in different industry contexts.* Different types of acquisitions are seen with greater frequency at different stages of the industry life cycle. During the introduction stage, acquisitions tend to be by firms in related segments acquiring technology (R&D acquisitions) or products of startups (product extensions). During the growth phase of the industry life cycle, several types of acquisitions are common. Some R&D acquisitions of a now-proven technology by later-moving established companies from related industry segments still take place. But given that in the growth phase, products have achieved more accepted status, many more product-extension acquisitions are seen. The geographic roll-up tends to appear at the waning stages of the growth phase. In high-velocity industries, industry-convergence acquisitions also start to appear. During the maturity stage, overcapacity acquisitions start to emerge, and roll-ups and product-extension acquisitions continue. Overcapacity acquisitions continue throughout industry decline. Industry turbulence, such as technological change, demographic change, geopolitical change, trade liberalization, and deregulation are all forms of industry shock that tend to increase acquisition activity because they change the competitive landscape.

350

Review Questions

1. What is an acquisition?

2. Why would firms use acquisitions rather than create a new business internally?

3. What are the possible motives for acquisitions?

4. What are the ways in which synergies can be created in acquisitions?

5. How easy or difficult is it to achieve the alternative types of synergies?

6. What are the various types of acquisitions?

7. How do market-extension acquisitions and geographic roll-ups differ?

8. Give examples of product extension, overcapacity, and R&D acquisitions.

9. What is an acquisition premium?

10. How can you calculate the synergies that must be extracted from an acquisition with a given premium?

11. How do acquisitions tend to be used in different stages of the industry life cycle?

Experiential Activities

Group Exercises

1. Pick a firm of interest to your group. Identify potential acquisition candidates. Explain why these companies would make sense as an acquisition target. Evaluate and describe possible implementation barriers to this acquisition.

2. Pick a firm of interest and peruse its annual reports over a 5- to 10-year period. Assess the information presented on M&As in the annual reports. Do you see any explicit mention of the link between strategy formulation and implementation with respect to the acquisition mentioned in the annual reports? (As a starting place, see the chairman's letter to the shareholders.) What are the before-and-after scenarios that you find regarding the M&As?

Ethical Debates

1. During the due diligence phase of a pharmaceutical company's acquisition, you discover that an executive of the potential target may have funneled payments to government regulators overseeing the company's drug approval process. The case in question only represents a minor drug in the target's portfolio of therapies. What should you do?

2. While negotiating a possible buyout with the management of a firm, the CEO of the target starts to play hardball. He continues to add contingencies to the deal. In addition, he has recently raised the issue of a golden parachute for himself if he can convince the largest shareholder to agree to the deal. The CFO of the target pulls you aside and indicates that he can persuade the largest shareholder to sell and that he can do it for much less than the CEO is asking for in his golden parachute. What should you do?

How Would YOU DO THAT?

1. Identify a company that has recently announced an acquisition. Study the terms of the deal and identify to the extent possible the market value of the target, its intrinsic value, and the acquisition price. What was the acquisition premium? Using the synergy trap formula presented in the box entitled "How Would *You* Do That? 1," determine the performance improvements required to justify this acquisition premium. Calculate the required performance improvements with different assumptions as to how long it will take to implement them in, say, one, three, and five years. What is the difference in these required performance improvements if the acquisition premium is 50 percent lower than what was paid? What if it is 50 percent higher?

Go on to see How Would You Do That at www.prenhall.com/ carpenter&sanders

Endnotes

1. N. Wingfield and J. Sapsford, "eBay to Buy PayPal for $1.4 Billion," *Wall Street Journal*, July 9, 2002, A6; N. Wingfield, "eBay Completes PayPal Deal, Gaining Web-Payments Heft," *Wall Street Journal*, October 4, 2002, B8; N. Wingfield, "eBay's Profit More Than Triples as Transaction Revenue Surges," *Wall Street Journal*, October 18, 2002, B4; Adam Lashinsky, "Building eBay 2.0," *Fortune*, October 5, 2006; "Interview Transcript: Meg Whitman, eBay," *Financial Times*, June 18, 2006; "Analysis: eBay's Growth To Come From Community" *InformationWeek*, June 19, 2006; "eBay Inc. Announces Financial Results for First Quarter 2007," *M2 Presswire*, April 19, 2007; "eBay Quarterly Net Beats Expectations, Raises Outlook," *eWeek*, April 18, 2007.

2. "Kerkorian Files Briefs in Lawsuit Alleging Deception by Daimler," *Wall Street Journal*, June 19, 2001, A4.

3. See R. F. Bruner, *Applied Mergers and Acquisitions* (Hoboken, NJ: John Wiley & Sons, 2004).

4. P. Wright, M. Kroll, and D. Elenkov, "Acquisition Returns, Increase in Firm Size, and Chief Executive Officer Compensation: The Moderating Role of Monitoring," *Academy of Management Journal* 45 (2002), 599–608.

5. Y. Amihud and B. Lev, "Risk Reduction as a Managerial Motive for Conglomerate Acquisitions," *The Bell Journal of Economics* 12 (1983), 605–617.

6. R. Roll, "The Hubris Hypothesis of Corporate Takeovers," *Journal of Business* 59 (1986), 197–216.

7. O. E. Williamson, *The Economic Institutions of Capitalism* (New York: Free Press, 1985).

8. Adapted from Hambrick and Fredrickson, "Are You Sure You Have a Strategy?" *Academy of Management Executive* 15:4 (2001), 48–59.

9. Data drawn from U.S. Department of Commerce sources.

10. P. Haunschild, "How Much Is That Company Worth?: Interorganizational Relationships, Uncertainty, and Acquisition Premiums," *Administrative Science Quarterly* 39 (1994), 391–411; W. G. Sanders, "Behavioral Responses of CEOs to Stock Ownership and Stock Option Pay," *Academy of Management Journal* 44 (2001), 477–492.

11. Data compiled from SDC Platinum, a product of Thompson Financial.

12. Data compiled from SDC Platinum, a product of Thompson Financial.

13. R. F. Bruner, *Deals from Hell: M&A Deals That Rise Above the Ashes* (New York: Wiley, 2005).

14. Figure is adapted. This typology was developed by J. T. Bower, "Not All M&As Are Alike—and That Matters," *Harvard Business Review* 79:3 (2001), 92–101.

15. Bower, "Not All M&As Are Alike."

16. M. L. Sirower, *The Synergy Trap: How Companies Lose at the Acquisition Game* (New York: Free Press, 1997).

17. Haspeslagh and Jemison, *Managing Acquisitions*; D. B. Jemison and S. B. Sitkin, "Corporate Acquisitions: A Process Perspective," *Academy of Management Review* 11:1 (1986), 145–163.

18. Brunner, *Applied Mergers and Acquisitions*; Haspeslagh and Jemison, *Managing Acquisitions*.

19. Haspeslagh and Jemison, *Managing Acquisitions*, 42.

20. Haspeslagh and Jemison, *Managing Acquisitions*.

21. Haspeslagh and Jemison, *Managing Acquisitions*.

22. Brunner, *Applied Mergers and Acquisitions*, 88.

23. S. L. Brown and K. M. Eisenhardt, *Competing on the Edge: Strategy as Structured Chaos* (Boston: Harvard Business School Press, 1998).

Index